HTML
Illustrated Complete

Elizabeth Eisner Reding
Sasha Vodnik

COURSE
TECHNOLOGY

ONE MAIN STREET, CAMBRIDGE, MA 02142

an International Thomson Publishing company I(T)P®

Cambridge • Albany • Bonn • Boston • Cincinnati • London • Madrid • Melbourne • Mexico City
New York • Paris • San Francisco • Singapore • Tokyo • Toronto • Washington

HTML—Illustrated Complete is published by Course Technology

Associate Publisher:	Carolyn Henderson
Senior Product Manager:	Jeanne Herring
Contributing Author:	Donald I. Barker
Development Editors:	Rachel Bunin, Pam Conrad
Production Editor:	Melissa Panagos
Composition House:	GEX, Inc.
QA Manuscript Reviewer:	Jon Greacen, Brian McCooey, Alex White
Text Designer:	Joseph Lee
Cover Designer:	Joseph Lee

© 1999 by Course Technology—I(T)P®

For more information contact:

Course Technology
One Main Street
Cambridge, MA 02142

International Thomson Editores
Seneca 53
Colonia Polanco
11560 Mexico D.F. Mexico

ITP Europe
Berkshire House 168-173
High Holborn
London WCIV 7AA
England

ITP GmbH
Königswinterer Strasse 418
53227 Bonn
Germany

Nelson ITP/Australia
102 Dodds Street
South Melbourne, 3205
Victoria, Australia

ITP Asia
60 Albert Street, #15-01
Albert Complex
Singapore 189969

ITP Nelson Canada
1120 Birchmount Road
Scarborough, Ontario
Canada M1K 5G4

ITP Japan
Hirakawacho Kyowa Building, 3F
2-2-1 Hirakawacho
Chiyoda-ku, Tokyo 102
Japan

ISBN 0-7600-5842-3

Printed in the United States of America

5 6 7 8 9 BM 02 01 00

Exciting New Illustrated Products

The Illustrated Projects™ Series: The Quick, Visual Way to Apply Computer Skills

Looking for an inexpensive, easy way to supplement almost any application text and give your students the practice and tools they'll need to compete in today's competitive marketplace? Each text includes more than 50 real-world, useful projects—like creating a resume and setting up a loan worksheet—that let students hone their computer skills. These two-color texts have the same great two-page layout as the Illustrated Series.

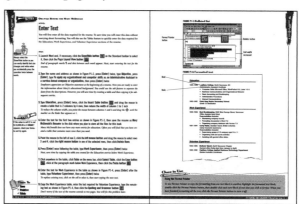

Illustrated Projects titles are available for the following:

▶ Microsoft Access
▶ Microsoft Excel
▶ Microsoft Office Professional
▶ Microsoft Publisher
▶ Microsoft Word

▶ Creating Web Sites
▶ World Wide Web
▶ Adobe PageMaker
▶ Corel WordPerfect

Illustrated Interactive® Series: The Safe, Simulated Way to Learn Computer Skills

The Illustrated Interactive Series uses multimedia technology to teach computer concepts and application skills. Students learn via a CD-ROM that simulates the actual software and provides a controlled learning environment in which every keystroke is monitored. Plus, all products in this series feature the same step-by-step instructions as the Illustrated Series. An accompanying workbook reinforces the skills that students learn on the CD.

Illustrated Interactive titles are available for the following applications:*

▶ Microsoft Office 97
▶ Microsoft Word 97
▶ Microsoft Excel 97

▶ Microsoft Access 97
▶ Microsoft PowerPoint 97
▶ Computer Concepts

Standalone & networked versions available. Runs on Windows 3.1, 95, and NT. CD-only version available for Computer Concepts and Office 97.

CourseKits™: Offering You the Freedom to Choose

Balance your course curriculum with Course Technology's mix-and-match approach to selecting texts. CourseKits provide you with the freedom to make choices from more than one series. When you choose any two or more Course Technology products for one course, we'll discount the price and package them together so your students pick up one convenient bundle at the bookstore.

Contact your sales representative to find out more about these Illustrated products.

Preface

Welcome to *HTML – Illustrated Complete!* This highly visual book offers new users a hands-on introduction to HTML and Web-page creation and also serves as an excellent reference for future use.

► Organization and Coverage

This text contains fourteen units that cover basic through advanced HTML skills. In these units students learn how to create Web pages using HTML, add hyperlinks, graphics, tables, frames, and forms, consider design when creating Web pages, and understand the role of scripting. They also learn how to use JavaScript and Cascading Style Sheets to create dynamic text and images, control positioning, and bind data to a Web page. The last unit of the book introduces students to the basics of XML. An appendix at the end of the book contains information about publishing a site to the Web, as well as reference tables for HTML tags, color names, and special characters, JavaScript objects and operators, and Cascading Style Sheets.

► About this Approach

What makes the Illustrated approach so effective at teaching software skills? It's quite simple. Each skill is presented on two facing pages, with the step-by-step instructions on the left page, and large screen illustrations on the right. Students can focus on a single skill without having to turn the page. This unique design makes information extremely accessible and easy to absorb, and provides a great reference for after the course is over. This hands-on approach also makes it ideal for both self-paced or instructor-led classes.

Each lesson, or "information display," contains the following elements:

Each 2-page spread focuses on a single skill.

Clear step-by-step directions explain how to complete the specific task, with what students are to type in red. When students follow the numbered steps, they quickly learn how each procedure is performed and what the results will be.

Concise text that introduces the basic principles discussed in the lesson. Procedures are easier to learn when concepts fit into a framework.

Creating an Image Map

HTML

Pixel coordinates are stored in a separate document that identifies which Web site the reader will jump to when the image is clicked. In an online Web session, clicking an image map connects you to the site identified in the image map document. When not online, clicking an image map results in the pointer changing to an hourglass while your computer searches for the site. You can also create an e-mail link so readers can send mail directly to the page administrator. Grace creates the image map document that contains the pixel coordinates to other Web sites that she will insert later.

Steps

1. Click the **text editor program button** on the taskbar
   The image map document is created in a new document in the editor.

2. Click **File** on the menu bar, click **New**, then click **OK**
   You determined a single point in each image that links to Web sites that you insert later. In addition to the pixel coordinates, you can include comment lines to identify the sites by name. Each comment line begins with the pound sign (#). You type placeholders for the real Web sites.

   Trouble?
   If you are using a text editor other than WordPad, open a new document.

3. Type the **comment lines and coordinates** shown in Figure C-11
   You have typed the coordinates for each image.

4. Save the file as a text document with the filename **Nomad image.map**
   The image map document is complete, so when you view the original document, Nomad Home Page.htm, it can refer to the image map.

   Trouble?
   Verify that this file has been saved with the .map extension, not .txt.

5. Click the **browser program button** on the taskbar, then view the changes to Nomad Home Page.htm by refreshing your screen
   The image is updated, as shown in Figure C-12. You can return to the image map document later and insert the Web site locations that the reader will jump to when each image is clicked.

6. Print the browser document

TABLE C-1: Common graphic file formats

format	extension	support provided
Graphics Interchange Format	GIF	Native
Joint Photographic Experts Group	JPEG, JPG	Native
PC Paintbrush	PCX	External
Tagged Image File Format	TIFF	External
Windows Bitmap	BMP	External

► HTML C-12 **ADDING GRAPHICS AND MULTIMEDIA**

Tips as well as trouble-shooting advice right where you need it — next to the step itself.

Quickly accessible summaries of key terms, toolbar buttons, or keyboard alternatives connected with the lesson material. Students can refer easily to this information when working on their own projects at a later time.

Every lesson features large-size, full-color representations of what the students' screen should look like after completing the numbered steps.

Other Features

The two-page lesson format featured in this book provides the new user with a powerful learning experience. Additionally, this book contains the following features:

▶ **Real-World Case**
The skills used throughout the textbook are designed to be "real-world" in nature and representative of the kinds of activities that students encounter when working with HTML. With a real-world case, the process of solving problems will be more meaningful to students.

▶ **End of Unit Material**
Each unit concludes with a Concepts Review that tests students' understanding of what they learned in the unit. The Concepts Review is followed in each skills-based unit by a Skills Review, which provides students with additional hands-on practice of the skills they learned in the unit. The Skills Review is followed by Independent Challenges, which pose case problems for students to solve. At least one Independent Challenge in each unit asks students to use the World Wide Web to solve the problem as indicated by a Web Work icon. The Visual Workshops that follow the Independent Challenges help students develop critical thinking skills. Students are shown completed Web pages or screens and are asked to recreate them from scratch.

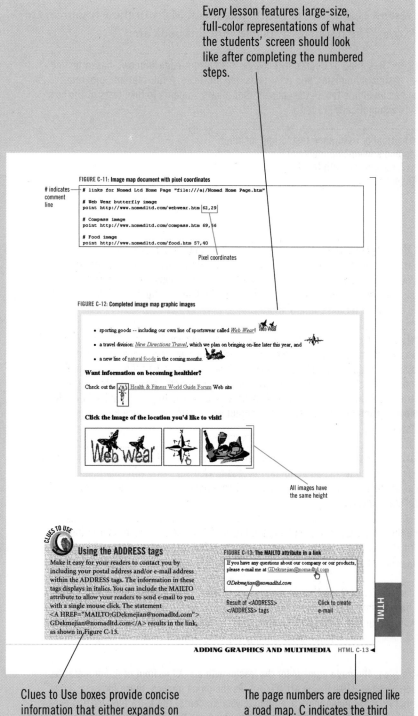

FIGURE C-11: Image map document with pixel coordinates

# indicates comment line

```
# links for Nomad Ltd Home Page "file:///a|/Nomad Home Page.htm"

# Web Wear butterfly image
point http://www.nomadltd.com/webwear.htm 62,29

# Compass image
point http://www.nomadltd.com/compass.htm 69,56

# Food image
point http://www.nomadltd.com/food.htm 57,40
```

Pixel coordinates

FIGURE C-12: Completed image map graphic images

- sporting goods -- including our own line of sportswear called *Web Wear*
- a travel division: *New Directions Travel*, which we plan on bringing on-line later this year, and
- a new line of natural foods in the coming months.

Want information on becoming healthier?

Check out the Health & Fitness World Guide Forum Web site

Click the image of the location you'd like to visit!

All images have the same height

Using the ADDRESS tags

Make it easy for your readers to contact you by including your postal address and/or e-mail address within the ADDRESS tags. The information in these tags displays in italics. You can include the MAILTO attribute to allow your readers to send e-mail to you with a single mouse click. The statement
<A HREF="MAILTO:GDekmejian@nomadltd.com">
GDekmejian@nomadltd.com</A> results in the link, as shown in Figure C-13.

FIGURE C-13: The MAILTO attribute in a link

If you have any questions about our company or our products, please e-mail me at GDekmejian@nomadltd.com

GDekmejian@nomadltd.com

Result of <ADDRESS> </ADDRESS> tags

Click to create e-mail

HTML

Clues to Use boxes provide concise information that either expands on one component of the major lesson skill or describes an independent task that is in some way related to the major lesson skill.

The page numbers are designed like a road map. C indicates the third unit, and 13 indicates the page within the unit.

Instructor's Resource Kit

The Instructor's Resource Kit is Course Technology's way of putting the resources and information needed to teach and learn effectively into your hands. With an integrated array of teaching and learning tools that offer you and your students a broad range of technology-based instructional options, we believe this kit represents the highest quality and most cutting edge resources available to instructors today. Many of these resources are available at www.course.com. The resources available with this book are:

Course Test Manager   Designed by Course Technology, this cutting-edge Windows-based testing software helps instructors design, administer, and print tests and pre-tests. A full-featured program, Course Test Manager also has an online testing component that allows students to take tests at the computer and have their exams automatically graded.

Instructor's Manual   Quality assurance tested and includes:
- Solutions to all lessons and end-of-unit material
- Detailed lecture topics for each unit with teaching tips
- Extra Independent Challenges
- Task References
- Transparency Masters
- Project Files

WWW.COURSE.COM   We encourage students and instructors to visit our web site at www.course.com to find articles about current teaching and software trends, featured texts, interviews with authors, demos of Course Technology's software, Frequently Asked Questions about our products, and much more. This site is also where you can gain access to the Faculty Online Companion or Student Online Companion for this text — see below for more information.

Course Faculty Online Companion   Available at www.course.com, this World Wide Web site offers Course Technology customers a password-protected Faculty Lounge where you can find everything you need to prepare for class, including the Instructor's Manual in an electronic Portable Document Format (PDF) file and Adobe Acrobat Reader software. Periodically updated items include any updates and revisions to the text and Instructor's Manual, links to other Web sites, and access to project and solution files. This site will continue to evolve throughout the semester. Contact your Customer Service Representative for the site address and password.

Course Student Online Companion   Available at www.course.com, this book features its own Student Online Companion where students can go to gain access to Web sites that will help them complete the Web Work Independent Challenges. These links are updated on a regular basis. These sites will continue to evolve throughout the semester.

Project Files   To use this book students must have the Project Files. See the inside front or inside back cover for more information on the Project Files. Adopters of this text are granted the right to post the Project Files on any stand-alone computer or network.

X-tra files   Now it's even easier to teach the skills you want to teach! Every two-page spread in this book requiring a project file now includes a project file or an X-tra file. An X-tra file is a project file in the exact format needed to work through that one particular lesson. X-tra files are not available for lessons in which project files are not needed or in which a project file is explicitly opened or created as part of the lesson steps.

The filename of each X-tra file is the page number for the lesson with an "X" in front of it. For instance, the X-tra file for the lesson on page HTML B-6 is XHTML B-6. As the name implies, these files are "extra" and you can choose whether or not to make them available to your students. The X-tra files for this book are provided separately from the Project Files in the Instructor's Resource Kit and on the Faculty Online Companion.

Brief Contents

Contents

HTML

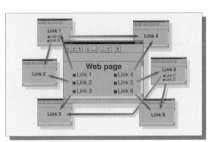

Contents

Controlling HTML Text · HTML B-1

Nomad Ltd's *Web Wear*!

Welcome to the world of *Web Wear*,
where the clothing is comfy and the livin' is easy!

What's available

Web Wear is available in the following designs:

1. **Mega way-cool bitmapped T-Shirt**
2. **Awesome elegant T-Shirt**
3. **Whatsamatta T-Shirt**
4. **On-line Chat T-Shirt**

What's the difference between the designs?

Mega way-cool bitmapped T-Shirt
     An original creation, 100% cotton, in navy blue or crimson.

Adding Graphics and Multimedia

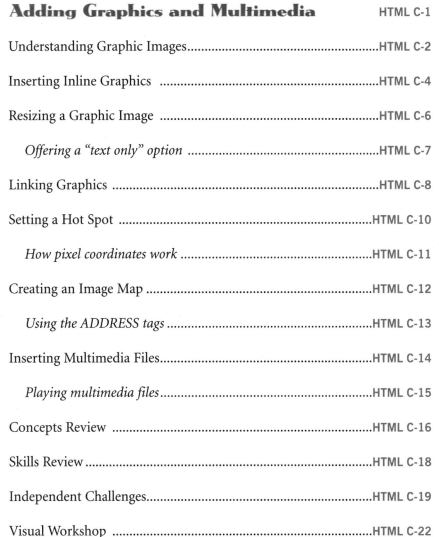

Contents

Using Forms to Control Input HTML D-1

Working with Tables

HTML E-1

Tour	Description	Duration
	Domestic	
Athlete	For the sports-minded. Bicycling, kayaking, and hiking occur throughout the year.	2-7 days
	Domestic or International	
Arts	Dedicated to the performing arts. An assortment of museums, music, and theater.	3-21 days
	International	
Leisure	Relax and spend time in beautiful settings. Lavish accommodations and gourmet meals.	2-15 days

Contents

Using Frames
HTML F-1

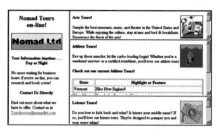

Designing Web Pages

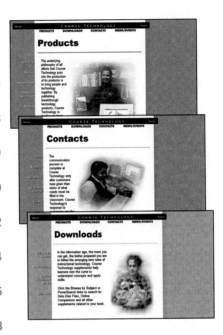

Contents

Scripting for HTML HTML H-1

Working with Dymamic HTML (DHTML)

window
- location
- frames
- history
- navigator
- event
- screen
- document
  - links
  - anchors
  - images
  - filters
  - forms
  - applets
  - embeds
  - plug-ins
  - frames
  - scripts
  - all
  - selection
  - stylesheets
  - body

Contents

Specifying Style Dynamically HTML J-1

Frequently Asked Questions about

Dynamic HTML (DHTML)

Nomad Ltd

♦ **What is Dynamic HTML?**
Dynamic HTML (DHTML) describes a set of new technologies for designing Web pages that allow new and more precise formatting features, along with faster access for users.

♦ **Is DHTML a new language?**
DHTML is not a new language. DHTML is simply a snazzy name for a set of new features that recent Web browsers are equipped to interpret and use. DHTML features work only within the context of a standard HTML document.

♦ **How does DHTML work?**
DHTML uses two new pieces in concert with HTML. The first is scripts that run on the user's browser, written in a scripting language such as JavaScript or VBScript. The other is Cascading Style Sheets, a new method of specifying exact styles for a Web page's elements.

Controlling Content Dynamically

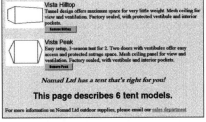

Contents

Positioning with DHTML

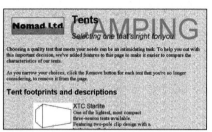

Implementing Advanced DHTML Features

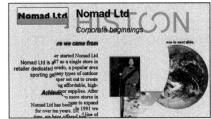

Contents

Structuring Data with XML
HTML N-1

Appendix HTML AP-1

Creating
an HTML document

You already know how to navigate the World Wide Web. Now you'll learn how to create beautiful Web pages using markup codes called HTML. You'll also learn how to link Web sites, include graphic images and sound files, and create user-friendly forms. ◢═ As the Web manager for the Nomad Ltd travel and sporting goods company, Grace Dekmejian needs to create an attractive series of pages that will ultimately allow customers to place orders using the World Wide Web.

HTML

Understanding HTML

HTML is an acronym for HyperText Markup Language. It allows all types of computers to interpret information on the World Wide Web in the same way. HTML is a series of tags, sometimes called **elements**, **containers**, or **codes**, that surround text you are coding for special treatment much like parentheses or quotation marks. Text in an HTML document can be controlled, just as in word processing, by adding formatting attributes such as bolding. In addition, you can insert graphic images, sound files, and multimedia clips. A Web user accesses these elements by clicking "links" on the Web page. Figure A-1 shows a Web page created using HTML. Grace wants Nomad Ltd's Web site to look professional and be easy to use so customers can find what they're looking for. By using an HTML Web page, she can:

Details

Include text that is attractive and professional-looking

With HTML tags, you can easily create high-impact text by using various type sizes and fonts and enhance text with bolding, underlining, and italics.

Link Web sites

In your own experience using the Web, you've probably gone from one location to another using links. **Links**, or **hyperlinks**, are other Web site addresses (called **uniform resource locators** or **URLs**) that are coded into an HTML document. Since Nomad cooperates in a variety of environmental projects, you include links to take readers directly to information that may be of interest to them. The ability to link Web sites—even those not belonging to Nomad—creates an informative, easy-to-use series of pages. As URLs change, links can be continuously updated and modified. Figure A-2 shows the relationships that can exist between Web pages.

Create tables and lists

HTML codes easily create numbered and bulleted lists for items in the catalog or steps to follow. In addition, tables can be created to make columnar text or data easy to read.

Include graphic images, sound files, and multimedia clips

Web pages without graphic images would be dull. Nomad's Web site must be exciting and interesting to visit. You want to include plenty of graphic images and sound files.

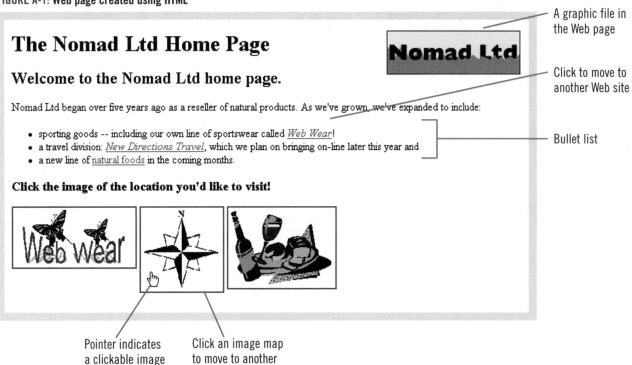

The Nomad Ltd Home Page

Welcome to the Nomad Ltd home page.

Nomad Ltd began over five years ago as a reseller of natural products. As we've grown, we've expanded to include:

- sporting goods -- including our own line of sportswear called *Web Wear*!
- a travel division: *New Directions Travel*, which we plan on bringing on-line later this year and
- a new line of natural foods in the coming months.

Click the image of the location you'd like to visit!

A graphic file in the Web page

Click to move to another Web site

Bullet list

Pointer indicates a clickable image

Click an image map to move to another Web site

FIGURE A-2: Possible relationships between Web pages

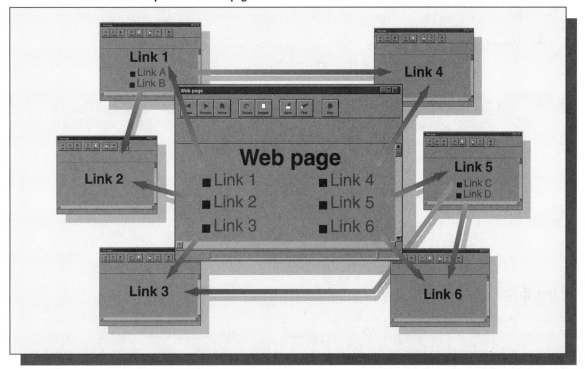

HTML

Planning an HTML Document

Before writing an HTML document, you should plan what elements you want on the page. Although you'll probably modify your initial page format, it is a good idea to have a master plan. Grace reviews the steps for planning and creating her Web page:

Details

Create an outline
The first step in creating a Web page is to prepare an outline. The outline should include a list of all the elements for your page, including its title, an introductory paragraph, links to other sites, an optional graphic image, and a contact address, as shown in Figure A-3.

Enter the text in a document
Use a text editor to create the document that will be the Web page.

Insert HTML tags around each element on the page
Type HTML tags around the elements in your document.

Add graphics
Insert HTML-compatible graphic files to add value to your page and make it attractive.

Add links to other Web sites
Create links in your document to other Web sites that would be of interest to your readers.

Save the document
Save your work often to prevent loss of data.

View the page
Periodically examine your page using a Web browser, as shown in Figure A-4. Correct any errors to the HTML codes as you go.

Test the links
Make sure the links in your HTML page are correct and function properly. Verify that you have entered the URLs correctly and go to those sites to be sure they are still active.

CLUES TO USE

Using a text editor versus a word processor

Many word processors, such as Microsoft Word, offer a Save as HTML command in the File menu that translates an ordinary document into one usable on the Web. Instead of typing tags—as is done in the exercises in this book—you type text and the program determines what types of tags are needed. For this reason, this book makes use of a plain text editor (such as WordPad or NotePad). If your word processor offers an HTML document type, this may be suitable to create a plain text document.

FIGURE A-3: Sample outline of a Web page

I Title: The Nomad Ltd on-line catalog!
   (display company logo)

II Description
      a. company, philosophy
      b. products

III Web links
      a. to our products
      b. to order form
      c. to additional information

IV Closing
      a. thank you
      b. e-mail and U.S. mail addresses

FIGURE A-4: Completed Web page

The Nomad Ltd on-line catalog!

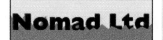

Welcome to the **Nomad Ltd** on-line catalog. As merchants of fine sporting goods and other natural products, our company has been thriving for over five years. We are pleased to offer a new line of clothing called *"Web Wear"* to our on-line customers!

Exclusively for our on-line customers,
Web Wear is designed for the active Web surfer.
You'll find our styles comfy and our materials politically correct.
We hope you enjoy *Web Wear*!

Enjoy browsing through our catalog!

Unisex *Web Wear* is way cool!
Order form so you get *Web Wear* fast!

HTML

Writing an HTML Document

Once you've planned what elements you want to include in your document, it's time to create it. Any word processor or text editor can be used to type an HTML document. When you save the document, make sure the document type is a text file using the extension **.htm**. Newer word-processors have a "Save as HTML" option that automatically inserts HTML codes into uncoded documents. When a Web browser views an HTML document, it ignores uncoded line spaces and whether the tags are in upper or lowercase letters. HTML tags are enclosed in brackets (< >), and sometimes occur in pairs (both before and after the text they surround). Tags that do not occur in pairs are sometimes called **empty containers**. The ending tag differs from the beginning tag: it contains a slash (/) as the first character within the brackets. Grace decides to create her HTML document using the WordPad text editor included with Windows. You can use any word processor that can save a text file to create an HTML document.

QuickTip

Use a plain text editor, such as WordPad or NotePad, to ensure results like those found in these lessons.

1. **Click Start on the taskbar, point to Programs, point to Accessories, click WordPad, then maximize the screen, if necessary**
   A blank WordPad document opens. Every HTML document contains tags that identify it as an HTML document, and tags for the Head, Title, and Body text. Table A-1 lists the tags necessary for a basic HTML document.

2. **Type <HTML> then press [Enter]**
   The typed text appears and the insertion point moves to the next line. You can use upper- and lowercase letters, line spaces, and hard returns to make your HTML code easier to read without affecting its appearance on the Web.

3. **Type the remaining text shown in Figure A-5**
   Now the initial text is entered. Saving documents is an important step in any work session.

4. **Insert your Project Disk into the appropriate drive**

Trouble?

Using a Save as HTML command on a document created with a word processor may produce unusual results if the document contains typed tags.

5. **Click File on the menu bar, then click Save**
   The Save As dialog box opens. See Figure A-6. These lessons assume that your Project Disk is in drive A.

6. **Click the Save in list arrow, then click 3½ Floppy (A:) or (B): (*whichever drive contains your Project Disk*)**
   If you are using a different drive or storing your practice files on a network, click the appropriate drive. If you are using a text editor other than WordPad, save the document as Nomad.htm and skip to the next lesson.

7. **Double-click Document in the File name box, then type Nomad.htm to replace the default filename**

8. **Make sure Text Document appears in the Save as type list box, then click Save**
   The Save As dialog box closes, and the filename appears in the title bar at the top of the document.

FIGURE A-5: **Document with HTML tags**

```
<HTML>

<HEAD>
<TITLE>The Nomad Ltd on-line catalog</TITLE>
</HEAD>

<BODY>
Welcome to the Nomad Ltd on-line catalog!
</BODY>

</HTML>
|
```

FIGURE A-6: **Save As dialog box**

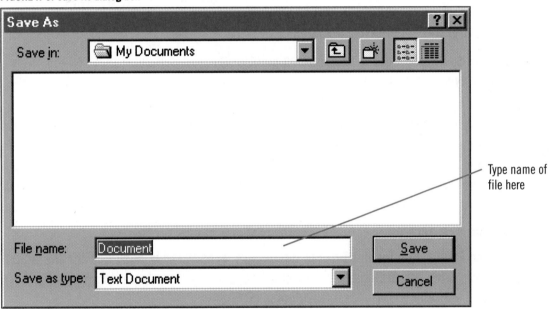

Type name of
file here

TABLE A-1: **Tags in a basic HTML document**

tags	purpose	example
<HTML></HTML>	Identifies the document as one consisting of HTML tags. Without these tags, the document could be misinterpreted as "text only."	<HTML><HEAD><TITLE> The Nomad Ltd on-line catalog </TITLE></HEAD><BODY> We hope you love our merchandise!</BODY></HTML>
<HEAD></HEAD>	The head element identifies the first part of your HTML-coded document that contains the title. The title is shown as part of your browser's window.	<HEAD><TITLE> The Nomad Ltd on-line catalog </TITLE></HEAD>
<TITLE></TITLE>	A required element that indicates the document's title, which appears in the title bar, and is often used by Web indexing systems.	<TITLE>The Nomad Ltd on-line catalog</TITLE>
<BODY></BODY>	Contains the bulk of the document, including headings, text, lists, links, graphics, and multimedia.	<BODY>We hope you love our merchandise!</BODY>

HTML

HTML

Editing and Viewing an HTML Document

Like any document, an HTML document is rarely written perfectly the first time. When editing an HTML document, you use the same editing techniques used in word processing. HTML documents can have up to six sizes of headings. Although each Web browser can display headings differently, Table A-2 shows the relative size of HTML headings. Grace wants to expand the body text in her document and add headings to give impact to special text. She begins the body of the page with a large heading.

Steps

1. Click to the left of the word Welcome, type <H1>The Nomad Ltd on-line catalog!</H1>, then press [Enter]
   This text will be the largest size heading.

2. Click to the right of the exclamation point in the next sentence, press [Backspace], then type a period (.)
   The exclamation point is replaced with a period.

QuickTip

HTML is easier to read and write in WordPad if the Wrap to ruler option is selected on the Text tab in the Options dialog box.

3. Press [Spacebar], type As merchants of fine sporting goods and other natural products, our company has been thriving for over five years. We are pleased to offer a new line of clothing called "Web Wear" to our on-line customers!, then press [Enter]
   A new paragraph can be added using the <P> tag.

4. Type <P> then press [Enter]

5. Type Exclusively for our on-line customers, Web Wear is designed for the active Web surfer. You'll find our styles comfy and our materials politically correct. We hope you enjoy Web Wear!, then press [Enter]
   A level 2 heading is smaller than a level 1 heading.

6. Type <H2>Enjoy browsing through our catalog!</H2>, then press [Enter]
   Compare your document with Figure A-7.

Trouble?

If the text editor prompts you when saving an existing file, Make sure you save the file as a text document.

7. Save the document
   Once your document is saved, it can be viewed using your browser.

8. Start your browser, cancel any dial up operations, then open the file Nomad.htm
   Note: You do not have to be online to complete the steps. Compare your page with Figure A-8. You can leave your browser open so you can easily see your progress; use the taskbar to switch between the browser and text editor.

9. Click the text editor program button on the taskbar

FIGURE A-7: New text and headings added

```
<HTML>

<HEAD>
<TITLE>The Nomad Ltd on-line catalog></TITLE>
</HEAD>

<BODY>
<H1>The Nomad Ltd on-line catalog!</H1>
Welcome to the Nomad Ltd on-line catalog. As merchants of fine sporting
goods and other natural products, our company has been thriving for over
five years. We are pleased to offer a new line of clothing called "Web
Wear" to our on-line customers!
<P>
Exclusively for our on-line customers, Web Wear is designed for the
active Web surfer. You'll find our styles comfy and our materials
politically correct. We hope you enjoy Web Wear!
<H2>Enjoy browsing through our catalog!</H2>
|
</BODY>

</HTML>
```

— Heading 1 added
— Paragraph tag
— Heading 2 added

FIGURE A-8: Document viewed in the browser

The Nomad Ltd on-line catalog! ———— Heading 1

Welcome to the Nomad Ltd on-line catalog. As merchants of fine sporting goods and other natural products, our company has been thriving for over five years. We are pleased to offer a new line of clothing called "Web Wear" to our on-line customers!

Exclusively for our on-line customers. Web Wear is designed for the active Web surfer. You'll find our styles comfy and our materials politically correct. We hope you enjoy Web Wear! ———— New paragraph

Enjoy browsing through our catalog! ———— Heading 2

TABLE A-2: HTML headings

heading tags	sample	result
<H1> </H1>	<H1>Heading 1</H1>	# Heading 1
<H2> </H2>	<H2>Heading 2</H2>	## Heading 2
<H3> </H3>	<H3>Heading 3</H3>	### Heading 3
<H4> </H4>	<H4>Heading 4</H4>	Heading 4
<H5> </H5>	<H5>Heading 5</H5>	Heading 5
<H6> </H6>	<H6>Heading 6</H6>	Heading 6

HTML

Linking Documents to Other Web Sites

One of the most exciting features of HTML documents is the ability to go from one Web site to another by clicking a link. **Links**, or **hyperlinks**, display on a page in a different color and are jumps to other Web sites. When the mouse pointer is over a link, it changes to 🖑. Links can be created using URL or local file addresses and can be created before the link file is even created. You may notice that familiar DOS symbols look different in HTML. ━━ Grace wants to add two links to the document: one to a page showing different Web Wear styles, and a second one to an order form page.

Steps

1. Click below the <H2> </H2> heading line
Each link refers to an HTML file that you will create and save later. The link is defined in the first <A> tag. The information between the first and second tags is what displays, and clicking it moves you to the site.

Trouble?

The pipe symbol (|) is often located on the same key as the backslash symbol(\).

2. Type <A HREF=file:///al/Nomad2.htm>Unisex Web Wear</A> is way cool!, then press [Enter]
On a real Web page, you would not link files to a file stored on a disk drive, but to other sites on the Web. In these steps, you link files to the drive containing your student files.

3. Type <A HREF=file:///al/Nomad3.htm>Order now</A> to get Web Wear fast., then press [Enter]
Compare your document with Figure A-9.

4. Click the Save button on the toolbar, click Save as Text Document (if necessary), then click the browser program button on the taskbar
Since this file is already open, you can refresh, or reload, the image to view the latest changes through the browser.

Trouble?

Depending upon the browser you are using, you will either have a Reload or a Refresh button on the toolbar. You click this button to update the document to view the changes in the browser.

5. View the saved version of Nomad.htm by refreshing your screen
The image is updated to display the links added to the file. When the pointer passes over the link, it changes to 🖑, and the site displays in the status area of the browser.

6. Move 🖑 over the text Order now, *but don't click the mouse button*
Compare your document with Figure A-10.

7. Click the text editor program button on the taskbar

CLUES TO USE

Translating DOS symbols to HTML

DOS symbols such as the backslash (\ ) and colon (:) look different in an HTML document. The backslash, used to indicate filename locations, is replaced with a slash (/). The colon, used to note a storage volume—such as a diskette—is replaced with a pipe (|). That's why the statement "file:\\\a:\Nomad.htm" was typed as "file:///al/Nomad2.htm." This change in symbols enables a wide range of computers to understand the link.

```
<HTML>

<HEAD>
<TITLE>The Nomad Ltd on-line catalog></TITLE>
</HEAD>

<BODY>
<H1>The Nomad Ltd on-line catalog!</H1>
Welcome to the Nomad Ltd on-line catalog. As merchants of fine sporting
goods and other natural products, our company has been thriving for over
five years. We are pleased to offer a new line of clothing called "Web
Wear" to our on-line customers!
<P>
Exclusively for our on-line customers, Web Wear is designed for the
active Web surfer. You'll find our styles comfy and our materials
politically correct. We hope you enjoy Web Wear!
<H2>Enjoy browsing through our catalog!</H2>
<A HREF=file:///a|/Nomad2.htm>Unisex Web Wear</A> is way cool!
<A HREF=file:///a|/Nomad3.htm>Order now</A> to get Web Wear fast.

</BODY>

</HTML>
```

Link to other page or
site doesn't display in
browser

Click to move to
a new location

FIGURE A-10: Links displayed in the Web page

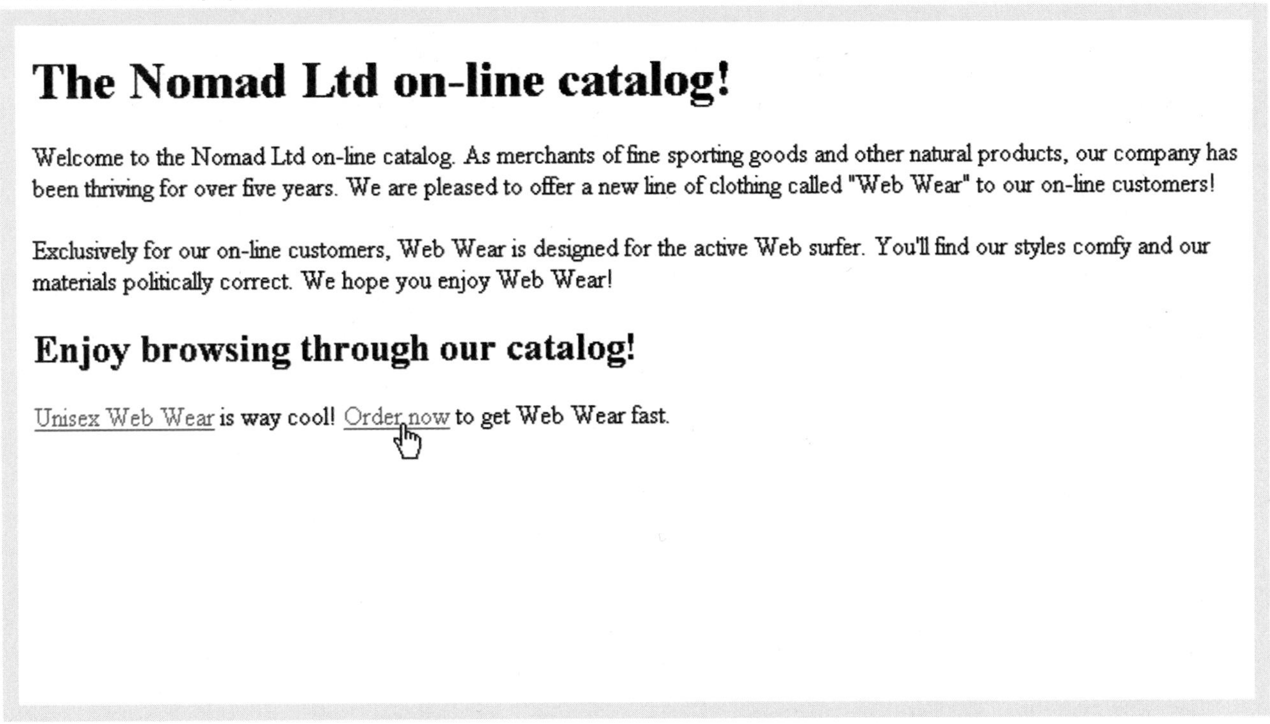

The Nomad Ltd on-line catalog!

Welcome to the Nomad Ltd on-line catalog. As merchants of fine sporting goods and other natural products, our company has been thriving for over five years. We are pleased to offer a new line of clothing called "Web Wear" to our on-line customers!

Exclusively for our on-line customers, Web Wear is designed for the active Web surfer. You'll find our styles comfy and our materials politically correct. We hope you enjoy Web Wear!

Enjoy browsing through our catalog!

Unisex Web Wear is way cool! Order now to get Web Wear fast.

HTML

Printing an HTML Document

To keep records of your work, it's important to be able to print documents. Due to their tags, HTML documents are not very attractive; however, you might need to give a co-worker a copy of a document, or you might want to keep a copy for your records. Most browsers make it possible to view and then print the HTML tags of the active document from within the browser. A Web browser can be assigned to whichever HTML editor you use. ✐ Grace wants to print the HTML document and the browser page.

Steps

1. **Click the Print button on the toolbar**
   A single copy of the document prints from the text editor. The HTML tags look slightly different from within the browser.

2. **Click the browser program button on the taskbar**
   Every browser has menu commands to view the HTML source document. Depending on which browser you are using, the menu commands to view the source document may vary.

Trouble?

Depending on which browser you are using, a document's source may be displayed in a text editor, such as Notepad or Wordpad. Your HTML source codes may display in a different window.

3. **Click View on the menu bar, then click Source (or Page Source)**
   The HTML tags for the current document display in the window, as shown in Figure A-11.

4. **Click the Close button on the title bar**
   You can print the Web page using a button on the toolbar.

5. **Click the Print button on the toolbar, then follow any directions to print the page**
   The active page is sent to the printer. You are finished with the initial work on this Web page and decide to close the browser and text editor.

QuickTip

You can close a program quickly by clicking the Close button on the program's title bar.

6. **Click File on the browser menu bar, then click Exit**

7. **Click File on the text editor menu bar, then click Exit**

FIGURE A-11: HTML tags displayed

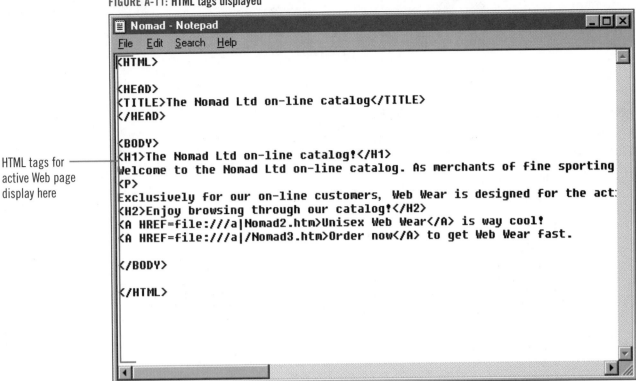

HTML tags for
active Web page
display here

Viewing codes with an HTML editor

HTML editors that show you exactly what your Web
page will look like as you create it also let you see
your codes. In FrontPage Express, you can see color-
coded HTML codes that make it easy to distinguish
codes from Web page text. To examine the HTML
codes, click View on the menu bar, then click HTML.
The View or Edit HTML dialog box opens, as shown
in Figure A-12. Using the FrontPage Express editor,
you can modify a Web page using tags or WYSIWYG
("What You See Is What You Get") view.

FIGURE A-12: Color-coded tags in an HTML editor

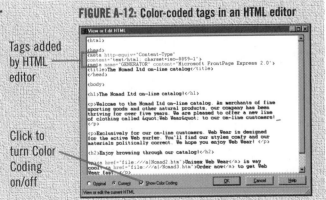

Tags added
by HTML
editor

Click to
turn Color
Coding
on/off

HTML

Practice

► Concepts Review

Label each element of the WordPad screen shown in Figure A-13.

FIGURE A-13

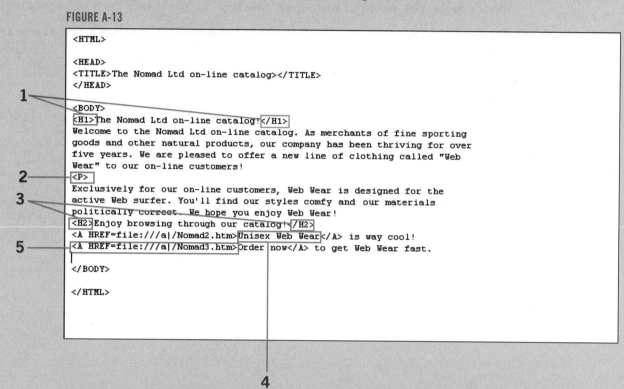

```
<HTML>

<HEAD>
<TITLE>The Nomad Ltd on-line catalog></TITLE>
</HEAD>

<BODY>
<H1>The Nomad Ltd on-line catalog!</H1>
Welcome to the Nomad Ltd on-line catalog. As merchants of fine sporting
goods and other natural products, our company has been thriving for over
five years. We are pleased to offer a new line of clothing called "Web
Wear" to our on-line customers!
<P>
Exclusively for our on-line customers, Web Wear is designed for the
active Web surfer. You'll find our styles comfy and our materials
politically correct. We hope you enjoy Web Wear!
<H2>Enjoy browsing through our catalog!</H2>
<A HREF=file:///a|/Nomad2.htm>Unisex Web Wear</A> is way cool!
<A HREF=file:///a|/Nomad3.htm>Order now</A> to get Web Wear fast.

</BODY>

</HTML>
```

1

2

3

5

4

Match each statement with the term or button that it describes.

6. Updates a browser image
7. Displays an HTML link in a browser
8. Jumps to another Web page
9. Displays HTML tags in a browser
10. Opens the active document in WordPad

a. 📄 Nomad - WordPad
b. View, Source
c. Reload/Refresh
d. Hyperlink
e. 🖑

Select the best answer from the list of choices.

11. **Which tags are used to create the largest heading?**
    a. <H6> </H6>
    b. <Lheading> </Lheading>
    c. <H1> </H1>
    d. <H1> <\H1>

12. **When typing HTML tags, you should type the tags using**
    a. uppercase only
    b. lowercase only
    c. either upper- or lowercase
    d. uppercase for the opening tag; lowercase for the closing tag

13. **Which menu is used to open a local file in a browser?**
    a. File
    b. Edit
    c. View
    d. Format

14. **In HTML, which symbol replaces the colon (:) used in a DOS filename address?**
    a. /
    b. ;
    c. }
    d. |

15. **HTML stands for**
    a. HypertText Modern Language
    b. HyperText Markup Language
    c. HyperTool Modern Linkage
    d. HyperTool Markup Linkage

16. **Tags used by computers to interpret information on the Web are called?**
    a. Keylinks
    b. Webwords
    c. Containers
    d. Samifars

17. **URL stands for**
    a. Universal Resource Locator
    b. Universal Resource Location
    c. Uniform Resource Link
    d. Uniform Resource Location

18. Which tags contain the bulk of an HTML document?
   a. <BODY></BODY>
   b. <HTML></HTML>
   c. <TITLE></TITLE>
   d. <HEAD></HEAD>

19. Which HTML tag creates a new paragraph?
   a. <PARA>
   b. <NEW>
   c. <P>
   d. <NP>

Skills Review

1. Start the text editor.
   a. Open a blank document.
   b. Become familiar with the toolbar buttons.
   c. If you are using WordPad make sure the Wrap to ruler button is selected.

2. Write an HTML document.
   a. Type the initial <HTML> tag at the beginning of the document.
   b. Type the remaining information shown in Figure A-14.
   c. Save your work as a text document called Crystal Clear Opticals.htm.

FIGURE A-14

```
<HTML>

<HEAD>
<TITLE>Crystal Clear Opticals</TITLE>
</HEAD>

<BODY>
Welcome to the Crystal Clear Opticals Web page. We're offering super-
cool looking eyewear at phenomenal discounts. If you're looking for the
sharpest looks on the Web . . . look no further!
</BODY>

</HTML>
```

3. **Edit and view an HTML document.**
   a. Add "Home Page" to the end of the Title text.
   b. Add the largest possible heading after the initial Body tag that says "The Crystal Clear Opticals Web page."
   c. Add a paragraph tag after ". . . look no further!".
   d. Type a new paragraph as follows: "Crystal Clear Opticals has been in business since 1972, and has always been dedicated to offering the best looking eyewear at the lowest prices."
   e. Add a smaller size heading under the previous paragraph that says "We know you'll find an attractive style to suit your needs!"
   f. Save your work.
   g. Open your browser, then open and view the Crystal Clear Opticals.htm file.
   h. Leave your browser open, then return to the text editor.

4. **Link documents to other sites.**
   a. Create a link to a file called Women's fashions.htm. The clickable text should read "Women, check these out!"
   b. Create a link to a file called Men's fashions.htm. The clickable text should read "Hey, Men, great looking shades!"
   c. Save your work.
   d. Return to your browser and refresh the Crystal Clear Opticals.htm file.

5. **Print an HTML document.**
   a. Print the browser document.
   b. View the HTML tags while in your browser.
   c. Return to the text editor, then print the Crystal Clear Opticals document.
   d. Exit the text editor.
   e. Exit your browser.

▶ Independent Challenges

1. Your computer consulting business, Star Dot Star, now has a "Web presence." Using the skills you learned in this unit, plan and create a Web page for your consulting firm. Use a text editor to write your HTML tags, then use your browser to view the finished page. Your page should include at least two headings, as well as links to other Web pages or sites.

To complete this independent challenge:

a. Create an outline that includes all the topics you want to cover in your Web page.

b. Decide which HTML tags you'll need and which outline elements they'll be assigned to.

c. Decide if you'll want to use any graphic images, which you'll insert at a later date. Where will you insert these images?

d. Add at least two links to your Web page.

e. Save your work as a text document called My Web Page.htm.

f. Print the document in your text editor and in your browser.

2. Your local Board of Realtors has hired you to create a Web page for your community. Because you are familiar with the area and HTML, you'll be able to design a professional-looking page that will help attract potential real estate customers.

To complete this independent challenge:

a. Create an outline that includes all the items you want to include in your Web page. What qualities about your community do you want to mention?

b. Decide which HTML tags you'll need and which outline elements they'll be assigned to.

c. Decide if you'll want to use any graphic images, which you'll insert at a later date. Where will you insert these images?

d. Add at least three links on your Web page.

e. Save your work as a text document called Real Estate.htm on your Student Disk.

f. Print the document in your text editor and in your browser.

3. Use the Web to find examples of personal pages you might use as a model for a page you want to develop on your own. Personal pages are typically individuals' pages who display their interests on hobbies on their Web site.
To complete this independent challenge:

a. Establish an Internet connection.
b. Use any search engine to locate at least two personal Web pages. (*Hint:* you might start looking at a home page for an Internet Service Provider in your area.)
c. Print these pages as well as their source codes.
d. Identify HTML tags that are familiar by circling them on the page.
e. Disconnect from the Internet.
f. Exit your browser.

4. Use the Web to find examples of interesting business pages.
To complete this independent challenge:

a. Establish an Internet connection.
b. Use any search engine to locate at least two business Web pages. (*Hint:* you might start looking at a home page for an Internet Service Provider in your area.)
c. Print these pages as well as their source codes.
d. Identify HTML tags that are familiar.
e. Disconnect from the Internet.
f. Exit your browser.

HTML

Visual Workshop

Use the skills you learned in this unit to create the Web page shown in Figure A-15. Save your HTML file as a text document called Marvelous Musicals.htm, then print the document in your text editor and your browser.

FIGURE A-15

The Marvelous Musicals Web page

If you love musicals from the 1930s through the 1960s, you've come to the right place!

Marvelous Musicals is dedicated to celebrating the 'golden age' of movie musicals and their artists. Click here to see a complete list of the movies and artists we're featuring.

In months to come, we'll keep adding pages to this Web site, so stay tuned . . .

Currently, we're featuring pages on the following:

Gene Kelly was elegant and athletic! Fred Astaire was always debonair! On the Town is an on-location romp through New York City! The King and I: Yul Brynner at his best!

HTML Unit **B**

Controlling
HTML Text

Objectives

▶ Plan document formats
▶ Create ordered and definition lists
▶ Create unordered lists
▶ Format text
▶ Add line breaks
▶ Use preformatted text
▶ Create a table

Now that you know how to create a simple Web page and link sites to it, it's time to learn how to control the text within it. You can format HTML text in many ways to make it more attractive and dynamic when viewed with a Web browser. Grace wants to enhance the text on Nomad Ltd's Web page to attract customers to visit other Nomad sites.

HTML

Planning Document Formats

HTML documents can contain a variety of formatted text. As you learned previously, a Web document's appearance is controlled by its HTML tags. These tags control whether the text has numbers or bullets before each line, and how each level of the text is indented or displayed. Common HTML formats found in Web documents are shown in Table B-1. Grace decides how she wants her text to appear on the page. Using common HTML tags, she can display her text using:

Details

Ordered lists
Sometimes referred to as a *numbered list*, each line of text in the list is preceded by a number. If Grace decides to change the order of the items in the list, HTML will automatically renumber the list correctly.

QuickTip

An easy way to remember HTML list tags is that UL is short for an unordered list, OL is short for an ordered list, DL is short for a definition list, and DIR is short for a directory list.

Unordered lists
Each item in an unordered or *bulleted list* is preceded by a dark, round circle, as shown in Figure B-1. Each item in an unordered list displays with a hanging indent, in which each new line of the text appears directly underneath the previous line. Use an unordered list to call attention to specific products.

Directory lists
Like a telephone directory, a directory list appears as multiple columns across a Web page. This type of list is used to display items of equal importance in a wide, space-saving format.

Menu lists
Items in a menu list display left-justified one beneath another; they contain neither numbers nor bullets, and have no hanging indent. This type of list is appropriate when displaying related items that don't have any special order.

Definition lists
A definition list, also shown in Figure B-1, is a handy way of displaying a term or short group of words with an indented description under each term.

Nested lists
Most outlines contain not only headings, but subheadings as well. A nested list allows you to create expanded ordered and unordered lists by combining their tags within an existing list.

FIGURE B-1: Web page with sample lists

The Nomad Ltd on-line directory!

Welcome to the **Nomad Ltd** on-line directory.
We invite you to visit the Nomad Ltd Web site nearest you! Our sites feature some of the following items . . .

Unordered list ———

- Natural Clothing
- Memorable Tours
- Bicycle and Kayaking equipment
- Travel agents

Our Web pages guide you through the following product areas:

Definition list ———

Unisex clothing
　Clothing for men, women, and children. Our clothing has been designed especially for Nomad, and for the *elite* Web surfer.
Travel Tours
　Our tours are exciting and will provide you with a lifetime of memories! Each tour is specificially designed for our customers -- who expect the best!

TABLE B-1: Common HTML formats

description	tags	description	tags
Ordered list	<OL> <LI>*Item 1*</LI> <LI>*Item 2*</LI> </OL>	**Unordered list**	<UL> <LI>*Item 1*</LI> <LI>*Item 2*</LI> </UL>
Directory list	<DIR> <LI>*Item 1*</LI> <LI>*Item 2*</LI> </DIR>	**Menu list**	<MENU> <LI>*Item 1*</LI> <LI>*Item 2*</LI> </MENU>
Definition list	<DL> <DT>*Item 1*</DT> <DD>*description*</DD> <DT>*Item 2*</DT> <DD>*description*</DD> </DL>	**Nested list**	<OL> <LI>*Item A*</LI> <UL> <LI>*Item 1*</LI> <LI>*Item 2-a*</LI> <LI>*Item 2-b*</LI> </UL></OL>

CLUES TO USE

Using a text editor versus a word processor

Many word processors, such as Microsoft Word, offer a Save as HTML command in the File menu that translates an ordinary document into one usable on the Web. Instead of typing tags—as is done in the exercises in this book—you type text and the program determines what types of tags are needed. For this reason, this book makes use of a plain text editor (such as WordPad or NotePad). If you save a document that is coded with HTML tags using the Save as HTML command, it can result in HTML tags appearing twice.

HTML

Creating Ordered and Definition Lists

Arranging text in a list format is an effective way of displaying information. Depending on how it's arranged, a document with one or more lists can be easier to read than one with text in paragraph form. You can use an ordered list to show items of varied importance or a sequential list; an unordered list works well for displaying text of equal importance. Grace wants to organize her Web page so customers can easily see Nomad's online items. She's already started her HTML document and has inserted placeholders where she wants the lists to occur.

Steps

1. Start the **text editor**, open the file **HTML B-1.htm**, then save it as a text document with the filename **Nomad2.htm**
   You start an ordered list by typing the <OL> initial tag. A selected placeholder is automatically replaced by typing.

2. Select the **PLACE ORDERED LIST HERE** text, type **<OL>**, then press **[Enter]**
   Each of the individual items in the list must be surrounded by the HTML tags <LI> and </LI>.

3. Type **<LI>Mega way-cool bitmapped T-Shirt</LI>**, then press **[Enter]**
   A blank line appears after the first list item.

4. Type the three items highlighted in Figure B-2, then press **[Enter]**
   An ordered list ends using the </OL> HTML tag.

5. Type **</OL>**
   A definition list is used to explain each of the designs. Unlike the ordered list, the definition list uses three groups of HTML tags. The initial definition tag is <DL>.

6. Select the **PLACE DEFINITION LIST HERE** text, type **<DL>**, then press **[Enter]**
   A definition list consists of a text line, usually containing the term to be defined. The <DT> tag is used.

7. Type **<DT>Mega way-cool bitmapped T-Shirt</DT>**, then press **[Enter]**
   The explanation uses the <DD> tag.

8. Type **<DD>An original creation, 100% cotton, in navy blue or crimson.</DD>**, press **[Enter]**, then type **</DL>**
   The definition or explanation appears indented on the line beneath the term. Compare your document with Figure B-2.

Trouble?

Cancel any dial-up activities.

9. Save the file **Nomad2.htm** as a text document, start your browser, open the file **Nomad2.htm**, then scroll through the file to view all the lists
   Compare your work with Figure B-3.

FIGURE B-2: HTML document with ordered and definition list tags

Type these tags for ordered list

Tags for definition list

```
Web Wear is available in the following designs:
<OL>
<LI>Mega way-cool bitmapped T-Shirt</LI>
<LI>Awesome elegant T-Shirt</LI>
<LI>Whatsamatta T-Shirt</LI>
<LI>On-line Chat T-Shirt</LI>
</OL>
<H2>What's the difference between the designs?</H2>
<DL>
<DT>Mega way-cool bitmapped T-Shirt</DT>
<DD>An original creation, 100% cotton, in navy blue or crimson.</DD>
</DL>
<H2>Sizes and Styles</H2>
Nomad Ltd's Web Wear is conveniently sized for both genders and is
available in the following styles:
PLACE UNORDERED LIST HERE
```

FIGURE B-3: Web page with ordered and definition lists

Ordered list

Definition list

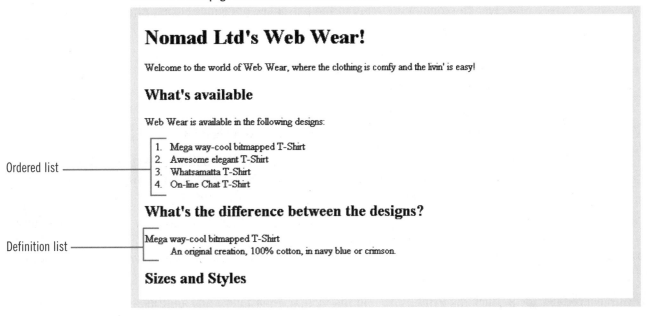

Nomad Ltd's Web Wear!

Welcome to the world of Web Wear, where the clothing is comfy and the livin' is easy!

What's available

Web Wear is available in the following designs:

1. Mega way-cool bitmapped T-Shirt
2. Awesome elegant T-Shirt
3. Whatsamatta T-Shirt
4. On-line Chat T-Shirt

What's the difference between the designs?

Mega way-cool bitmapped T-Shirt
An original creation, 100% cotton, in navy blue or crimson.

Sizes and Styles

Creating Unordered Lists

An unordered list makes it possible to display text with bullet characters preceding each line. This is an effective way of calling attention to each item in the list. An unordered list is created in the same manner as an ordered list, except that the initial and final tags are <UL> and </UL>. Grace wants to include an unordered list on her Web page. She begins by opening the HTML document in the text editor, but leaves her browser open so she can review her progress.

Steps

1. Click the text editor program button on the taskbar
The Nomad2.htm document appears.

2. Select the text PLACE UNORDERED LIST HERE, type <UL>, then press [Enter]
As in an ordered list, each of the individual items in the unordered list are surrounded by the HTML tags <LI> </LI>.

3. Type <LI>Long sleeves, crew neck</LI>, then press [Enter]

4. Type the remaining items in the list below pressing [Enter] after each line:
<LI>Long sleeves, turtleneck</LI>
<LI>Short sleeves, crew neck</LI>
<LI>Short sleeves, turtleneck</LI>
Your list contains four items.

5. Type </UL>
Compare your completed HTML document with Figure B-4.

6. Click the Save button on the toolbar to save Nomad2.htm as a text document
Next, you can view the document in your browser. When you switch back to view the changes in the browser, you have to reload or refresh the document.

> **QuickTip**
>
> In Netscape Navigator, click Reload on the toolbar to refresh your screen.

7. Click the browser program button on the taskbar, then view the saved version of Nomad2.htm by refreshing your screen
Compare your page with Figure B-5; you might have to scroll down the screen. It is often helpful to have a hard copy version of your work.

> **Trouble?**
>
> Depending on your browser, the Print button will look different. You can also always find the Print command on the File menu.

8. Click the Print button on the toolbar, then follow any additional instructions to print

FIGURE B-4: Tags for unordered list

```
<OL>
<LI>Mega way-cool bitmapped T-Shirt</LI>
<LI>Awesome elegant T-Shirt</LI>
<LI>Whatsamatta T-Shirt</LI>
<LI>On-line Chat T-Shirt</LI>
</OL>
<H2>What's the difference between the designs?</H2>
<DL>
<DT>Mega way-cool bitmapped T-Shirt</DT>
<DD>An original creation, 100% cotton, in navy blue or crimson.</DD>
</DL>
<H2>Sizes and Styles</H2>
Nomad Ltd's Web Wear is conveniently sized for both genders and is
available in the following styles:
<UL>
<LI>Long sleeves, crew neck</LI>
<LI>Long sleeves, turtleneck</LI>
<LI>Short sleeves, crew neck</LI>
<LI>Short sleeves, turtleneck</LI>
</UL>
<P>
```

Unordered list tags

FIGURE B-5: Unordered list in browser

Web Wear is available in the following designs:

1. Mega way-cool bitmapped T-Shirt
2. Awesome elegant T-Shirt
3. Whatsamatta T-Shirt
4. On-line Chat T-Shirt

What's the difference between the designs?

Mega way-cool bitmapped T-Shirt
    An original creation, 100% cotton, in navy blue or crimson.

Sizes and Styles

Nomad Ltd's Web Wear is conveniently sized for both genders and is available in the following styles:

- Long sleeves, crew neck
- Long sleeves, turtleneck
- Short sleeves, crew neck
- Short sleeves, turtleneck

Indented unordered list in browser

HTML

Formatting Text

You can enhance text in an HTML document by adding formatting tags for bolding, italics, and underlining (although some Web browsers do not display underlining). Most HTML formatting tags must surround the text they enhance, however, not all HTML tags require this. By typing a single tag, you can create a dividing line (also known as a horizontal rule) to separate sections on the screen, or a line break to force a line to end before the right margin. Table B-2 lists some common HTML formatting tags. Grace wants to enhance the text in her Web page to make it look more attractive. She'll insert additional HTML tags in the existing document.

Steps

1. **Click the text editor program button on the taskbar**
   You want the words "Web Wear" in the initial heading in the document to be in italics.

2. **Click to the left of the word Web in the first heading below the <BODY> tag, then type <I>**
   The initial italics tag defines the beginning of italicized text.

3. **Click to the right of the word Wear in the first heading below the <BODY> tag, then type </I>**
   Since the words "Web Wear" are generally in italics whenever the product line is printed, you decide to add italics tags around each occurrence throughout the document, except within the title tags.

QuickTip

Use the keyboard shortcut [Ctrl][→] or [Ctrl][←] to move from word to word within text.

4. **Complete Steps 2 and 3 for every occurrence of the words Web Wear in the body of the document**
   Compare your document with Figure B-6. To separate the introductory text from the "What's available" heading, you can add a horizontal rule to the page.

5. **Click to the right of … the livin' is easy!, press [Enter], then type <HR>**
   Although you can't see text formatting or the rule in the text editor, you can view the formatting in your browser.

6. **Save Nomad2.htm as a text document, then click the browser program button on the taskbar**

7. **View the saved version of the document by refreshing your screen**
   The modified Web page appears, as shown in Figure B-7.

FIGURE B-6: Italics tags added to document

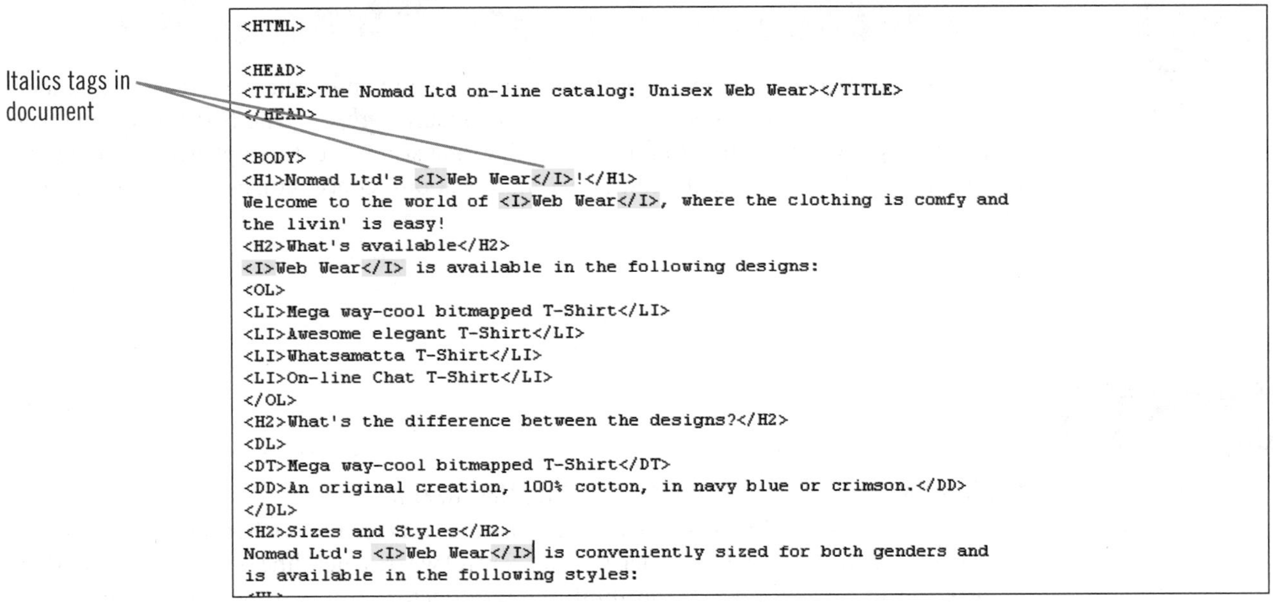

Italics tags in document

```
<HTML>

<HEAD>
<TITLE>The Nomad Ltd on-line catalog: Unisex Web Wear></TITLE>
</HEAD>

<BODY>
<H1>Nomad Ltd's <I>Web Wear</I>!</H1>
Welcome to the world of <I>Web Wear</I>, where the clothing is comfy and
the livin' is easy!
<H2>What's available</H2>
<I>Web Wear</I> is available in the following designs:
<OL>
<LI>Mega way-cool bitmapped T-Shirt</LI>
<LI>Awesome elegant T-Shirt</LI>
<LI>Whatsamatta T-Shirt</LI>
<LI>On-line Chat T-Shirt</LI>
</OL>
<H2>What's the difference between the designs?</H2>
<DL>
<DT>Mega way-cool bitmapped T-Shirt</DT>
<DD>An original creation, 100% cotton, in navy blue or crimson.</DD>
</DL>
<H2>Sizes and Styles</H2>
Nomad Ltd's <I>Web Wear</I> is conveniently sized for both genders and
is available in the following styles:
```

FIGURE B-7: Modified text in browser

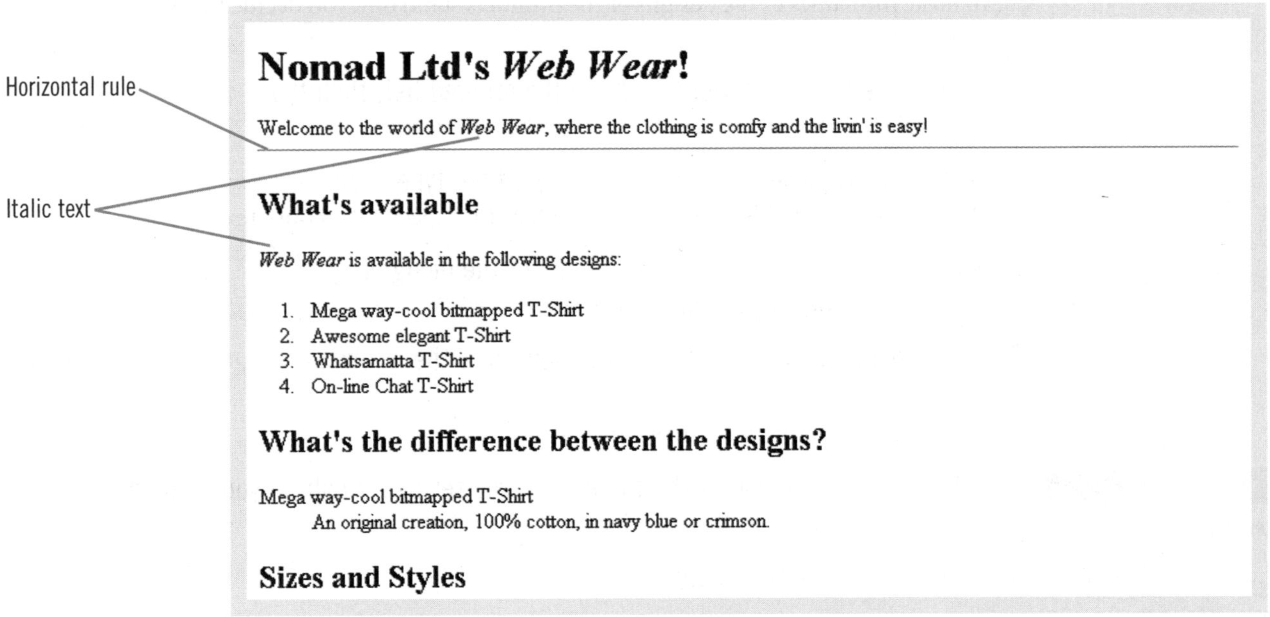

Horizontal rule

Italic text

Nomad Ltd's *Web Wear*!

Welcome to the world of *Web Wear*, where the clothing is comfy and the livin' is easy!

What's available

Web Wear is available in the following designs:

1. Mega way-cool bitmapped T-Shirt
2. Awesome elegant T-Shirt
3. Whatsamatta T-Shirt
4. On-line Chat T-Shirt

What's the difference between the designs?

Mega way-cool bitmapped T-Shirt
   An original creation, 100% cotton, in navy blue or crimson.

Sizes and Styles

TABLE B-2: HTML text formatting tags

description	tag(s)	description	tag(s)
Boldface text	<B> </B>	Italicize text	<I> </I>
Underline text	<U> </U>	Line break	
Horizontal rule	<HR>		

HTML

Adding Line Breaks

Sometimes you might want to end a line to emphasize a point and make the text easier to understand. A line break is used to end a line of text manually. ✎ The first line on the page seems too long, so Grace wants to force a new line. She also wants to emphasize some important text. Before she completes the rest of her modifications, Grace returns to the document.

Steps

1. **Click the text editor program button on the taskbar**
   In most cases, the width of your Web browser window determines when a line of text wraps around to a new line. The <BR> tag lets you control where a new line of text will begin when displayed in a Web browser. You think the introductory text will have more impact if it appears on two lines.

2. **Click to the left of where in the line that starts Welcome to the world of, type
 (after the comma), then press [Enter] and delete the unnecessary space**
   To make the names of the designs of the products stand out, you decide to display the names as bold text.

3. **Click to the left of the word Mega in the ordered list, then type <B>**
   The final tag </B> determines the end of the bold text.

4. **Click to the right of the word bitmapped, then type </B>**
   The word bitmapped is surrounded with tags that specify it as bold text.

5. **Type <B> and </B> tags around each of the designs**
   Compare your document with Figure B-8.

6. **Save the file as a text document, then click the browser program button on the taskbar**
   The browser becomes the active window.

Trouble?

If a text enhancement tag doesn't display as you thought it would, it might not be supported by your Web browser.

7. **View the saved version of the file in the browser by refreshing your screen**
   The page is updated, as shown in Figure B-9.

8. **Print the browser document**

FIGURE B-8: Line break and bold tags added to document

Line break tag

Bold tags

```
<HTML>

<HEAD>
<TITLE>The Nomad Ltd on-line catalog: Unisex Web Wear></TITLE>
</HEAD>

<BODY>
<H1>Nomad Ltd's <I>Web Wear</I>!</H1>
Welcome to the world of <I>Web Wear</I>, <BR>
where the clothing is comfy and the livin' is easy!
<HR>
<H2>What's available</H2>
<I>Web Wear</I> is available in the following designs:
<OL>
<LI><B>Mega way-cool bitmapped</B> T-Shirt</LI>
<LI><B>Awesome elegant</B> T-Shirt</LI>
<LI><B>Whatsamatta</B> T-Shirt</LI>
<LI><B>On-line Chat</B>| T-Shirt</LI>
</OL>
<H2>What's the difference between the designs?</H2>
<DL>
<DT>Mega way-cool bitmapped T-Shirt</DT>
<DD>An original creation, 100% cotton, in navy blue or crimson.</DD>
</DL>
<H2>Sizes and Styles</H2>
Nomad Ltd's <I>Web Wear</I> is conveniently sized for both genders and
```

FIGURE B-9: Web page with line break and bold enhancements added

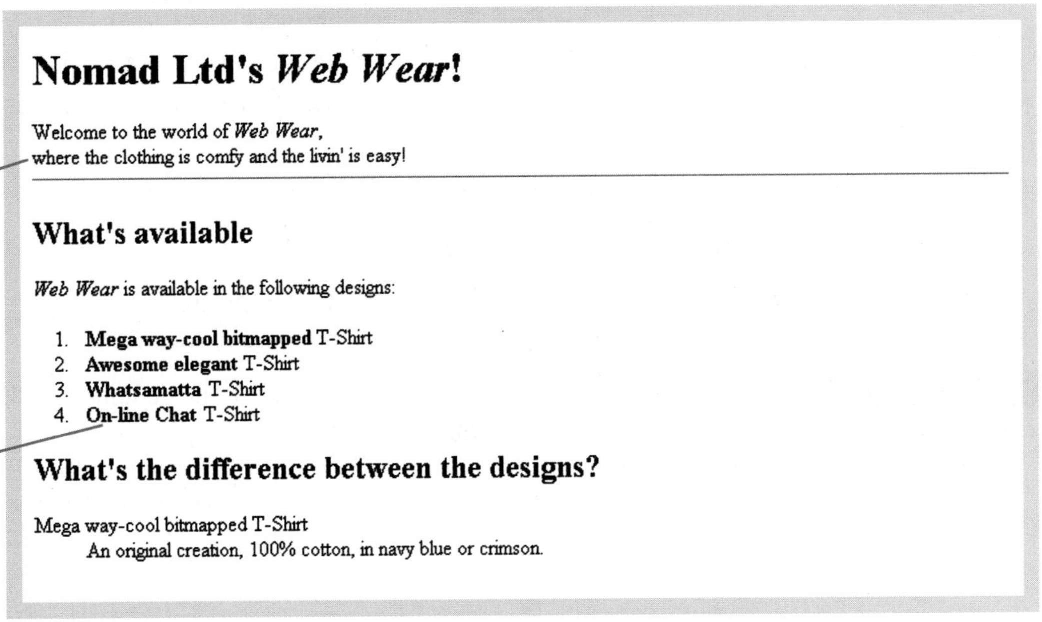

Nomad Ltd's *Web Wear*!

Welcome to the world of *Web Wear*,
where the clothing is comfy and the livin' is easy!

Line break causes new line to start here

What's available

Web Wear is available in the following designs:

1. **Mega way-cool bitmapped** T-Shirt
2. **Awesome elegant** T-Shirt
3. **Whatsamatta** T-Shirt
4. **On-line Chat** T-Shirt

Bold text

What's the difference between the designs?

Mega way-cool bitmapped T-Shirt
    An original creation, 100% cotton, in navy blue or crimson.

Using Preformatted Text

Your Web browser determines how HTML tags are interpreted and how formatted text, such as bold, italics, and bulleted lists will look when displayed. Since there are a variety of browsers currently in use, there is a possibility your text won't look quite the way you want. For that reason, it's possible to include preformatted text in your HTML document. The text within the preformatted tags (<PRE> </PRE>) will be spaced exactly the way you type it in your document. Grace wants to make sure text in her Web page is displayed exactly as she types it.

Steps

1. Open the document HTML B-2.htm, then save it as a text document with the filename Nomad3.htm

Preformatted text can include enhancements, such as bolding and italics, and allows you to include your own line spaces and breaks without having to include the <P> and
 HTML tags inserted in regular text. You want to include preformatted text in the document.

2. Select the INSERT PREFORMATTED TEXT HERE text, then type the following text exactly as follows, pressing [Tab] to indent the lines and [Enter] to insert line breaks and blank lines as needed

```
<PRE>Web surfers
          from Boston to Bermuda
              love <I>Web Wear</I>!


          <B>Quick . . . order yours now!!!</B>
                  Don't be the only surfer without
                      <I>Web Wear</I>! </PRE>
```

3. Press [Enter]

Compare your document with Figure B-10.

4. Save Nomad3.htm as a text document

5. Click the browser program button on the taskbar

Since this file is not already displayed, you open it using the menu.

Trouble?

Depending on your browser the command on the File menu to Open a File or Page may vary slightly.

6. Click File on the menu bar, click Open to open the document, select the Nomad3.htm file, then click Open to view the page

The Web page appears, as shown in Figure B-11. Text within the <PRE></PRE> tags display in a *monotype font* in which each character occupies the same amount of space.

FIGURE B-10: HTML tags for preformatted text

```
<HTML>

<HEAD>
<TITLE>The Nomad Ltd on-line catalog: Order Form</TITLE>
</HEAD>

<BODY>
<H1>Nomad Ltd's <I>Web Wear</I> Order Form!</H1>
<HR>
<PRE>Web surfers
        from Boston to Bermuda
                love <I>Web Wear</I>!

                <B>Quick . . . order yours now!!!</B>
                        Don't be the only surfer without
                                <I>Web Wear</I>!</PRE>

<HR>
```

Preformatted text and tags ———

FIGURE B-11: Preformatted text displayed in browser

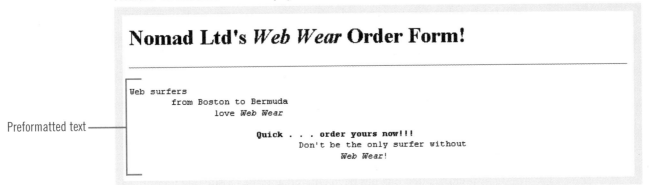

Nomad Ltd's *Web Wear* Order Form!

```
Web surfers
        from Boston to Bermuda
                love Web Wear

                Quick . . . order yours now!!!
                        Don't be the only surfer without
                                Web Wear!
```

Preformatted text ———

Using an HTML editor

You can make the process of writing HTML code easier by using one of the many HTML editors available. These editors, such as Microsoft FrontPage Express or Netscape Composer, make creating HTML documents very easy. Instead of having to type beginning and ending tags, you can insert tags around selected text with the click of a toolbar button or drop-down list. Figure B-12 shows the choice of tags in the FrontPage Express Change Style drop down list.

FIGURE B-12: Document in FrontPage Express

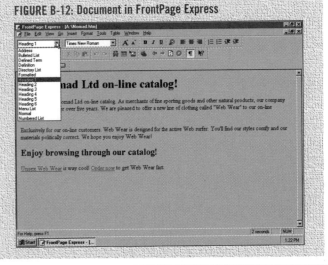

Creating a Table

One of the ways the <PRE> HTML tag can be used is to create a table. A table is created using the preformatted text tags, by typing the text exactly the way you want it to display on the page. Most text on a Web page displays in proportional type (such as Times New Roman), but preformatted text displays in nonproportional type (such as Courier) *exactly* as it is typed, including line breaks and spacing. Some Web browsers support an HTML tag designed specifically for tables (<TABLE> </TABLE>). Since these tags are not supported by all Web browsers, it's safer to use preformatted text. ⬛▬▬ Grace wants to add a table to the text document that shows the colors available for each design.

Steps

1. **Click the text editor program button on the taskbar**
   A placeholder already exists in the document. You replace the placeholder with preformatted text that contains the table. You want the column titles to be bold.

2. **Select the INSERT TABLE HERE text, type <PRE><B>, then press [Enter]**
   When creating a table, you can control the space between columns better if you use the Spacebar rather than [Tab], since the Spacebar allows you to create an exact amount of space between columns.

3. **Type the table data shown in Figure B-13, then press [Enter]**
   Once the table data is typed, you type the final preformatted text tag.

4. **Type </PRE> then press [Enter] if necessary**
   The preformatted text has been entered and the closing tag identifies the end of the text to be included.

5. **Save Nomad3.htm as a text document**

6. **Print the text document**

7. **Click the browser program button on the taskbar**

8. **View the saved version of Nomad3.htm by refreshing your screen, then scroll down the page, if necessary, to see the preformatted text**
   The active page is displayed with the preformatted text, as shown in Figure B-14.

9. **Print the browser document**

10. **Close your browser and text editor**

FIGURE B-13: Table data entered as preformatted text

```
<TITLE>The Nomad Ltd on-line catalog: Order Form</TITLE>
</HEAD>

<BODY>
<H1>Nomad Ltd's <I>Web Wear</I> Order Form!</H1>
<HR>
<PRE>Web surfers
        from Boston to Bermuda
                love <I>Web Wear</I>!

                <B>Quick . . . order yours now!!!</B>
                        Don't be the only surfer without
                                <I>Web Wear</I>!</PRE>

<HR>
<H2>Here's a recap of our designs!</H2>
<PRE><B>
Design                    Color 1            Color 2</B>
Mega way-cool bitmapped   navy blue          crimson
Awesome elegant           yellow             orange
Whatsamatta               purple             red
On-line Chat              green              berry
</PRE>

</BODY>

</HTML>
```

Preformatted tags surround table data

Use the Spacebar to create space between columns

FIGURE B-14: Completed table in browser

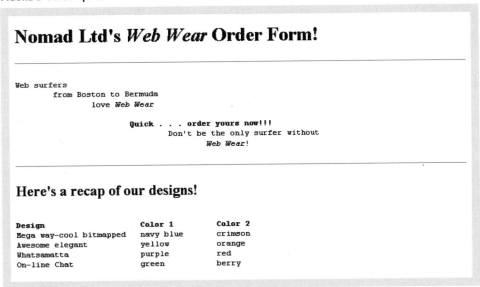

Nomad Ltd's *Web Wear* Order Form!

```
Web surfers
        from Boston to Bermuda
                love Web Wear

                Quick . . . order yours now!!!
                        Don't be the only surfer without
                                Web Wear!
```

Here's a recap of our designs!

```
Design                    Color 1      Color 2
Mega way-cool bitmapped   navy blue    crimson
Awesome elegant           yellow       orange
Whatsamatta               purple       red
On-line Chat              green        berry
```

CLUES TO USE

Using <TABLE> tags to create tables

For browsers that support the <TABLE> tags, this is a much easier way to create professional-looking tables. A bordered table is surrounded with the <TABLE BORDER> </TABLE> tags, and uses the <TR> </TR> tags to define each row within the table. Data in each cell in a row is surrounded by the <TD> </TD> tags, and is displayed as bold and centered using the <TH> </TH> tags (for headings, for example). Figure B-15 shows a table created using TABLE tags.

FIGURE B-15: Table with border created with TABLE tags

Here's a recap of our designs!

Design	Color 1	Color 2
Mega way-cool bitmapped	navy blue	crimson
Awesome elegant	yellow	orange
Whatsamatta	purple	red
On-line Chat	green	berry

HTML

Practice

► Concepts Review

Identify the function of each HTML tag labeled in Figure B-16.

FIGURE B-16

```
<HTML>

<HEAD>
<TITLE>The Nomad Ltd on-line catalog: Unisex Web Wear></TITLE>
</HEAD>

<BODY>
<H1>Nomad Ltd's <I>Web Wear</I>!</H1>
Welcome to the world of <I>Web Wear</I>, <BR>
where the clothing is comfy and the livin' is easy!
<HR>
<H2>What's available</H2>
<I>Web Wear</I> is available in the following designs:
<OL>
<LI><B>Mega way-cool bitmapped</B> T-Shirt</LI>
<LI><B>Awesome elegant</B> T-Shirt</LI>
<LI><B>Whatsamatta</B> T-Shirt</LI>
<LI><B>On-line Chat</B> T-Shirt</LI>
</OL>
<H2>What's the difference between the designs?</H2>
<DL>
<DT>Mega way-cool bitmapped T-Shirt</DT>
<DD>An original creation, 100% cotton, in navy blue or crimson.</DD>
</DL>
<H2>Sizes and Styles</H2>
Nomad Ltd's <I>Web Wear</I> is conveniently sized for both genders and
```

1
2
3
4
5

Match each statement with the HTML tags it describes.

6. Opening and closing preformatted text tags   a. <U> </U>
7. Opening and closing italics tags   b. <PRE> </PRE>
8. Opening and closing list item tags   c. <MENU> </MENU>
9. Opening and closing underline tags   d. <I> </I>
10. Opening and closing menu list tags   e. <LI> </LI>

Select the best answer from the list of choices.

11. **Which tag(s) are used to create a horizontal rule?**
    a.
    b. <HR></HR>
    c. <RL>
    d. <HR>

12. **Which key do you press to create column spaces when typing preformatted text?**
    a. [Spacebar]
    b. [Tab]
    c. either [Spacebar] or [Tab]
    d. [Ctrl]

13. **Which tag creates a new line?**
    a.
    b. <HR>
    c. <RL>
    d. <NL>

14. **Which tag ends a numbered list?**
    a. <OL>
    b. </NL>
    c. </OL>
    d. </LI>

15. **Which tag starts a bulleted list?**
    a. <BL>
    b. </BL>
    c. <UL>
    d. <OL>

16. **Which tags are used to boldface text?**
    a. <U></U>
    b. <B><B>
    c. <EM></EM>
    d. <B></B>

17. **Which type of list contains bullets?**
    a. Ordered
    b. Definition
    c. Unordered
    d. Menu

▶ Skills Review

1. Create unordered list.

a. Start your text editor, open the file HTML B-3.htm, then save it as a text document with the filename Interstellar Pizza.htm.

b. Select the INSERT UNORDERED LIST HERE text.

c. Type the initial unordered list tag, then press [Enter].

d. Type the text for the list items, including the beginning and ending HTML tags, as shown in Table B-3.

TABLE B-3: Interstellar Pizza

```
<LI>imported cheeses</LI>
<LI>organically grown ingredients</LI>
<LI>farm-fresh crust</LI>
<LI>organic spices</LI>
```

e. Press [Enter] after all the items are typed, then type the ending HTML unordered list tag.

f. Save your work.

g. View the document in your browser.

2. Format text.

a. Return to the text editor.

b. Bold the text "Interstellar on-line pizzeria!".

c. Italicize each of the remaining headings.

d. Add a horizontal rule in the line above the heading "Nothing but the best for you!".

3. Add a line break.

a. Create a line break after the space that follows "We make the finest pizza".

b. Save your work.

c. Reload the changes to the document in your browser.

4. Use preformatted text.

   a. Return to the text editor

   b. Select the INSERT PREFORMATTED TEXT HERE text.

   c. Type the initial preformatted text tag, then press [Enter].

   d. Type the preformatted text shown in Figure B-17.

   e. Press [Enter] after the last line of preformatted text, type the closing preformatted text tag, then press [Enter].

   f. Save your work.

   g. Reload the changes to the document in your browser.

FIGURE B-17

```
<HTML>

<HEAD>
<TITLE>Interstellar on-line pizza Web page</TITLE>
</HEAD>

<BODY>
<H1><B>Interstellar on-line pizzeria!</B></H1>
We make the finest pizza <BR>this side of the galaxy.<BR>
<PRE>
Throughout the galaxy,
        aliens and earthlings have enjoyed
                Interstellar pizza for ages!
Isn't it time you joined our
        cosmic friends in the best pizza ever?
</PRE>
```

5. Create a table.

   a. Return to the text editor.

   b. Select the text INSERT TABLE HERE.

   c. Type the initial preformatted text tag, then press [Enter].

   d. Type the text shown in Table B-4.

TABLE B-4: Table text

Pizza Type	Topping(s)	Size
Safety zone	cheese	10" and 14"
Surfer's special	pepperoni, onions	6" and 14"
Alien madness	onions, garlic, sausage	14"
Planetary revenge	SURPRISE!!!	6", 10", and 14"

   e. Type the closing preformatted text tag on a new line below the table.

   f. Type the opening bold tag after the opening preformatted text tag.

   g. Type the closing bold tag after "Size."

   h. Save your work.

   i. Print the text document.

   j. Refresh the changes to the document in your browser.

   k. Print the browser page.

   l. Close and exit your browser and text editor.

▶ Independent Challenges

1. The Star Dot Star computer consulting firm is ready to expand its Web page. Using the document you previously created, expand it by adding lists and text formatting. Your page should contain at least two types of lists, and some text formatting such as bolding or italicizing.

To complete this independent challenge:

a. Start your text editor, open the file HTML B-4.htm, then save it as a text document with the filename Star Dot Star-page 1.htm.

b. Replace the "ADD SERVICES HERE" placeholder with a definition list that defines the types of services you provide.

c. Add an unordered list that describes the types of clients you have.

d. Add horizontal rules, line breaks, and text formatting where appropriate.

e. Print the document using the text editor.

f. Open your browser.

g. Print the document in your browser.

h. Close the browser.

i. Exit the text editor.

2. Your work with your local Board of Realtors continues. They have been very happy with your initial work on their Web page, and they would like for you to add text enhancements and lists to the existing page.

To complete this independent challenge:

a. Start your text editor, open the file HTML B-5.htm, then save it as a text document with the filename Realtors-1.htm.

b. Identify at least three geographic regions where houses are sold in your area, then create a definition list that identifies where these houses are located for prospective customers.

c. Use a definition list to describe the three regions you listed in Step 2 and replace the "LIST NEIGHBORHOODS HERE" placeholder with your list.

d. Add text enhancements where appropriate to add impact to the page.

e. Save your work.

f. Print the document using the text editor.

g. Open your browser.

h. Print the document in your browser.

i. Close your browser.

j. Exit your text editor.

3. You've recently opened your own video store, Film Clips, and you've decided to design an in-store information system that uses HTML and a browser. With this system, customers can learn more about the movies in the store. Film Clips specializes in your favorite kind of movies—horror, comedies, recent blockbusters—whatever you like.

To complete this independent challenge:

a. Open a blank document using your text editor and save it as a text document with the filename Film Clips-1.htm.

b. Design an outline for your store's Web page.

c. Include a list of the types of movies available in your store on the page.

d. Include a list of some of the prominent stars featured in these films.

e. Add text enhancements where appropriate to add impact to the page.

f. Save your work.

g. Print the document using the text editor.

h. Print the document in your browser.

i. Exit your browser and text editor.

4. You have been hired to design a Web page for a local astrologer, Madam Zylog. Madam Zylog reads horoscopes and tells fortunes. She specializes in palmistry, or reading a person's fortune, and wants to emphasize that she is particularly gifted in predicting a person's economic and romantic future. To help design this page, you've decided to research similar Web sites.

To complete this independent challenge:

a. Establish an Internet connection.

b. Use any search engine to locate at least two Web pages with similar topics.

c. Print out the home page for each of the two Web sites.

d. Create an outline that includes all the items you want to include in your Web page.

e. Start your text editor, open a new document, then save it as a text document with the filename Madam Zylog-1.htm.

f. Include at least two types of lists in this page.

g. Include text enhancements where necessary to add impact to the page.

h. Save your work.

i. Print the document using the text editor.

j. Open your browser.

k. Print the document in your browser.

l. Close your Internet connection.

m. Exit the text editor and your browser.

Visual Workshop

Use the skills you learned in this unit to create the Web page shown in Figure B-18. Save your HTML file in your text editor as a text document called Barbara's Bakery.htm, then print the document using the text editor and your browser.

FIGURE B-18

Welcome to Barbara's Bakery!

In business for 22 years,

- We create the most superb baked goods.
- We use only the finest ingredients.
- We create the freshest, most delicious pastries!

We mail order the following baked goods:

```
                 sold by                    sold by
Bagels           dozen      French bread    loaf
Baggettes        dozen      Rye bread       loaf
Cookies          dozen      Wheat bread     loaf
Chocolate cakes  each       White bread     loaf
```

Please allow 4 days for delivery! We at **Barbara's Bakery** wish to *thank you* for your business!

Adding
Graphics and Multimedia

Objectives

► Understand graphic images
► Insert inline graphics
► Resize a graphic image
► Link graphics
► Set a hotspot
► Create an image map
► Insert multimedia files

While text conveys the message in your Web page, pictures can add spice and pizzazz. In an HTML document, pictures are inserted as graphic images or electronic art files that are displayed by your Web browser. Sound can be used to identify key themes or simply enhance the page. Grace wants to include Nomad's logo and other graphic images to make Nomad's Web pages more attractive and interesting. She also adds sound to enhance specific parts of the page.

Understanding Graphic Images

When a graphic image, or picture, is displayed on a Web page, it is not actually saved in the HTML source document. You can display a graphic image in a Web browser by using HTML tags to point to the location of the image. Graphic images are available in a variety of formats, and most images can be viewed by Web browsers. Some graphic images are displayed *natively* by browsers (meaning they are displayed without additional assistance); other graphic images, however, are not supported natively (they require the *external* assistance of helper programs). The most common graphic image file formats supported by Web browsers are shown in Table C-1. Grace considers what options she has when using graphic images in her Web documents:

Use common file formats

A GIF image is the most common natively supported graphic file format and can be displayed by most graphics-capable Web browsers. GIF images work well for displaying images with a small number of colors. JPEG images are not supported natively by all browsers, but they have smaller file sizes and look better when displaying images that have a lot of colors. By using the GIF format, you can be assured that the images will look good and can be displayed by all Web browsers.

Use inline images

A graphic image can be inserted into an HTML document as an inline image. An **inline image** displays in a Web page, as shown in Figure C-1. They require no helper programs, don't have to be downloaded to be viewed, and can be aligned with text using special HTML tags. Since inline images make a document look great, you include several of them, including the Nomad logo.

Trouble?

If an image displays as an icon, the image's file format might not be natively supported by your browser, or you may have not typed the HTML tags correctly.

Explanatory text following images

There are still some Web browsers being used that cannot display images. For users of text-only browsers, you can include descriptive text following inline images. This text is helpful to those without graphic browsers, and can add valuable explanations to displayed images.

Create links between images and Web sites

Just as clicking linked text in a Web page can take you to a different Web site, an image can also be linked to other sites. In addition to making an image "clickable," clicking specific areas of an inline image can take you to different Web locations. Linked images display in a Web page surrounded by a dark border. When you pass the mouse pointer over the clickable image the pointer changes to a pointing hand as shown in Figure C-1.

The Nomad Ltd Home Page

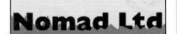

Welcome to the Nomad Ltd home page.

Nomad Ltd began over five years ago as a reseller of natural products. As we've grown, we've expanded to include:

- sporting goods -- including our own line of sportswear called _Web Wear_!
- a travel division: _New Directions Travel_, which we plan on bringing on-line later this year and
- a new line of natural foods in the coming months.

Click the image of the location you'd like to visit!

Pointer changes
in linked image

Dark border surrounds
linked image

Inline graphic image

TABLE C-1: Common graphic file formats

format	extension	support provided
Graphics Interchange Format	GIF	Native
Joint Photographic Experts Group	JPEG, JPG	Native
PC Paintbrush	PCX	External
Tagged Image File Format	TIFF	External
Windows Bitmap	BMP	External

HTML

Inserting Inline Graphics

An inline graphic image is easy to add to an HTML document. The HTML image tag is <IMG SRC="*image_location*">; it is an empty container, so it does not require a closing tag. Once this tag is in the document, additional codes can be used to affect the size, position, and alignment of the graphic image on the page. Commonly used codes, or **attributes**, are defined in Table C-2. Grace has a graphics file containing the Nomad Ltd logo that she wants to add to her Web page.

Steps

1. Start your text editor, open the file HTML C-1.htm, then save it as a text document with the filename Nomad Home Page.htm

There are several text placeholders in the document to help position graphic images correctly.

2. Select the INSERT INLINE GRAPHIC HERE text

A graphic file is inserted into a Web document by using the image tag, IMG, and the attribute that defines the source, SRC. The ALIGN attribute can be typed before or after the SRC code in the IMG container. ALIGN attributes may be typed in upper- or lowercase. An inline graphic image is automatically left-aligned when it's inserted into a document unless you specify otherwise.

3. Type <IMG SRC="file:///al/nomad.jpg" ALIGN="right">

Refer to Figure C-2. The ALIGN attribute lets you position an image on a page, as well as where text on the same line appears. The LEFT and RIGHT options let you specify the margin alignment of the image; the TOP, MIDDLE, and BOTTOM options let you specify where the image will display relative to text on the same line.

4. Save the file Nomad Home Page.htm as a text document

5. Start your browser, then open the file Nomad Home Page.htm

Compare your Web page with Figure C-3.

> **Trouble?**
>
> If you are using a drive other than A for your project files and the file Nomad.jpg is in another directory, substitute the correct drive letter and path in the HTML tag.

FIGURE C-2: Inline image container with alignment attribute

```
<HTML>

<HEAD>
<TITLE>Nomad Ltd Home Page></TITLE>
</HEAD>

<BODY>
<IMG SRC="file:///a|/nomad.jpg" ALIGN="right">
<H1>The Nomad Ltd Home Page</H1>
```

Affect image position
using ALIGN

FIGURE C-3: Right-aligned inline image

The Nomad Ltd Home Page

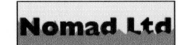

Welcome to the Nomad Ltd home page.

Nomad Ltd began over five years ago as a reseller of natural products. As we've grown, we've expanded to include:

- sporting goods -- including our own line of sportswear called *Web Wear*!
- a travel division: *New Directions Travel*, which we plan on bringing on-line later this year, and
- a new line of natural foods in the coming months.

Click the image of the location you'd like to visit!

INSERT CODES FOR CLICKABLE WEBWEAR IMAGE HERE INSERT CODES FOR CLICKABLE NEW DIRECTIONS IMAGE HERE INSERT CODES FOR CLICKABLE NATURAL FOODS IMAGE HERE

TABLE C-2: Common IMG attributes

attribute	description	status
ALIGN	Physically aligns image on the page	Optional
ALT	Specifies alternative text a user can also click	Optional
ISMAP	Specifies that image is an image map	Optional
SRC	Specifies an image source or location	Necessary

Resizing a Graphic Image

Inline graphics are easy to insert into a Web document, but unfortunately, they might not be the right size. Using the additional ALIGN attributes HEIGHT and WIDTH, you can make your graphic images any size you want. Since some Web browsers do not have graphics capabilities, you can offer readers a "text only" option. ◄▬▬ Grace wants to display a small graphic image for each of the items in her unordered list at the end of each line so they are the same size.

Steps 1 2 3 4

1. **Click the text editor program button on the taskbar**
   The Nomad Home Page document displays. You use the IMG container, with the added attributes of HEIGHT and WIDTH, to size a graphic image. Each image should be the same height on the line.

2. **Click to the right of the Web Wear bulleted line, then press [Enter]**
   The .jpg files are stored on your Project Disk. HEIGHT and WIDTH attributes are measured in pixels and are relative to the actual dimensions of the original image. They force an image to be scaled to new dimensions.

3. **Type <IMG SRC="file:///al/webwear.jpg" HEIGHT=35 WIDTH=60>**
   Figure C-4 shows the completed tag. You have to add graphic images to the remaining bulleted lines. The logo for New Directions Travel is compass.jpg; the logo for the natural foods line is food.jpg.

   QuickTip

   You can copy and paste repeating text to assist your coding the HTML tags.

4. **Click to the right of each of the remaining bulleted lines, refer to Figure C-4, then type an IMG statement referencing the graphic image for each file**
   Your text document should look like Figure C-4. Each image will scale to the same size.

5. **Save the file Nomad Home Page.htm as a text document**

6. **Click the browser program button on the taskbar, then view the saved version of Nomad Home Page.htm by refreshing your screen**
   Compare your browser page with Figure C-5.

7. **Print the browser document**

FIGURE C-4: Graphic images with HEIGHT and WIDTH attributes

```
<H2>Welcome to the <B>Nomad Ltd</B> home page.</H2>
Nomad Ltd began over five years ago as a reseller of natural products.
As we've grown, we've expanded to include:
<UL>
<LI>sporting goods -- including our own line of sportswear called <A
HREF=file:///a|/webwear.htm><I>Web Wear</I></A>!</LI>
<IMG SRC="file:///a|webwear.jpg" HEIGHT=35 WIDTH=60>
<LI>a travel division: <A HREF=file:///a|/ndt.htm><I>New Directions
Travel</I></A>, which we plan on bringing on-line later this year,
and</LI>
<IMG SRC="file:///a|compass.jpg" HEIGHT=35 WIDTH=60>
<LI>a new line of <A HREF=file:///a|/food.htm>natural foods</A> in the
coming months.</LI>
<IMG SRC="file:///a|food.jpg" HEIGHT=35 WIDTH=60>
</UL>
<H3>Click the image of the location you'd like to visit!</H3>
INSERT CODES FOR CLICKABLE WEBWEAR IMAGE HERE
```

Each image is scaled to the same size

FIGURE C-5 : Scaled inline images

Nomad Ltd began over five years ago as a reseller of natural products. As we've grown, we've expanded to include:

- sporting goods -- including our own line of sportswear called *Web Wear*!

- a travel division: *New Directions Travel*, which we plan on bringing on-line later this year, and

- a new line of natural foods in the coming months.

Click the image of the location you'd like to visit!

Inline images

Spacing between lines in a list changes when images are added

Offering a "text only" option

Since some Web browsers cannot display graphic images due to software or hardware limitations, you can include a "text only" option in a Web page containing graphic images. For example, the following statement: **Click <A HREF="file:///a|/plain.htm">here</A> for a "text only" version of this page** can be added to your HTML document. The file plain.htm is the same HTML document with the graphic images deleted. This makes your Web page more meaningful to those users who cannot view graphic images, as shown in Figure C-6.

FIGURE C-6: A "text only" statement in a Web page

- a new line of natural foods in the coming months.

Click here for a "text only" version of this page.

Click the image of the location you'd like to visit!

Link to an HTML document with no graphics

Linking Graphics

You've already learned how to link one Web page to another by clicking text. You've also learned how to insert a graphic image on a Web page. So, doesn't it make sense to be able to link one Web page to another by clicking a graphic image? Of course. In fact, the same HTML tag you used to create the text link <A HREF="*location*"> can be combined with the <IMG SRC="*location*"> tag. You can also include additional text with a graphic image so Web users who lack graphic capabilities can view the link. ◀━━━ Grace wants to create links on the Nomad Web page to other Web sites that can be accessed by clicking a graphic image or text.

QuickTip

Web sites used as examples in these lessons are fictitious.

1. **Click the text editor program button on the taskbar**
   Since Nomad's customers are health conscious, you want readers of the page to be able to jump to a fitness Web site called the Health & Fitness World Guide Forum by clicking a graphic image.

2. **Click to the right of the </UL> tag, then press [Enter]**
   You want to create a heading for this link.

3. **Type <H3>Want information on becoming healthier?</H3>, then press [Enter]**
   Next you set up the link to the Health & Fitness World Guide Forum Web site by creating a clickable graphic image and clickable text.

4. **Type *(but do not press [Enter])* Check out the <A HREF="http://www.worldguide.com/ Fitness/hf.html"><IMG SRC="file:///al/fitness.jpg"> Health & Fitness World Guide Forum</A> Web site**
   You want to align the text on this line with the top of the image, so you add the ALIGN attribute to the IMG container.

5. **Click to the right of "file:///al/fitness.jpg", press [Spacebar], then type ALIGN="top" HEIGHT=60 WIDTH=30**
   Compare your work with Figure C-7.

6. **Save the file as a text document, then click the browser program button on the taskbar**
   Since changes have been made in the text document, you have to refresh your browser page to view the aligned images.

7. **View the saved version of Nomad Home Page.htm by refreshing your screen**
   The Web page displays, as shown in Figure C-8. Notice that the image is surrounded by a blue outline which indicates that the image is linked. By clicking either the image or the text following it, the reader jumps to the linked Web site.

FIGURE C-7: **HTML tags for linked image**

```
<IMG SRC="file:///a|compass.jpg" HEIGHT=35 WIDTH=60>
<LI>a new line of <A HREF=file:///a|/food.htm>natural foods</A> in the
coming months.</LI>
<IMG SRC="file:///a|food.jpg" HEIGHT=35 WIDTH=60>
</UL>
<H3>Want information on becoming healthier?</H3>
Check out the <A HREF="http://www.worldguide.com/Fitness/hf.html"><IMG
SRC="file:///a|fitness.jpg" ALIGN="top" HEIGHT=60 WIDTH=30> Health &
Fitness World Guide Forum</A> Web site
```

Your text may wrap
differently

Link to Web site

FIGURE C-8: **Linked image and text**

The Nomad Ltd Home Page

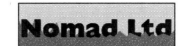

Welcome to the Nomad Ltd home page.

Nomad Ltd began over five years ago as a reseller of natural products. As we've grown, we've expanded to include:

- sporting goods -- including our own line of sportswear called *Web Wear*!

- a travel division: *New Directions Travel*, which we plan on bringing on-line later this year, and

- a new line of natural foods in the coming months.

Want information on becoming healthier?

Check out the Health & Fitness World Guide Forum Web site

Click the image of the location you'd like to visit!

http://www.worldguide.com/Fitness/hf.html   My Computer

Link displays in
status line

Click text or image to
jump to link

HTML

Setting a Hot Spot

The instinct to click an image is natural; clicking different areas within an image can take you to different Web sites. You can set up a single graphics file as an **image map** "button" that will take the reader to another Web site when it is clicked. Creating an image map can be tricky; each clickable area, or **hot spot**, within an image must be identified using pixel coordinates. You can set the hot spot by adding the ISMAP attribute to the IMG container in your HTML document. ✏️ Grace wants to create image maps that will link readers to different Web sites. She uses her browser to determine the pixel coordinates before creating the images to click.

Steps

1. Click the text editor program button on the taskbar
   You need to determine the pixel coordinates that will jump readers to other Web sites.

2. Select the INSERT CODES FOR CLICKABLE WEB WEAR IMAGE HERE text, then type
   <A HREF="file:///al/Nomad image.map"><IMG SRC="file:///al/webwear.jpg"
   HEIGHT=100 ISMAP></A>, then press [Enter]
   The pixel coordinates for the images in this page will be stored in a separate file called Nomad image.map. You create that file after determining all the coordinates for webwear.jpg, compass.jpg, and food.jpg.

3. Select the text placeholders for the IMG tags, type the tags shown in Figure C-9, then press [Enter]

4. Save the file as a text document

5. View the saved version of the file by refreshing your screen
   The image is updated. You use the mouse pointer to determine the pixel coordinates you'll reference in the image map document.

Trouble?

Clicking an unavailable or fictitious Web site results in your browser displaying an error message.

6. Move the mouse pointer over each of the new images, *but don't click the mouse button*
   Notice that as the pointer moves over an image, its pixel coordinates are displayed in the browser's status bar, as shown in Figure C-10. You note the pixel coordinates at the center of each image you will use to create the Nomad image.map file.

FIGURE C-9: Completed IMG tags

```
<IMG SRC="file:///a|compass.jpg" HEIGHT=35 WIDTH=60>
<LI>a new line of <A HREF=file:///a|/food.htm>natural foods</A> in the
coming months.</LI>
<IMG SRC="file:///a|food.jpg" HEIGHT=35 WIDTH=60>
</UL>
<H3>Want information on becoming healthier?</H3>
Check out the <A HREF="http://www.worldguide.com/Fitness/hf.html"><IMG
SRC="file:///a|fitness.jpg" ALIGN="top" HEIGHT=60 WIDTH=30> Health &
Fitness World Guide Forum</A> Web site
<H3>Click the image of the location you'd like to visit!</H3>
<A HREF="file:///a|Nomad image.map"><IMG SRC="file:///a|webwear.jpg"
HEIGHT=100 ISMAP></A>
<A HREF="file:///a|Nomad image.map"><IMG SRC="file:///a|compass.jpg"
HEIGHT=100 ISMAP></A>
<A HREF="file:///a|Nomad image.map"><IMG SRC="file:///a|food.jpg"
HEIGHT=100 ISMAP></A>
|
<ADDRESS>
```

Additional image
map tags

FIGURE C-10: Determining pixel coordinates in browser

Mouse pointer

Pixel coordinates
of mouse pointer

How pixel coordinates work

When a point in an image is clicked, the closest referenced point in the image map is activated. Since the likelihood that a reader will click the exact coordinates you specified in your image map document is low, it is important to choose the coordinates carefully. Make sure multiple points are not too close to one another, or your reader might accidentally jump to the wrong Web site.

HTML

Creating an Image Map

Pixel coordinates are stored in a separate document that identifies which Web site the reader will jump to when the image is clicked. In an online Web session, clicking an image map connects you to the site identified in the image map document. When not online, clicking an image map results in the pointer changing to an hourglass while your computer searches for the site. You can also create an e-mail link so readers can send mail directly to the page administrator. ✒ Grace creates the image map document that contains the pixel coordinates to other Web sites that she will insert later.

Steps

1. Click the text editor program button on the taskbar

The image map document is created in a new document in the editor.

Trouble?

If you are using a text editor other than WordPad, open a new document.

2. Click File on the menu bar, click New, then click OK

You determined a single point in each image that links to Web sites that you insert later. In addition to the pixel coordinates, you can include comment lines to identify the sites by name. Each comment line begins with the pound sign (#). You type placeholders for the real Web sites.

3. Type the comment lines and coordinates shown in Figure C-11

You have typed the coordinates for each image.

Trouble?

Verify that this file has been saved with the .map extension, not .txt.

4. Save the file as a text document with the filename Nomad image.map

The image map document is complete, so when you view the original document, Nomad Home Page.htm, it can refer to the image map.

5. Click the browser program button on the taskbar, then view the changes to Nomad Home Page.htm by refreshing your screen

The image is updated, as shown in Figure C-12. You can return to the image map document later and insert the Web site locations that the reader will jump to when each image is clicked.

6. Print the browser document

FIGURE C-11: **Image map document with pixel coordinates**

# indicates comment line

```
# links for Nomad Ltd Home Page "file:///a|/Nomad Home Page.htm"

# Web Wear butterfly image
point http://www.nomadltd.com/webwear.htm 62,29

# Compass image
point http://www.nomadltd.com/compass.htm 69,56

# Food image
point http://www.nomadltd.com/food.htm 57,40
```

Pixel coordinates

FIGURE C-12: **Completed image map graphic images**

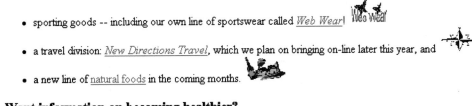

- sporting goods -- including our own line of sportswear called *Web Wear*!

- a travel division: *New Directions Travel*, which we plan on bringing on-line later this year, and

- a new line of natural foods in the coming months.

Want information on becoming healthier?

Check out the Health & Fitness World Guide Forum Web site

Click the image of the location you'd like to visit!

All images have the same height

Using the ADDRESS tags

Make it easy for your readers to contact you by including your postal address and/or e-mail address within the ADDRESS tags. The information in these tags displays in italics. You can include the MAILTO attribute to allow your readers to send e-mail to you with a single mouse click. The statement
<A HREF="MAILTO:GDekmejian@nomadltd.com">
GDekmejian@nomadltd.com</A> results in the link, as shown in Figure C-13.

FIGURE C-13: **The MAILTO attribute in a link**

If you have any questions about our company or our products, please e-mail me at GDekmejian@nomadltd.com

GDekmejian@nomadltd.com

Result of <ADDRESS> </ADDRESS> tags

Click to create e-mail

Inserting Multimedia Files

Most computers used today are capable of displaying beautiful images and playing videos with sound. Full-motion videos and sound files are commonly referred to as **multimedia**. Full-motion videos tend to have larger file sizes that make them cumbersome on the Internet. Audio files have varying sizes, are simple to use, and can be heard through a standard computer speaker. To see or hear multimedia files on your computer, you need to configure your browser to work with **plug-ins** or **add-ins**, which are independent programs that let you use multimedia files. ✏️ Grace wants to add an audio file to her Web page to take advantage of the Web's multimedia capabilities.

Steps

1. Click the text editor program button on the taskbar
   You decide to add an audio file at the end of the "Welcome to the Nomad Ltd home page" heading.

2. Open the file Nomad Home Page.htm

3. Click to the left of the </H2> tag, then press [Enter]
   Inserting a multimedia file requires two HTML tags: the <A HREF></A> tag identifies the location of the audio file, and the <IMG SRC> tag allows the reader to see or hear the file. You plan to use sound files that come with Windows.

   Trouble?

   If you do not have a Windows folder or any files, see your instructor or technical support person for assistance

4. Type <A HREF="file:///cl/windows/media/The Microsoft Sound.wav">, then press [Enter]
   You can substitute any .wav file if you cannot find the Microsoft sound. The image sound.jpg is a familiar icon for sound. You can click the image to hear the sound.

5. Type <IMG SRC="file:///al/sound.jpg"></A>
   Compare your document with Figure C-14.

6. Save the file as a text document

7. Click the browser program button on the taskbar, then view the saved version of the file by refreshing your screen
   The document displays with a linked image following the Welcome heading, as shown in Figure C-15.

   Trouble?

   If the File Download dialog box opens, select Open this file from its current location, then click OK.

8. Click the linked image then click the Play button on the toolbar

9. Close the media player, close your browser, then close the text editor

FIGURE C-14: **HTML tags for a multimedia file**

```
<HTML>

<HEAD>
<TITLE>Nomad Ltd Home Page></TITLE>
</HEAD>

<BODY>
<IMG SRC="file:///a|/nomad.jpg" ALIGN="right">
<H1>The Nomad Ltd Home Page</H1>
<H2>Welcome to the <B>Nomad Ltd</B> home page.
<A HREF="file:///c|/windows/media/The Microsoft Sound.wav">
<IMG SRC="file:///a|/sound.jpg"></A></H2>
Nomad Ltd began over five years ago as a reseller of natural products.
As we've grown, we've expanded to include:
<UL>
<LI>sporting goods -- including our own line of sportswear called <A
HREF=file:///a|/webwear.htm><I>Web Wear</I></A>!</LI>
<IMG SRC="file:///a|/webwear.jpg" HEIGHT=35 WIDTH=60>
<LI>a travel division: <A HREF=file:///a|/ndt.htm><I>New Directions
Travel</I></A>, which we plan on bringing on-line later this year,
and</LI>
<IMG SRC="file:///a|/compass.jpg" HEIGHT=35 WIDTH=60>
<LI>a new line of <A HREF=file:///a|/food.htm>natural foods</A> in the
coming months.</LI>
<IMG SRC="file:///a|/food.jpg" HEIGHT=35 WIDTH=60>
</UL>
```

Audio file added
to document

FIGURE C-15: **Inline image linked to an audio file**

The Nomad Ltd Home Page

Nomad Ltd

Welcome to the Nomad Ltd home page.

Nomad Ltd began over five years ago as a reseller of natural products. As we've grown, we've expanded to include:

Click to hear
the audio file

CLUES TO USE

Playing multimedia files

A browser can be configured to show pictures, play videos and animations, and play sounds. Although this technique differs among browsers, it is usually a fairly straightforward process. In Microsoft Internet Explorer 4, you can check the current status of your Internet Options. Do this by clicking View on the menu bar, then clicking Internet Options and selecting the Advanced tab. Scroll down to the multimedia section and you will see your current settings. Figure C-16 shows that all multimedia options are enabled.

FIGURE C-16: **Multimedia options in browser**

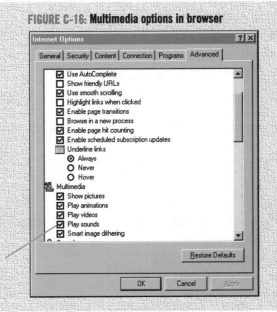

Check indicates
option is enabled

HTML ⌐ Practice

► Concepts Review

Label each element of the browser screen shown in Figure C-17.

FIGURE C-17

Match each statement with the HTML attributes it describes.

6. Italicizes address
7. Adds linked text to linked image
8. Indicates image map
9. Indicates image source
10. Determines text/margin position

a. ALIGN
b. ADDRESS
c. SRC
d. ISMAP
e. HREF

Select the best answer from the list of choices.

11. Which is not a common Internet graphics file format?
    a. AUZ
    b. JPG
    c. TIFF
    d. BMP
12. You can identify image map locations by using
    a. helper programs
    b. addressable images
    c. pixel coordinates
    d. local access points

13. **All of the following are attributes of ALIGN,** *except*
    a. top
    b. right
    c. bottom
    d. under

14. **The appearance of a linked image differs from a non-linked image in that it**
    a. is double-underlined
    b. has an outline
    c. has no outline
    d. displays in shades of red

15. **What happens when browsing a document whose graphic image is incorrectly entered?**
    a. The image displays in shades of red.
    b. The image displays as an icon.
    c. The browser window closes.
    d. A warning chime sounds.

16. **The border of linked images appears in what color?**
    a. Red
    b. Black
    c. Green
    d. Blue

17. **Each of the following is a common IMG attribute,** *except*
    a. ALT
    b. ALIGN
    c. JPG
    d. SRC

18. **HEIGHT and WIDTH attributes are measured in**
    a. pixels
    b. inches
    c. centimeters
    d. millimeters

19. **Which tag lets you send e-mail as part of a hyperlink?**
    a. <MAILTO>
    b. <SEND>
    c. <ADDRESS>
    d. <ZIPTO>

Skills Review

1. Insert graphics.

a. Start the text editor and open the file HTML C-2.htm, then save it as a text document with the filename Pizza home page.htm.

b. Select the INSERT LOGO HERE text.

c. Type <IMG SRC="file:///al/pizza.jpg"> then press [Enter]. (*Note:* These steps assume your files are on a disk in drive A.)

d. Add the attribute ALIGN="right" to the IMG statement.

e. Save your work.

f. View your work in your browser, then return to your text editor.

2. Resize a graphic image.

a. Select the INSERT SMALL LOGO HERE text.

b. Insert the pizza.jpg file using Height=40 and Width=50 attributes.

c. Select the INSERT IMAGE #1 HERE text, and insert the stress.jpg file from your Project Disk using a height and width of 40.

d. Select the INSERT IMAGE #2 HERE text, and insert the pressure.jpg file from your Project Disk using a height and width of 40.

e. Save your work.

f. View the document in your browser.

g. Print the document in your browser.

3. Link graphics.

a. Return to the text editor.

b. Select the INSERT LINKED GRAPHIC HERE text.

c. Type an HTML tag that creates a link to the (fictitious) Web site http://www.istellar.pizza.com/faqs.htm.

d. Type an IMG tag that links to pizza.jpg on your Project Disk.

e. Save your work.

f. View the changes to the document in your browser.

g. Print the document in your browser.

4. Set a hot spot.

a. Return to the text editor

b. Select the INSERT IMAGE #3 HERE text.

c. Write an HTML tag referencing the image map file Pizza image.map (to be created later) that links the pixel coordinates of the four buttons in menu.jpg.

d. Use your browser to determine pixel coordinates for each of the four buttons at the bottom of the graphic image.

e. Write down the four pixel coordinates.

5. Create an image map.

a. Open a new document and save it as a text document with the filename Pizza image.map on your Project Disk.

b. Create four statements: one that points to each set of pixel coordinates, then save your work. Assume that clicking each button jumps the reader to a Web site (using the fictitious site http://www.istellar.pizza.com/) where you make up the name of each file. (For example, the Web site for the first button on the left could be called http://www.istellar.pizza.com/Safety.htm.)

c. Save your work.

d. Print the document in your text editor.

    e. View the changes to the Pizza Home Page document in your browser. (*Note:* Clicking any of the buttons in the image will result in an error message, since you have created fictitious Web sites.)

    f. Print the document in your browser.

6. Insert a multimedia file.

    a. Return to your text editor.

    b. Place the insertion point after "Allow one light year for delivery!".

    c. Type an HTML tag that links the chimes.wav audio file (located in the c:\windows\media\ folder). (*Note:* If you can't locate this file, find and link to any other appropriate .wav file.)

    d. Type an IMG tag that links the multimedia file to sound.jpg on your Project Disk.

    e. Save your work.

    f. Print the text editor document.

    g. View the changes to the document in your browser.

    h. Play the sound image.

    i. Close the media player when the sound is finished.

    j. Print the document in your browser.

    k. Exit the media player.

    l. Close and exit your browser and text editor.

▶ Independent Challenges

1. You'd like to incorporate the Star Dot Star consulting firm's logo into its Web page and to use other graphic images to make your pages more effective and attractive. You've already created the logo and have other graphics files, now you'll insert these files and create links to other sites.

    To complete this independent challenge:

    a. Open the file HTML C-3.htm in your text editor, then save it as a text document with the filename Star Dot Star-home page.htm.

    b. Insert the logo file, stardot.jpg, by replacing the INSERT LOGO HERE text with the correct tag.

    c. Insert the same file in an additional location, but scaled to a smaller size.

    d. Create a link to the (fictitious) Web site http://www.hi-tech.com using a graphic image of your choice, as well as text.

    e. Create a text-only text link to your page.

    f. Add one additional inline image (from any available source) to the page.

    g. Print the document in your text editor.

    h. Print the document in your browser.

    i. Close your browser.

    j. Exit your text editor.

2. The Board of Realtors loves your work so much they've created a new logo for you to incorporate into their Web site. Realtors know that presentation is very important, so they've asked you to jazz up their Web pages with graphic images, links, and sounds.

To complete this independent challenge:

a. Open the file HTML C-4.htm and save it as Realtors Home Page.htm.

b. Make any necessary modifications to the text as you see fit.

c. Insert the Board of Realtors logo file, realtors.jpg, on your Project Disk by replacing the INSERT LOGO HERE text with the correct tag.

d. Find a (real) Web site that prospective home buyers might find interesting, and create a link to it.

e. Add at least two sounds to your page using the .wav files provided in the c:\windows\media folder on your hard drive or server.

f. Use the sound.jpg file as a link to the sounds.

g. Insert a smaller version of realtors.jpg elsewhere on the page.

h. Save your work.

i. Print the document in your text editor.

j. Print the document in your browser.

k. Close your browser.

l. Exit your text editor.

3. The reaction to your in-store information system at Film Clips is very encouraging. In fact, you've decided to enhance your Web pages by adding sounds and graphic images. Many images are available on the Web, and here's your opportunity to do some quality surfing. You've also designed a logo and have that in electronic form. Film Clips specializes in your favorite kind of movies.

To complete this independent challenge:

a. Create an outline for an explanatory page about a retrospective about your favorite movie star.

b. Open a blank text editor document, and save it as a text document called Film Clips Home Page.htm.

c. Type the outline in the document, using the appropriate HTML tags.

d. Insert the logo, filmclip.jpg, located on your Project Disk. Use any alignment for the logo you feel is appropriate.

e. Find at least one graphic image of your movie star. (*Note:* You can use the Web to find images.)

f. Include this graphic image on your page.

g. Create a fictitious Web site containing information on this movie star, then create a link so your customers can click the image in Step 6 to jump to this Web site. (*Note:* If you want, you can locate a real site on the Web.)

h. Save your work.

i. Print the document in your text editor.

j. Print the document in your browser.

k. Close your browser.

l. Exit your text editor.

4. Madam Zylog, your client, is determined to be the foremost astrologer, fortune teller, and palm reader on the World Wide Web. She's pleased with your work so far, and has had a vision of many graphic images on her page. Madam Zylog feels strongly that you are the one to provide these images. Consult the Web to find images used in sites similar to Madam Zylog.

To complete this independent challenge:

a. Establish an Internet connection.

b. Locate a Web site with relevant downloadable graphic images.

c. Download a new graphic image (or use her logo) and determine three pixel coordinates using an available art program.

d. Create an outline for a new Web page that will concentrate on Madam Zylog's talents.

e. Start your text editor, open a new document, then save it as a text document called Madam Zylog Home Page 1.htm.

f. Insert her logo, Zylog.jpg, found on your Project Disk.

g. Insert a sound on the page using a scaled version of her logo as the clickable image that starts the Media Player application.

h. Create an image map that connects to each of these Web sites in a new text document called Madam Zylog.map.

i. Save your work.

j. Print out the text editor and browser documents.

k. Close and exit text editor and your browser.

► Visual Workshop

Use the skills you learned in this unit to create the Web page shown in Figure C-18. Save the HTML file as a text document called Barbara's Home Page.htm, then print the document in your text editor and your browser. Use the graphics files barbaras.jpg and cookie.jpg on your Project Disk; use the fictitious Web site http://www.barbaras.com/recipes.htm.

FIGURE C-18

Welcome to the *Barbara's Bakery* Home Page!

We're new to the World Wide Web, but we want
everyone to know about our fresh and wholesome baked goodies!

In fact, this month we're featuring mouth-watering **chocolate chip cookies**!

Think about it . . . don't you *need* delicious,
home-made chocolate chip cookies? We think so!!!

And if you'd like to purchase the recipe for this

baked wonder-of-the-world, click here

Any questions about our fabulous baked goods? Contact me at Barbara@barbsbakery.com and I'll be sure to get back to you ASAP!

Link to fictitious
Web site

Create link to fictitious
e-mail address

Using

Forms to Control Input

► **Plan a form**
► **Create a text entry field**
► **Use radio buttons**
► **Use checkboxes**
► **Create a pull-down menu**
► **Create a scroll box**
► **Use push buttons with preset values**

Businesses using the World Wide Web to introduce customers to their products can also use their Web pages to take customer's orders. HTML has a variety of tags that can be used to create helpful forms that easily accept user input. ◢ The purpose of Nomad's Web pages is not only to introduce its products to a wider audience, but also to make online purchases simple. Grace wants to include a form that makes it easy for customers to make purchases.

HTML

Planning a Form

A form is a great way of gathering information for later use. For a business that uses the Web, a form is a great way of collecting information about customer preferences and taking orders. A Web page form can accept input by allowing a user to type text or click radio buttons, check-boxes, or labeled buttons to make selections. Table D-1 lists the three HTML tags that are used to create these items on a form. Grace decides what types of fields she wants in the Nomad order form based on the type of data she has to collect from the customer.

Details

 Single-line text entries

A user can simply type information in a text box, much like on a paper form. When the text box is defined, you can set its maximum length to ensure a professional look. A text box is used for the customer to enter his/her name in the form.

 Checkboxes and radio buttons

Many forms are simplified by allowing a user to select from a list of options or choices. A Web page is no exception. Choices are commonly displayed in the form using checkboxes and radio buttons, as shown in Figure D-1. Frequently, the user is asked to choose one item from a list (although it is possible to make multiple selections using special tags). In addition to giving the user a list of choices, you can also supply a default selection—an item that is automatically selected because it is the most likely choice—to make filling out the form that much quicker.

 Pull-down menus and scroll boxes

To avoid cluttering a form with lengthy lists, a more attractive option can be a scroll box or pull-down menu. Each of these selection methods can also display an automatic default value. For items with several options, use a pull-down menu.

 Multi-line text areas

Even though a form should require as little typing as possible for the user, it's nice to offer customers the option of commenting without restriction. You include an area in which a customer can freely comment on Nomad and its products.

Push buttons with preset functions

Once a customer makes selections on the order form, the information must be sent to an order desk where it is processed for delivery and billing. You design a single button that a customer clicks when the order form is finished. By clicking this button the information is sent to the Nomad Web server.

CLUES TO USE

Printing a Web page

To print a Web page so it displays elements such as checkboxes and radio buttons, you must take a "picture" of what is on your screen by pressing the Print Screen button on your keyboard; this places an image of your screen on the computer's Clipboard. Then you can start the Paint program that comes with Windows, click Edit on the menu bar, then click Paste. To fit the image on a single sheet of paper, change the paper orientation to landscape by clicking File on the menu bar, then clicking Page Setup. To print the image, click File on the menu bar, then click Print.

Nomad Ltd's *Web Wear* Order Form!

Nomad Ltd

Please tell us your name: [   ]

Which style would you like to order?

Please select a *style*:
(Mega way-cool bitmapped   (Awesome elegant   (Whatsamatta   (On-line Chat

What size?

Please select a *size*: [ ] Small [✓] Medium [ ] Large [ ] X-Large

And the color?

Please select a *color*: [Navy blue ▾]

Click here to submit this form. [Send data now!]

Click radio button to make a selection

Pull down menu with default selection

Checkbox options with a default already selected

Type text entry here

TABLE D-1: HTML field creation tags

tag	result
INPUT	Creates a variety of fields: single text lines, radio buttons, checkboxes, and push buttons
SELECT	Creates a field in which a user makes choices from a scroll box or pull-down menu
TEXTAREA	Creates a field that accepts multiple lines of user text

Creating a Text Entry Field

A single line of text is the simplest type of entry field to create on a form. A text entry field is created using the <INPUT TYPE> tags. Other INPUT attributes are listed in Table D-2. Regardless of the type of field, each fill-out form begins and ends with the <FORM> </FORM> tags. You can have many forms in a document. Each <FORM> tag must also indicate how the information on the form is transmitted. The initial <FORM> tag is used in combination with either the ACTION or METHOD attribute in order to correctly send the completed form.
Grace started her document and left spaces to fill in necessary information. She begins by adding a field for a customer to enter his/her name.

Steps

1. Start your **text editor**, then open the file **HTML D-1.htm** and save it as a text document with the filename **Nomad on-line order form.htm**
   The first HTML tag necessary when creating a form field is the <FORM> tag. This tag must be accompanied by the attributes ACTION or METHOD, so the information is properly sent.

QuickTip

Try to eliminate clutter on a form; include only what's necessary or your page will look messy.

2. Click in the **blank line under the <HR> tag**, then type **<FORM ACTION="URL">**
   By including the ACTION attribute in this statement, you can send the information in the form to a URL location (which you supply later to replace the URL placeholder).

3. Type **Please tell us your name:**, then press **[Enter]**
   Text fields are created using the TEXT attribute. You use additional attributes to define the field's size and name.

4. Type **<INPUT TYPE="TEXT" SIZE=20 NAME="yourname">**, then press **[Enter]**
   A form ends with the final <FORM> tag.

5. Type **</FORM>**
   Compare your document with Figure D-2.

6. Save the file **Nomad on-line order form.htm** as a text document
   You start your browser and view the document.

7. Start your browser, then open the file **Nomad on-line order form.htm**
   Compare your Web page with Figure D-3. The defined text area appears on the screen.

FIGURE D-2: HTML tags for text field

```
<HTML>

<HEAD>
<TITLE>The Nomad Ltd on-line catalog: Order Form</TITLE>
</HEAD>

<BODY>
<IMG SRC="file:///a|/nomad.jpg" ALIGN="right">
<H1>Nomad Ltd's <I>Web Wear</I> Order Form!</H1>
<HR>
<FORM ACTION="URL">Please tell us your name:
<INPUT TYPE="TEXT" SIZE=20 NAME="yourname">
</FORM>
```

Begins a form

Tag determines type and size of field

Ends a form

FIGURE D-3: Text field in form

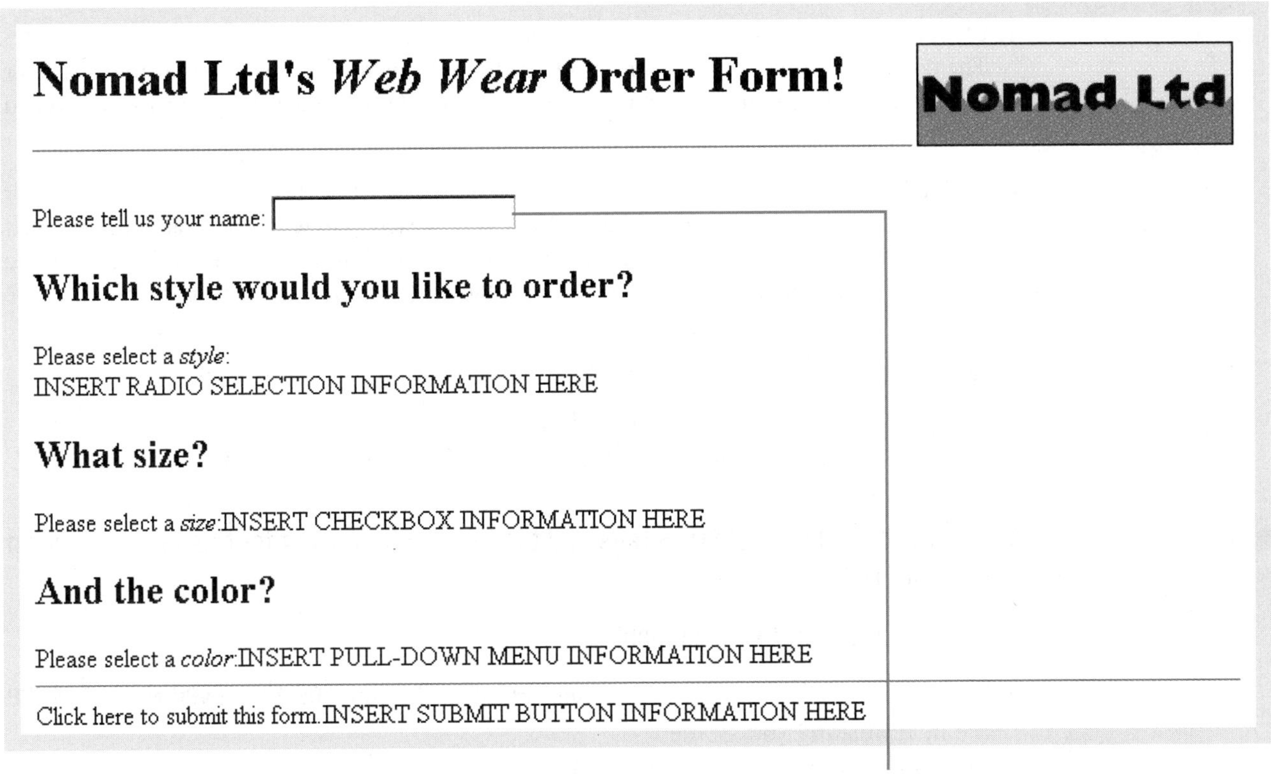

Nomad Ltd's Web Wear Order Form!
Nomad Ltd
Please tell us your name:
Which style would you like to order?
Please select a style:
INSERT RADIO SELECTION INFORMATION HERE
What size?
Please select a size:INSERT CHECKBOX INFORMATION HERE
And the color?
Please select a color:INSERT PULL-DOWN MENU INFORMATION HERE
Click here to submit this form.INSERT SUBMIT BUTTON INFORMATION HERE

User types text here

TABLE D-2: HTML INPUT attributes

attribute	description
NAME	Defines the name of the data; a required field
SIZE	Determines the size of the field; measured in characters
MAXLENGTH	Determines the maximum number of allowable characters
VALUE	Defines the default value to be displayed
CHECKED	Determines which radio button or checkbox value is selected; works only with these two INPUT attributes
TYPE	Sets the input field to "text," "password," "radio," "checkbox," "reset," or "submit"

HTML

Unit
D

HTML

Using Radio Buttons

Making selections on a form should be as simple and error-free as possible. By providing radio buttons and checkboxes in a form, you limit the choices and assure easy and accurate data entry. Both radio buttons and checkboxes use the INPUT TYPE tags. Items in a list are grouped together by sharing a common NAME. Items displayed using checkboxes or radio buttons can be arranged using list tags or line break tags. ◢▬▬ Grace uses radio buttons to allow customers to choose which style Web Wear T-shirt they want to order.

Steps

1. **Click the** text editor program button **on the taskbar**
   The document appears. You want to add radio buttons to this form so that the customer simply has to click a button to make a selection. The <FORM> tags have already been typed for the radio buttons.

2. **Select the** INSERT RADIO SELECTION INFORMATION HERE **text**
   The INPUT TYPE for each entry will be "RADIO" as each item will have a radio button next to it. Each item in the group is given the NAME "style," and each item will have a unique VALUE. The text outside the <INPUT> tag will display on the page to help the reader make a choice.

3. **Type** <INPUT TYPE="RADIO" NAME="style" VALUE="Mega way-cool bitmapped"> Mega way-cool bitmapped, **then press** [Enter]
   Each remaining item in the radio button list is similar, but has a different VALUE and different text.

   QuickTip
   Use copy and paste to assist your data entry.

4. **Type the remaining** <INPUT> **tags and the final** <FORM> **tag for this form, as shown in Figure D-4**

5. **Save the file as a text document**

6. **Click the** browser program button **on the taskbar, then view the saved version of the file by refreshing your screen**
   Compare your document with Figure D-5.

```
<H2>Which style would you like to order?</H2>
<FORM ACTION="URL">Please select a <I>style</I>:<BR>
<INPUT TYPE="RADIO" NAME="style" VALUE="Mega way-cool bitmapped">Mega
way-cool bitmapped
<INPUT TYPE="RADIO" NAME="style" VALUE="Awesome elegant">Awesome elegant
<INPUT TYPE="RADIO" NAME="style" VALUE="Whatsamatta">Whatsamatta
<INPUT TYPE="RADIO" NAME="style" VALUE="On-line Chat">On-line Chat
</FORM>
<H2>What size?</H2>
<FORM ACTION="URL">Please select a <I>size</I>:INSERT CHECKBOX
INFORMATION HERE
</FORM>
<H2>And the color?</H2>
```

Input tags   Closing form tag   Creates a radio button display   Displays next to the radio button

FIGURE D-5: **Radio buttons in HTML form**

Nomad Ltd's *Web Wear* Order Form!

Nomad Ltd

Please tell us your name: [   ]

Which style would you like to order?

Please select a *style*:

○ Mega way-cool bitmapped   ○ Awesome elegant   ○ Whatsamatta   ○ On-line Chat

What size?

Please select a *size*:INSERT CHECKBOX INFORMATION HERE

And the color?

Please select a *color*:INSERT PULL-DOWN MENU INFORMATION HERE

Click here to submit this form.INSERT SUBMIT BUTTON INFORMATION HERE

Radio buttons with no default selection

Displaying radio buttons and checkboxes using a list format

Radio button and checkbox selections can be displayed horizontally (within a line of text, for example) or in a vertical list using ordered or definition list tags, or by inserting <BR> tags where you want each line to end. Definition tags (<DL><DT><DD>) can be used to create an indented effect, as shown in Figure D-6.

FIGURE D-6: **Definition list tags create indented radio buttons**

Nomad Ltd's *Web Wear* Order Form!   **Nomad Ltd**

Please tell us your name: [   ]

Which style would you like to order?

Please select a *style*:
- ○ Mega way-cool bitmapped
- ○ Awesome elegant
- ○ Whatsamatta
- ○ On-line Chat

List tags can be used with input types to change appearance

HTML

HTML

Using Checkboxes

Checkboxes are similar to radio buttons in that the user can make a selection from several items. When creating either checkboxes or radio buttons, you can select a default value—which automatically appears as selected—using the CHECKED attribute. ▰▰▰▰ Grace wants to use a checkbox field so customers can select a size; she wants the default size, Medium, to be checked.

Steps 1 2 3 4

1. **Click the text editor program button on the taskbar**
   Text placeholders mark the location of the tags in this document.

2. **Select the INSERT CHECKBOX INFORMATION HERE text**
   Since the <FORM> tags have already been typed, you need the INPUT TYPE attributes for the checkbox fields. The sizes available are small, medium, large, and x-large.

3. **Type <INPUT TYPE="CHECKBOX" NAME="sizes" VALUE="Small"> Small, then press [Enter]**
   The Medium checkbox will be the default value. An item appears as checked (or on, for a radio button) by including the CHECKED attribute in the INPUT statement.

4. **Type <INPUT TYPE="CHECKBOX" NAME="sizes" VALUE="Medium" CHECKED> Medium, then press [Enter]**
   The four items in the checkbox list will display across the line.

5. **Type the remaining checkbox items, as shown in Figure D-7**

6. **Save the file, then click the browser program button on the taskbar**
   The page without the changes displays in your browser screen.

> **Trouble?**
> When you first create checkboxes, some items might appear as checked when they shouldn't be. Reopening the file from the File menu correctly displays the checked items.

7. **View the saved changes to the file by refreshing the screen**
   The Web page appears, as shown in Figure D-8. The Medium checkbox automatically appears with a checkmark, as this is the default selection.

```
</HEAD>

<BODY>
<IMG SRC="file:///a|/nomad.jpg" ALIGN="right">
<H1>Nomad Ltd's <I>Web Wear</I> Order Form!</H1>
<HR>
<FORM ACTION="URL">Please tell us your name:
<INPUT TYPE="TEXT" SIZE=20 NAME="yourname">
</FORM>
<H2>Which style would you like to order?</H2>
<FORM ACTION="URL">Please select a <I>style</I>:<BR>
<INPUT TYPE="RADIO" NAME="style" VALUE="Mega way-cool bitmapped">Mega
way-cool bitmapped
<INPUT TYPE="RADIO" NAME="style" VALUE="Awesome elegant">Awesome elegant
<INPUT TYPE="RADIO" NAME="style" VALUE="Whatsamatta">Whatsamatta
<INPUT TYPE="RADIO" NAME="style" VALUE="On-line Chat">On-line Chat
<H2>What size?</H2>
<FORM ACTION="URL">Please select a <I>size</I>:<INPUT TYPE="CHECKBOX"
NAME="sizes" VALUE="Small">Small
<INPUT TYPE="CHECKBOX" NAME="sizes" VALUE="Medium" CHECKED>Medium
<INPUT TYPE="CHECKBOX" NAME="sizes" VALUE="Large">Large
<INPUT TYPE="CHECKBOX" NAME="sizes" VALUE="X-Large">X-Large
</FORM>
<H2>And the color?</H2>
<FORM ACTION="URL">Please select a <I>color</I>:INSERT PULL-DOWN MENU
INFORMATION HERE
</FORM>
```

Input tags to type   Creates a checkbox display   Indicates a default selection

FIGURE D-8: Checkboxes on a Web page

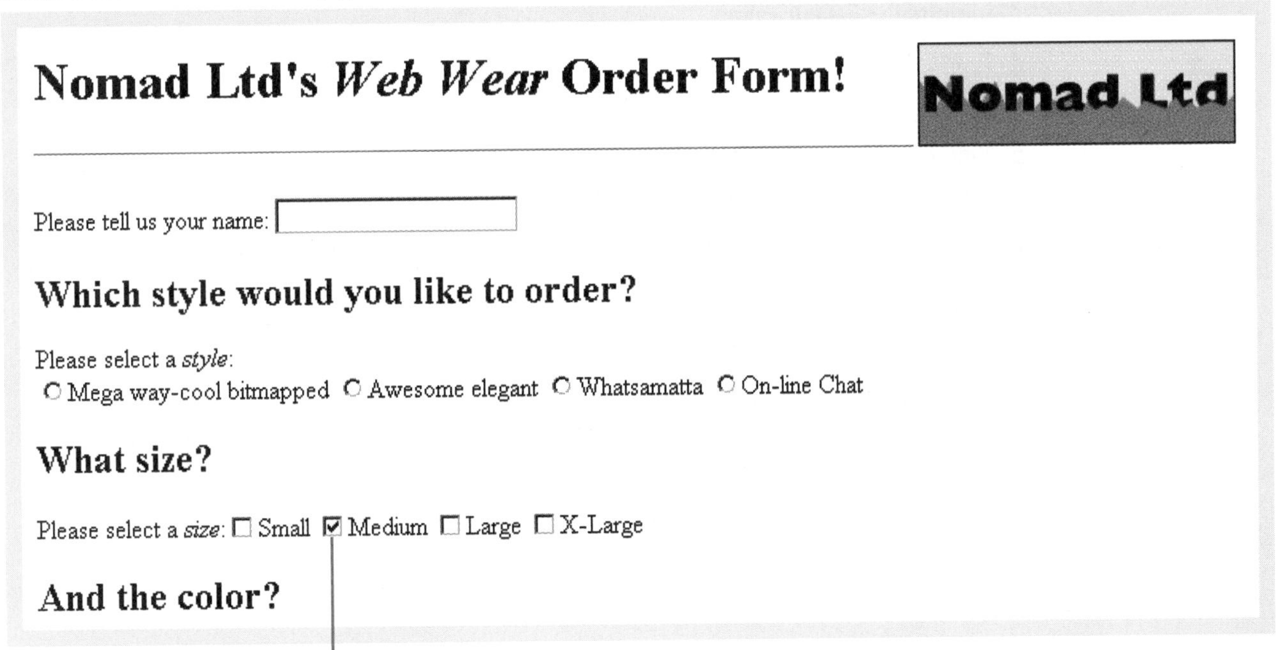

Nomad Ltd's *Web Wear* Order Form!

Nomad Ltd

Please tell us your name: [   ]

Which style would you like to order?

Please select a *style*:
○ Mega way-cool bitmapped ○ Awesome elegant ○ Whatsamatta ○ On-line Chat

What size?

Please select a *size*: ☐ Small ☑ Medium ☐ Large ☐ X-Large

And the color?

Default selection
is automatically
selected

Creating a Pull-down Menu

Depending on the layout of your Web page, you might want to offer choices to readers without displaying all the options on the page. Pull-down menus and scroll boxes use the <SELECT> tag; each of these display methods can be assigned a default value using the SELECTED attribute. The <SELECT> tag has a variety of attributes that affect the appearance of the list. These attributes are described in Table D-3. Grace wants to list the T-shirt color choices in a pull-down menu.

Steps 1 2 3 4

1. Click the text editor program button on the taskbar
The document has a text placeholder with the information needed for a simple pull-down menu.

2. Select the text INSERT PULL-DOWN MENU INFORMATION HERE
A pull-down menu begins and ends with the initial <FORM ACTION> tag, but the closing </FORM> tag is not used. The SELECT tag defines the options in the list, and the first item in the list defines the name of the field.

3. Type <SELECT NAME="color">, then press [Enter]
The first item in the list will be the default value. You include the SELECTED attribute to indicate the default value.

4. Type <OPTION SELECTED>Navy blue, then press [Enter]
The list ends using the final <SELECT> tag.

5. Type the remaining colors and tags using Figure D-9 as a guide
All the information is typed. The </SELECT> tag ends this form.

6. Save the file as a text document

7. Click the browser program button on the taskbar
The page without this new pull-down menu displays on the screen.

8. View the saved version of the file by refreshing your screen
The Web page appears, as shown in Figure D-10 use the scroll bar if necessary to see the pull-down menu.

9. Click the arrow on the pull-down menu to see all the items

TABLE D-3: SELECT tag attributes

attribute	description
NAME	Defines the name of the data; a required field
SIZE	Determines how many items display. If omitted, choices appear as pop-up menu; if set to 2 or more, appears as scroll box
MULTIPLE	Allows more than one selection to be made; appears as a scroll box
VALUE	The value to be assigned to a choice; an optional attribute that doesn't need to have the same value displayed on the page
SELECTED	The choice to be the default option

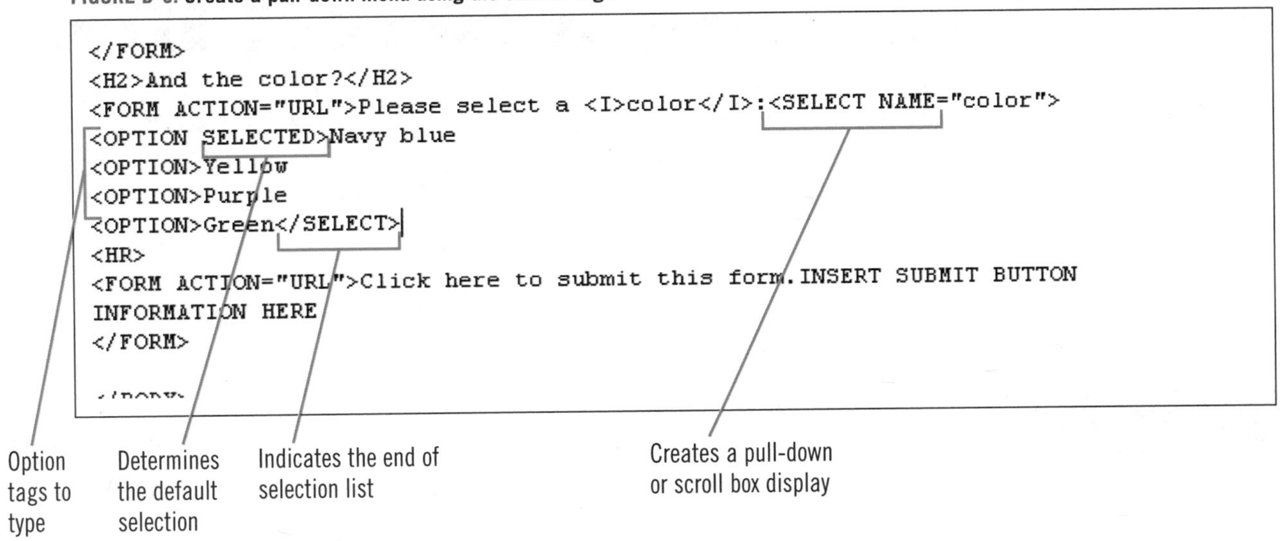

```
</FORM>
<H2>And the color?</H2>
<FORM ACTION="URL">Please select a <I>color</I>:<SELECT NAME="color">
<OPTION SELECTED>Navy blue
<OPTION>Yellow
<OPTION>Purple
<OPTION>Green</SELECT>
<HR>
<FORM ACTION="URL">Click here to submit this form.INSERT SUBMIT BUTTON
INFORMATION HERE
</FORM>
```

Option tags to type

Determines the default selection

Indicates the end of selection list

Creates a pull-down or scroll box display

FIGURE D-10: Pull-down menu with a default value

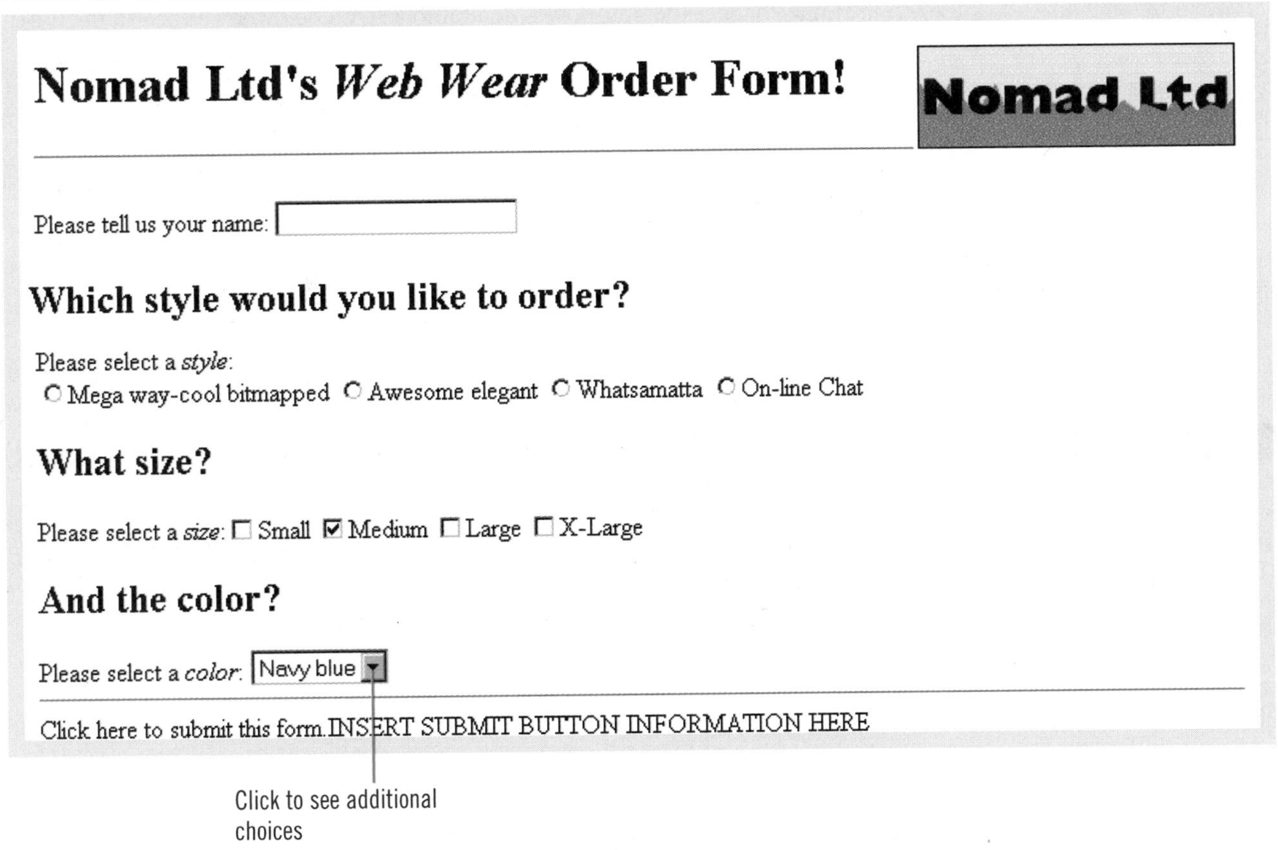

Nomad Ltd's *Web Wear* Order Form!

Nomad Ltd

Please tell us your name: [   ]

Which style would you like to order?

Please select a *style*:
○ Mega way-cool bitmapped   ○ Awesome elegant   ○ Whatsamatta   ○ On-line Chat

What size?

Please select a *size*: ☐ Small ☑ Medium ☐ Large ☐ X-Large

And the color?

Please select a *color*: [Navy blue ▾]

Click here to submit this form.INSERT SUBMIT BUTTON INFORMATION HERE

Click to see additional choices

Creating a Scroll Box

You've seen how a simple pull-down menu can be created using the <SELECT> tags. Existing HTML tags can be modified to change a pull-down menu into a scroll box by adding the optional SIZE attribute to the SELECT statement. ✐ Grace needs to add additional colors to the list of choices and to change the pull-down menu into a scroll box.

Steps 1 2 3 4

1. Click the **text editor program button** on the taskbar
You want to add more T-shirt colors to the list.

2. Click to the right of the word **Green**, then press **[Enter]**

Trouble?

If the items added to an <OPTION> list don't appear in your Web browser after reloading the document, close the browser then reopen the file.

3. Type **<OPTION>Teal**, press **[Enter]**, type **<OPTION>Orange**, press **[Enter]**, then type **<OPTION>Berry**
The SIZE attribute changes the pull-down menu into a scroll box when added to the initial SELECT tag.

4. Click to the right of **color** in the **<SELECT>** tag, press **[Spacebar]**, then type **SIZE=3**
Compare your document with Figure D-11. Three items are visible in the scroll box.

5. Save the file, then click the **browser program button** on the taskbar
These changes can be viewed by viewing the Web page in the browser.

6. View the saved version of the document in your browser by refreshing your screen
The image is updated, as shown in Figure D-12.

Sharing Web pages with colleagues is helpful during the design phase. The Paint program provided with Windows is useful to create printouts of Web pages.

Trouble?

Can't find the Print Screen key on your keyboard? There are many variations of this key. It might appear as "Print Scrn" or "PrtSc," depending on the type of keyboard you have. It is usually located to the right of the [F12] key.

7. Press **[Print Screen]**, start **Paint** (click **Start** on the taskbar, point to **Programs**, point to **Accessories**, then click **Paint**)

8. Click **Edit** on the menu bar, click **Paste**, enlarge the image if necessary, click **Page Setup**, change the orientation to landscape, click **OK**, click **File**, click **Print**, then click **OK**
Compare your printed page to the screen image.

```
<H2>And the color?</H2>
<FORM ACTION="URL">Please select a <I>color</I>:<SELECT NAME="color"
SIZE=3>
<OPTION SELECTED>Navy blue
<OPTION>Yellow
<OPTION>Purple
<OPTION>Green
<OPTION>Teal
<OPTION>Orange
<OPTION>Berry</SELECT>
<HR>
<FORM ACTION="URL">Click here to submit this form.INSERT SUBMIT BUTTON
INFORMATION HERE
</FORM>
```

Number indicates how many choices are displayed in scroll box

Additional entries

FIGURE D-12: Scroll box on a Web page

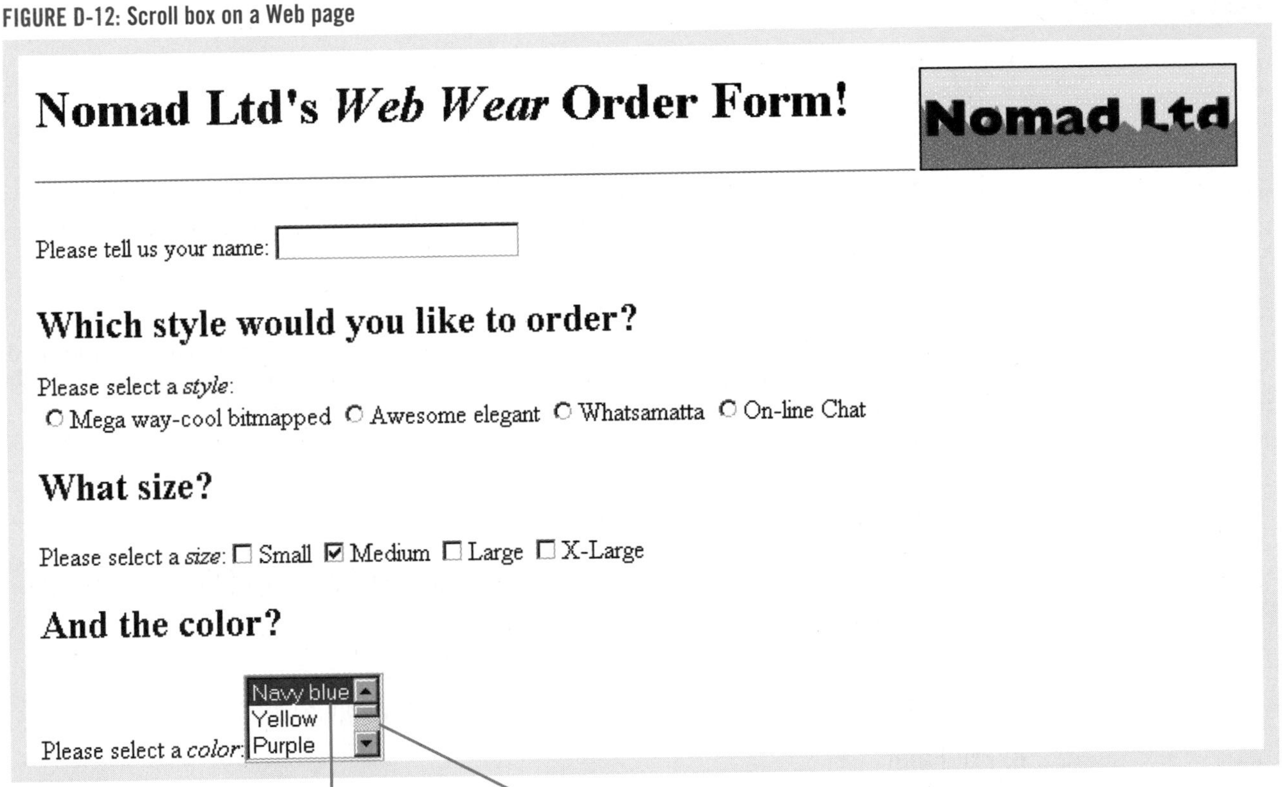

Nomad Ltd's *Web Wear* Order Form!

Nomad Ltd

Please tell us your name: [   ]

Which style would you like to order?

Please select a *style*:
○ Mega way-cool bitmapped   ○ Awesome elegant   ○ Whatsamatta   ○ On-line Chat

What size?

Please select a *size*: ☐ Small   ☑ Medium   ☐ Large   ☐ X-Large

And the color?

Please select a *color*: [Navy blue / Yellow / Purple]

Default selection   Click to see additional choices

CLUES TO USE

Creating a multi-line text area

As a courtesy to your Web page readers, you can add a comment section that permits them to type text in a free-form style. You create a text box using the TEXTAREA tag and options that control the height and width of the displayed box. For example, the box shown in Figur D-13 was created using the following tags: <TEXTAREA NAME="comments" ROWS=5 COLS=40></TEXTAREA>. By default, a 4-row by 40-column text box is created, but this can be modified, as shown in the tag.

FIGURE D-13: TEXTAREA tags create a multi-line text box

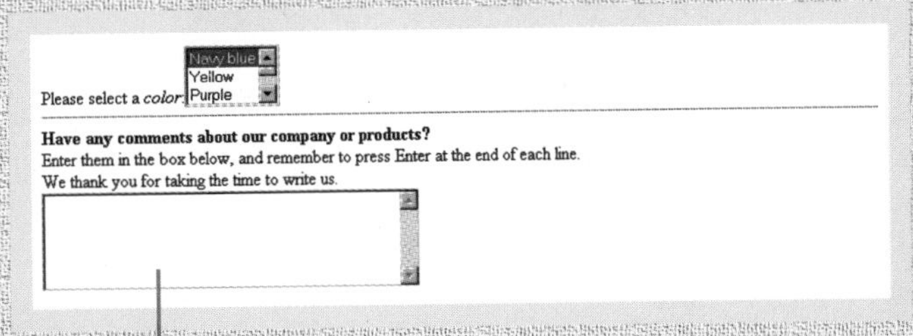

Please select a *color* [Navy blue / Yellow / Purple]

Have any comments about our company or products?
Enter them in the box below, and remember to press Enter at the end of each line.
We thank you for taking the time to write us.

Box automatically scrolls as displayed area is filled

HTML

Using Push Buttons with Preset Values

The information in a form is of little use if it is not sent to a Web address where it can be read or processed. In most cases, the data in a form is sent to a Web server using a URL address, and the easiest way to send data is to supply a push button on the Web page. The SUBMIT attribute is designed to send form data to the server for processing. You can also use a push button to reset the default settings in your form. ✒ Once the form is filled out, Grace wants customers to be able to send the information by clicking a single button.

Steps

1. **Click the text editor program button on the taskbar**
   The document includes a placeholder with information for the Submit button.

2. **Select the text INSERT SUBMIT BUTTON INFORMATION HERE**
   The SUBMIT attribute displays the default value "Submit Query," on the face of the button. You want the button to be more expressive; the VALUE attribute can contain any message you want to display on the button.

3. **Type <INPUT TYPE="SUBMIT" VALUE="Send data now!">**
   Compare your text document with Figure D-14. In a live Web session, the user would send the data to the designated URL, as determined by the Webmaster. This button has no function since you have not supplied its URL.

4. **Save the file as a text document**

5. **Print the text file in the text editor**

6. **Click the browser program button, then view the saved version of the file by refreshing your screen**
   The document with the Submit button is shown in Figure D-15.

7. **Use the Print Screen button, then open Paint to print your Web page**

8. **Exit Paint**

9. **Close your browser and text editor**

```
<HR>
<FORM ACTION="URL">Click here to submit this form.<INPUT
TYPE="SUBMIT" VALUE="Send data now!"></FORM>

</BODY>
```

Creates a
button type

Replaces default button text

FIGURE D-15: **Displaying creative text on a Submit button**

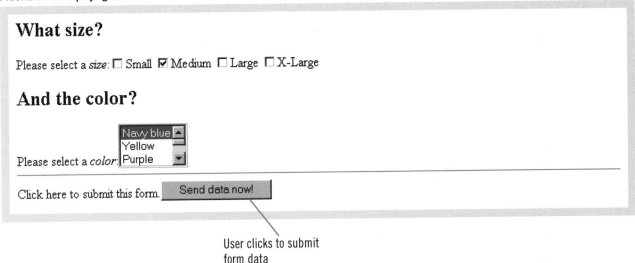

User clicks to submit
form data

Supplying a Reset button

Another common use of an on-screen button is to allow users to reset all the default values for form fields. This feature gives the user a chance to "do over" all the selections he or she has made. Like the Submit button, the function of the Reset button is preset. By using the VALUE attribute, you can replace the default "Reset" value on the button face with any text you want. Figure D-16 was created using the code <INPUT TYPE="RESET" VALUE="Clear all entries!">.

FIGURE D-16: **Reset button with creative text**

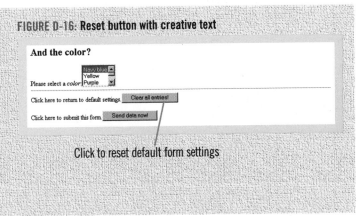

Click to reset default form settings

Practice

▶ Concepts Review

Label each element of the browser screen shown in Figure D-17.

FIGURE D-17

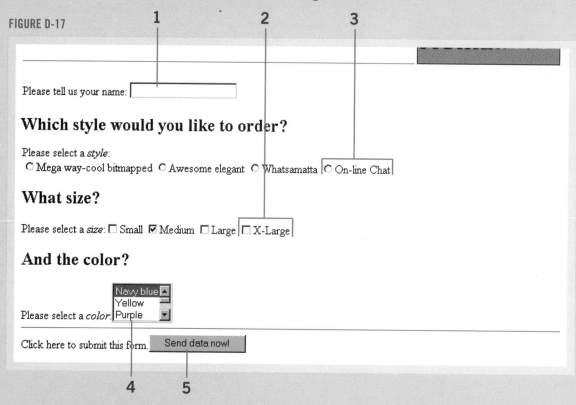

Match each statement with the HTML INPUT attribute it describes.

6. Sends data to a specified location   a. TYPE
7. Determines the kind of input   b. NAME
8. Creates a default selection   c. SIZE
9. Determines the number of displayed items   d. CHECKED
10. Defines the field name   e. SUBMIT

Select the best answer from the list of choices.

11. **Each of the following uses the INPUT tag, *except***
    a. checkbox
    b. scroll box
    c. radio button
    d. text box

12. **Which attribute changes a pull-down menu into a scrollbox?**
    a. SHAPE
    b. TYPE
    c. KIND
    d. SIZE

13. **Which attribute creates a multi-line text box?**
    a. TEXTBOX
    b. SCROLLBOX
    c. TEXTAREA
    d. MULTILINE

14. **The attribute that creates a button that returns a form to its default settings is**
    a. SEND
    b. RESET
    c. SUBMIT
    d. RETURN

15. **Which input attribute defines the displayed entry field text?**
    a. NAME
    b. VALUE
    c. CHECKED
    d. TYPE

16. **Which attribute determines the default value of a radio button or checkbox?**
    a. CHOSEN
    b. SELECTED
    c. CHECKED
    d. DEFAULT

HTML

17. **Which attribute determines the default value of a pull-down menu?**
    a. CHOSEN
    b. SELECTED
    c. CHECKED
    d. DEFAULT

18. **Which attribute is required in a pull-down menu?**
    a. NAME
    b. SIZE
    c. VALUE
    d. SELECTED

19. **Which tag concludes a form?**
    a. <FORM>
    b. </END FORM>
    c. </FORM>
    d. </FORM END>

▶ Skills Review

1. **Create a text entry field.**
   a. Start the text editor, open the file HTML D-2.htm, then save it as a text document with the filename Interstellar Pizza order form.htm.
   b. In the blank line above "Who is ordering this pizza?" type <FORM ACTION="URL">.
   c. Select the text INSERT TEXT BOX HERE.
   d. Type <INPUT TYPE="TEXT" SIZE=25 NAME="orderby">.
   e. Press [Enter] then type </FORM>.
   f. Save your work.
   g. View your work in your browser.

2. **Use checkboxes.**
   a. Return to your text editor.
   b. Select the text INSERT CHECKBOX INFORMATION HERE.
   c. Type an INPUT TYPE="CHECKBOX" statement for a field named "Ptype." The VALUE field and displayed text information is shown in Table D-4.

TABLE D-4

value field	display information
Szone	Safety zone
Sspecial	Surfer's special
Amadness	Alien madness
Prevenge	Planetary revenge

   d. Make Alien madness the default value.
   e. Save your work.
   f. Refresh the changes to the document.

3. Use radio buttons.
   a. Return to your text editor.
   b. Select the text INSERT RADIO BUTTON INFORMATION HERE.
   c. Type an INPUT TYPE="RADIO" statement for a field named "topping." The VALUE field and displayed text information is shown in Table D-5.

TABLE D-5

value field	display information
Cheese	Cheese
Pepons	Pepperoni, onions
Ongarsa	Onions, garlic, sausage
Surprise	SURPRISE!!!

   d. Make the Pepperoni, onions topping the default value.
   e. Save your work.
   f. Refresh changes to the browser.

4. Create a pull-down menu.
   a. Return to the text editor.
   b. Select the text INSERT PULL-DOWN MENU INFORMATION HERE.
   c. Type a SELECT NAME tag for a field named "size."
   d. Type an OPTION tag for each of the following sizes: 6 inches, 10 inches, and 14 inches.
   e. Make the 10-inch size the default value.
   f. Save your work.

5. Create a scroll box

 a. Add an additional option to the list: "Surprise me!"

 b. Change the pull-down menu to a scroll box by adding the SIZE=3 statement to the SELECT NAME tag.

 c. Select the text INSERT MULTI-LINE TEXT BOX INFORMATION HERE.

 d. Type a TEXTAREA tag that creates a 4-row by 50-column text box for a field named "tellus."

 e. Save your work.

 f. Refresh the changes to the document in your browser.

6. Use push buttons with preset values.

 a. Return to your text editor.

 b. Select the text INSERT RESET INFORMATION HERE.

 c. Type an INPUT TYPE statement for a Reset button that displays "Help - do over!" on its face.

 d. Select the text INSERT SUBMIT INFORMATION HERE.

 e. Type an INPUT TYPE statement for a Submit button that displays "Order up!" on its face.

 f. Save your work.

 g. Print the text editor document.

 h. Refresh the changes to the document in your browser.

 i. Use Print Screen and the Paint program to print your browser document.

 j. Exit Paint, then close your browser and text editor.

▶ Independent Challenges

1. Many of the Star Dot Star consulting firm's clients are avid World Wide Web users. In order to find out how many clients are using the Web, you've decided to add a questionnaire to your series of Web pages.

 To complete this independent challenge:

 a. Create a new text document and save it as Star Dot Star customer profile.htm.

 b. Insert the logo file supplied on your Project Disk, stardot.jpg, on the page. If you wish, you can reduce or enlarge its size.

 c. To preserve your client's anonymity, create a text field for the client's zip code.

 d. Create a series of checkboxes that asks the client how recently he/she has used your services. Some possible choices are last three days, week, month, year, etc.

 e. Create radio buttons that let the client select the type of service he/she values most from your firm (such as consulting, repairing software problems, installing upgrades, etc.).

 f. Create a multi-line text box for the client to provide optional free-form comments.

 g. Print the document in your text editor.

 h. Use Print Screen and the Paint program to print your browser document.

 i. Exit Paint, then close and exit your browser and text editor.

2. To help rate the success of the Web pages you've designed for the Board of Realtors, they've asked you to develop a questionnaire that readers can answer online. The Board is interested in reader satisfaction with your Web pages, and how readers like the services performed by Board members.

To complete this independent challenge:

a. Create a new text document and save it as BOR customers.htm.

b. Insert the Board of Realtors logo file supplied on your Project Disk, realtors.jpg, anywhere on the page.

c. Create a series of radio buttons that determines the age bracket of the respondent (for example, 18–24, 25–34, 35–44, etc.).

d. Create a series of checkboxes that determines if the respondent currently rents or owns a home.

e. Create a pull-down menu that asks renters if their apartment is in a home or apartment complex.

f. Create a multi-line text box that lets clients describe the kind of property they are interested in purchasing.

g. Create a Submit button that sends the form data to a URL.

h. Save your work.

i. Print the document in your text editor.

j. Use Print Screen and the Paint program to print your browser document.

k. Exit Paint, then close and exit your browser and text editor.

3. Not only do the Film Clips customers love your Web pages, they've indicated a desire to tell you what videos they want so you can make better video purchases. You decide to add a questionnaire to your Web page that lets customers tell you what videos they want to see in the store.

To complete this independent challenge:

a. Create a new document and save it as Film Clips requests.htm.

b. Create a text box in which the customer can enter his/her first and last name.

c. Create a series of radio buttons that lets the customer select a favorite type of movie, such as drama, action, documentary, or comedy.

d. Create a series of checkboxes that lets a customer choose black & white, color, or both types of movies.

e. Provide three text boxes in which your customers can enter the names of their favorite movie stars.

f. Save your work.

g. Print the document in your text editor.

h. Use Print Screen and the Paint program to print your browser document.

i. Exit Paint, then close your browser and exit your text editor.

4. Madam Zylog is interested in collecting information from her clients using a form on the World Wide Web. She's indicated to you that a person's date and time of birth is crucial information she'll need to make accurate projections.

To complete this independent challenge:

a. Establish an Internet connection.

b. Use any search engine to locate a Web site that contains a form. Use this as a model for the rest of this Independent Challenge.

c. Print out the Web site through your browser, then close your Internet connection.

d. Create a new text document and save it as Zylog customer form.htm.

e. Insert the logo supplied on your Project Disk, Zylog.jpg.

f. Create a text field in which a customer enters his/her date of birth.

g. Create a text field in which a customer enters his/her time of birth.

h. Create checkboxes for the customer to enter whether the time of birth was AM or PM.

i. Create a scroll box in which a customer can select his/her astrological sign.

j. Create a field on the form to ask the customer if they have ever been to another astrologer. The customer should be able to respond using YES/NO radio buttons.

k. Save your work.

l. Print out the text editor and browser documents.

m. Close the text editor and your browser.

▶ Visual Workshop

Use the skills you learned in this unit to create the Web page shown in Figure D-18. Save your HTML file as a text document called Barbara's Bakery order form.htm, then print the document in your text editor and your browser. The Barbara's Bakery logo is stored in the graphics file barbaras.jpg supplied on your Project Disk. Barbara's Bakery makes bagels in the following flavors: plain, onion, garlic, cinnamon-raisin, green chili, and sesame seed; the plain flavor is the default choice.

FIGURE D-18

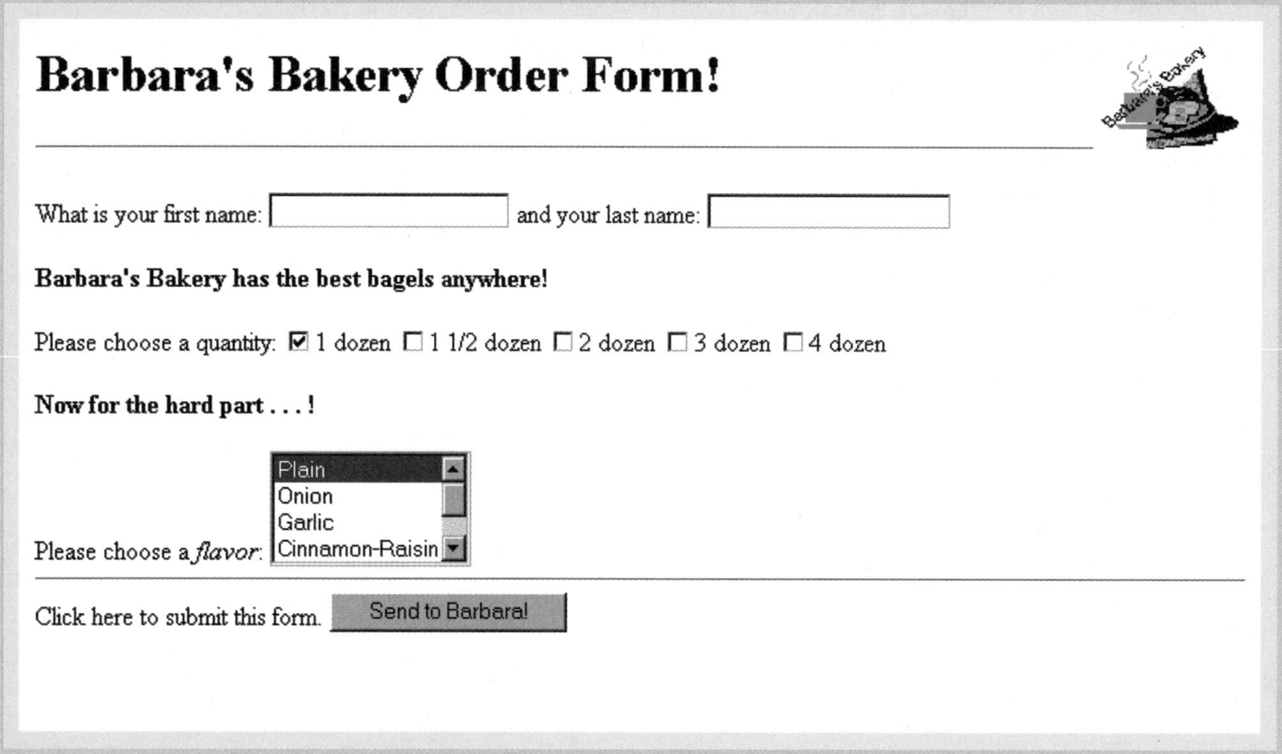

Barbara's Bakery Order Form!

What is your first name: [   ] and your last name: [   ]

Barbara's Bakery has the best bagels anywhere!

Please choose a quantity: ☑ 1 dozen ☐ 1 1/2 dozen ☐ 2 dozen ☐ 3 dozen ☐ 4 dozen

Now for the hard part . . . !

Please choose a *flavor*:

| Plain |
| Onion |
| Garlic |
| Cinnamon-Raisin |

Click here to submit this form. [Send to Barbara!]

Working

with Tables

Objectives

► **Create a simple table**
► **Span columns**
► **Format a border**
► **Align text**
► **Add color**
► **Modify a border**
► **Change table dimensions**
► **Control page layout**

Web pages often contain tabular data, which is displayed as a **table** in a series of columns and rows. It wasn't that long ago that unless a Web page used preformatted data tags (e.g., <PRE> </PRE>), a browser might not have the capability to display data in a tabular format. Now, browsers that can display tables are the rule rather than the exception. ✐ James Chavez is in charge of putting Nomad's tours online. Because there is so much tour data, James wants to use a tabular format to organize and present the information.

Creating a Simple Table

A tabular format—using a grid—is often the best way of organizing and displaying a list of complex data. With HTML tags, you can create both simple and complex tables. Table E-1 lists the tags used to create a basic table. A table is composed of columns and rows, with data contained in individual boxes, or **cells**. Most browsers display the text in the first row in a table, the **table header**, bold and centered. Subsequent rows generally are shown using standard body text. James created a basic HTML document earlier and now creates a simple table that lists the types of tours Nomad has to offer.

Steps

QuickTip
To control the word wrapping in the text document, in Notepad, click Edit on the Menu bar, then click Word Wrap; in WordPad, click View on the menu bar, click Options, then click Wrap to Ruler.

1. **Start your text editor, open the file HTML E-1, then save it as a text document with the filename Nomad tour types.htm**
   This document contains the basic information for the Web page. The initial table tag defines a table. The **Border** attribute adds a border around the table.

2. **Select the INSERT TABLE HERE text, type <TABLE BORDER>, then press [Enter]**
   The tags that follow the initial <TABLE> container define a caption, individual rows, the table header, and cells within the table. A **caption** is text centered above the table, but not within the table.

3. **Type <CAPTION>Nomad Tours</CAPTION>, then press [Enter]**
   The caption describes the contents of the table: for this table, it is Nomad Tours. The <TR> tag defines the beginning of each new row. The table header—usually the first row in a table—contains the name of each column.

QuickTip
Most browsers allow you to omit the final tag for a table header </TH>, row </TR>, and cell </TD>.

4. **Type <TR>, press [Enter], type <TH>Tour<TH>Description<TH>Duration, then press [Enter]**
   The table header helps organize the table. The <TR> tag precedes each additional row, and <TD> tags define each cell.

5. **Type <TR>, press [Enter], type <TD>Athlete<TD>For the sports-minded. Bicycling, kayaking, and hiking occur throughout the year.<TD>2-7 days, then press [Enter]**
   The second row in the table is the first tour type. There are two additional tour types that must be entered.

6. **Type the remaining tours and descriptions, including the final </TABLE> tag, as shown in Figure E-1**
   The table is now complete.

7. **Click the Save button on the toolbar, and save Nomad tour types.htm as a text document**
   You can view your code by loading the document in your browser.

8. **Open your browser, cancel any dialup activities, then open the file Nomad tour types.htm**
   Compare your document to Figure E-2.

FIGURE E-1: Tags for simple table

Adds a border to the table

```
<BODY>
<IMG SRC="nomad.jpg" ALIGN="right">
<H1>Nomad Tours on-line!</H1>
<H2>Get Tour Information Anytime: Day or Night</H2>
Nomad Ltd's fine tours and equipment are now available on-line.<BR>
Imagine, our years of experience in creating exciting tours are now<BR>
available to you at the click of your mouse -- 24 hours a day!<BR>
No more waiting for business hours; if you're at your computer,<BR>
you can research our tours and book one!
<P>
<H2>Types of Nomad Tours</H2>
<TABLE BORDER>
<CAPTION>Nomad Tours</CAPTION>
<TR>
<TH>Tour<TH>Description<TH>Duration
<TR>
<TD>Athlete<TD>For the sports-minded. Bicycling, kayaking, and hiking
occur throughout the year.<TD>2-7 days
<TR>
<TD>Arts<TD>Dedicated to the performing arts. An assortment of museums,
music, and theater.<TD>3-21 days
<TR>
<TD>Leisure<TD>Relax and spend time in beautiful settings. Lavish
accommodations and gourmet meals.<TD>2-15 days
</TABLE>
<H2>Find Out More About Each Type of Tour</H2>
```

Defines a new row

Final table tag

Caption appears centered above table

FIGURE E-2: Simple table completed

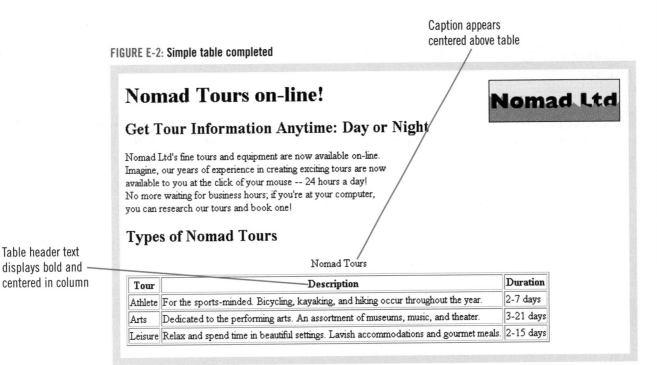

Table header text displays bold and centered in column

TABLE E-1: Basic table tags

tag	function	closing tag
<TABLE> </TABLE>	These are the primary table containers, which surround the rest of the table	required
<TH> </TH>	Denotes the table header—usually, the first row of a table	optional
<TR> </TR>	Defines each row in a table	optional
<TD> </TD>	Signifies the beginning/ending of a cell	optional

Spanning Columns

In most tables, a cell occupies space within a single column, but occasionally you may want a row to be wider than one column. Rows and columns can be **spanned**, or enlarged, by combining them with adjacent cells. The COLSPAN or ROWSPAN attribute is used with the <TD> tag to determine the number of columns or rows you want spanned. James wants the table to indicate whether tours are domestic or international. He inserts rows that span the columns for each tour and tells whether a tour type stays in this country, goes abroad, or both.

Steps

1. Click the **text editor program button** on the taskbar

The text document displays. The additional information will be in a new row above the tour it refers to, span two columns, and be centered.

2. Click to the left of **<TD>Athlete**

The insertion point is at the beginning of the line containing the Athlete tour. The first cell in the new row will be empty, and the cell spanning two columns will indicate that this is a domestic tour. Because empty cells display differently in different browsers, the HTML entity ** ** (nonbreaking space—an invisible character) ensures that all browsers treat empty cells equally.

QuickTip

The COLSPAN and ALIGN attributes can be put in a single tag.

3. Type **<TD> <TD COLSPAN=2 ALIGN=CENTER>Domestic**, press **[Enter]**, type **<TR>**, then press **[Enter]**

The new row—with data spanning columns 2 and 3—is inserted above the Athlete row.

QuickTip

When adding new rows, make sure there are sufficient <TR> tags for each row.

4. Click to the left of **<TD>Arts**, type **<TD> <TD COLSPAN=2 ALIGN= CENTER>Domestic or International**, press **[Enter]**, type **<TR>**, then press **[Enter]**

The row above the Arts tour indicates this is a Domestic or International tour.

5. Click to the left of **<TD>Leisure**, type **<TD> <TD COLSPAN=2 ALIGN= CENTER>International**, press **[Enter]**, type **<TR>**, then press **[Enter]**

The row above the Leisure tour indicates this is an International tour. The destinations of all tour types have been indicated. Compare your work to Figure E-3.

6. Save the file **Nomad tour types.htm** as a text document

Once the text document is saved, you can view the changes in your browser.

QuickTip

If you are using Netscape Navigator, refresh your screen by clicking the Reload button. If you are using Internet Explorer, click the Refresh button.

7. Click the **browser program button** on the taskbar, then view the saved version of **Nomad tour types.htm** by refreshing the screen

Compare your document to Figure E-4.

FIGURE E-3: **COLSPAN and ALIGN attribute tags**

Centers text over spanned column

```
<TR>
<TH>Tour<TH>Description<TH>Duration
<TR>
<TD> <TD COLSPAN=2 ALIGN=CENTER>Domestic
<TR>
<TD>Athlete<TD>For the sports-minded. Bicycling, kayaking, and hiking
occur throughout the year.<TD>2-7 days
<TR>
<TD> <TD COLSPAN=2 ALIGN=CENTER>Domestic or International
<TR>
<TD>Arts<TD>Dedicated to the performing arts. An assortment of museums,
music, and theater.<TD>3-21 days
<TR>
<TD> <TD COLSPAN=2 ALIGN=CENTER>International
<TR>
<TD>Leisure<TD>Relax and spend time in beautiful settings. Lavish
accommodations and gourmet meals.<TD>2-15 days
</TABLE>
```

Nonbreaking space   Spans 2 columns

FIGURE E-4: **Table containing spanned columns**

Types of Nomad Tours

Nomad Tours

Tour	Description	Duration
	Domestic	
Athlete	For the sports-minded. Bicycling, kayaking, and hiking occur throughout the year.	2-7 days
	Domestic or International	
Arts	Dedicated to the performing arts. An assortment of museums, music, and theater.	3-21 days
	International	
Leisure	Relax and spend time in beautiful settings. Lavish accommodations and gourmet meals.	2-15 days

CLUES TO USE

Controlling table text

In addition to determining how table elements are aligned, you also can control where text breaks within cells. You can use the <BR> tag to create a line break at a specific location within a cell. Also, you can include inline images, links, and form elements within a table. Figure E-5 shows the results of using line breaks and links within a table.

FIGURE E-5: **Line breaks and links in a table**

Types of Nomad Tours

Nomad Tours

Tour	Description	Duration
	Domestic	
Athlete	For the sports-minded. Bicycling, kayaking, and hiking occur throughout the year. For more information, see our Athlete tour page.	2-7 days
	Domestic or International	
Arts	Dedicated to the performing arts. An assortment of museums, music, and theater. For more information, see our Arts tour page.	3-21 days
	International	
Leisure	Relax and spend time in beautiful settings. Lavish accommodations and gourmet meals. For more information, see our Leisure tour page.	2-15 days

Link in a table cell   Line break tag here

HTML

Formatting a Border

Entering information in a table is only part of table creation; if the table isn't well-designed, no one will read it. Increasing the size of a table's border—using the default border color—gives it a three-dimensional look. A thicker border draws the reader's eye into the table, which makes the table easier to read. ✐▬▬ James wants the table border to be thicker.

Steps

1. **Click the text editor program button on the taskbar**
   The document displays. The table already has the default border defined in the <TABLE BORDER> tag. Border width is measured in **pixels**, a fixed number of dots whose height and width determine the size of a file or image. Pixel dimensions, along with the size and setting of the monitor, determine how large an image appears on-screen.

2. **Click to the right of BORDER in the <TABLE BORDER> tag, then type =20**
   When viewed in your browser, the border will be significantly thicker than before.

3. **Save the file Nomad tour types.htm as a text document**
   Once the text document is saved, you can view the changes to the table border in your browser.

4. **Click the browser program button on the taskbar, then view the saved version of Nomad tour types.htm by refreshing your screen**
   The 20-pixel border appears raised off the page, as shown in Figure E-6. For this page, it seems too thick.

5. **Click the text editor program button on the taskbar, click to the left of 20 in the <TABLE BORDER> tag, press [Delete], then type 1**
   The width of the border is now decreased to 10 pixels.

6. **Save the file Nomad tour types.htm as a text document**
   Once the text document is saved, you can view the changes in your browser.

7. **Click the browser program button on the taskbar, then view the saved version of Nomad tour types.htm by refreshing your screen**
   The table still appears to be raised off the page with the 10-pixel border. However, it is not as severe as the border that was specified with 20 pixels. Compare your document to Figure E-7.

FIGURE E-6: Changing border width

Depth added to border

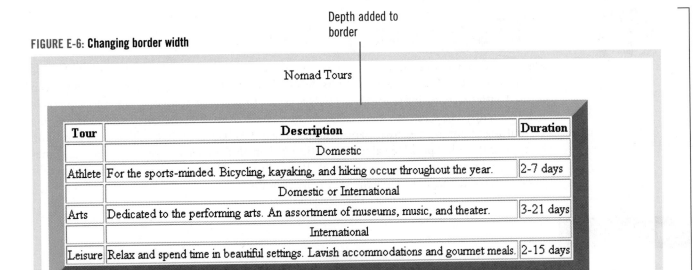

Nomad Tours

Tour	Description	Duration
	Domestic	
Athlete	For the sports-minded. Bicycling, kayaking, and hiking occur throughout the year.	2-7 days
	Domestic or International	
Arts	Dedicated to the performing arts. An assortment of museums, music, and theater.	3-21 days
	International	
Leisure	Relax and spend time in beautiful settings. Lavish accommodations and gourmet meals.	2-15 days

FIGURE E-7: Table with thick border

Types of Nomad Tours

Nomad Tours

Tour	Description	Duration
	Domestic	
Athlete	For the sports-minded. Bicycling, kayaking, and hiking occur throughout the year.	2-7 days
	Domestic or International	
Arts	Dedicated to the performing arts. An assortment of museums, music, and theater.	3-21 days
	International	
Leisure	Relax and spend time in beautiful settings. Lavish accommodations and gourmet meals.	2-15 days

10 pixel border has a 3-D look

Aligning Text

Elements within a table can be positioned in a variety of ways using the ALIGN attribute. The default value of <ALIGN> varies with its tag, as shown in Table E-2. The ALIGN attribute can be used with the following tags: <CAPTION>, <TR> to align row contents, <TH> to align table head contents, and <TD> to align cell contents. The <VALIGN> attribute lets you determine vertical alignment of an element. The default value of VALIGN is middle, with top, bottom, and baseline as the other possible values. To vertically align all the cells in a row so all their baselines match use the following tag: <TR VALIGN=BASELINE>. James wants data within cells to be centered to make the table more visually appealing.

Steps

1. **Click the text editor program button on the taskbar**
   The document displays. Although the ALIGN attribute can be inserted in each <TD> tag, the easiest way to center all the cells in a row is to modify the <TR> tag.

2. **Click to the right of TR above Athlete, press [Spacebar], then type ALIGN=CENTER**
   Compare your document to Figure E-8. The contents of each cell in the Athlete row will appear centered. This attribute must be added to each row in order to center the contents of the two remaining tour rows.

3. **Click to the right of TR above Arts, press [Spacebar], then type ALIGN=CENTER**
   This addition center-aligns the contents of the Arts row.

4. **Click to the right of TR above Leisure, press [Spacebar], then type ALIGN=CENTER**
   This addition center-aligns the contents of the Leisure row.

5. **Save the file Nomad tour types.htm as a text document**
   Once the text document is saved, you can view the changes to the alignment in your browser.

6. **Click the browser program button on the taskbar, then view the saved version of Nomad tour types.htm by refreshing your screen**
   Compare your document to Figure E-9.

FIGURE E-8: **ALIGN attribute added to TR tag**

```
<H2>Types of Nomad Tours</H2>
<TABLE BORDER=10>
<CAPTION>Nomad Tours</CAPTION>
<TR>
<TH>Tour<TH>Description<TH>Duration
<TR>
<TD> <TD COLSPAN=2 ALIGN=CENTER>Domestic
<TR ALIGN=CENTER>
<TD>Athlete<TD>For the sports-minded. Bicycling, kayaking, and hiking
occur throughout the year.<TD>2-7 days
<TR>
<TD> <TD COLSPAN=2 ALIGN=CENTER>Domestic or International
<TR ALIGN=CENTER>
<TD>Arts<TD>Dedicated to the performing arts. An assortment of museums,
music, and theater.<TD>3-21 days
<TR>
<TD> <TD COLSPAN=2 ALIGN=CENTER>International
<TR ALIGN=CENTER>
<TD>Leisure<TD>Relax and spend time in beautiful settings. Lavish
accommodations and gourmet meals.<TD>2-15 days
</TABLE>
<H2>Find Out More About Each Type of Tour</H2>
```

Centers the contents
of all cells in the row

FIGURE E-9: **Centered cells in table**

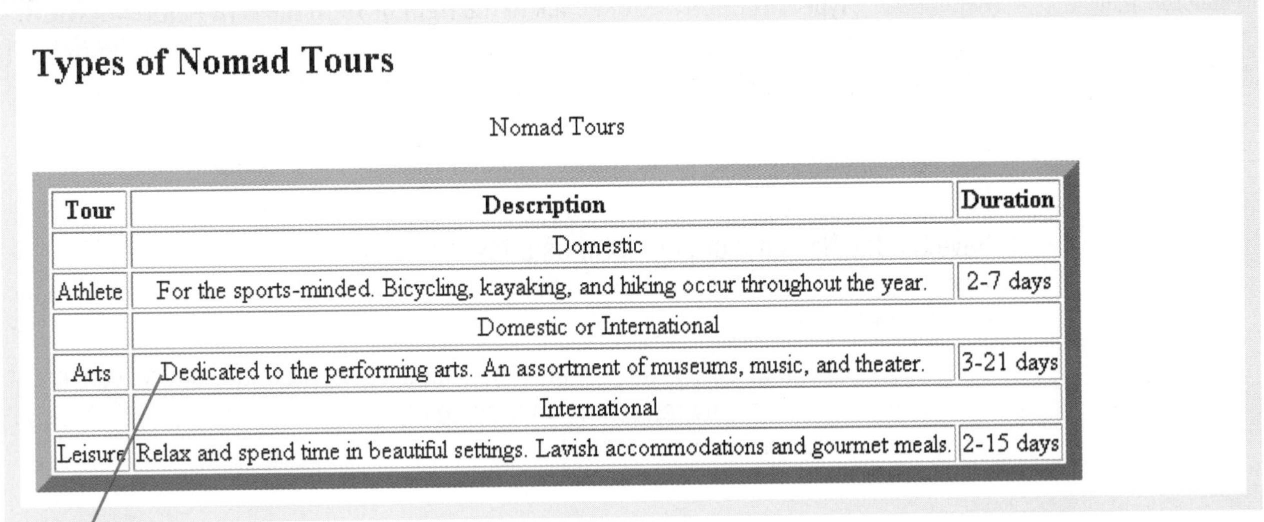

Types of Nomad Tours

Nomad Tours

Tour	Description	Duration
	Domestic	
Athlete	For the sports-minded. Bicycling, kayaking, and hiking occur throughout the year.	2-7 days
	Domestic or International	
Arts	Dedicated to the performing arts. An assortment of museums, music, and theater.	3-21 days
	International	
Leisure	Relax and spend time in beautiful settings. Lavish accommodations and gourmet meals.	2-15 days

Contents of all cells
centered in the rows

TABLE E-2: **ALIGN attributes**

tag	possible attributes
<CAPTION>	TOP (default) and BOTTOM
<TR>	LEFT (default), RIGHT, and CENTER
<TH>	LEFT, RIGHT, and CENTER (default)
<TD>	LEFT (default), RIGHT, and CENTER

Adding Color

Adding color to a table can enhance any Web page. You can use color in a cell background or in a table's border to distinguish and organize data. Although you can apply color liberally, it should always add value to the data—that is, colors used within the table should make the data easier to read and should not compete with the data. Table E-3 lists colors that can be used as border or background colors. ✎ James wants to add colors to the table to make data in the cells stand out.

Steps

1. **Click the text editor program button on the taskbar**
   The document displays. Color can be added to the background of a row by adding the BGCOLOR attribute into the <TR> tag.

Trouble?

ALIGN, BORDER, or BGCOLOR must be within the brackets, such as <TR BGCOLOR=RED>.

2. **Click to the right of TR in the <TR> tag 1 line beneath the <CAPTION> tag, press [Spacebar], then type BGCOLOR=YELLOW**
   The background of the table header row is now set to yellow. Color should be coordinated on a Web page; yellow and aqua work well with the colors in the Nomad logo.

QuickTip

Add the BGCOLOR attribute to the <TD> tag to add color to the background of a cell.

3. **Click to the right of TR in the <TR ALIGN=CENTER> tag above the Athlete row, press [Spacebar], type BGCOLOR=AQUA, click to the right of TR in the <TR ALIGN=CENTER> tag above the Arts row, press [Spacebar], type BGCOLOR=AQUA, click to the right of TR in the <TR ALIGN=CENTER > tag above the Leisure row, press [Spacebar], then type BGCOLOR=AQUA**
   The aqua color will display in the Athlete, Arts, and Leisure rows. Compare your document to Figure E-10.

4. **Save the file Nomad tour types.htm as a text document**
   Once the text document is saved, you can view the changes to the background colors in the rows in your browser.

5. **Click the browser program button on the taskbar, then view the saved version of Nomad tour types.htm by refreshing your screen**
   Compare your document to Figure E-11.

FIGURE E-10: BGCOLOR attributes added to document

```
you can research our tours and book one!
<P>
<H2>Types of Nomad Tours</H2>
<TABLE BORDER=10>
<CAPTION>Nomad Tours</CAPTION>
<TR BGCOLOR=YELLOW>
<TH>Tour<TH>Description<TH>Duration
<TR>
<TD> <TD COLSPAN=2 ALIGN=CENTER>Domestic
<TR BGCOLOR=AQUA ALIGN=CENTER>
<TD>Athlete<TD>For the sports-minded. Bicycling, kayaking, and hiking
occur throughout the year.<TD>2-7 days
<TR>
<TD> <TD COLSPAN=2 ALIGN=CENTER>Domestic or International
<TR BGCOLOR=AQUA ALIGN=CENTER>
<TD>Arts<TD>Dedicated to the performing arts. An assortment of museums,
music, and theater.<TD>3-21 days
<TR>
<TD> <TD COLSPAN=2 ALIGN=CENTER>International
<TR BGCOLOR=AQUA ALIGN=CENTER>
<TD>Leisure<TD>Relax and spend time in beautiful settings. Lavish
accommodations and gourmet meals.<TD>2-15 days
</TABLE>
<H2>Find Out More About Each Type of Tour</H2>
```

Multiple attributes assigned to TR tag

FIGURE E-11: Color added to table

Types of Nomad Tours

Nomad Tours

Tour	Description	Duration
	Domestic	
Athlete	For the sports-minded. Bicycling, kayaking, and hiking occur throughout the year.	2-7 days
	Domestic or International	
Arts	Dedicated to the performing arts. An assortment of museums, music, and theater.	3-21 days
	International	
Leisure	Relax and spend time in beautiful settings. Lavish accommodations and gourmet meals.	2-15 days

TABLE E-3: HTML border and background colors

color	sample	color	sample	color	sample	color	sample
Black		Silver		Gray		Navy	
White		Maroon		Red		Blue	
Purple		Fuchsia		Green		Teal	
Lime		Olive		Yellow		Aqua	

HTML

Modifying a Border

Color plays an important part in a table's appearance. In addition to changing its width, you can modify the color of a border. Using the BORDERCOLOR attribute and the same colors used in cell backgrounds, the appearance of a border can be coordinated to match the color scheme of the Web page. James wants to enhance the page by taking advantage of the color options available in his border design.

Steps

1. **Click the text editor program button on the taskbar**
   A border's color is specified within the <TABLE> tag using the BORDERCOLOR attribute.

2. **Click to the right of TABLE in the <TABLE BORDER> tag, press [Spacebar], type BORDERCOLOR=NAVY**
   The color of the table's border is specified to navy. The BORDERCOLOR attribute can be used in the <TD> or <TR> tags to color a specific cell or row.

3. **Click to the right of TR beneath the TH row, press [Spacebar], type BORDERCOLOR=RED**
   The row containing "Domestic" is specified with a red outline.

4. **Type the attribute BORDERCOLOR=RED in the <TR> tags for the rows containing the text Domestic or International and International**
   Compare your document to Figure E-12.

5. **Save Nomad tour types.htm as a text document**

Trouble?

If the border color does not match Figure E-13, this attribute mat not be supported by your browser.

6. **Click the browser program button on the taskbar, then view the saved version of Nomad tour types.htm by refreshing your screen**
   The border of the table should appear in navy, as shown in Figure E-13. Notice that the border color of each cell in the table has also changed to red .

FIGURE E-12: **BORDERCOLOR attribute inserted**

```
<H2>Types of Nomad Tours</H2>
<TABLE BORDERCOLOR=NAVY BORDER=10>
<CAPTION>Nomad Tours</CAPTION>
<TR BGCOLOR=YELLOW>
<TH>Tour<TH>Description<TH>Duration
<TR BORDERCOLOR=RED>
<TD> <TD COLSPAN=2 ALIGN=CENTER>Domestic
<TR BGCOLOR=AQUA ALIGN=CENTER>
<TD>Athlete<TD>For the sports-minded. Bicycling, kayaking, and hiking
occur throughout the year.<TD>2-7 days
<TR BORDERCOLOR=RED>
<TD> <TD COLSPAN=2 ALIGN=CENTER>Domestic or International
<TR BGCOLOR=AQUA ALIGN=CENTER>
<TD>Arts<TD>Dedicated to the performing arts. An assortment of museums,
music, and theater.<TD>3-21 days
<TR BORDERCOLOR=RED>
<TD> <TD COLSPAN=2 ALIGN=CENTER>International
<TR BGCOLOR=AQUA ALIGN=CENTER>
<TD>Leisure<TD>Relax and spend time in beautiful settings. Lavish
accommodations and gourmet meals.<TD>2-15 days
```

Color of individual
cell borders is
changed

FIGURE E-13: **Color of border modified**

Tour	Description	Duration
	Domestic	
Athlete	For the sports-minded. Bicycling, kayaking, and hiking occur throughout the year.	2-7 days
	Domestic or International	
Arts	Dedicated to the performing arts. An assortment of museums, music, and theater.	3-21 days
	International	
Leisure	Relax and spend time in beautiful settings. Lavish accommodations and gourmet meals.	2-15 days

HTML

Changing Table Dimensions

The height and width of a table (or individual cells) can be measured in pixels, or as a percentage of the browser window. Use the pixel measurement when you want to control the size of a table; use a percentage when you want the table to occupy space based on the browser window's dimension. This attribute gives added control of the table's dimensions. The amount of space surrounding each cell—giving the effect of a margin—can be changed using the CELLPADDING attribute. ✎ James adds attributes to control the dimensions of the table.

Steps 1 2 3 4

1. Click the text editor program button on the taskbar
Table dimension attributes are added within the <TABLE> tag.

QuickTip

If a line of code is too crowded, press [Enter] to drop text down to a new line.

2. Click to the right of 10 in the BORDER=10 tag, press [Spacebar], then type WIDTH=90% CELLPADDING=5
The WIDTH attribute specifies the percentage of the browser's window that will be taken up with the table. In this case, 90% of the window is slightly larger than the amount of space currently used by the table. The CELLPADDING attribute adds a cushion of space to each cell, increasing the height of each cell. Using a width of 90% of the window surrounds the table with an attractive "cushion" of white space.
Compare your document to Figure E-14.

3. Save Nomad tour types.htm as a text document

4. Click the browser program button on the taskbar, then view the saved version of Nomad tour types.htm by refreshing the screen
The Web page displays, as shown in Figure E-15.

FIGURE E-14: **WIDTH and CELLPADDING attributes added**

```
<P>
<H2>Types of Nomad Tours</H2>
<TABLE BORDERCOLOR=NAVY BORDER=10 WIDTH=90% CELLPADDING=5>
<CAPTION>Nomad Tours</CAPTION>
<TR BGCOLOR=YELLOW>
<TH>Tour<TH>Description<TH>Duration
<TR BORDERCOLOR=RED>
<TD> <TD COLSPAN=2 ALIGN=CENTER>Domestic
<TR BGCOLOR=AQUA ALIGN=CENTER>
<TD>Athlete<TD>For the sports-minded. Bicycling, kayaking, and hiking
occur throughout the year.<TD>2-7 days
```

Specifications added
to the TABLE tag

FIGURE E-15: **Table dimensions changed**

Tour	Description	Duration
	Domestic	
Athlete	For the sports-minded. Bicycling, kayaking, and hiking occur throughout the year.	2-7 days
	Domestic or International	
Arts	Dedicated to the performing arts. An assortment of museums, music, and theater.	3-21 days
	International	
Leisure	Relax and spend time in beautiful settings. Lavish accommodations and gourmet meals.	2-15 days

Cellpadding adds
spacing to the text

10% of the window
is unused

Controlling Page Layout

In most—but not all—cases, a table is created with a border, which gives the table more form and makes it easier for readers to organize its data. A borderless table can be used not only to display data, but as an organizational tool for nontabular data. ✐ James creates a borderless table that contains an image and a final thought.

Steps

1. **Click the text editor program button on the taskbar**
   A borderless table can be used with nontabular data or to successfully display an image next to text. When you eliminate the BORDER attribute in the <TABLE> tag, no border will be displayed.

2. **Press [Page Down] to view the end of the document, click to the left of the </BODY> tag, type <P>One final thought, press [Enter], type <TABLE>, then press [Enter]**
   Since this table is used to contain an image and text, no heading row is needed.

3. **Type <TR>, press [Enter], type <TD><IMG SRC="serene.jpg">, then press [Enter]**
   The first cell in the table contains the graphic image, serene.jpg.

4. **Type <TD>, type Everyone works hard in their life and at their chosen profession.
Be kind to yourself and recharge your batteries.
Take a break., then press [Enter]**
   Each line break advances the text to the next line in the cell.

5. **Type </TABLE>, then press [Enter]**
   The final tag concludes the table. Compare your document to Figure E-16.

6. **Save Nomad tour types.htm as a text document**

7. **Click your browser's program button on the taskbar, then refresh the screen; press [Page Down] to view the borderless table in the document**
   Compare your browser's document to Figure E-17. The image appears to the left of the text.

8. **Print the Nomad tour types Web page, then exit your browser**

9. **Print the Nomad tour types.htm text document, then exit the text editor**

FIGURE E-16: Table contains image and text

```
<H2>Contact Us Directly</H2>
Find out more about what we have to offer. Contact the tour office at <A
HREF="MAILTO:Tourdirector@nomadltd.com">Tourdirector@nomadltd.com</A>
<P>One final thought.
<TABLE>
<TR>
<TD><IMG SRC="serene.jpg">
<TD>Everyone works hard in their life and at their chosen profession.
<BR>Be kind to yourself and recharge your batteries.<BR>Take a break.
</TABLE>
</BODY>
```

Creates a borderless
table

Image contained
in a cell

FIGURE E-17: Borderless table containing image

Contact Us Directly

Find out more about what we have to offer. Contact the tour office at Tourdirector@nomadltd.com

One final thought.

 Everyone works hard in their life and at their chosen profession.
Be kind to yourself and recharge your batteries.
Take a break.

Line break advances
text to the next line

CLUES TO USE

Unconventional table data

A borderless table can display any type of data. Such a table format can be used to display data that should be separated from other cells, as shown in Figure E-18. This figure uses a borderless table to organize menu information and a graphic image.

FIGURE E-18: Image and text in a borderless table and a borderless table used as a menu

```
<BODY BGCOLOR=TAN>
<IMG SRC="file:///a|nomad.jpg" ALIGN="right">
<H1>Nomad Coffee Shop</H1>
<H2 ALIGN=CENTER>Bill of Fare</H2>
<TABLE ALIGN=CENTER WIDTH=50%>
<TR ALIGN=CENTER>
<TH> <TH>Flavor<TH>Available As . . .
<TR ALIGN=CENTER>
<TD ROWSPAN=6><IMG SRC="coffee.jpg">
<TD>House Blend<TD>Cup
<TR ALIGN=CENTER>
<TD> <TD>Latte
<TR ALIGN=CENTER>
<TD> <TD>Double-Whammy
<TR ALIGN=CENTER>
<TD>Kenya<TD>Latte
<TR ALIGN=CENTER>
<TD> <TD>Frozen Surprise
<TR ALIGN=CENTER>
<TD> <TD>Tall Skinny
</TABLE>
</BODY>
```

Nomad Coffee Shop   Nomad Ltd
             Bill of Fare

              Flavor   Available As . . .
           House Blend   Cup
                               Latte
                            Double-Whammy
              Kenya   Latte
                           Frozen Surprise
                             Tall Skinny

Practice

► Concepts Review

Label each of the HTML tags shown in Figure E-19.

FIGURE E-19

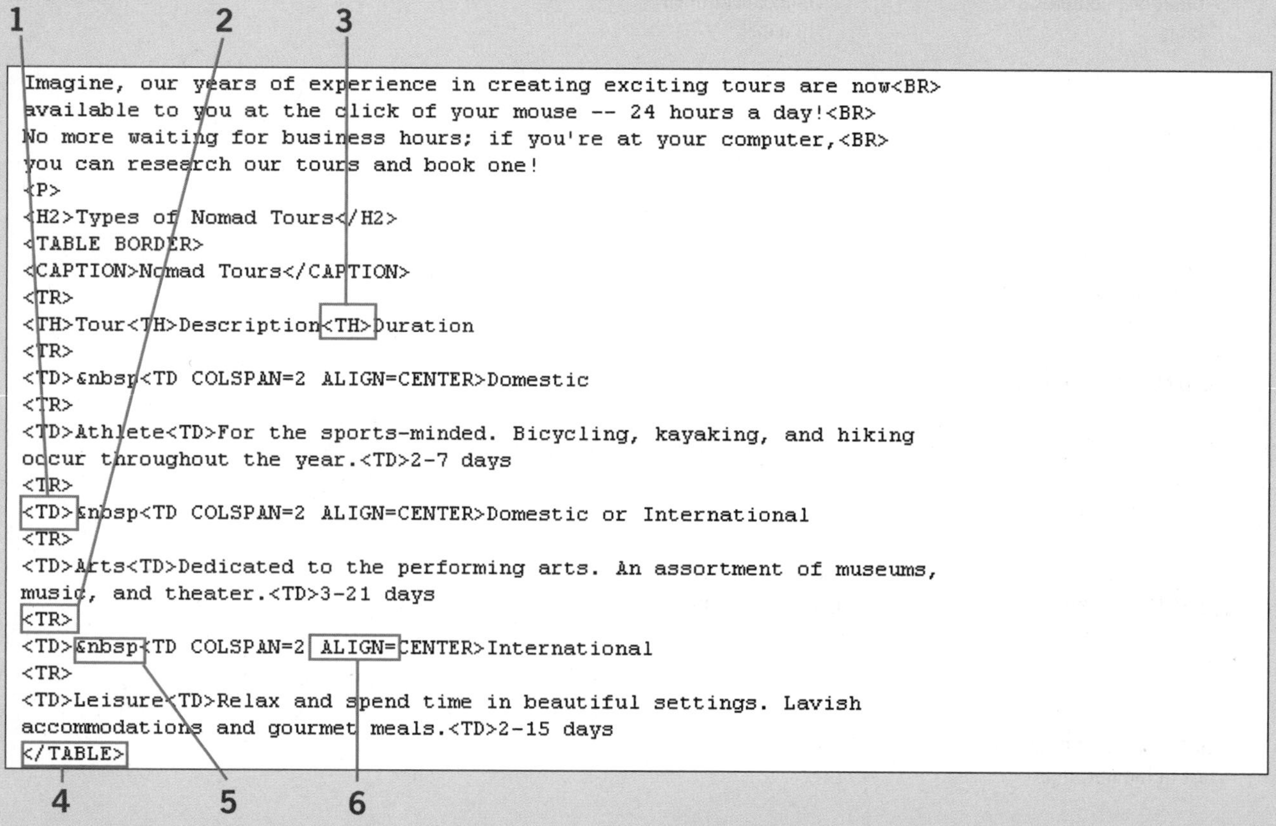

1   2   3

```
Imagine, our years of experience in creating exciting tours are now<BR>
available to you at the click of your mouse -- 24 hours a day!<BR>
No more waiting for business hours; if you're at your computer,<BR>
you can research our tours and book one!
<P>
<H2>Types of Nomad Tours</H2>
<TABLE BORDER>
<CAPTION>Nomad Tours</CAPTION>
<TR>
<TH>Tour<TH>Description<TH>Duration
<TR>
<TD> <TD COLSPAN=2 ALIGN=CENTER>Domestic
<TR>
<TD>Athlete<TD>For the sports-minded. Bicycling, kayaking, and hiking
occur throughout the year.<TD>2-7 days
<TR>
<TD> <TD COLSPAN=2 ALIGN=CENTER>Domestic or International
<TR>
<TD>Arts<TD>Dedicated to the performing arts. An assortment of museums,
music, and theater.<TD>3-21 days
<TR>
<TD> <TD COLSPAN=2 ALIGN=CENTER>International
<TR>
<TD>Leisure<TD>Relax and spend time in beautiful settings. Lavish
accommodations and gourmet meals.<TD>2-15 days
</TABLE>
```

4   5   6

Match each statement with the HTML tag it describes.

7. Spanned column	a. BORDER
8. Adds border to table	b. _____
9. Table header	c. <TH> </TH>
10. Text centered above a table	d. <TR> </TR>
11. New table row	e. COLSPAN
12. Invisible character	f. <CAPTION> </CAPTION>

Select the best answer from the list of choices.

13. The BORDERCOLOR attribute can be added to each tag, *except*
    a. <TD>
    b. <TABLE>
    c. <TR>
    d. </TABLE>

14. Which entity is used to create an empty table cell?
   a. !nbsp
   b.
   c. $nbsp
   d. *nbsp

15. Which attribute is used to create a column that spans across rows?
   a. COLSPAN
   b. SPANROW
   c. BRIDGEROW
   d. ROWSPAN

16. Each of the following is true about a table header, *except*
   a. It displays bold.
   b. It displays underlined.
   c. It displays centered.
   d. It is generally the first row in a table.

17. A table border is measured in
   a. pixels.
   b. centimeters.
   c. inches.
   d. units.

18. Each of the following is a table formatting attribute, *except*
   a. ALIGN.
   b. BGCOLOR.
   c. TH.
   d. BORDER.

19. Which tag is used to create a new cell?
   a. <TH>
   b. <TR>
   c. <TD>
   d. <TC>

20. Which attribute is used to add color to a cell background?
   a. BACKGROUNDCOLOR
   b. BGCOLOR
   c. COLOR
   d. BCOLOR

21. Which attribute is used to change the default border width?
   a. BORDER
   b. BORDERWIDTH
   c. BWIDTH
   d. BRWIDTH

▶ Skills Review

1. Create a simple table.

 a. Open your text editor.

 b. Open the file HTML E-2.htm, and save it as a text document with the name PVP Table.htm.

 c. Select the INSERT TABLE HERE text and create a bordered table using the data in Table E-4.

 d. Save your work.

 e. Open your browser, and display the PVP Table.htm file.

TABLE E-4: **Simple table**

film type	title	year
Comedy	Some Like It Hot	1959
Comedy	Arsenic and Old Lace	1944
Drama	Witness for the Prosecution	1957
Comedy	His Girl Friday	1940
Drama	Citizen Kane	1941
Comedy	Bringing Up Baby	1938

2. Span columns.

 a. Return to your text editor.

 b. Add a row directly beneath the table header row that spans all three columns and has centered text. The text in this row should read: "All in glorious black & white!"

 c. Save your work.

 d. Return to your browser, and view the changes to the document.

3. Format a border.

 a. Return to your text editor.

 b. Change the border width to 5.

 c. Save your work.

 d. Return to your browser, and view the changes to the document.

4. Align text.

 a. Click the text editor program button on the taskbar.

 b. Center the contents of the Film Type column.

 c. Align the table so it is centered on the screen.

 d. Save your work.

 e. Return to your browser, and view the changes to the document.

5. **Add color.**

    a. Return to your text editor.

    b. Change the background color of the spanned row to silver.

    c. Change the background color of the cells containing the Film Type to aqua.

    d. Change the background color of the table header row to purple.

    e. Save your work.

    f. Return to your browser, and view the changes to the document.

6. **Modify a border.**

    a. Return to your text editor.

    b. Change the color of the border to black.

    c. Return to your browser, and view the changes.

    d. Return to the text editor.

    e. Return the border color to its default.

    f. Save your work.

    g. Return to your browser, and view the changes.

7. **Change table dimensions.**

    a. Return to your text editor.

    b. Change the table so it occupies 50% of the browser window.

    c. Add the cellpadding attribute, with a value of 10.

    d. Save your work.

    e. Return to your browser, and view the changes.

    f. Print the document.

8. **Control page layout.**

    a. Return to your text editor.

    b. Click to the left of the </BODY> tag, and type an initial table tag for a borderless table.

    c. Center the table on the page.

    d. Create a row and cell that contain the following text: "We would love to hear any suggestions you might have. Please feel free to e-mail us at the above address. We will try to respond to your suggestions within 24 hours."

    e. Insert the serene.jpg image into the first column of the table.

    f. Add a tag that closes the borderless table.

    g. Save your work.

    h. Return to your browser, and view the changes.

    i. Print the document.

    j. Exit your browser and text editor.

► Independent Challenges

1. Your Hometown Humane Society, where you volunteer, has decided to try its hand at the Web. You've been asked to design a Web page that describes some of the pets available for adoption. While the initial pages are complete, you want to display some information on available pets in table form.

To complete this independent challenge:

a. Start your text editor, open the file HTML E-3.htm, and then save it as a text document with the filename Humane Society Table.htm.

b. Add a simple table that describes at least five available pets. (Make up this data yourself.)

c. Center-align the table.

d. Use a background color of aqua.

e. Use a border width of 10.

f. Add any other formatting features of your choice.

g. Save your work.

h. View the document in your browser.

i. Print the document in your browser.

j. Exit your text editor and browser.

2. A local elementary school has hired you to produce a newsletter as a morale-booster for its staff. You've begun working on the project and need to complete the project.

To complete this independent challenge:

a. Start your text editor, open the file HTML E-4.htm, and save it as a text document with the filename Trumble Catalog.htm.

b. Create a table containing course, title, credit hours, and instructor's name, containing at least eight rows of data. Create this data yourself, or use the information in Table E-5.

c. Format the alignment in a specific column.

d. Use a background color in at least one row in the table.

e. Add other formatting features of your choice.

f. Save your work.

g. Print the document in your text editor.

h. Open the document in your browser.

i. Print the document in your browser.

j. Exit your text editor and browser.

TABLE E-5: **Catalog data**

course	title	credits	instructor
COMP 101	Introduction to Computers	3	Stein
ENG 121	Wit of Shakespeare	4	Welch
COMP 142	Intermediate HTML	3	Gruff
COMP 143	HTML Lab	1	Eliott
HLTH 105	EMT-Basic	5	Hagerty
HLTH 107	EMT-Intermediate	3	Reding
HIST 240	Vietnam War	4	Grace
BIOL 125	Introduction to Chemistry	4	Wadsworth

3. Your local CD shop—Play It Loud—has decided to list some music selections on its Web page. They have asked you to design a page and create a simple table that displays the store's CD offerings.

To complete this independent challenge:

a. Start your text editor, open a new file, then save it as a text document with the filename Play It Loud.htm

b. Create a simple table that describes at least five types of music (make up this data yourself) the store carries.

c. Add the following formatting features: alignment, a table border, and background colors.

d. Save your work.

e. View the document in your browser.

f. Print the document in your browser.

g. Exit your text editor and browser.

4. Your local public television station—WOOF—wants to display its programming on a page within its Web site. They've asked you to design a page that can display its schedule from a tabular data source.

To complete this independent challenge:

a. Connect to the Internet, then go to http://www.pbs.org.

b. Find at least five shows you would like to include in your Web site.

c. Start your text editor, open a new file, then save it as WOOF.htm.

d. Create table data for the station's schedule for three days. Make up data for this file, including a field for the day, show title, length, and show type. Make sure the file contains at least 10 entries (including the five from your Internet search).

e. Add your choice of formatting.

f. Save your work.

g. View the document in your browser.

h. Print the document in your browser.

i. Exit your text editor and browser.

Visual Workshop

Open the file HTML E-5 and save it as a text document with the filename Carla's Collectibles.htm. Use your text editor to modify the document so it looks like Figure E-20 when viewed in your browser. Save and print the document in your text editor and browser. (*Hint*: Use a border width of 10 and red and lime as background colors.)

FIGURE E-20

Welcome to Carla's Collectibles!

Carla's specializes in obscure collectibles: stuff you just can't find anywhere else!

Carla's Collectibles: Just what you were looking for!

Collection	Item	Description
60's	Lava Lamp	Lamp with soothing, flowing, oozing goo in a variety of colors.
60's	Star Trek cards	Various characters, including Captain Kirk and Mr. Spock.
50's	Betty Boop	10" high Statue in excellent condition.
40's	Daniel Boone cap	Vintage fake-fur cap with tail.

Receive Our Catalog!

Find out more about what we have to offer. Contact us at Carla's Collectibles.
You can send us e-mail at Carla@carlascollectibles.com and we'll send you a
complete full-color catalog.

Using
Frames

Objectives

► **Understand frames**
► **Create the main frame**
► **Format a frame**
► **Modify a frame**
► **Control frames**
► **Target hyperlinks**
► **Understand frame navigation**
► **Create a navigation bar**

Information on a Web page is designed using HTML tags. Pages display in windows. This information can be organized—and expanded—through the use of frames. Frames divide the screen into independent sections. By using frames, readers can get a lot more information organized on the screen in a clear and understandable format. ✎ Sarah Klein is working on expanding the Nomad tour Web site. She wants to use frames to provide more information within the confines of a computer screen.

Understanding Frames

In the context of Web pages, **frames** are scroll-capable windows that are created independently and tiled together. With frames, you can present more information on a single screen. Like tables, frames are useful in organizing data. Unlike tables, however, frames organize your browser's display window. Sarah feels that framed Web pages are more visually appealing than tables and provide the reader with easier access to more information.

Details

Frames can be arranged horizontally and vertically within the display window
Arranging Web pages in multiple windows visually organizes the information, provides easier access, and makes the content simpler to understand. Sarah knows that the right number of horizontal and vertical frames helps organize a page: Good design dictates that too many frames can look cluttered. Figure F-1 contains a sample page with horizontal and vertical frames.

One document determines the organization and arrangement of its frames
A single HTML file, called a **FRAME document**, dictates the number and location of horizontal and vertical frames, as well as the placement of the documents within its windows. The FRAME document illustrated in Figure F-2 contains instructions that determine how frames contained in other documents are organized. A document within a frame can be updated without affecting other framed documents because each individual document contains its own text, graphics, links, and formatting. Sarah plans to have a FRAME document that organizes the other Nomad pages as frames on the Web site.

Scrolling within framed windows can be programmed to occur automatically
Not all frames have scrollbars. As in many other programs, scroll bars appear if the contents don't fit within the parameters of the window. In frames, scrolling occurs automatically as needed, but can be turned off or on—even if it's not needed.

Frame margins and borders can be formatted
Within framed windows, Sarah can determine the width and height of margins. She also can set the width of borders in each frame. Individual frame borders can be turned on and off or assigned a color.

The designer determines whether or not frames can be resized
In most cases, the user can resize Web-page frames by dragging the edge of the frame. Although this is a good feature, there are times when you don't want the frame arrangement changed. Sarah can prevent frames from being resized as she sees fit.

Use frames to control navigation
In addition to being attractive, frames can be used to navigate within a Web site or from one Web site to another. Sarah can place a hyperlink within a frame that, when clicked, is replaced with a new site.

FIGURE F-1: Multi-frame Web page

Frame

Frame (no border)

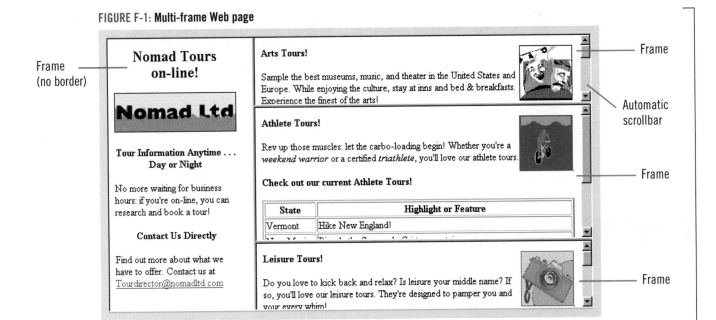

Automatic scrollbar

Frame

Frame

FIGURE F-2: Framed Web page structure

Doc1.htm

Doc2.htm

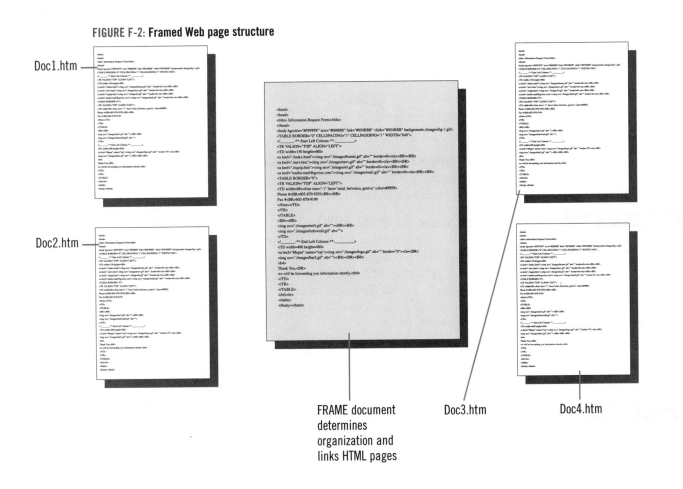

FRAME document determines organization and links HTML pages

Doc3.htm

Doc4.htm

HTML

Creating the Main Frame

A framed Web page is organized in a single document, the FRAME document. This page uses the <FRAMESET> </FRAMESET> container instead of the <BODY> </BODY> tags that define nonframed Web pages. Organizational instructions are defined within the FRAMESET containers. The number of vertical and horizontal frames and the amount of space each occupies is established in an initial <FRAMESET> tag, although a separate FRAMESET container is needed for columns and for rows. Table F-1 lists the attributes and tags used within a FRAME-SET. ✐ Sarah started a document that contains the frame instructions. She creates the FRAMESET for the Nomad Web site.

Steps 1234

1. **Open your text editor, open the file HTML F-1.htm, then save it as a text document with the filename Frame info.htm**
   The text document displays. The FRAMESET instructions determine where columns and rows occur as well as which documents display in the frames. Columns and rows can be defined in pixels, percentages, a proportional division of available space, or actual numbers of columns and rows. Columns define vertical frames, and rows define horizontal frames. If you don't define at least one row or column in a FRAMESET, your browser will completely ignore all the frames.

2. **Select the INSERT FRAMESET INFO HERE text, type <FRAMESET COLS="30,70">, then press [Enter]**
   This statement defines two columns: the first frame occupies 30% of the screen, and the second occupies 70%, or the remaining portion of the screen. (If your totals don't total 100%, percentages will be automatically scaled up or down.) The location, or source, of the frame's contents follows the initial <FRAMESET> tag.

3. **Press [Tab], type <FRAME SRC="nomad-main.htm">, then press [Enter]**
   This text establishes the source of the first column. The second column will include three rows—each containing a different HTML file.

4. **Press [Tab], type <FRAMESET ROWS="1,2,1">, then press [Enter]**
   The FRAMESET statement for the ROWS is **nested** within the initial FRAMESET statement. The space is proportionally divided so that the second horizontal frame takes up twice the space as the top or bottom frame. [1+2+1=4; frame 1 takes up ¼ of the screen, frame 2 takes up ¾ (or half), frame 3 takes up ¼.] Percentage values that work well in one browser may not translate well in another. Proportionally dividing available space, however, works well in most browsers.

5. **Press [Tab] twice, type <FRAME SRC="arts.htm">, press [Enter], press [Tab] twice, type <FRAME SRC="athlete.htm">, press [Enter], press [Tab] twice, type <FRAME SRC="leisure.htm">, then press [Enter]**

6. **Press [Tab], type </FRAMESET>, press [Enter], then type </FRAMESET>**
   The sources of each frame, as shown in Figure F-3, have been established. Each FRAMESET is followed by a concluding </FRAMESET> tag.

7. **Save the file Frame info.htm as a text document**

8. **Open your browser, cancel any dialup operations, then open the file Frame info.htm**
   Compare your document to Figure F-4. Note that, depending on the display settings of your monitor, the left column may have scroll bars.

Trouble?

Frame tags and attributes are not supported by all browsers.

Trouble?

Be sure that all the project files are copied into the same directory as the file Frame info.htm to allow correct viewing of all the frames.

FIGURE F-3: FRAMESET tags created

```
<HTML>

<HEAD>
<TITLE>Nomad Tours on-line</TITLE>
</HEAD>

<FRAMESET COLS="30,70">
      <FRAME SRC="nomad-main.htm">
      <FRAMESET ROWS="1,2,1">
            <FRAME SRC="arts.htm">
            <FRAME SRC="athlete.htm">
            <FRAME SRC="leisure.htm">
      </FRAMESET>
</FRAMESET>

<NOFRAMES>
Your browser cannot display frames.
</FRAMES>

</HTML>
```

Nested FRAMESET

FIGURE F-4: Document with four frames

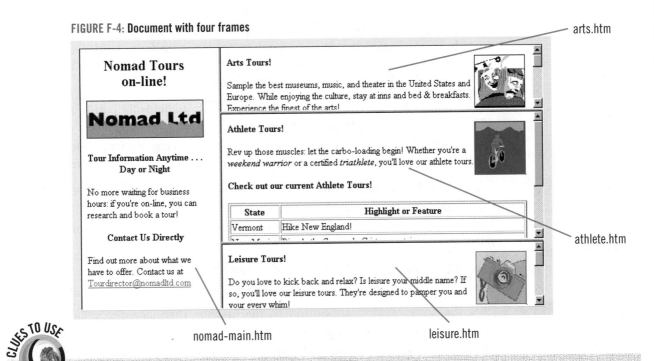

arts.htm

athlete.htm

nomad-main.htm

leisure.htm

CLUES TO USE

Alternative for frame-incapable browsers

Although most browsers allow viewing of frames, not all do. By adding the <NOFRAMES></NOFRAMES> container within your frame document, you can provide an alternative for nonframe browsers. Any codes found within these tags appear in browsers with no frame capabilities; frame-capable browsers ignore the NOFRAMES containers. You don't have to use the <BODY> tags within the NOFRAMES containers unless you want to include graphic images.

TABLE F-1: FRAMESET tags and attributes

tag/attribute	function
ROWS	Creates horizontal frames
COLS	Creates vertical frames
<FRAME>	Defines a single frame
SRC	Locates a frame's content
<NOFRAMES> </NOFRAMES>	Provided for browsers without frame capabilities

HTML

Formatting a Frame

HTML provides a variety of methods for formatting a frame. While the actual framed document contains tags for individual background colors, you can control frame and border colors as well as alter the frame border's width from within the FRAMESET. If no value is given, the default border width is 5. Table F-2 contains these attributes and their associated tags. ✎ Sarah would like to modify the border widths and add some color to a frame.

Steps

1. **Click the text editor program button on the taskbar**
   Whether the FRAMEBORDER attribute is added to the <FRAMESET> or <FRAME> tag depends on which property you want to affect. To change the frame border width to effect all the frames within the set, you add the FRAMEBORDER attribute to the <FRAMESET> tag; add it to the <FRAME> tag to affect specific frames.

2. **Click to the left of SRC in the <FRAME SRC="nomad-main.htm"> tag, type FRAMEBORDER="NO", then press the [Spacebar]**
   This tag turns off the frame border in the column frame. Change the frame border using the BORDER attribute; add color to borders using the BORDERCOLOR attribute.

QuickTip

To create a page with all borderless frames, define the initial <FRAMESET> tag with FRAMEBORDER="NO" and the BORDER=0.

3. **Click to the left of ROWS, type BORDER=15 BORDERCOLOR=BLUE, then press the [Spacebar]**
   This statement creates a 15-pixel width blue border for all the horizontal frames within the frameset.

4. **Save the file Frame info.htm as a text document**
   You can use your browser to view the changes to the borders.

Trouble?

Frame tags and attributes are not supported by all browsers.

5. **Click the browser program button on the taskbar, then view the saved version of Frame info.htm by refreshing your screen**
   The border between the frames looks attractive but obscures data because it is too wide.

6. **Click the text editor program button on the taskbar, double-click 15, then type 7**
   The resulting thinner border should divide the frames without overpowering them. Your text document should look like Figure F-5.

7. **Save the file Frame info.htm as a text document**
   You can use your browser to view the saved changes to the borders.

8. **Click the browser program button on the taskbar, then view the saved version of Frame info.htm by refreshing your screen**
   Compare your work to Figure F-6.

```
<HTML>

<HEAD>
<TITLE>Nomad Tours on-line</TITLE>
</HEAD>

<FRAMESET COLS="30,70">
     <FRAME FRAMEBORDER="NO" SRC="nomad-main.htm">
     <FRAMESET BORDER=7 BORDERCOLOR=BLUE ROWS="1,2,1">
          <FRAME SRC="arts.htm">
          <FRAME SRC="athlete.htm">
          <FRAME SRC="leisure.htm">
     </FRAMESET>
</FRAMESET>

<NOFRAMES>
Your browser cannot display frames.
</FRAMES>
```

Turns border attribute off in the frame

Changes border width and color in the FRAMESET

FIGURE F-6: Borders formatted

No border

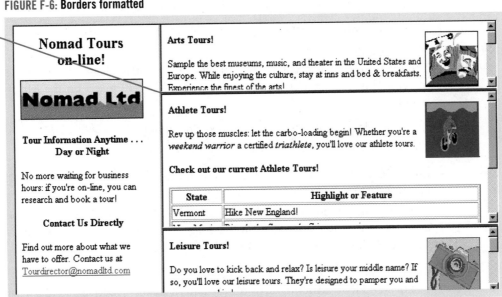

TABLE F-2: Frame border attributes and tags

attribute	associated tag	function
BORDER	<FRAMESET>	Sets the width of all borders
FRAMEBORDER	<FRAMESET> or <FRAME>	Has a value of "YES" (the default) or "NO"
BORDERCOLOR	<FRAMESET> or <FRAME>	Can be assigned a color name or hexadecimal value

HTML

Modifying a Frame

A frame's interior margins—height and width—can be controlled using the MARGINWIDTH and MARGINHEIGHT attributes. The interior margins, measured in pixels, create a "frame" of space surrounding the document. These attributes added to the <FRAME> tag. Scrollbars that display when a document's content exceeds its window space are automatic (the default) but can also be turned on or off. Sarah wants to alter the interior margins of the document in the column frame so the document appears centered within the column. She also wants to remove the scrollbar from this frame.

Steps

1. Click the text editor program button on the taskbar

Adding the appropriate attributes to the <FRAME> tag controls the interior margins.

2. Click to the left of FRAMEBORDER, type MARGINWIDTH="20" MARGINHEIGHT="20", then press the [Spacebar]

The total number of pixels in the attribute statement is divided between the areas in the margin. This statement creates an interior margin of 10 pixels on the left, right, top, and bottom.

3. Save the file Frame info.htm as a text document

The saved changes can be viewed using your browser.

4. Click the browser program button on the taskbar, then view the saved version of Frame info.htm by refreshing your screen

Increasing the interior margins had a negligible effect on the document's appearance but it automatically created a scrollbar in this frame, as Figure F-7 shows. This scrollbar adds no value to the frame and should be turned off.

5. Click the text editor program button on the taskbar

The SCROLLING attribute turns off the automatically occurring scrollbar when added to the <FRAME> tag.

6. Click to the left of FRAMEBORDER, type SCROLLING="NO", then press [Spacebar]

This attribute suppresses the scrollbar. Compare your document to Figure F-8.

7. Save the file Frame info.htm as a text document

8. Click the browser program button on the taskbar, then view the saved version of Frame info.htm by refreshing your screen

Compare your work to Figure F-9.

FIGURE F-7: Interior margins adjusted, with scrollbar

Each interior margin contains 10 pixels

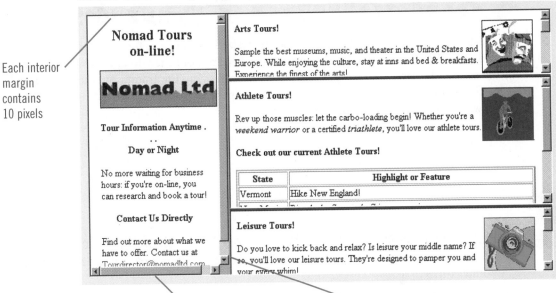

Bottom interior margin not visible   Scrollbar automatically displays

FIGURE F-8: Interior margins adjusted, scrollbar suppressed

Defines interior margins

Turns off automatic scrollbar

```
<HTML>

<HEAD>
<TITLE>Nomad Tours on-line</TITLE>
</HEAD>

<FRAMESET COLS="30,70">
     <FRAME MARGINWIDTH="20" MARGINHEIGHT="20"
SCROLLING="NO" FRAMEBORDER="NO" SRC="nomad-main.htm">
     <FRAMESET BORDER=7 BORDERCOLOR=BLUE ROWS="1,2,1">
          <FRAME SRC="arts.htm">
          <FRAME SRC="athlete.htm">
          <FRAME SRC="leisure.htm">
     </FRAMESET>
</FRAMESET>

<NOFRAMES>
Your browser cannot display frames.
</FRAMES>

</HTML>
```

FIGURE F-9: Browser shows interior margins adjusted and scrollbar suppressed

No scrollbar

Interior margins "frame" the document

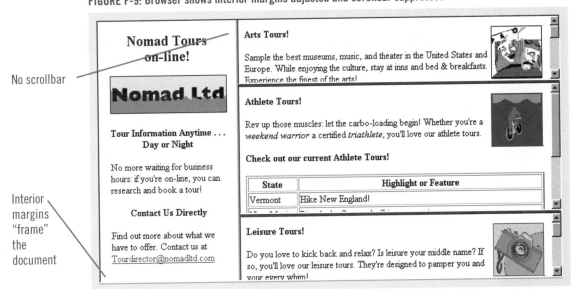

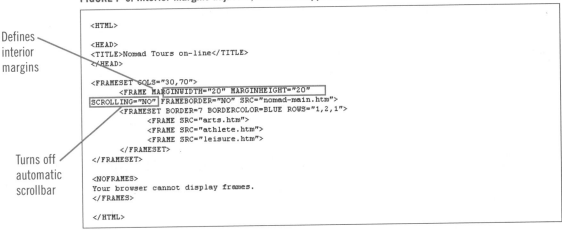

HTML

Controlling Frames

HTML

In most cases, frames within Web pages can be resized by dragging the corner of the frame in the window. These changes are only temporary, of course, but they do affect how information in the frames displays. You can prevent a user from resizing the frames in your Web page by using the NORESIZE attribute. Since she spent so much time designing these frames, Sarah wants to prevent users from resizing them.

Steps

Trouble?

Different browsers may display different pointers.

1. Place the pointer on the vertical frame border to the left of Athlete Tours!
The pointer turns to ←→. When the pointer is on the border of a horizontal frame, the pointer turns to ↕.

2. Press and hold the mouse button when the pointer looks like ←→
The vertical frame border changes to indicate that it is selected.

3. Drag the ←→ pointer so the frame edge is between the words "Arts" and "Tours!," as shown in Figure F-10, then release the mouse button
The frame has been resized.

Trouble?

If refreshing or reloading doesn't restore the frame border, click Start on the taskbar, point to Documents, then click Frame info.htm.

4. Refresh the image in your browser
The appearance of the image is restored.

5. Click the text editor program button on the taskbar
The NORESIZE attribute prevents users from changing a frame's dimensions when added directly to the <FRAME> tag.

6. Click to the left of SRC in the SRC="nomad-main.htm" tag, type NORESIZE, then press [Spacebar]
See Figure F-11.

7. Save the file Frame info.htm as a text document

8. Click the browser program button on the taskbar, then view the saved version of Frame info.htm by refreshing your screen

9. Position the mouse pointer over the column border and notice that the pointer *does not* change to ←→

FIGURE F-10: Resizing a frame

Temporary location of frame border

Mouse pointer changes when over frame border

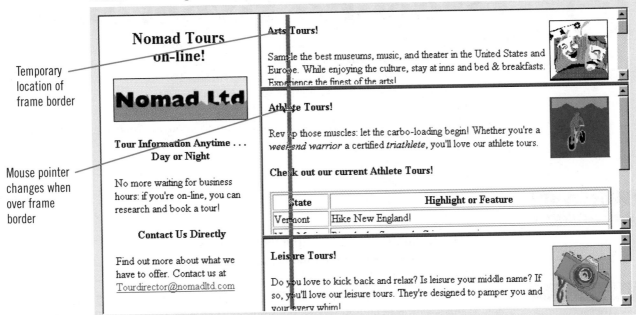

FIGURE F-11: **NORESIZE attribute prevents frame resizing**

Prevents resizing

```
<HTML>

<HEAD>
<TITLE>Nomad Tours on-line</TITLE>
</HEAD>

<FRAMESET COLS="30,70">
      <FRAME MARGINWIDTH="20" MARGINHEIGHT="20"
SCROLLING="NO" FRAMEBORDER="NO" NORESIZE SRC="nomad-main.htm">
      <FRAMESET BORDER=7 BORDERCOLOR=BLUE ROWS="1,2,1">
            <FRAME SRC="arts.htm">
            <FRAME SRC="athlete.htm">
            <FRAME SRC="leisure.htm">
      </FRAMESET>
</FRAMESET>

<NOFRAMES>
Your browser cannot display frames.
</FRAMES>
```

Targeting Hyperlinks

At first glance, frames seem limited to creating interesting-looking Web pages. However, they have far-greater uses. Their real strength is as a navigational tool. Frames can be named and targeted so that when a link is clicked, the user jumps to a different site. This function uses the NAME and TARGET attributes. The TARGET attribute also can be used with the AREA, FORM, and BASE tags. Table F-3 describes these two attributes and their locations. Sarah would like readers to be able to click a link and have one frame jump to another. She begins by naming the Athlete document; she already created the target for that existing frame.

Steps

1. Click the **text editor program button** on the taskbar

The Frame info.htm document displays. The NAME attribute is used to assign a name that will be referenced in a hyperlink.

Trouble?

Type the NAME attribute outside the FRAME tag to open the target file in a separate window.

2. Click to the right of **athlete** in the <FRAME SRC="athlete.htm"> tag, type **2**, click to the left of the **>** in the same line, press **[Spacebar]**, then type **NAME="ATHLETETARGET"**

You had to rename the reference to the athlete.htm document to athlete2.htm. The ATHLETETARGET name is referenced in the Frame info.htm and athlete2.htm documents. Once the frame is named, the hyperlink is created in the document initially displayed in the frame. You must name a frame if the frame's contents will be changing by clicking a link.

3. Save the **Frame info.htm** file as a text document, then open the file **HTML F-2.htm** and save it as a text document with the filename **athlete2.htm**

The table information in this document will be replaced with a hyperlink, which is needed to "call" the newly created target to the frame.

Trouble?

Make sure to check your code carefully.

4. Click to the left of the <TABLE BORDER= 2> tag, press and hold the mouse button, drag to select **all the table data up to and including the </TABLE> tag**, type **<A HREF="moreath.htm" TARGET="ATHLETETARGET">Click here to see our athlete tours.</A>**, then press **[Enter]**

Compare your document to Figure F-12. When the link is clicked in the Web page, the frame will jump to the moreath.htm document.

5. Save the file **athlete2.htm** as a text document

Use your browser to view the saved changes.

6. Click the **browser program button** on the taskbar, then view the saved version of Frame info.htm by refreshing your screen

Compare your page to Figure F-13. Notice that the new link appears in the second horizontal frame.

7. Click the **Click here to see our athlete tours.** link

Clicking the link causes the frame to change to the moreath.htm document, as shown in Figure F-14.

8. Print the browser document, then close the browser

9. Click the **text editor program button** on the taskbar, then print the text document

TABLE F-3: Navigation attributes

attribute	description	location
NAME	Assigns a name to a frame; used to link to the frame	Within the <FRAME> tag; in the FRAME document
TARGET	References the name of the frame	Within the framed document, in the <A HREF> tag

FIGURE F-12: Name and target in frame

```
<HTML>

<HEAD>
<TITLE>Nomad Athlete Tours</TITLE>
</HEAD>

<BODY>
<IMG SRC="athlete.jpg" HEIGHT=90 WIDTH=90 ALIGN="right">
<H4>Athlete Tours!</H4>
Rev up those muscles: let the carbo-loading begin! Whether you're a
<I>weekend warrior</I> or
a certified <I>triathlete</I>, you'll love our athlete tours.<P>

<H4>Check out our current Athlete Tours!</H4>
<A HREF="moreath.htm" TARGET="ATHLETETARGET">Click here to see our
athlete tours.</A>

</BODY>

</HTML>
```

Calls the moreath.htm document

FIGURE F-13: Targeted link displayed in frame

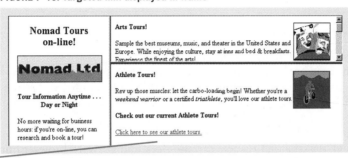

Click link to jump to new frame

FIGURE F-14: Result of clicking target link

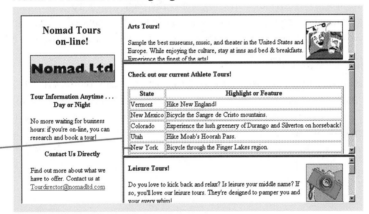

New document replaces contents of previous frame

Naming frames

You can use almost any name when naming frames, with a few exceptions. These reserved names begin with the underscore character instead of names composed of alphanumeric characters (such as TARGETATHLETE). The underscore (_) is reserved for implicit names built into HTML. There are four reserved implicit frame names, which control how the target is called. These reserved frame names are described in Table F-4. The name "_blank" in the tag <A HREF="moreath.htm" TARGET="_blank"> results in the moreath.htm document displaying in its own browser window.

TABLE F-4: Reserved implicit frame names

name	purpose
_blank	Clicking the link opens a new browser window with the contents of the new document
_self	Clears the current frame and replaces it with the new document
_parent	Loads the called document into the initial (parent) frameset; if none exists, this is the same as _self
_top	Loads the called document into the top-level frameset related to the calling frame; if none exists, this is the same as _self

Understanding Frame Navigation

You may have a fabulous series of Web pages, but if readers find them difficult to navigate, your Web site won't get used. If you've ever maneuvered through a unidirectional site—that is, one in which going deeper into the levels is easy, but returning to previous levels is almost impossible—you understand that easy access to all your pages is a vital aspect of Web design. Sarah reviews the importance of Web-page navigation.

Details

Indicate position

Like the "you are here" signs in department stores or office buildings, some indication of where a Web-page reader is in your site is important and comforting. Letting readers know where they are within a Web site provides a sense of context and adds to the site's organizational structure.

Navigation methods

Although it's true that readers can use Back and Forward browser buttons, these buttons work only relative to the most recently viewed pages. Readers who move from your pages in nonlinear ways will have difficulty finding a specific page again. Page buttons or links to specific pages within your site provide readers with the easiest means of navigating your site. Figure F-15 shows a Web site with navigation tools across the top and on the left edge of the page.

Provide a "way out"

Because many Web sites are composed of layered pages, readers must know how to return to the home page or get back to some other specific page. It's unrealistic to assume readers will "bookmark" a specific location; not offering navigation options may add to readers' frustration. Pages that are difficult to navigate can spell fewer reader "hits." Figure F-16 shows navigation tools at the bottom of the page.

FIGURE F-15: Navigation in a Web site

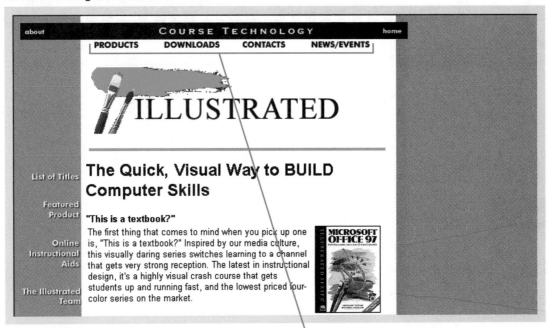

Click to jump to a site

FIGURE F-16: Site navigation tools

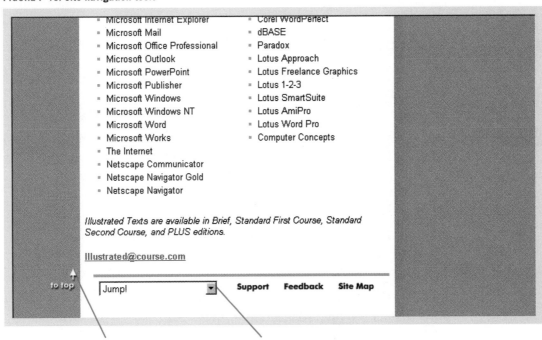

Moves to top of page   Re-directs to different page within the site

Creating a Navigation Bar

Easy Web site navigation is a courtesy to your readers. With a simple series of hyperlinks, you can create a navigation bar within a frame that lets a reader jump to other sites. Often, navigation bars offer a variety of links to complex Web sites. Navigation bars at the bottom of sites, allowing a reader to return to a page top, to a home page, or to other pages within a site. Sarah creates a navigation bar at the bottom of an existing framed page. She begins by adding a new nested frame to the FRAME document.

Steps

1. Verify that Frame info.htm is displayed in your text editor
   A fourth horizontal frame is needed at the bottom of the page.

2. Click to the right of the second 1 in the ROWS= "1,2,1" tag, type ,1
   This addition creates a fourth horizontal frame at the bottom of the page. A new nested <FRAME> tag is needed to reference the document containing the navigation links.

3. Click to the right of > in the <FRAME SRC="leisure.htm"> tag, press [Enter], press [Tab] twice, then type <FRAME SRC="navigate.htm">
   The document containing the navigation links as referenced in the Frame info.htm file is called navigate.htm.

4. Save the file Frame info.htm as a text document

5. Open the file HTML F-3.htm, then save it as a text document with the filename navigate.htm
   The navigation bar consists of simple hyperlinks that reference Nomad sites.

Trouble?

Be sure to type "nbsp" and then the pipe symbol (I).

6. Select the INSERT NAVIGATION LINKS HERE text, type <A HREF=Nomad Home.htm TARGET= "_blank">Nomad Home Page</A> l , then press [Enter]
   This first link takes the reader to the (yet unwritten) Nomad home page. A space and the pipe (|) character separate each link in this navigation bar. The remaining links are typed in the document.

7. Type <A HREF=Nomad Tour Types.htm TARGET="_blank">Tour Types</A> l , press [Enter], <A HREF=Arts.htm TARGET="_blank">Art tours</A> l , press [Enter], <A HREF=Athlete.htm TARGET="_blank">Athlete tours</A> l , press [Enter], <A HREF=Leisure.htm TARGET="_blank">Leisure tours</A> l , then press [Enter]
   Each of the links has been entered in the navigation bar, as shown in Figure F-17.

8. Save the file navigate.htm as a text document, click the browser program button on the taskbar, then view the saved version of Frame info.htm by refreshing your screen
   The navigation bar displays in the fourth frame of the browser page, as shown in Figure F-18.

9. Print the browser page, close and exit the browser, then close and exit the text editor

FIGURE F-17: Code containing the navigation bar

Pipe used to create a vertical line

Nonbreaking space used to create space

Filenames in tags are not case-sensitive

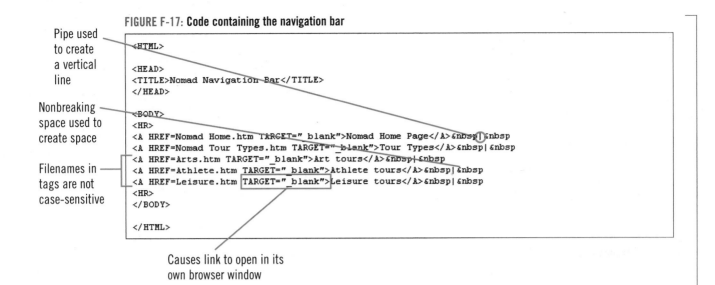

```
<HTML>

<HEAD>
<TITLE>Nomad Navigation Bar</TITLE>
</HEAD>

<BODY>
<HR>
<A HREF=Nomad Home.htm TARGET="_blank">Nomad Home Page</A> | 
<A HREF=Nomad Tour Types.htm TARGET="_blank">Tour Types</A> | 
<A HREF=Arts.htm TARGET="_blank">Art tours</A> | 
<A HREF=Athlete.htm TARGET="_blank">Athlete tours</A> | 
<A HREF=Leisure.htm TARGET="_blank">Leisure tours</A> | 
<HR>
</BODY>

</HTML>
```

Causes link to open in its own browser window

FIGURE F-18: Navigation bar displayed in a frame

Click hyperlink to jump to a page

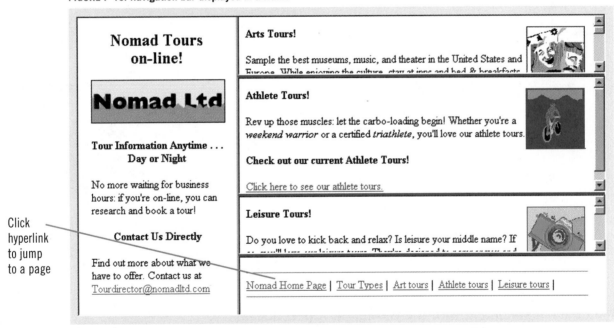

Practice

► Concepts Review

Describe the function of each HTML tag shown in Figure F-19.

FIGURE F-19

```
1    <HTML>

2    <HEAD>
     <TITLE>Nomad Tours on-line</TITLE>
     </HEAD>

3    <FRAMESET COLS="30,70">
         <FRAME MARGINWIDTH="20" MARGINHEIGHT="20"
     SCROLLING="NO" FRAMEBORDER="NO" NORESIZE SRC="nomad-main.htm">
         <FRAMESET BORDER=7 BORDERCOLOR=BLUE ROWS="1,2,1">
4            <FRAME SRC="arts.htm">
             <FRAME SRC="athlete.htm">
             <FRAME SRC="leisure.htm">
5        </FRAMESET>
     </FRAMESET>

6    <NOFRAMES>
     Your browser cannot display frames.
     </FRAMES>

     </HTML>
```

Match each statement with the HTML tag it describes.

7. NOFRAMES
8. SCROLLING
9. <FRAMESET> tags
10. BORDER
11. SRC
12. FRAMEBORDER

a. Holds organizational instructions for a framed Web page.
b. Turns border on or off.
c. Provides content for frame-incapable browsers.
d. Can only be added to the FRAMESET tag.
e. Affects display of scroll bars.
f. Locates a FRAME's content.

Select the best answer from the list of choices.

13. **Which attribute is used to prevent users from changing frame dimensions?**
    a. NORESIZE
    b. NOFRAMES
    c. NOSCROLLING
    d. NOCHANGE

14. **When the pointer changes to ←→ when placed over a column border you can**
    a. Delete the border.
    b. Change the color of the border.
    c. Change the width of the frame.
    d. Change the height of the frame.

15. **Which attribute is used in a hyperlink when referencing a named document?**
    a. JUMPTO
    b. NAME
    c. LINK
    d. TARGET

16. **Reserved implicit frame names begin with what character?**
    a. *
    b. #
    c. _
    d. %

17. **You can extend and expand the capabilities of a Web page by using**
    a. Attributes.
    b. Scripts.
    c. Browsers.
    d. Objects.

18. **Each of the following is a component of a script, *except***
    a. Handling.
    b. Object.
    c. Container.
    d. Event.

19. **FRAMESETS within a FRAMESET are considered to be**
    a. nestled.
    b. confined.
    c. nested.
    d. contained.

20. Which implicit frame name opens a link in its own window?
   a. _empty
   b. _blank
   c. _single
   d. _window

21. Which tag defines an individual frame?
   a. <FRAMESET>
   b. <SRC>
   c. <FRAME>
   d. <FRAMER>

► Skills Review

1. Create the main frame.
   a. Open your text editor.
   b. Open the file HTML F-4.htm, and save it as PVP-frame.htm.
   c. Select the INSERT FRAMESET INFO HERE text and create tags using the parameters in Table F-5.
   d. Save your work.
   e. Open your browser, and display the PVP-frame.htm file.
   f. Print the browser document.

TABLE F-5: Frame parameters

frame	type	percentages	contents	location
1	Horizontal	25, 15, 60	PVP-main.htm	Top frame
			PVP-order.htm	Middle frame
			(contains vertical frames)	Bottom frame
2	Vertical	25, 75	PVP-studios.htm	Left frame
			PVP-table.htm	Right frame

2. Format a frame.
   a. Return to your text editor.
   b. Change the color of the vertical frame border to Navy.
   c. The width of the vertical border should be 10.
   d. Save your work.
   e. Start the browser, and open the file to view the PVP-frame.htm file.
   f. Print the browser document.

3. Modify a frame.

a. Return to your text editor.

b. Change the margin width of the top horizontal frame to 20.

c. Use the SCROLLING attribute to add a scroll bar to the frame containing the PVP-order.htm file.

d. Save your work.

e. Return to your browser and view the changes by refreshing the image.

f. Print the browser document.

4. Control frames.

a. Resize the vertical frame containing the PVP-table file so the border appears between the words "Vintage" and "Prestige" in the frame containing the PVP-main file.

b. Return to the text editor.

c. Add the NORESIZE attribute to the frame containing the PVP-table document.

d. Save your work.

e. Return to your browser and view the changes to the document.

f. Print the browser document.

5. Target hyperlinks.

a. Return to your text editor.

b. Assign the name "MGM" to the MGM.htm file.

c. Modify the name "PVP-studios.htm" to "PVP-studios2.htm".

d. Save your work.

e. Open the file PVP-studios.htm in the text editor and save it as a text document with the name PVP-studios2.htm.

f. In PVP-studios2.htm, modify the hyperlink containing the MGM.htm file so it references the target "MGM".

g. Save your work.

h. Return to your browser and refresh the image.

i. Click the link for Metro Goldwyn Mayer.

j. Print the browser document.

6. Create a navigation bar.

a. Return to your text editor and open the PVP-frame.htm file.

b. Replace the reference to the PVP-order.htm file with the file PVP-nbar.htm.

c. Save your work.

d. Open the file HTML F-5 and save it as the text document PVP-nbar.htm.

e. Select the INSERT NAVIGATION LINKS HERE text and replace it with information in Table F-6.

f. After each link, insert a pipe surrounded by a non-breaking space.

g. Each link should open in its own window.

h. Save your work as a text document.

i. Open the browser and refresh the image.

j. Print the browser document.

k. Click the link to Metro Goldwyn Mayer.

l. Exit the text editor and browser.

TABLE F-6: PVP navigation information

link to	display text
PVP-main.htm	PVP Home page
PVP-studios.htm	Studio info
Warner.htm	Warner Brothers
Columbia.htm	Columbia Pictures
MGM.htm	Metro Goldwyn Mayer

HTML

► Independent Challenges

1. Your Web-page design for the Hometown Humane Society (HHS) has been so popular that HHS has asked you to revise it. HHS would like you to create a page containing several frames. Like the initial pages you designed, these also will have information about some of the pets HHS has available for adoption.

To complete this independent challenge:

a. Start your text editor, open the file HTML F-6.htm, then save it as a text document with the filename HHS-frame.htm.

b. Create frames in any order you choose using the following files: HHS-main.htm, HHS-pets.htm, and HHS-call.htm.

c. Add a colorful frame border to your frames.

d. Save your work.

e. View the document in your browser.

f. Print the document in your browser.

g. Exit your text editor and browser.

2. Independence Community College has hired you to produce a framed Web page to illustrate the types of courses they offer.

To complete this independent challenge:

a. Start your text editor, open the file HTML F-7.htm, then save it as a text document with the filename ICC-frame.htm.

b. Create frames in any order you choose using the following files: ICC-main.htm, ICC-course.htm, and ICC-call.htm.

c. Create your own course listing and add it (in table format) in the ICC-course.htm document.

d. Turn off scrolling in a frame.

e. Make it impossible for a viewer to resize a frame.

f. Save your work.

g. View the document in your browser.

h. Print the document in your browser.

i. Exit your text editor and browser.

3. You've been asked to create a state-of-the-art framed Web page for the local CD shop, Play It Loud. Use your knowledge of music and HTML page design to create a framed page that includes a targeted hyperlink.
  To complete this independent challenge:

a. Start your text editor, create a frame document, and save it as PIL-frame.htm.

b. Create documents that will occupy at least three frames. One document should give address information on the store; another should talk about the types of music sold; and the third can be on a featured artist.

c. Arrange the frames any way you choose.

d. Add formatting to frames as you see fit.

e. Save your work.

f. View the document in your browser.

g. Print the document in your browser.

h. Exit your text editor and browser.

4. Your local independent television station (WOOF) wants its Web site to include a framed page. The station has asked you to design a framed page that can display a partial schedule and give listeners some additional information about the station.
  To complete this independent challenge:

a. Connect to the Internet and use your favorite search engine to find a home page for a local television station in your area.

b. Print the browser page.

c. Start your text editor, create a frame document, and save it as WOOF-frame.htm.

d. Create documents that will occupy at least three frames. Use the printed Web page as a model for the documents you create.

e. Arrange the frames any way you choose.

f. Add a navigation bar to a frame.

g. Add color borders, scroll bars, and limit frame resizing as you see fit.

h. Save your work.

i. View the document in your browser.

j. Print the document in your browser.

k. Exit your text editor and browser.

▶ Visual Workshop

Open the file HTML F-8.htm, and save it as Carla's frame.htm. Use your text editor to modify the document so it looks like Figure F-20. Save and print the document in your text editor and browser. (*Hint*: The completed frame uses the following documents: Carla-main.htm, Specialize.htm, and Catreq.htm.)

FIGURE F-20

Welcome to Carla's Collectibles!

Carla's specializes in obscure collectibles: stuff you just can't find anywhere else!

Carla's Collectibles: Just what you were looking for!

Collection	Item	Description
60's	Lava Lamp	Lamp with soothing, flowing, oozing goo in a variety of colors.
60's	Star Trek cards	Various characters, including Captain Kirk and Mr. Spock.
50's	Betty Boop	10" high Statue in excellent condition.
40's	Daniel Boone cap	Vintage fake-fur cap with tail.

Receive Our Catalog!

Find out more about what we have to offer. Contact us at Carla's Collectibles. You can send us e-mail at Carla@carlascollectibles.com and we'll send you a complete full-color catalog.

Designing
Web pages

When you set out to paint a room, you need to know more than how to dip a brush into a gallon of white semi-gloss; likewise, when you set out to design Web pages, knowing how to write a technically advanced script will not guarantee a well-designed, usable Web site. You can use many techniques to "wow" Web readers, but sometimes, the most valuable tool is restraint. Sarah Klein is the corporate Webmaster responsible for the overall content and appearance of all of Nomad's pages. She examines the outward appearance and code submitted by her designers and approves them for Web publication.

Designing Effective Web Pages

A Web page—or series of pages—is not unlike a highway billboard: there is a limited amount of space and time to get the reader's attention and send a message. How you do this depends on your knowledge of design tactics and how to best "deliver the goods." Some Web pages may yell and scream, using arguably awful colors and, perhaps, distasteful language. These pages may be sensational, but do they have any substance? Sarah uses several principles for general Web page evaluation.

Details

Use headings judiciously

Make sure that every line of text is not a heading. Careful—and limited—use of headings advises your readers about the start of an important passage. If every line of text is huge, readers will not be able to distinguish what is important.

Strive for a "clean" look

White space (i.e., space on your page that has no text or graphics), while seemingly empty, provides much-needed visual relief. Make good use of these areas, and use them to manipulate your reader into focusing on what you want seen. The page in Figure G-1 has white space that "frames" the primary text.

Control your page as much as possible

You don't know which browser or what computer system a reader will use to access the Web. If you build inflexibility into your page, you can control how a page will look. Unless flexibility is part of the usability of your Web page, or an activity at the site, place graphics and text in fixed positions and don't allow for resizing of frames.

Be thoughtful

Remember that some users may not have graphics- or Java-capable browsers. They also may not have modems that are as fast as the one you use in development. Use small-size graphics files and provide a "text-only" or frames-incapable option. Use high-contrast colors between background and text, or background and images. You don't want your text to get lost in the background, and you don't want readers straining to read text or see images. Each image—especially those with captions—should fit within a window. (This means that you should test Web pages using the minimum resolution possible: 640 × 480.)

Proofread and test before publishing

Make sure your links work and your script is debugged. Your Web site—especially a business-oriented one—should inspire confidence. A poorly scripted site tells your readers you (or your designers) are sloppy and thoughtless. Keep in mind that the Web site represents you and your business.

Be purposeful

Rather than showing off Web tricks, give your reader useful information in an attractive, practical way. Using special effects for no good reason is arrogant and annoying. Provide a navigation bar so readers can easily jump between sites. Links to relevant sites are also helpful.

Follow-up

Provide hyperlinks within a site as a courtesy to your readers. With that courtesy comes the responsibility for making sure that either the links are stable or, at least, updated.

Citizenship

Even though the Web has no government regulation, it is up to each Web author and publisher to act responsibly. Although good taste is highly subjective, you should strive to avoid profanity and potentially offensive topics and wording.

Nomad Ltd Home Page!

Nomad Ltd

Learn About Our Company's Philosophy

Nomad Ltd has been in business for over ten years. During that time, we have offered tours to exotic (and simple) lands and sold sporting equipment (for bicycling, hiking, and other activities). In all that time, we have always been aware that our employees are our corporate ambassadors, and our customers are our royalty. We know that any company can make a buck here and there, but we want to do more than make a profit. We want you to enjoy shopping at our stores and make Nomad a fun and interesting place to shop.

We know that as a business, we are community members. Nomad wants to contribute to community efforts and make each town a better place in which to live. We hire from the community, offer educational and financial benefits to our employees, and become involved in community efforts.

Nomad Home Page | Tour Types | Art Tours | Athlete Tours | Employment Opportunities | Store Locations | Talk To Us

White space "frames" the text

Navigation bar to clearly identified sites

Simple heading using a different font and color

HTML file interpretation

If you decide to use an HTML editor, rather than a text editor, to create your Web page, you may find that the HTML code itself looks different when both editors are compared. (The browser page looks identical, regardless of the editor.) The same document is shown in Figure G-2, yet one is viewed by a text editor, whereas the other is viewed by an HTML editor. Notice that the STYLE containers in the text editor look different.

FIGURE G-2: Document in text editor

Named text handled differently

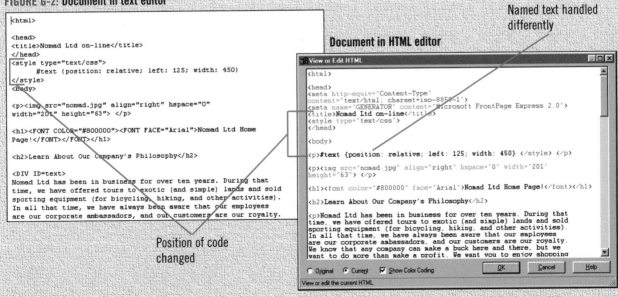

Position of code changed

Document in HTML editor

HTML

Formatting Text

Text can be **formatted** by changing its size, color, and font. Formatting is divided into two primary classes: logical and physical. **Logical formatting** indicates how an author wants text to look in comparison to other text on the page. This formatting leaves the appearance of the page up to the browser. **Physical formatting** indicates exactly how the author wants the text to look and gives the author more control over its appearance. Table G-1 shows commonly used logical and physical tags.  Sarah is editing a Web page submitted by one of her designers and adds physical formatting to the text where she feels it is necessary.

1. Open your text editor, open the file **HTML G-1.htm**, then save it as a text document with the filename **Nomad mission statement.htm**
   Seeing how the file looks in the browser helps you visualize where text formatting is needed.

2. Open your browser, then open the file **Nomad mission statement.htm**
   After looking at the document, you decide the font of the level 1 heading: Nomad Ltd Home Page!, would look better as Arial and in the color Maroon. Using the **hexadecimal value** for the color gives you more control over its appearance because these values translate more exactly between various browsers and computer platforms.

   > **QuickTip**
   >
   > When changing font faces, choose fonts most people own. If a font is not resident on a user's computer, the request will be ignored.

3. Click the text editor program button on the taskbar, click to the left of Nomad in the `<h1>` line, type `<FONT COLOR="800000"><FONT FACE="Arial">`
   The closing tag for the font color and font face is identical: `</FONT>`.

4. Click to the right of ! in the same line, then type `</FONT></FONT>`
   The first `</FONT>` tag completes the font change; the second `</FONT>` tag completes the font color change. Additional text to be modified is held within the DIV container. The DIV tag is used with style sheets when an entire text block style is defined. Adding bold to the full corporate name within the body text gives a more forceful appearance to the page.

   > **Trouble?**
   >
   > Not adding the second `</FONT>` tag results in the entire document displaying in the new font color.

5. Click to the left of Nomad in the next paragraph, type `<B>`, click to the right of Ltd (in the same line), then type `</B>`
   This company name will appear in boldface when viewed in the browser.

   > **QuickTip**
   >
   > Many HTML editors let you select text to be formatted, and then allow you to click a toolbar button to bold, italicize, format color, or underline.

6. Save Nomad mission statement.htm as a text document
   Compare your document to Figure G-3. Once the text document is saved, you can view the changes in your browser.

7. Click the browser program button on the taskbar, then view the saved version of Nomad mission statement.htm by refreshing the screen
   Compare your document to Figure G-4. Notice that formatting changes enhance the page's overall appearance, highlighting important text without detracting from the content.

TABLE G-1: Logical and physical formatting tags

tag	description	type
`<EM> </EM>`	Indicates emphasis; generally shown in italics	Logical
`<STRONG> </STRONG>`	Indicates importance; generally shown in boldface	Logical
`<SAMP> </SAMP>`	Indicates literal characters; generally shown in monotype font	Logical
`<B> </B>`	Displays in boldface	Physical
`<I> </I>`	Displays in italics	Physical
`<TT> </TT>`	Displays in monotype font	Physical
`<U> </U>`	Underlines text	Physical

FIGURE G-3: Formatting added to text

Hexadecimal
color value

Closes the font
face tag

Closes the font
color tag

```
<head>
<title>Nomad Ltd on-line</title>
</head>
<style type="text/css">
      #text {position: relative; left: 125; width: 450}
</style>
<body>

<p><img src="nomad.jpg" align="right" width="201" height="63"> </p>

<h1><FONT COLOR="800000"><FONT FACE="Arial">Nomad Ltd Home
Page!</FONT></FONT></h1>

<h2>Learn About Our Company's Philosophy</h2>

<DIV ID=text>
<B>Nomad Ltd</B> has been in business for over ten years. During that
time, we have offered tours to exotic (and simple) lands and sold
sporting equipment (for bicycling, hiking, and other activities).
```

FIGURE G-4: Color and font changed

Nomad Ltd Home Page!

Nomad Ltd

Learn About Our Company's Philosophy

Nomad Ltd has been in business for over ten years. During that time, we have offered tours to exotic (and simple) lands and sold sporting equipment (for bicycling, hiking, and other activities). In all that time, we have always been aware that our employees are our corporate ambassadors, and our customers are our royalty. We know that any company can make a buck here and there, but we want to do more than make a profit. We want you to enjoy shopping at our stores and make Nomad a fun and interesting place to shop.

We know that as a business, we are community members. Nomad wants to contribute to community efforts and make each town a better place in which to live. We hire from the community, offer educational and financial benefits to our employees, and become involved in community efforts.

Nomad Home Page | Tour Types | Art Tours | Athlete Tours | Employment Opportunities | Store Locations | Talk To Us

Bold text

Hexadecimal 80000
is a maroon color

Arial is a commonly
available font

Colors and their values

Colors, like formatting attributes, can be described logically or physically. Although it is easier for the Web author to use the logical attribute RED to describe the desired color, the actual appearance is still left up to the browser. The hexadecimal value is a much more accurate way of indicating what color you want displayed. Hexadecimal values use combinations of letters and numbers to create color codes.

HTML

Learning Graphic Design Principles

A well-designed Web page doesn't just "happen." It should be the result of thoughtful planning and design execution. Page design can make or break a Web site: although certain elements such as images and colors can improve appearances, it's important to use them judiciously. Sarah reviews specific graphic-design principles to inspire her work on the Nomad Web site.

Details

Know how your pages will be used

Although you can never know for certain how your pages will be used, you can make some basic assumptions. Pages with large amounts of text may be printed for later reading, shorter documents will probably be read online, and pages with reference information or important facts may be printed or faxed. Although graphics enhance a page, people want the information in the text on most pages. Therefore, it is wise to consider how long it will take to load a page with currently available modem speeds before adding graphic images.

Know the primary task of graphic design

Any page's design is used to organize the information it is presenting. Place the most important information at the beginning of a document to ensure your readers see it. Use headings and attributes to add emphasis to important topics and draw your readers' attention. Do not make all the text the same size, color, and depth.

Understand visual hierarchy

Initially, readers see a page as a mass with a particular shape and color. As they proceed, they notice specifics such as a graphic image, a headline, or a paragraph. Later, the finer details, such as individual headlines and words, are recognized. The organizational scheme of graphic design is called **visual hierarchy**. Tools used within this hierarchy include color, typography, and layout.

Strive for consistency

Decide on a common look for your pages and use it repeatedly. A theme provides a comfort level for readers and informs them that they're still within your site. Figure G-5 shows three pages from a Web site that are unified with a common visual design.

Understand page construction

Because Western languages such as English are read from left-to-right, top-to-bottom, this is the direction most Web pages take. The top of a page is the most important location because it is the first item visible to all viewers. You have no control over the size or resolution of a viewer's monitor, so it is important that a successful page design start at the top.

Choose elements carefully

Background colors should not be jarring: avoid loud colors unless they are necessary for emphasis. Elements such as bullets, icons, or horizontal rules should be accents, not themes. Overuse of these elements can make a page boring and may suggest "form over substance" to your audience.

Common
design
elements

Using Color and Images

Colors and images affect what we think and how we perceive products and companies. You will never see the words "Coca-Cola®" written in green or McDonalds® golden arches in purple. A company can have its corporate logo color-contrasted to allow its use as a background image, or watermark. Logos can be tiled or centered on the page. Tiling creates multiple images from a single image in a geometric pattern. A **watermark** is a light-toned image used as a background that reminds the reader of the corporate image while not competing with the main information on the page. You also can add a solid color to the page background.　　 Sarah had the art department create a Nomad corporate image watermark using a special graphics program. She thinks the page needs softening and wants to see how it looks in the Web page background.

Steps

1. Click the text editor program button on the taskbar
   The watermark file is referenced in the initial <BODY> tag because it affects the entire body of the page.

2. Click to the right of body in the <body> tag, press the [Spacebar], then type BACKGROUND="WATRMARK.JPG"
   Each time you make a change, see how it looks in the browser.

3. Save the text document, click your browser program button on the taskbar, then view the saved changes by refreshing the image
   The watermark displays in the background of the document, as shown in Figure G-6. You realize the watermark makes the design look too "busy" and detracts from the page content. A subtle color might be a better solution for the page background.

   | Trouble? |
   Make sure you type hexadecimal codes correctly: use a zero, *not* the letter "O."

4. Click the text editor program button on the taskbar, select BACKGROUND= "WATRMARK.JPG", then type BGCOLOR="#C0C0C0"
   This hexadecimal value replaces the watermark image with a soothing background color.

5. Save your text document
   Compare your work to Figure G-7.

6. Click your browser program button on the taskbar, then view the saved version of the document by refreshing the image
   Compare your work to Figure G-8. The silver background looks better: it is not busy, has a soothing appearance, and enhances the page.

FIGURE G-6: Watermark in page background

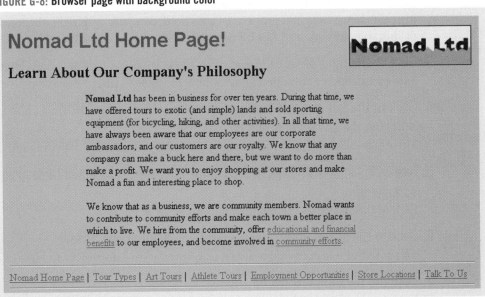

FIGURE G-7: Revised code with background color

Hexadecimal value for "silver"

```
<html>

<head>
<title>Nomad Ltd on-line</title>
</head>
<style type="text/css">
    #text {position: relative; left: 125; width: 450}
</style>
<body BGCOLOR="#C0C0C0">

<p><img src="nomad.jpg" align="right" width="201" height="63"> </p>

<h1><FONT COLOR="800000"><FONT FACE="Arial">Nomad Ltd Home
Page!</FONT></FONT></h1>
```

FIGURE G-8: Browser page with background color

Nomad Ltd Home Page!

Nomad Ltd

Learn About Our Company's Philosophy

Nomad Ltd has been in business for over ten years. During that time, we have offered tours to exotic (and simple) lands and sold sporting equipment (for bicycling, hiking, and other activities). In all that time, we have always been aware that our employees are our corporate ambassadors, and our customers are our royalty. We know that any company can make a buck here and there, but we want to do more than make a profit. We want you to enjoy shopping at our stores and make Nomad a fun and interesting place to shop.

We know that as a business, we are community members. Nomad wants to contribute to community efforts and make each town a better place in which to live. We hire from the community, offer educational and financial benefits to our employees, and become involved in community efforts.

Nomad Home Page | Tour Types | Art Tours | Athlete Tours | Employment Opportunities | Store Locations | Talk To Us

CLUES TO USE

Using color effectively

Proper use of a background color can make or break a page. A page whose background and text have too little contrast, such as in Figure G-9, is difficult to read. The reader's eye is drawn to the lightest element on the page, which is the corporate logo. Unfortunately, the logo should be an "accent," and the point of the page is for the text to be read. This design forces the reader away from the text to the least important element on the page.

FIGURE G-9: Poorly adjusted contrast between text and background

Your eye is drawn here

Designing a Form Correctly

A form is a Web page that requires some input from the reader. Input devices, such as radio buttons, checkboxes, drop-down lists, and text boxes are the instruments you use to collect your reader's responses. How those pages look can, directly or indirectly, influence many responses you get or how truthfully they are completed. An unattractive, disorganized form may not get as many responses as a more pleasant-looking form. In addition, an unprofessional-looking form reflects poorly on the company's image. ▰▰▰ Sarah prepares to examine the form area of the current document.

Steps

1. **Scroll your browser window down to the bottom of the page**
   Text boxes display that enable a reader to fill in a name and address and then send Nomad this data to request information. The text boxes, as shown in Figure G-10, are disorganized, cluttered, and appear unprofessional.

2. **Click the text editor program button on the taskbar, then scroll so the HTML codes containing the form is visible**
   Text boxes can be aligned in a variety of ways. One method is to use preformatted text. Using this technique, any text within these tags is converted to a monotype font and is displayed exactly as it appears in the code. You prefer to create a borderless table with right-aligned descriptions. To do this, you must insert <TABLE> tags in the form data to create the table's cells.

3. **Click to the right of <FORM ACTION="URL">, press [Enter], then type <TABLE>**
   Tags and attributes are added to determine the table's cells.

4. **Click to the left of First Name, type <TR><TD ALIGN=RIGHT>, click to the right of Name: in the same line, then type <TD>**
   These tags define the first row of the table and right-align the data in the first cell.

5. **Type <TR> and <TD> tags to each of the remaining rows in the table, using Figure G-11 as a guide**
   Each of the text boxes is contained within the table.

6. **Click to the left of <BR>, type </TABLE>, then press [Enter]**
   The </TABLE> tag concludes the table. Compare your document to Figure G-11.

7. **Save the file as a text document**
   Your new changes will be visible in the browser when the image is refreshed.

8. **Click the browser program button on the taskbar, then view the saved version of the Nomad mission statement.htm document by refreshing the image**
   Compare the formatted text boxes to Figure G-12.

FIGURE G-10: Disorganized text boxes

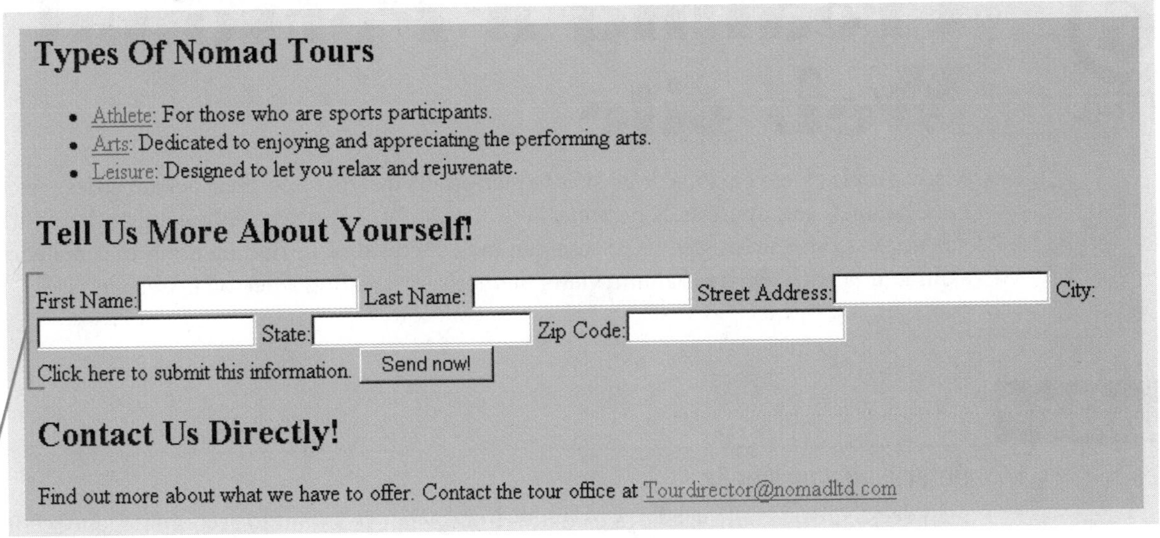
Types Of Nomad Tours
Athlete: For those who are sports participants.
Arts: Dedicated to enjoying and appreciating the performing arts.
Leisure: Designed to let you relax and rejuvenate.
Tell Us More About Yourself!
First Name:
Last Name:
Street Address:
City:
State:
Zip Code:
Click here to submit this information.
Send now!
Contact Us Directly!
Find out more about what we have to offer. Contact the tour office at Tourdirector@nomadltd.com

Text boxes are confusing

FIGURE G-11: Text boxes organized within a table

```
<h2>Tell Us More About Yourself!</h2>
<TABLE>
<FORM ACTION="URL">
<TR><TD ALIGN=RIGHT>First Name:<TD><INPUT TYPE="TEXT" SIZE=20
NAME="firstname">
<TR><TD ALIGN=RIGHT>Last Name:<TD> <INPUT TYPE="TEXT" SIZE=20
NAME="lastname">
<TR><TD ALIGN=RIGHT>Street Address:<TD><INPUT TYPE="TEXT" SIZE=20
NAME="address">
<TR><TD ALIGN=RIGHT>City: <TD><INPUT TYPE="TEXT" SIZE=20 NAME="city">
<TR><TD ALIGN=RIGHT>State:<TD><INPUT TYPE="TEXT" SIZE=20 NAME="state">
<TR><TD ALIGN=RIGHT>Zip Code:<TD><INPUT TYPE="TEXT" SIZE=20
NAME="zipcode">
</TABLE>
<BR>Click here to submit this information. <INPUT TYPE="SUBMIT"
VALUE="Send now!">
</FORM>

<h2>Contact Us Directly!</h2>
```

Concludes table

Not part of table

FIGURE G-12: Table containing text boxes

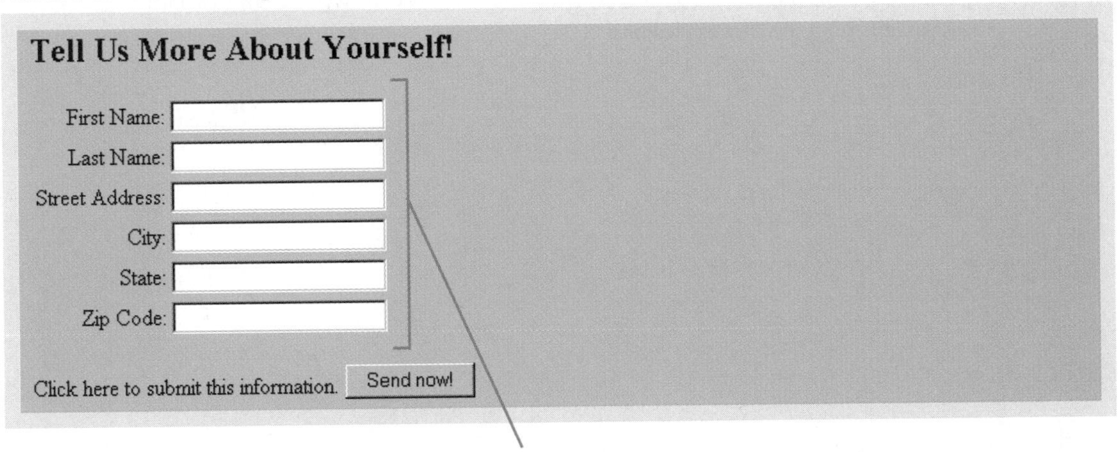
Tell Us More About Yourself!
First Name:
Last Name:
Street Address:
City:
State:
Zip Code:
Click here to submit this information.
Send now!

Looks less cluttered

Creating a Personal Web site

Many people create personal Web sites to give others insights into their personalities, special talents, hobbies, and interests. A personal Web site can be a great way of meeting others with similar interests and sharing ideas. It also can be a useful tool in finding a job that matches your skills and talents. ✐ Sarah reviews methods for creating a personal Web site.

Details

Determine your needs

First decide if you really need a personal Web site, what you want to accomplish, and whom you want to attract. You also should find out from your Internet Service Provider (ISP) what the space limitations and the fees for document storage on their Web server are, if any.

Plan ahead

Once you've decided to go ahead with developing your personal Web site, outline your page. Determine how many images you'll need and their availability. You may wish to photograph yourself, any special projects you have created, your pets, or your family.

Write code using a text editor or HTML editor

Use your favorite text or HTML editor to create your own page. With these tools, you can use your imagination—and HTML writing skills—to create the page that will represent you. HTML editors, however, have no Help screens or user assistance to aid you in designing the pages.

Use a specially designed Web design Wizard in your word processor

Word processors, such as Microsoft Word, often include a Web Page Wizard, such as the one shown in Figure G-13 that helps you lay out a variety of Web pages, including a personal home page. With it, you can create a variety of Web page types that meet specific needs.

Use an online Wizard

There are many easy-to-use Wizards that can be used through corporate Web sites. The Netscape Page Wizard, shown in Figure G-14, is one such site. This site works in combination with various Netscape products and offers assistance and helpful design features.

Locate other Web Wizard products

Use your favorite search engine, such as Yahoo! or WebCrawler, to find Web design products. These products—and there are a lot of them—may be freely downloadable, as shown in Figure G-15, or available on a fee-for-service basis.

FIGURE G-13: Microsoft Word Web Page Wizard

Suggested headings and topics

Types of Web pages that can be designed

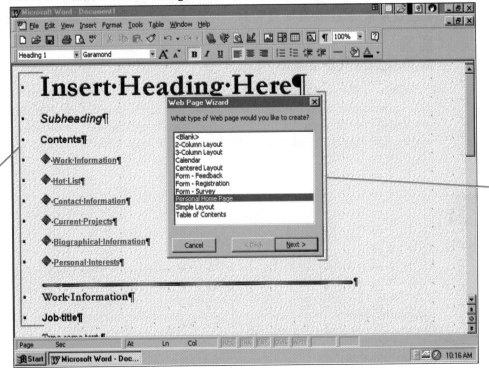

FIGURE G-14: Netscape Web Page Wizard

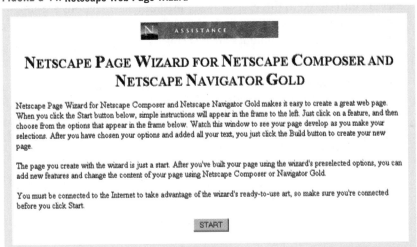

FIGURE G-15: Downloadable Web Page Wizard

Locating Web Design Resources

Unit G
HTML

If you do a search on Web design, you'll find hundreds of sites offering advice or fee-paid service organizations. Several sites, however, exist that can help with basic Web design issues. These sites do not contain topical information; they usually contain links to other sites. ✐ Sarah reviews several helpful Web sites that explain design principles.

Details

Style guides

A style guide may be your best resource. When conducting a search on this topic, the keywords *style guide* will yield the best results. Figure G-16 shows the initial page for the *Yale C/AIM Web Style Guide.* This guide provides in-depth information to issues, including site design, page layout, graphic use and optimization, and multimedia and animation. Another style resource is the Sun Microsystems Guide to Web style, shown in Figure G-17.

Current information

Because each of these style guides is on the Web, they can be kept up-to-date. As new technologies are introduced to this ever-growing medium, new sections are added and existing ones are amended. Style guides such as those shown here not only explain how to create specific effects, but also why certain techniques are less effective than others.

Professional designers

You may not want to take the time to design your own series of Web pages. If that is the case, a query using your favorite search engine(s) will show you that there are many opportunities to hire professional Web site designers. These companies combine the latest Web programming techniques and use your graphics or create them. Often, periodic Web site maintenance is included in their fee.

FIGURE G-16: Yale C/AIM Web Style Guide

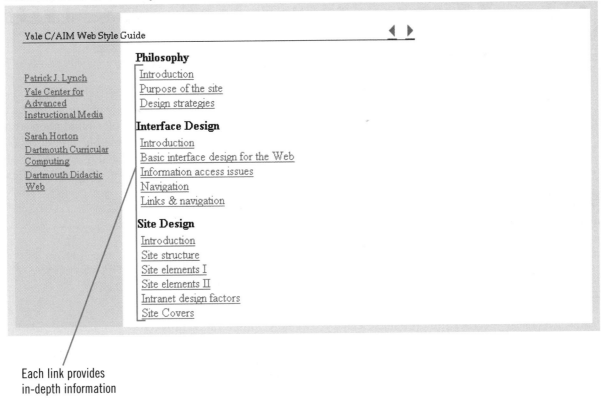

Each link provides
in-depth information

FIGURE G-17: Sun Microsystems Guide to Web Style

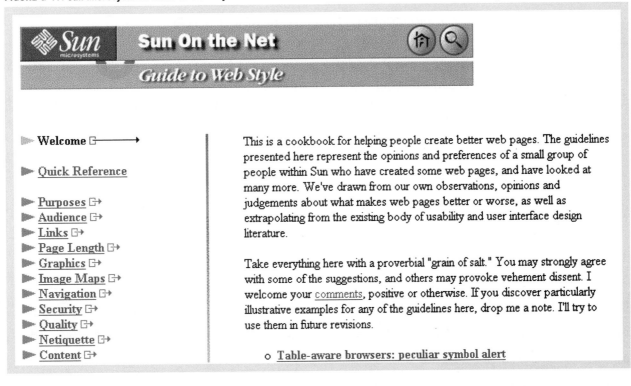

Designing for Special-needs Audiences

The Web's vast audience includes readers with specialized needs. The Web-using population includes visually impaired as well as hearing impaired users. The visually impaired may be color blind or have limited vision, or they may have complete blindness. Color-blind people cannot distinguish between two or more colors. (The most common form of color blindness occurs with the colors red and green.) Table G-2 contains design suggestions that may prove helpful to colorblind users. Sarah reviews Web page design considerations for special-needs audiences and makes several changes to help this audience.

Steps

1. **Click the text editor program button on the taskbar**
   The current background may make the page difficult for some groups to read. A lighter background would ensure easy readability to most readers.

QuickTip

For most people, it is helpful to design pages with a high contrast between font and background colors.

2. **Double-click the BGCOLOR code COCOCO, then type FFFFFF**
   Each time you make a change, see how it looks in the browser.

3. **Save the text document, click your browser program button on the taskbar, then view the saved changes by refreshing the image**
   Figure G-18 shows how the change in color adds more contrast between the text and background. Applying color to the boldface name of the company adds contrast to the text.

4. **Click the text editor program button on the taskbar, click to the left of Nomad beneath the <DIV> tag, type <FONT COLOR="800000">, click to the right of Ltd in the same line, then type </FONT>**

5. **Save your text document, then print the text document**
   Compare your text document to Figure G-19.

6. **Click your browser program button on the taskbar, then view the saved version of the document by refreshing the image**
   Compare your work to Figure G-20. Using the same color for the company name visually unites the text.

7. **Print the browser document**

8. **Exit the browser, then exit the text editor**

TABLE G-2: Design suggestions for colorblind users

do/don't	suggestion
Do	Use a dark shade for text; a light shade for backgrounds
Do	Associate use of colored text with a different font; if readers can't see the color, they may be able to see the different font
Do	Examine your page on a monitor with monochrome settings
Don't	Use a highly textured background; the color can make text difficult to read
Don't	Use green and red in any combination of text and background

FIGURE G-18: Light-color background creates higher contrast

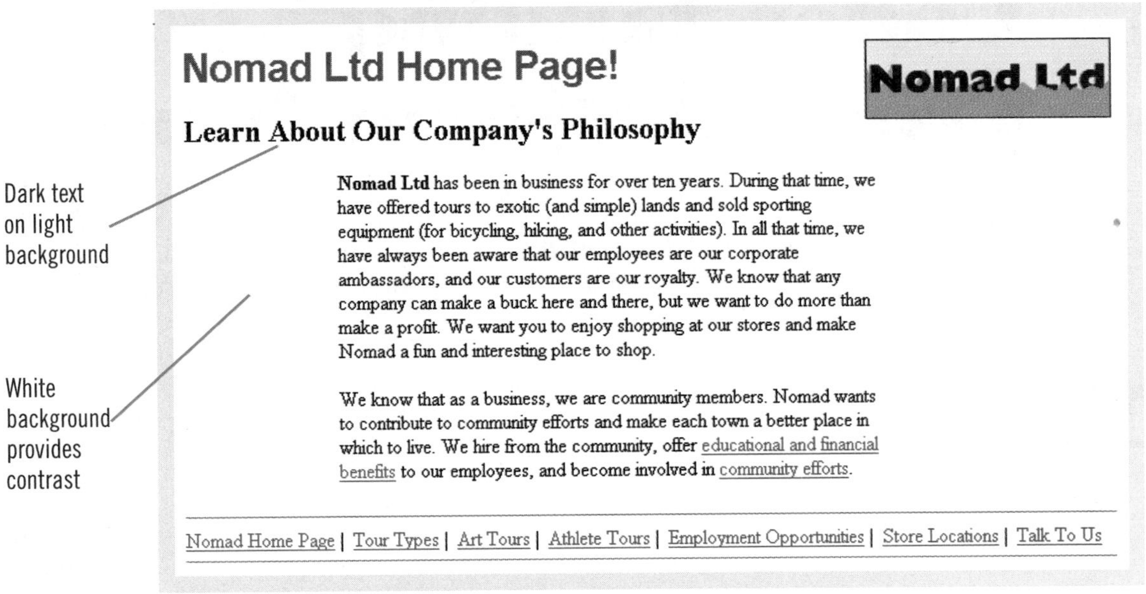

Nomad Ltd Home Page!

Nomad Ltd

Learn About Our Company's Philosophy

Dark text on light background

White background provides contrast

Nomad Ltd has been in business for over ten years. During that time, we have offered tours to exotic (and simple) lands and sold sporting equipment (for bicycling, hiking, and other activities). In all that time, we have always been aware that our employees are our corporate ambassadors, and our customers are our royalty. We know that any company can make a buck here and there, but we want to do more than make a profit. We want you to enjoy shopping at our stores and make Nomad a fun and interesting place to shop.

We know that as a business, we are community members. Nomad wants to contribute to community efforts and make each town a better place in which to live. We hire from the community, offer educational and financial benefits to our employees, and become involved in community efforts.

Nomad Home Page | Tour Types | Art Tours | Athlete Tours | Employment Opportunities | Store Locations | Talk To Us

---

FIGURE G-19: Background and font color changes

Font color changed

```
</style>
<body BGCOLOR="FFFFFF">

<p><img src="nomad.jpg" align="right" width="201" height="63"> </p>

<h1><FONT COLOR="800000"><FONT FACE="Arial">Nomad Ltd Home
Page!</FONT></FONT></h1>

<h2>Learn About Our Company's Philosophy</h2>

<DIV ID=text>
<B><FONT COLOR="800000">Nomad Ltd</FONT></B> has been in business for
over ten years. During that
time, we have offered tours to exotic (and simple) lands and sold
```

FIGURE G-20: Completed Web page

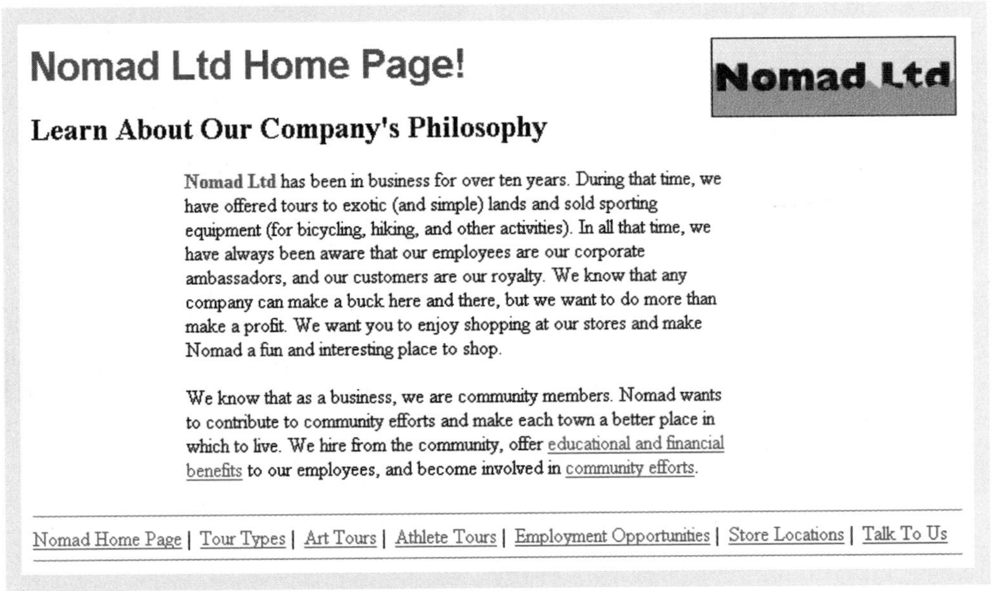

Nomad Ltd Home Page!

Nomad Ltd

Learn About Our Company's Philosophy

Nomad Ltd has been in business for over ten years. During that time, we have offered tours to exotic (and simple) lands and sold sporting equipment (for bicycling, hiking, and other activities). In all that time, we have always been aware that our employees are our corporate ambassadors, and our customers are our royalty. We know that any company can make a buck here and there, but we want to do more than make a profit. We want you to enjoy shopping at our stores and make Nomad a fun and interesting place to shop.

We know that as a business, we are community members. Nomad wants to contribute to community efforts and make each town a better place in which to live. We hire from the community, offer educational and financial benefits to our employees, and become involved in community efforts.

Nomad Home Page | Tour Types | Art Tours | Athlete Tours | Employment Opportunities | Store Locations | Talk To Us

Understanding Cross-platform Issues

Designing Web pages is fraught with many challenges, such as variations in users' monitor sizes and video-display resolution settings. To complicate matters, not everyone uses the same computer/operating system combination, or **platform**. All these variables are additional factors that the designer must consider. ◄━━━━ Sarah considers platform-dependent design issues.

Details

Browser interpretation

Browser wars—the continuing debate over which Internet browser is better—involves more than loyalty to a specific program. Each browser has exclusive capabilities creating incompatibilities between the browsers when viewing Web pages. In addition, as technology evolves, the capabilities of browsers are continually advanced creating a system of users at different levels of technology using the same browsers but different versions. For example, although all browsers may view JavaScript, VBScript may only be visible in some. Generally, it is safe to assume that newer browsers have all the capabilities of older browsers, but the reverse is seldom true. For this reason, you may find that HTML tags and coding vary between browsers, thereby creating different displays in different systems.

Differing resolutions

You can easily bet that what you see on your screen is not exactly what other users see. There are so many monitors and video cards on the market that it would be virtually impossible to test a page on every monitor. Also, monitor resolution, the setting that determines how "real estate" is visible on a single screen, also varies. The **resolution** is the number of pixels displayed on the screen. In many cases, the default setting is 640 × 480, but many people set their resolution at 800 × 600 or 1024 × 768. Figure G-21 shows a Web page at 640 × 480, while Figures G-22 and G-23 show the same page at 600 × 800 and 1024 × 768, respectively. Notice that as the resolution increases, so do the image clarity and the amount of the page you can see on the screen.

Appearance of images

Gamma settings, the degree of contrast between mid-level gray values in an image, vary across platforms. The variation of these settings can cause image appearance to differ markedly. An image with heavy contrast on a Macintosh may look very dark on a PC, whereas high-contrast Windows images may look flat and washed out on a Macintosh. Gamma settings can be optimized for either environment using graphics programs such as Adobe PhotoShop.

Text-size variations

An additional issue concerns variations in text sizes. Macintosh font sizes generally appear two sizes smaller than their PC counterparts. Although testing your HTML document on both platforms would be optimal, it is not always practical or possible. For insight into how font sizes look on the other platforms, PC users should use the <FONT SIZE="-2"> tag, and Macintosh users should use the <FONT SIZE="+2"> tag.

FIGURE G-21: Web page at 640 X 480 resolution

FIGURE G-22: Web page at 800 X 600 resolution

FIGURE G-23: Web page at 1024 X 768 resolution

Practice

► Concepts Review

Label the function of each HTML tag shown in Figure G-24.

FIGURE G-24

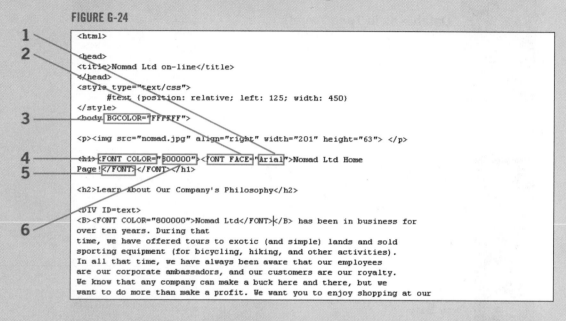

1
2
3
4
5
6

```
<html>

<head>
<title>Nomad Ltd on-line</title>
</head>
<style type="text/css">
        #text {position: relative; left: 125; width: 450}
</style>
<body BGCOLOR="FFFFFF">

<p><img src="nomad.jpg" align="right" width="201" height="63"> </p>

<h1><FONT COLOR="800000"><FONT FACE="Arial">Nomad Ltd Home
Page!</FONT></FONT></h1>

<h2>Learn About Our Company's Philosophy</h2>

<DIV ID=text>
<B><FONT COLOR="800000">Nomad Ltd</FONT></B> has been in business for
over ten years. During that
time, we have offered tours to exotic (and simple) lands and sold
sporting equipment (for bicycling, hiking, and other activities).
In all that time, we have always been aware that our employees
are our corporate ambassadors, and our customers are our royalty.
We know that any company can make a buck here and there, but we
want to do more than make a profit. We want you to enjoy shopping at our
```

Match each statement with the HTML tag or attribute it describes.

7. </FONT>
8. <TT>
9. COLOR
10. <EM>
11. FACE
12. BGCOLOR

a. Changes typeface.
b. Changes typeface color.
c. Indicates emphasis.
d. Restores typeface color to default.
e. Indicates a monotype font.
f. Changes background color.

Select the best answer from the list of choices.

13. Each of the following is true about using Web page design, *except*
    a. White space provides relief to the eyes.
    b. Using physical tags eliminates the guesswork about a page's appearance.
    c. Using logical tags eliminates the guesswork about a page's appearance.
    d. Make sure every line of text is not a heading.

14. Which formatting indicates how text should look in comparison to other page text?
    a. Physical
    b. Relative
    c. Absolute
    d. Logical

15. Which formatting indicates how text should look regardless of other page text?
    a. Physical
    b. Relative
    c. Absolute
    d. Logical

16. What characters surround a new font selection?
    a. * *
    b. " "
    c. ? ?
    d. < >

17. Which physical attribute is used to bold text?
    a. B
    b. STRONG
    c. EM
    d. I

18. Which tag is used to conclude the FONT FACE attribute?
    a. </FONT>
    b. </FACE>
    c. </FFACE>
    d. <FACE>

19. Which tag is used to conclude the FONT COLOR tag?
    a. </FONT COLOR>
    b. </FONT>
    c. </COLOR>
    d. </FCOLOR>

20. Each of the following is a valid hexadecimal color value, *except*:
    a. FFFFFFF
    b. 008080
    c. FFFFFF
    d. FF00FF

21. In which tag is a watermark inserted?
    a. BACKGROUND
    b. BODY
    c. BG
    d. WTRMRK

22. Resolution is measured in
    a. inches.
    b. centimeters.
    c. pixels.
    d. units.

23. Macintosh font sizes vary from PC font sizes by a factor of
   a. +2.
   b. -2.
   c. +4.
   d. -4.

24. The degree of contrast between mid-level gray values in an image is controlled by
   a. Gamma settings.
   b. Gamma quadrant.
   c. Alpha settings.
   d. Alpha quadrant.

25. The computer/operating system combination is referred to as a
   a. Jacquard arrangement.
   b. Platform.
   c. Techno-usage.
   d. Usage.

26. Each of the following is a cross-platform issue, *except*:
   a. Gamma settings.
   b. Hexadecimal values.
   c. Browser interpretation.
   d. Font sizes.

 # Independent Challenges

1. The Hometown Humane Society would like you to experiment with color and design within their Web page. Also, they would like you to design a form that will be used to collect a viewer's information.
   To complete this independent challenge:

   a. Start your text editor, open the file HTML G-2.htm, then save it as a text document with the filename HHS-design.htm.
   b. Replace the INSERT FORM AND TABLE TEXT HERE text with your own input text boxes that will collect information you think should be gathered from readers.
   c. The table should be designed in an appealing manner; use any colors you feel are appropriate.
   d. Add logical or physical formatting to add emphasis. Italicize or underline some text.
   e. Add a light background color, such as C0C0C0, or any appropriate watermark image you can find.
   f. Save your work.
   g. View the document in your browser.
   h. Print the document in your browser.
   i. Exit your text editor and browser.

2. The Independence Community College would like you to add formatting and color-design elements to a new Web page. To complete this independent challenge:

a. Start your text editor, open the file HTML G-3.htm, then save it as a text document with the filename ICC-design.htm.

b. Replace the INSERT TEXT HERE with your own creative text about the college.

c. Underline some text on the page.

d. Add a light background color (using silver or white) or any appropriate watermark image you can find.

e. Save your work, and print the text document.

f. View the document in your browser.

g. Print the document in your browser.

h. Exit your text editor and browser.

3. The Play It Loud CD shop would like you to find out how to modify its Web pages for visually impaired users.
To complete this independent challenge:

a. Connect to the Internet.

b. Use any search engine to locate information about visually impaired users.

c. Print at least one document on this topic.

d. Cancel the Internet connection.

e. Start a new document in your text editor, and save it as a text document with the filename PIL-design.htm.

f. Create a simple document that demonstrates a suggested design for this group.

g. Save and print your work.

h. View the document in your browser.

i. Print the document in your browser.

j. Exit your text editor and browser.

4. Using the Web as a research tool, locate information about creating a personal Web site.
To complete this independent challenge:

a. Connect to the Internet.

b. Use any search engine to locate reviews of at least three personal Web site design products.

c. Print these reviews.

d. Locate the corporate pages for each of these products.

e. Print the manufacturer's information for each product.

f. Disconnect from the Internet.

g. Exit your browser.

h. Write a brief paper comparing and contrasting the features of each of the products.

i. Conclude with a statement about which product best suits your needs and why.

Visual Workshop

Open the file HTML G-4, and save it as Carla's design.htm. Use your text editor—or available HTML editor—to modify the document so it looks like Figure G-25. Save and print the document in your text editor and browser.

FIGURE G-25

Welcome to Carla's Collectibles!

Carla's specializes in obscure collectibles: stuff you just can't find anywhere else!

Add Your Name To Our Mailing List

First Name: [ ]
Last Name: [ ]
Street Address: [ ]
City: [ ]
State: [ ]
Zip Code: [ ]
Item of Interest: [ ]

Click here to add your name to our mailing list. [Send now!]

Receive Our Catalog!

Scripting
for HTML

- ► **Understand scripting for HTML**
- ► **Create a script**
- ► **Debug a script**
- ► **Understand objects**
- ► **Use JavaScript event handlers**
- ► **Create a function**
- ► **Assign a variable**
- ► **Create a conditional**

HTML allows you to create basic Web pages easily. Using many of the newest features available in Web page design, however, requires the incorporation of **scripts**, which are programs in a Web page that run on the viewer's browser. Using scripts can expand the number of features you can add to your Web pages and can simplify some HTML commands. ✎ Lydia Burgos works in the information systems division of Nomad Ltd. Her supervisor heard about the advantages of scripts at a recent seminar and has asked Lydia to create a report on ways that scripts could enhance the company's current Web publication. Lydia begins by researching the fundamentals of **scripting**, which is the process of writing scripts.

Understanding Scripting for HTML

A **script** is a small program contained within an HTML document that can be executed by a Web browser. In the early days of the Web, scripts were separate files stored and run on a remote Web server. Today, Web page designers can place scripts within a page's standard HTML, and the scripts can run on each user's computer. This change is made possible by new techniques for data transfer on the Web as well as a new generation of more powerful home computers. Other forms of Web page programming (such as CGI files that process data from Web page forms) may also be referred to as scripts. However, scripts that run on a user's browser represent the most powerful and innovative form of scripting on the Web today. This is the definition we will use in this book. Figure H-1 shows the source code for a Web page containing a script, as well as the Web page generated by that code. In researching scripting fundamentals, Lydia Burgos has learned that using scripting in Web page development offers several advantages over using HTML alone. These advantages include the following:

 ### Flexibility

Scripting allows you to modify your Web pages in ways that are not yet part of standard HTML. Additionally, you can combine scripting codes in many different ways, which opens the door to more variety and creativity in your pages than with HTML alone. For example, you can have a message that runs automatically when the Web page is opened and that is updated automatically, such as a current list of top headlines for a news Web site.

 ### Simplification

You can script some tasks that you usually would code using HTML. In many cases, scripting is more efficient and allows you to create a more organized publication. One of the first areas in which scripting is replacing HTML is in assigning styles to text. Instead of adding attributes to the tags for each block of text in your publication, you can insert a small script that automatically assigns specific attributes, such as boldface type or text color, to specific blocks of text throughout an entire Web page or set of pages.

 ### Immediate response

Traditionally, to access many features available on a Web page, your browser contacts the Web site where the page resides and requests a linked Web page or new information based on your input. Embedded scripts eliminate the lag time involved in contacting the remote server, waiting for a response, and downloading new information. This is because the scripts run on your local computer and can change what your browser displays without downloading new information from the server.

 ### Improved interactivity

The quick response time that local scripting provides allows you to incorporate an impressive amount of user interactivity into your Web pages. Since script processing occurs locally, your script can react almost instantaneously to any user action. For example, your script could display a short summary of a link when the user simply moves the pointer over the link without clicking it.

Reduced server load

Local execution of scripts is an advantage not just for users, but for Web site administrators as well. The reduced demand on the server when some of the processing is shifted to local computers results in more free system resources. This may result in a decrease in download time for people viewing your site's pages and faster processing when a Web page does need to submit a request to the server.

```
<HTML>

<HEAD>
<TITLE>Nomad Ltd online</TITLE>

<SCRIPT LANGUAGE="javascript">
<!--
var name=prompt("For personal service, please type your first name and click
OK.","")

function submitted() {
        alert("Information submitted!")
}

function clearUp() {
        document.info.elements[0].value=""
        document.info.elements[1].value=""
        document.info.elements[2].value=""
        document.info.elements[3].value=""
        document.info.elements[4].value=""
        document.info.elements[5].value=""
}

//-->
</SCRIPT>
```

Script
embedded
in HTML
code

User
name
generated
by script

Welcome to the Nomad Ltd home page, Lydia!

Nomad Ltd

Learn About Our Company's Philosophy

Nomad Ltd is a national sporting goods retailer
dedicated to delivering high-quality sporting gear and
adventure travel.
Nomad Ltd has been in business for over ten years.
During that time, we have offered tours all over the
world and sold sporting equipment for bicycling, hiking,
and other activities. Like most companies, our main goal
is to make a profit. At the same time, we realize that as a
business, we are also community members. Nomad Ltd
is committed to contributing to community efforts and
making each town where we do business a better place
to live. We do that by hiring from the community,

Choosing a scripting language

Several languages are available when writing scripts
for an HTML document. These include **JavaScript**
and **JScript**, which are both adaptations of Sun
Microsystems' Java programming language, as well as
VBScript, which is Microsoft's adaptation of its
Visual Basic programming language for Web use.
Both Internet Explorer 4 and Netscape Navigator 4
are largely compatible with JavaScript. On the other
hand, JScript and VBScript are not universally compatible, meaning that users of certain browsers might
be unable to view the scripted elements of your page
if you used one of these languages. This text uses
JavaScript to create pages viewable by both Internet
Explorer and Netscape Navigator users.

Creating a Script

You can add a script to a Web page just as you would add to or edit the Web page's HTML code. To do this, you can use a text editor such as WordPad or Notepad or a Web page editor such as FrontPage Express or Composer. In order for a browser to recognize a script, the script must be contained within <SCRIPT> HTML tags. It is also good practice to surround each script with a set of HTML tags to make it invisible to browsers incompatible with scripts. This second set of HTML tags tells incompatible browsers to bypass the script. ✒ While researching scripting fundamentals, Lydia found a sample script that validates a form before submitting it to a server by checking the form to be sure information has been entered in each field. If information has not been entered in each field and the user tries to send the form, then this form validation script displays a warning box which reminds the user to complete each field. Lydia decides to try adding this script to the Nomad Ltd home page in order to better understand how to insert scripts into HTML code.

QuickTip

When saving a file as HTML, be sure to select Text (.txt) as the file type to be saved and include the extension .htm in the filename.

1. Start your text editor program, open the file **HTML H-1.htm**, then save it as a text document with the filename **Scripted page.htm**
   If you use WordPad or Notepad, which are text editors built into Windows 95, the source code for the Web page appears as text in the text editor. If you use an HTML editing tool, such as Microsoft FrontPage or Netscape Composer, you will see the graphical representation of the file code. You must select the option Page Source or HTML from the View menu to see the HTML code for the page.

2. Select the text **[replace with opening script tags]** below the TITLE tag, then press **[Delete]**

3. Type **<SCRIPT LANGUAGE="javascript">** and press **[Enter]**
   Now the beginning of the script is marked with the <SCRIPT> HTML tag and an attribute specifying the scripting language you're using, which is JavaScript.

QuickTip

All browsers ignore the remainder of the line after the <!-- tag; thus, some script writers add a normal language comment here, such as "HIDE," to make the script code easier for programmers to look at and understand.

4. Type **<!--** and press **[Enter]** twice
   The tag <!-- tells an incompatible browser (one that can't process your script) to ignore the code that follows. A compatible browser (one that can interpret your script) will go ahead and process the script that follows.

5. Select the text **[replace with closing script tags]**, then press **[Delete]**

6. Type **//-->** and press **[Enter]**, then type **</SCRIPT>** and press **[Enter]**
   These tags mark the end of the script. Figure H-2 shows the Web page source code containing the opening and closing script tags and the dialog box generated by the script.

7. Check the lines you added for errors, make changes as necessary, then save Scripted page.htm as a text document

Trouble?

If the Web page does not display correctly, or if a dialog box opens describing an error in your script, click OK if necessary, read the next lesson to learn about debugging scripts, then return to look for errors in your Web page code.

8. Start your Web browser program, cancel any dial-up activities, open the page **Scripted page.htm**, scroll down to the text fields near the bottom of the page, fill in sample information, then click the **Send now! button**
   The script runs and displays the dialog box shown in Figure H-2.

9. Click the **OK button**
   The browser simulates form submission to a server. This script will save time for people using the Nomad Ltd Web page, since they do not have to wait for the form to be submitted to the server and then wait for an error message to be transmitted back to their computer.

FIGURE H-2: Source code for Web page dialog box

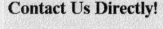

Opening script tags

Closing script tags

```
<HTML>

<HEAD>
<TITLE>Nomad Ltd online</TITLE>

<SCRIPT LANGUAGE="javascript">
<!--
function submitted() {
        alert("Information submitted!")
}
//-->
</SCRIPT>

</HEAD>

<BODY BACKGROUND="egg shell.jpg">

<IMG SRC="nomad.jpg" ALIGN="right" WIDTH=201 HEIGHT=63>

<H1>Nomad Ltd Home Page!</H1>

<H2>Learn About Our Company's Philosophy</H2>

<DIV ID=text>
Nomad Ltd has b
time, we have c
```

Script-generated dialog box

Types Of Nomad Tours

- Athlete: For those who are sports participants.
- Arts: Dedicated to enjoying and appreciating the performing arts.
- Leisure: Designed to let you relax and rejuvenate.

Tell Us More About Y

Microsoft Internet Explorer ☒

⚠ Information submitted!

OK

First Name: Lydia
Street Address: 733 Baker Street
City: Springfield   State:
Click here to submit this information. Send now!

Contact Us Directly!

Find out more about what we have to offer. Contact the tour office at
Tourdirector@nomadltd.com

CLUES TO USE

Linking to an external script

In addition to typing script code directly into a Web page, you can add scripts to your pages by using an HTML code that references a separate file containing script code. A script located in an external file that you can link to a Web page is known as a **scriptlet**. Scriptlets make it easier to share code and to reuse scripts on multiple pages by allowing you to use a script without needing to paste its code into each Web page.

Debugging a Script

No matter how carefully scripting code is entered, a script often contains errors, or **bugs**, the first time your browser processes it. In general, a bug causes the script to return unexpected and undesired results. These may include improper text formatting, the display of HTML or JavaScript code in the browser window, or, in the worst case, requiring you to exit and restart the browser. It's doubtful that simple errors you make entering the scripts in this book could hang your browser. However, when your results are different than those shown in this text, you can use a process called **debugging** to systematically identify and fix your script's bugs. Lydia reads up on debugging scripts and learns about several main culprits that cause undesired results. These are illustrated in Figure H-3.

Details

Capitalization
JavaScript is a **case-sensitive** language, meaning that it treats capital and lowercase versions of the same letter as different characters. Thus, depending on the script being entered, capitalizing or not capitalizing letters can result in errors. Always check that you have used capital letters where called for and that all the capital letters in your script are correct.

Spacing
When entering script code from a printed source, it is easy to add extra spaces or to leave spaces out. Some parts of JavaScript syntax allow for extra spaces, which makes code easier to view and understand. However, as in HTML, incorrect spacing in certain parts of a script can render otherwise-perfect code incomprehensible to the browser. The best way to avoid spacing errors is to pay careful attention to spacing while you enter code.

Parentheses ( ), brackets [ ], braces { }, and quotes " "
JavaScript often uses these four types of symbols to enclose arguments, values, or numbers upon which certain commands are executed. In more complex scripts, you may end up with several sets enclosing other sets, which makes it easy to forget to type one or more closing symbols. In lines or blocks of script where these symbols are concentrated, it can be difficult to check for accuracy. However, to ensure that your script will run properly, you must make sure that each one is paired with its counterpart.

Typographical errors (0 vs. O, 1 vs. I)
Another common source of errors when entering code from printed material is interchanging characters that appear similar, such as the number 0 and the letter O. Generally, the context provides good clues to figuring this out. For example, even if you don't know the function of the expression "value=0", the use of the word *value* gives you a good clue to type a number rather than a letter. Ultimately, the best way to avoid confusing these symbols is to analyze what the script is doing in the current line. Once you understand this, it should be obvious which character to type.

Others
Inevitably, various other sources of error will creep into your scripts. To help you deal with miscellaneous problems, as well as those detailed earlier, JavaScript-compatible browsers often display a JavaScript Error window, as shown in Figure H-4, when they can't interpret your code. Generally, the window describes the type of error the browser encountered and the error's location, referenced by its line number in the script. With this information, some investigation of your code, and a bit of thought, you can track down and fix most any bug that crops up.

Now that you understand the basics of working with scripts, you can begin to learn how to construct your own scripts.

FIGURE H-3: JavaScript containing common bugs

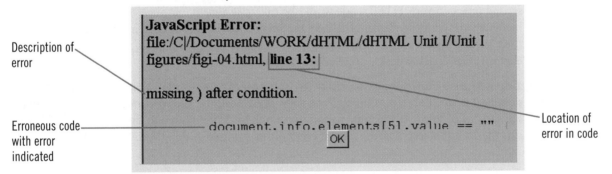

```
<HTML>

<HEAD>
<TITLE>Nomad Ltd online</TITLE>
<SCRIPT LANGUAGE="javascript">
<!--
function submit() {}

function verify() {
        if (document.info.elements[O].value == "" ||
        document.info.elements[1].value == "" ||
        Document.info.elements[2].value == "" ||
        document.info.elements[3].value == "" ||
        document. info.elements[4].value == "" ||
        document.info.elements[5].value == "" {
                alert("Please complete each field")
        }       else {
                submit()
        }
}
//-->
</SCRIPT>

</HEAD>

<BODY BACKGROUND="egg shell.jpg">
```

Unclosed parentheses

Incorrect capital

Extra space

Letter instead of number

FIGURE H-4: JavaScript Error window

Description of error

Erroneous code with error indicated

JavaScript Error:
file:/C|/Documents/WORK/dHTML/dHTML Unit I/Unit I figures/figi-04.html, line 13:

missing) after condition.

document.info.elements[5].value == ""
[OK]

Location of error in code

Commenting a script

While writing a script, it can be useful to include comments in ordinary language to explain what the script is doing at particular places. These notes can be helpful for you when editing or debugging your script or for someone else who wants to understand how the script works. To add a comment to the end of a line of the script, type // at the end of the line's script code, then type your comment. You also can mark several lines of text in a script as a comment by typing /* at the start of the block and */ at the end.

HTML

Understanding Objects

In order to organize and work with the various parts of the browser window, including the current Web page and each of its elements, JavaScript treats each element in the window as a unit called an **object**. JavaScript gives each object a default name and set of descriptive features based on its location and function. These features include **properties**, which are qualities such as size, location, and type. In a Web page containing a graphic, the IMG tag would be an object, and the WIDTH setting would be one of its properties. Each object also has associated **methods**, which are actions the object can carry out. For example, each frame in a browser window has an associated ALERT method, which allows you to create customized dialog boxes. JavaScript organizes objects in an **object hierarchy**, much like the system of folders used by Windows to keep track of disk contents. As Lydia researches the object hierarchy, she learns different ways to refer to the various elements in a document when writing a script.

To specify an object on a Web page, you need to detail its position in the hierarchy, beginning on the document level and then separating each level name with a period. This method of referencing objects in the hierarchy is called **dot syntax**. For example, to specify an image on a Web page, the name would begin *document.images*. Because a document can contain more than one image, each image is assigned a number, based on the order in which it appears in the Web page code. Other elements such as anchors, hyperlinks, and forms also are assigned numbers. It is important to note, however, that in JavaScript, this numbering begins with 0. Thus, when writing a script that refers to the first image in your HTML code, you would use the name *document.images[0]*. The second image in your HTML code would be called *document.images[1]* according to the object hierarchy. To specify an element such as a button or a text field contained inside a form you would use a slightly longer address. For example *document.forms[0].elements[0]* would refer to the first element created in the first form in a Web document.

You also use dot syntax to refer to an object's methods. For example, the code *document.write("Copyright Course Technology, 1999.")* calls on the *write* method of the *document* object. This code causes the information in parenthesis to be written to the document. Table H-1 lists the default objects that are part of every browser window, along with their methods.

TABLE H-1: Default JavaScript objects and methods

object name	method name	description
window	alert(message)	Displays a dialog box with a message in the window
	close()	Closes the window
	prompt(message, default_text)	Displays a dialog box prompting the user for information
	scroll(x, y)	Scrolls to the x.y coordinate in the window
frame	alert(message)	Displays a dialog box with a message in the frame
	close()	Closes the frame
	prompt(message, default_text)	Displays a dialog box prompting the user for information
history	back()	Returns to the previous page in the history list
	forward()	Goes to the next page in the history list
location	reload()	Reloads the current page
document	write()	Writes text and HTML tags to the current document
	writeln()	Writes text and HTML tags to the current document on a new line
form	reset()	Resets the form
	submit()	Submits the form

CLUES TO USE

Naming an object

When you initially create a page element, you can assign it an ID using the ID property. Then, you can refer to the object by its name instead of using its index number. For example, the code *<FORM ID="input">* assigns the ID *input* to the form. You can then use the form ID *input* rather than *forms[0]* to refer to the form or any elements within it.

You could now refer to this form as *document.input.elements[0]* rather than *document.forms[0].elements[0]*. By assigning a name to each element, such as check boxes or text boxes, you could eliminate the need for index numbers in the address as well.

HTML

Using JavaScript Event Handlers

HTML

In order for your Web pages to interact with users, your scripts must be able to recognize and respond to user actions. Each action by a user is known as an **event**. JavaScript can respond to a user's actions with **event handlers**, which are terms that specify possible user actions. By including an event handler along with a set of instructions, your script can respond to certain user actions when they happen. Table H-2 lists 12 event handlers and describes the event that each one names. ✎ Lydia has read about using event handlers. She wants the Nomad Ltd home page to display a message in the status bar window when a user moves the pointer over the e-mail address. She recognizes that this pointer positioning is an event, and that she can use a script containing an event handler to display the message.

Steps

1. Open HTML H-2.htm in your text editor and save it as a text document with the file-name Event handler.htm
Lydia wants to insert her script code in the <A> code near the bottom of the page.

2. Scroll to the end of the document, select the text [insert event handler here] in the <A> tag, then press [Delete]

Trouble?
Be sure you use two apostrophes, rather than a quotation mark, following *onMouseOut="window. status=.*

3. Type the following all on the same line, without pressing [Enter]:
onMouseOver="window.status='We will reply to your inquiry within 24 hours!';return true" onMouseOut="window.status='';return true"
The completed script is shown in Figure H-5. Even without pressing Enter, your text editor may wrap the text onto multiple lines. This will not affect the accuracy of your code. The window.status object refers to the status bar. In this script, the onMouseOver event handler instructs the browser to display the text typed between the apostrophes in the status bar when the pointer is over the hypertext link. In this script, the onMouseOut event handler instructs the browser to clear the text—that is, to display nothing in the status bar—when the mouse pointer is moved off the hypertext link. The text is cleared as indicated by the apostrophes containing no text or spaces that follow the second window.status.

4. Check the document for errors, make changes as necessary, then save Event handler.htm as a text document

5. Open the file Event handler.htm in your Web browser, then scroll to the bottom of the page
Notice that the status bar contains information about the loading status of the current Web page.

Trouble?
If your message does not appear correctly, check to be sure you have typed the script exactly as shown in Step 3.

6. Move the mouse pointer over the link Tourdirector@nomadltd.com, but do not click
The scripted message appears in the status bar, as shown in Figure H-6.

7. Move the mouse pointer off the link
The message no longer appears in the status bar.

FIGURE H-5: Completed script containing new event handlers

```
<H2>Tell Us More About Yourself!</H2>
<FORM NAME="info">
First Name:<INPUT TYPE="TEXT" SIZE=20 NAME="firstname">
Last Name: <INPUT TYPE="TEXT" SIZE=20 NAME="lastname"><BR>
Street Address:<INPUT TYPE="TEXT" SIZE=50 NAME="address"><BR>
City: <INPUT TYPE="TEXT" SIZE=20 NAME="city">
State:<INPUT TYPE="TEXT" SIZE=6 NAME="state">
Zip Code:<INPUT TYPE="TEXT" SIZE=15 NAME="zipcode">
<BR>Click here to submit this information. <INPUT TYPE="BUTTON" VALUE="Send
now!" onClick="submitted()">
</FORM>

<H2>Contact Us Directly!</H2>

Find out more about what we have to offer. Contact the tour
office at <A HREF="MAILTO:Tourdirector@nomadltd.com"
onMouseOver="window.status='We will reply to your inquiry within 24
hours!';return true" onMouseOut="window.status='';return
true">Tourdirector@nomadltd.com</A>

</BODY>
</HTML>
```

Event handler code entered

FIGURE H-6: Browser displaying status bar message

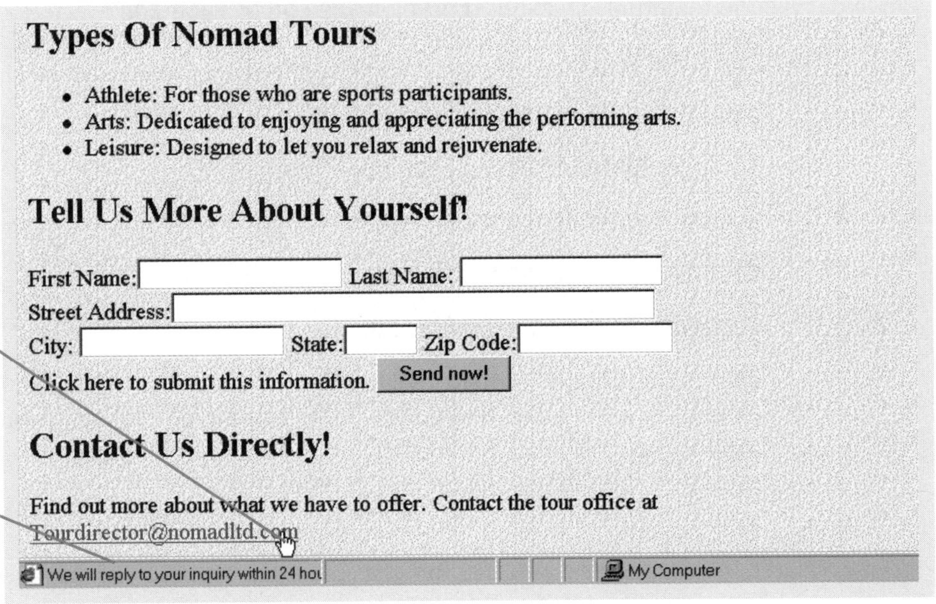

Types Of Nomad Tours

- Athlete: For those who are sports participants.
- Arts: Dedicated to enjoying and appreciating the performing arts.
- Leisure: Designed to let you relax and rejuvenate.

Tell Us About Yourself!

First Name: [   ]   Last Name: [   ]
Street Address: [   ]
City: [   ]   State: [   ]   Zip Code: [   ]
Click here to submit this information. [Send now!]

Contact Us Directly!

Find out more about what we have to offer. Contact the tour office at
Tourdirector@nomadltd.com

Event handler activated by position of pointer

Message in status bar triggered by event handler — We will reply to your inquiry within 24 hou   My Computer

TABLE H-2: JavaScript event handlers

event handler	triggering action	event handler	triggering action
onAbort	Page loading halted	onLoad	Page or image opens
onBlur	Object not current or highlighted	onMouseOut	Mouse pointer not over link
onChange	Object value changed	onMouseOver	Mouse pointer over link
onClick	Hyperlink or button clicked	onSelect	Text selected
onError	Error executing script	onSubmit	Form submitted
onFocus	Object current or highlighted	onUnload	Different page opened

HTML

Creating a Function

As your scripts become more complex, you will begin to incorporate many lines of code in each one to store and process information. To help keep your scripts organized, JavaScript allows you to group and name sets of script code in units called **functions**. A function is a set of code that performs a specific task. When you group the lines of your scripts into functions, the code is logically broken down into functional units, which makes it easier to understand and to debug. You usually define functions in a page's head section, which allows any programmer to quickly scan a page's code. Additionally, because each function has a name, you can easily refer to it in several different parts of a Web page. This means you do not need to duplicate code each time you want your page to repeat a procedure. Lydia wants to add a button to the Web page that will clear the user's input in the form. She writes a function to perform this task.

Steps 1234

1. Open the file **HTML H-3.htm** in your text editor, then save it as a text document with the filename **Function.htm**

   Generally, it's best to define functions at the beginning of a Web page, to make sure they are available for all subsequent uses.

2. Select the text **[replace with clearUp function]** in the page's head section, then press **[Delete]**

3. Type the following, pressing **[Enter]** at the end of each line

   function clearUp() {

       document.info.elements[0].value=""

       document.info.elements[1].value=""

       document.info.elements[2].value=""

       document.info.elements[3].value=""

       document.info.elements[4].value=""

       document.info.elements[5].value=""

   These lines define a function that assigns the value **null**, or nothing, to each of the six text fields on the page. This null value is defined with the paired quotation marks that follow each equal sign and that contain nothing between them.

4. Type }

   Figure H-7 shows the completed function, including the opening and closing braces. The code for a function is always demarcated with braces {}.

5. Scroll to the end of the document, select the text **[replace with Clear button code]**, then press **[Delete]**

6. Type **<INPUT TYPE="BUTTON" value="Clear form" onClick = "clearUp()">**

   The button tag includes an event handler to trigger, or **call**, the function clearUp() when a user clicks the button. Figure H-8 shows the completed button tag in the document.

7. Check the document for errors, make changes as necessary, then save Function.htm as a text document

8. Open **Function.htm** in your Web browser, fill in the six input fields, then click the **Clear form button**

   The browser clears each of the text input fields.

FIGURE H-7: Document containing clearUp() function code

```
<HTML>

<HEAD>
<TITLE>Nomad Ltd online</TITLE>

<SCRIPT LANGUAGE="javascript">
<!--
function submitted() {
      alert("Information submitted!")
}

function clearUp() {
      document.info.elements[0].value=""
      document.info.elements[1].value=""
      document.info.elements[2].value=""
      document.info.elements[3].value=""
      document.info.elements[4].value=""
      document.info.elements[5].value=""
}


//-->
</SCRIPT>

</HEAD>
```

Code defining new function

FIGURE H-8: Document containing clearUp() function reference

```
</UL>

<H2>Tell Us More About Yourself!</H2>
<FORM NAME="info">
First Name:<INPUT TYPE="TEXT" SIZE=20 ID="firstname">
Last Name: <INPUT TYPE="TEXT" SIZE=20 ID="lastname"><BR>
Street Address:<INPUT TYPE="TEXT" SIZE=50 ID="address"><BR>
City: <INPUT TYPE="TEXT" SIZE=20 ID="city">
State:<INPUT TYPE="TEXT" SIZE=6 ID="state">
Zip Code:<INPUT TYPE="TEXT" SIZE=15 ID="zipcode">
<BR>Click here to submit this information. <INPUT TYPE="BUTTON" VALUE="Send
now!" onClick="submitted()">
<BR>Click here to clear the form and start over.
<INPUT TYPE="BUTTON" VALUE="Clear form" onClick="clearUp()">
</FORM>

<H2>Contact Us Directly!</H2>

Find out more about what we have to offer. Contact the tour
office at <A HREF="MAILTO:Tourdirector@nomadltd.com"
onMouseOver="window.status='We will reply to your inquiry within 24
hours!';return true" onMouseOut="window.status='';return
true">Tourdirector@nomadltd.com</A>

</BODY>
</HTML>
```

Code referencing new function

Assigning a Variable

In scripting, you often instruct JavaScript to perform functions on pieces of information that you specify, known as **values**. For example, the text *We will reply to your inquiry within 24 hours!*, which you used earlier in conjunction with an event handler, is a value. Values can also include "true" and "false" and information about the user's browser, such as the width of the window in pixels. JavaScript can add or manipulate any numeric value mathematically. When values are composed of many characters, such as the message text above, or when they change in different situations, such as browser window dimensions, they can be cumbersome if you need to enter them several times in your script. You can make this process easier and more efficient by assigning the value to a **variable**, which serves as a nickname. When you assign a value to a variable, you enter or look up the value only one time and then you use the variable to refer to the value. Using variables saves you time when writing scripts. Variables provide added flexibility by allowing you to modify the value in only one place and have the modifications reflected instantaneously throughout the document as indicated by the variable. ✐ Lydia has modified the Nomad Ltd home page to personalize text by displaying the user's name. To finish her changes, she needs to define the variable she will use to represent the user's name, and then insert the variable name in the scripts.

Steps 1 2 3 4

1. Open the file HTML H-4.htm in your text editor, then save it as a text document with the filename Variable.htm

2. Select the text [replace with variable definition] near the top of the page, then press [Delete]

3. Type the following text on one line, without pressing [Enter]
   var name=prompt("For personal service, please type your first name and click OK.","")
   This line of script creates a dialog box that prompts the user to enter his or her first name and assigns the user's input to a variable named "name". Figure H-9 shows the document with this line of code inserted. The command "var" tells JavaScript that you are specifying a variable. The word following var—in this case, "name"—is the name of the variable you are creating. The value of the new variable follows the name after an equals sign. In this case, the value will be the result of user input in a dialog box created by the "prompt" method.

4. Scroll down to the beginning of the page's body section, select the text [replace with heading script], then press [Delete]
   Notice that Lydia has already inserted the opening and closing script tags.

5. Type the following text on one line, without pressing [Enter]
   document.write("<H1>Welcome to the Nomad Ltd home page, " + name + "!</H1>")
   This script writes a line of code to the Web page, containing H1 tags to format the text. Lydia uses the variable "name" to insert the user's name into the page heading.

6. Scroll down to the beginning of the form section, select the text [replace with second heading script], then press [Delete]

7. Type the following all on one line, without pressing [Enter]
   document.write("<H2>Please tell us more about yourself, " + name + ".</H2>")
   This script places the user's name at a second location in the Web page.

8. Check the document for errors, make changes as necessary, then save Variable.htm as a text document

9. Open the file Variable.htm in your Web browser, type your first name in the prompt dialog box, then click OK
   The Nomad Ltd home page is now personalized. The name the user enters in the prompt dialog box is displayed. See Figure H-10.

Trouble?

Be sure you type a space after the text **page**, and before the closing ".

FIGURE H-9: **Script creating a variable**

```
<HTML>

<HEAD>
<TITLE>Nomad Ltd online</TITLE>

<SCRIPT LANGUAGE="javascript">
<!--
var name=prompt("For personal service, please type your first name and click
OK.","")

function submitted() {
        alert("Information submitted!")
}

function clearUp() {
        document.info.elements[0].value=""
        document.info.elements[1].value=""
        document.info.elements[2].value=""
        document.info.elements[3].value=""
        document.info.elements[4].value=""
        document.info.elements[5].value=""
}

//-->
</SCRIPT>
```

Variable inserted in script

FIGURE H-10: **Web page incorporating user information**

Welcome to the Nomad Ltd home page, Lydia!

Nomad Ltd

Learn About Our Company's Philosophy

Nomad Ltd has been in business for over ten years. During that time, we have offered tours to exotic (and simple) lands and sold sporting equipment (for bicycling, hiking, and other activities). In all that time, we have always been aware that our employees are our corporate ambassadors, and our customers are our royalty. We know that any company can make a buck here and there, but we want to do more than that. We want you to enjoy shopping at our stores and contribute to making Nomad a fun and interesting place to shop. We also know that as a business, we are also community members. Nomad wants to contribute to community efforts and make each town we're in a better place to live and shop. How do we do that? By hiring from the community, offering educational and financial benefits to our employees, and becoming involved in various community efforts.

Types Of Nomad Tours

User name incorporated into Web page text generated by script

Manipulating variables

In addition to simply using variable values that a user enters or that a script looks up, your scripts can process values using **arithmetic operators**, which allow you to manipulate variables mathematically to create new values. For example, to count page headings, you could create a script that reads through your Web page code, adding 1 to a variable value each time it encounters a heading tag. You also could combine several values that a user enters using a mathematical equation.

Creating a Conditional

Sometimes, you want a script to be able to create different results depending on different user actions or on the value of a certain browser attribute. JavaScript allows you to set up this situation by creating a **conditional** in your script. A conditional allows your script to choose one of two paths, depending on a condition that you specify. For example, you might want a graphic to display at a smaller size if a user's window is not maximized, to keep it fully in view. You could use a conditional to check the dimensions of the user's browser window and then set the graphic dimensions to one of two preset choices. Conditionals allow you to create flexible, interactive scripts whose output can change in different situations. Nomad Ltd has had a problem with users submitting forms missing the zip code information. Lydia wants her Web page to verify that the user has completed the zip code form field before it submits the data to the server. Using a conditional, her page can prompt the user to complete the field if it is left blank.

Steps

1. Open the file HTML H-5.htm in your text editor, then save it as a text document with the filename Conditional.htm

2. Select [replace with verify function] in the page's head section and press [Delete]

3. Type the following code, pressing [Enter] at the end of each line

```
function verify() {
        if (document.info.elements[5].value == "") {
                alert("Please complete each field.")
        }       else {
                submitted()
        }
}
```

Figure H-11 shows the document containing the verify function. The "if" statement code checks if the value of the zipcode field is null, indicating that the user has left it blank. When the "if" statement returns a value of "true," the function executes the code that immediately follows it. Here, the "true" result triggers the "alert" command to create a dialog box prompting the user to complete each field. When the "if" statement returns a value of "false," the function executes the code following the word *else*. In Lydia's script, the else command runs a function called "submitted()" that sends the user's information to the Web server.

4. Scroll to the bottom of the form section, select the text [replace with event handler] in the tag for the Send now! button, then press [Delete]

5. Type onClick="verify()"

6. Check scripts you added for errors, make changes as necessary, then save Conditional.htm as a text document

7. Open Conditional.htm in your Web browser, enter your name, scroll down to the form, then click the Send now! button without filling in any of the fields
The script runs and displays the dialog box shown in Figure H-12.

8. Click the OK button, then fill in each of the fields with sample information and click the Send now! button
The script you added verifies that the zip code field contains information and then allows the form submit function to execute.

FIGURE H-11: Web document containing completed script

Condition

Conditional terms

"false" result

"true" result

```
                    document.info.elements[5].value=""
            }

function verify() {
        if (document.info.elements[5].value == "") {
                alert("Please complete each field.")
        }       else {
                submitted()
        }
}

//-->
</SCRIPT>

</HEAD>

<BODY BACKGROUND="egg shell.jpg">

<IMG SRC="nomad.jpg" ALIGN="right" WIDTH=201 HEIGHT=63>

<SCRIPT LANGUAGE="javascript">
<!--
document.write("<H1>Welcome to the Nomad Ltd home page, " + name + "!</H1>")
//-->
</SCRIPT>
```

FIGURE H-12: Browser showing alert dialog box

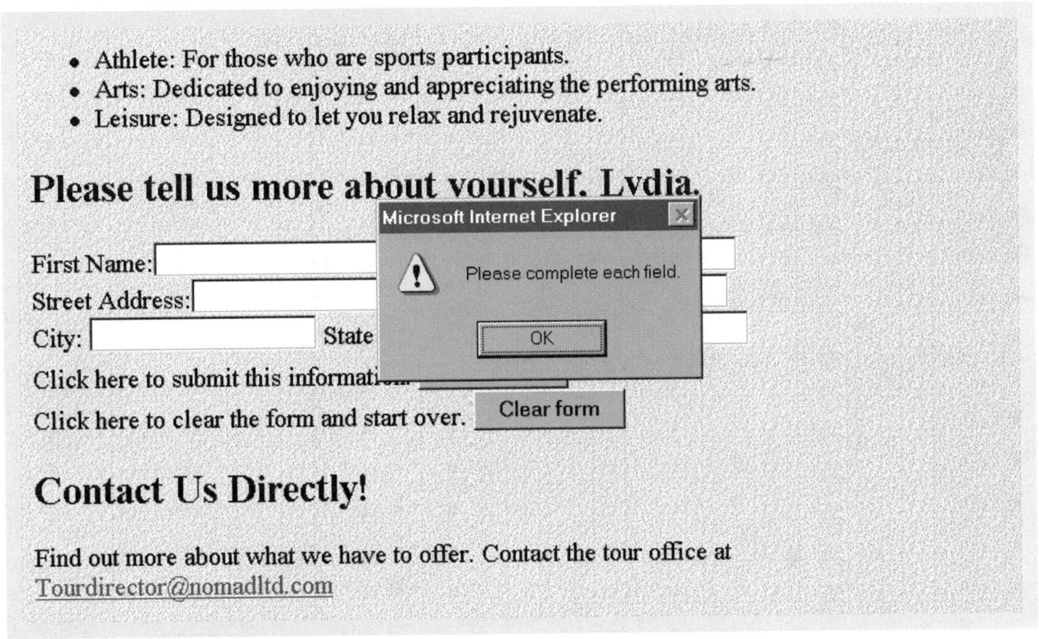

- Athlete: For those who are sports participants.
- Arts: Dedicated to enjoying and appreciating the performing arts.
- Leisure: Designed to let you relax and rejuvenate.

Please tell us more about yourself, Lydia,

First Name:
Street Address:
City: State

Microsoft Internet Explorer

⚠ Please complete each field.

OK

Click here to submit this informat...
Click here to clear the form and start over. Clear form

Contact Us Directly!

Find out more about what we have to offer. Contact the tour office at
Tourdirector@nomadltd.com

CLUES TO USE

Testing multiple conditions

In addition to using a conditional to test a single condition, you test multiple conditions using logical comparison operators. JavaScript recognizes three logical comparison operators: && ("and"), || ("or"), and ! ("not"). A conditional using the && operator between two or more conditions returns "true" only if all conditions are true. Linking multiple conditions with the || operator, however, returns "true" if any one of the conditions is true. The ! operator returns true if its associated condition is not true.

Practice

► Concepts Review

Label each item shown in Figure H-13.

FIGURE H-13

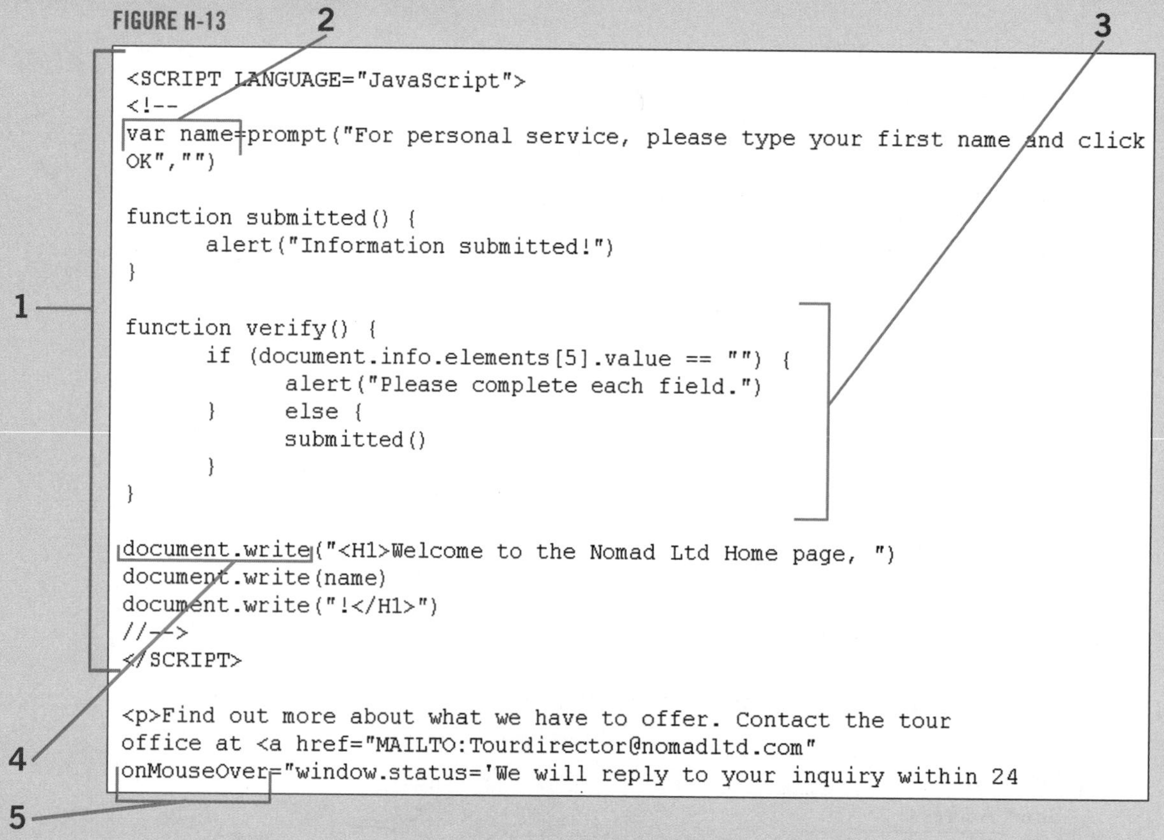

```
<SCRIPT LANGUAGE="JavaScript">
<!--
var name=prompt("For personal service, please type your first name and click
OK","")

function submitted() {
        alert("Information submitted!")
}

function verify() {
        if (document.info.elements[5].value == "") {
                alert("Please complete each field.")
        } else {
                submitted()
        }
}

document.write("<H1>Welcome to the Nomad Ltd Home page, ")
document.write(name)
document.write("!</H1>")
//-->
</SCRIPT>

<p>Find out more about what we have to offer. Contact the tour
office at <a href="MAILTO:Tourdirector@nomadltd.com"
onMouseOver="window.status='We will reply to your inquiry within 24
```

Match each statement with the term it describes.

6. Object hierarchy
7. Event handler
8. Bug
9. Method
10. JavaScript

a. Term specifying a possible user action
b. An error in a script
c. A Web page scripting language
d. JavaScript's object organization
e. Any action an object can carry out

Select the best answer from the list of choices.

11. **What HTML tagset marks the beginning and end of a script?**
    a. <JS>..</JS>
    b. <JAVASCRIPT>..</JAVASCRIPT>
    c. <SCRIPT>..</SCRIPT>
    d. <JAVASCRIPT>..<JAVASCRIPT>

12. **Which scripting language is compatible with both Netscape Navigator 4 and Microsoft Internet Explorer 4?**
    a. JScript
    b. JavaScript
    c. HTML
    d. VBScript

13. **Which of the following typing mistakes would not result in an error in your script?**
    a. Substituting the letter l for the number 1
    b. Inserting an extra space
    c. Omitting a closing bracket
    d. All of the above could result in errors.

14. **What would be the proper form of address in the object hierarchy for the second element in a form called "info"?**
    a. document.info.elements[1]
    b. document.info.elements[2]
    c. document.forms.info.elements[2]
    d. info.elements[2]

15. **What is the function of the string <!-- in scripting?**
    a. It is the HTML code for the beginning of a script.
    b. It is the HTML code for the end of a script.
    c. It tells an incompatible browser to ignore the code that follows.
    d. It tells the browser to display the text "--"

16. **Which comparison operator returns true only if the values before and after are both true?**
    a. &&
    b. ||
    c. !
    d. ==

17. **A set of script code grouped logically and named is called a(n)**
    a. Object.
    b. Variable.
    c. Hierarchy.
    d. Function.

▶ Skills Review

1. Create a script.

a. Open the text editor, open the file HTML H-6.htm, then save it as a text document with the filename Script review.htm.

b. Select the text [replace with script tags] in the page's head section, then press [Delete].

c. Type <SCRIPT LANGUAGE="javascript"> and press [Enter].

d. Type <!-- and press [Enter] twice.

e. Type //--> and press [Enter], then type </SCRIPT>.

f. Save Script review.htm as a text document.

g. Open Script review.htm in your Web browser.

2. Debug a script.

a. Open the file HTML H-7.htm in your browser, read the description of the error in the JavaScript Error dialog box, then click yes.

b. Open the file HTML H-7.htm in your text editor, then save it as a text document with the filename Debug review.htm.

c. Position the pointer in the third line of the clearUp() function, which begins document.info.elements[2].value, then insert a second quotation mark (") after the existing one at the end of the line.

d. Save Debug review.htm as a text document, open Debug review.htm in your Web browser, enter information in the form, then click the Clear form button.

3. Use JavaScript event handlers.

a. Open the file HTML H-8.htm in your text editor, then save it as a text document with the filename Event handler review.htm.

b. Scroll to the bottom of the document, select the text "[replace with event handler]" in the first <A> tag, then press [Delete].

c. Type the following without pressing [Enter]:
onMouseOver="window.status='Guidelines on scheduling vacation time';return true"
onMouseOut="window.status='';return true"

d. Review your typing for errors, then save Event handler review.htm as a text document.

e. Open Event handler review.htm in your Web browser, move the mouse pointer over the hypertext link "Additional vacation information" and verify that the message "Guidelines on scheduling vacation time" appears in the status bar.

f. If necessary, fix any errors in your text editor, then save and preview the page.

4. Create a function.

a. Open the file HTML H-9.htm in your text editor, then save it as a text document with the filename Function review.htm.

b. Select the text "[replace with date function]" in the page's head section, then press [Delete].

c. Type function writeDate() {

d. Press [Enter], then type document.write(month + "/" + today.getDate() + "/" + today.getYear() + ".")

e. Press [Enter], then type }

f. Select the text [replace with function call] near the bottom of the page, then type writeDate()

g. Save Function review.htm as a text document.

h. Open Function review.htm in your browser, verify that it displays the current date below the list of vacation dates, use your text editor to make changes if necessary, then save Function review.htm as a text document.

5. Assign a variable.

a. Open the file HTML H-10.htm in your text editor, then save it as a text document with the filename Variable review.htm.

b. Select the text [replace with variable code] in the page's head section, then type var name=prompt("Please type your first name and click OK","").

c. Select the text [replace with variable reference] at the top of the body section, then press [Delete].

d. Type document.write(name).

e. Save Variable review.htm as a text document, then open Variable review.htm in your browser.

f. Type your first name, then click OK.

g. Use your text editor to debug as needed.

6. Create a conditional.

a. Open the file HTML H-11.htm in your text editor, then save it as a text document with the filename Conditional review.htm.

b. Select the text [replace with conditional function] in the page's head section, then press [Delete].

c. Type the following code, pressing [Enter] at the end of each line:

```
function verify() {
        if (document.info.elements[0].value == "" ||
        document.info.elements[1].value == "" ||
        document.info.elements[2].value == "" ||
        document.info.elements[3].value == "" ||
        document.info.elements[4].value == "" ||
        document.info.elements[5].value == "") {
                alert("Please complete each field.")
        }       else {
                submitted()
        }
}
```

d. Review your code for typing errors, then save Conditional review.htm as a text document.

e. Open Conditional review.htm in your browser, fill in every field in the form except the last name field, click the "Submit now!" button, verify that your browser opens a dialog box asking you to complete all the fields, then click OK.

f. Close your text editor and browser.

HTML

► Independent Challenges

1. Green House, a local plant store, has hired you to add interactive features to their Web pages. You've decided to start by using an event handler to display link explanations in the status bar when users point to the page's links.

To complete this independent challenge:

a. Start your text editor program, open the file HTML H-12.htm, then save it as a text document with the filename Green House home.htm.

b. To define the text strings that will be displayed as variables, select the text [replace with variable script] at the top of the page, press [Delete], and insert the following script, pressing [Enter] at the end of each line:

```
<SCRIPT LANGUAGE="javascript">
<!--
var plants="An overview of our plant stock and sources"
var tips="Helpful growing hints on common houseplants"
var services="A guide to our professional plant care services"
//-->
</SCRIPT>
```

c. Select the text "[replace with first event handlers]" in the <A> tag for the first link at the bottom of the page, press [Delete], and type the following without pressing [Enter]:
onMouseOver="window.status=plants;return true"onMouseOut="window.status='';return true"

d. Repeat Step c to modify the second link with the following insertion:
onMouseOver="window.status=tips;return true" onMouseOut="window.status='';return true"

e. Repeat Step c to modify the third link with the following insertion:
onMouseOver="window.status=services;return true" onMouseOut="window.status='';return true"

f. Save Green House home.htm as a text document, then open the file Green House home.htm in your Web browser.

g. Use your text editor to make any changes necessary, always save the file as a text document, then close your text editor and browser.

2. You have designed a Web publication for Sandhills Regional Public Transit. You want to incorporate a function you've written to tell prospective riders which fare period is in effect. A sentence stating the fare period will display at the bottom of the Web page. This sentence will change depending on the time of day.

To complete this independent challenge:

a. Start your text editor program, open the file HTML H-13.htm, then save it as a text document with the filename SRPT home.htm.

b. Replace the text [replace with fare function] in the page's head section with the script located in the file HTML H-14.txt.

c. Scroll down immediately before the closing body section tag, delete the text [replace with function call script], enter the two opening script tags, type "schedTime()" (without the quotes) as the third line of the script, then enter the two closing script tags.

d. Save and preview your file in your Web browser program, debugging as necessary until you see no more JavaScript error messages.

3. You have been hired by Community Public School Volunteers to add advanced features to their Web publication using scripts. You have inserted a script into the home page they provided, but a JavaScript error dialog box opens when the page loads. To complete this independent challenge, preview the file HTML H-15.htm in your browser, noting the type of JavaScript error described and its location. Open the page in your text editor and save a copy as CPSV home.htm. Edit the script to fix the JavaScript error. Use the guidelines listed earlier in the unit to identify the types of errors that may be present. Continue to preview and edit the page until you no longer receive an error message, then save your work in your text editor as a text file.

4. Scripts are used in many Web pages on the WWW today to add features, as well as to create interesting formatting that is not possible with standard HTML coding. To complete this independent challenge, find two pages on the Web that contain scripts. (*Hint:* after opening a page in your browser, choose the HTML or Page Source option in your browser's View menu to check the document code for <SCRIPT> tags.) Print their HTML source code, and circle all scripts you see on your printouts. Circle and label any variables, conditionals, and functions you see in the documents.

▶ Visual Workshop

Open your text editor program, open the file HTML H-16.htm, and save it as a text document named Touchstone.htm. Then open Touchstone.htm in your browser. Scroll down to see the Send now! button. Click the Send now! button on the form without entering information in any of the fields. Use the form-verification script located in the file HTML H-17.txt and your text editor to modify the document Touchstone.htm. Change the event handler for the Send now! button to run the verify() function. Save the changes as a text document with the filename Touchstone.htm. Click the browser program button on the taskbar, and refresh your screen. Click the Send now! button again. Your screen should look like Figure H-14. Debug as necessary. (*Hint:* Remember to insert the verification script in the document header section between the beginning and ending script tags.)

FIGURE H-14

Working
with Dynamic HTML (DHTML)

Objectives

- ► **Define Dynamic HTML**
- ► **Understand the building blocks of DHTML**
- ► **Tour DHTML pages**
- ► **Understand the DHTML Object Model**
- ► **Understand browser variability**
- ► **Design DHTML pages**
- ► **Research code architecture**
- ► **Keep up with DHTML changes**

Once you have an understanding of standard HTML and Web page design, you can create well-structured Web pages that use effective style combinations and that allow basic user input. However, recent innovations in Web page design and scripting, collectively known as **Dynamic HTML** (or **DHTML** for short), have revolutionized Web page design. DHTML has greatly increased the degree of interactivity possible in Web page design. With DHTML, your Web pages are enlivened as text and graphics change color, grow, shrink, and move on and off the page in response to user actions. Lydia Burgos, who works in the information systems department at Nomad Ltd, has read about Dynamic HTML and wants to explore using it in her company's Web pages. She starts with some research to learn about what DHTML is and how it works.

Defining DHTML

During the early 1990's, all Web pages were simple documents that users downloaded and viewed on their local computers. Each Web page's interactivity was limited to hyperlinks, which opened other Web pages, opened new mail messages, or ran scripts on the server. Web pages that fit this description are known as **static HTML**. Today, however, many Web pages respond to and even interact with the user by changing their appearances based on user actions. Such pages use **dynamic HTML**, which describes a varied set of technologies that allow almost-immediate response to user actions in a Web page without accessing the Internet server. In her research, Lydia learns of several broad categories of design that DHTML allows.

Details

Dynamic style

When you create a page using standard HTML coding, you specify a style for each text element. These styles remain the same, regardless of user actions. The one exception to this is hyperlinks; their color may be changed by the browser if you have followed them recently. However, when you create a page using DHTML, you can incorporate styles—including font size, typeface, and color—that change immediately in response to user actions, such as moving the mouse pointer over a heading. This feature, known as **dynamic style**, allows your pages to emphasize an area when a user shows interest in it, without flooding the page with distracting large font sizes or bright colors. Figure I-1 provides an example of dynamic style. Notice on this DHTML page that the text color has changed, which is the result of DHTML. If the user selects this hyperlink, the color will change again to show that it has been viewed already.

Dynamic content

A DHTML Web page can display different content based on a user's activities, which is a feature known as **dynamic content**. Instead of taking the time to request, download, and display a new Web page (as standard HTML coding would do), DHTML utilities can simply hide or display blocks of text or other elements in the current page. This aspect of DHTML allows you to create a simple, well-organized, and visually appealing page that can instantly display extra information when the user is likely to be interested in it. Figure I-1 provides an example of dynamic content. Notice the message displayed in the status window, which is the result of DHTML.

Data-awareness

Standard HTML tools allow your Web pages to download chunks of information, such as database contents, from a Web server as a user requests access to them. With DHTML, this process is instantaneous for the user; for example, a DHTML Web page could be designed to download a complete database but then display only the information the user wants to view. A Web page equipped to work with data in this way is termed **data aware**, which means the user can work with information from a Web server without adding to Internet traffic by repeatedly requesting additional pieces of information. Also, data awareness can allow the user to manipulate and change the information right in the browser window.

Positioning

As with other formatting options, static HTML leaves many of the choices regarding the positioning of elements in a Web page to the browser's discretion. In addition to causing pages to display nonuniformly and unpredictably on different browsers, this aspect of HTML has prevented Web page design from rivaling the intricacy inherent in the best layouts of other media, such as magazines. DHTML represents an important step toward changing this by allowing Web page designers to specify precisely the location of all page elements, a feature known as **positioning**, which is unavailable in standard HTML. The Web page in Figure I-2, which is from an online tutorial on DHTML, uses DHTML to position text in combinations not possible with static HTML.

FIGURE I-1: Dynamic Web page

Classes to be offered, Fall 2000

- Introduction to Biology I
- Introduction to Biology II
- Plant Physiology
- Plant Chemistry
- Plant Field Practicum
- Marine Biology
- Introductory Microbiology
- Immunology
- Directed Study

Dynamic Web page on opening

Classes to be offered, Fall 2000

- Introduction to Biology I
- Introduction to Biology II
- Plant Physiology
- Plant Chemistry
- Plant Field Practicum
- Marine Biology
- Introductory Microbiology
- Immunology
- Directed Study

Text changes color when pointer positioned over it

Text appears in status window in response to pointer position

Fall registration begins August 15, 2000.   My Computer

FIGURE I-2: Web page formatted with DHTML positioning

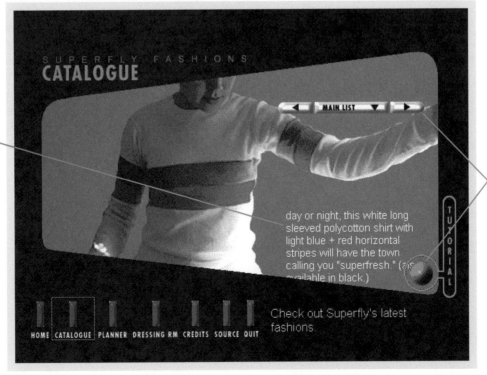

Text positioned over graphic

SUPERFLY FASHIONS
CATALOGUE

MAIN LIST

day or night, this white long sleeved polycotton shirt with light blue + red horizontal stripes will have the town calling you "superfresh." (also available in black.)

Check out Superfly's latest fashions.

HOME CATALOGUE PLANNER DRESSING RM CREDITS SOURCE QUIT

TUTORIAL

Graphics positioned over other graphic

Understanding the Building Blocks of DHTML

The creation of simple Web pages, while drawing on organization, design, and content-production skills, uses only HTML for arrangement and display in a browser. By contrast, DHTML is not a language or even a single technology, but, rather, a collection of Web page tools that, when used in various combinations, let designers create the effects specified in the previous lesson. As she reads more about DHTML, Lydia learns that DHTML is comprised of two main tools that work in tandem with standard HTML. These DHTML tools are included in the Web page source code shown in Figure I-3.

 Client-side scripts

Scripts are small programs that can be triggered by a user's action on a Web page. In the early days of the Web, browsers allowed only the use of **server-side scripts**, or scripts that were stored and run on the Web server. Using these server-side scripts was similar to triggering a hyperlink. Each time a server-side script was run, the Web page sent a message to the server instructing it to run the script. Users had to wait as the browser downloaded the results of the server-side script. The lag time involved in this setup made features such as dynamic content and dynamic style impractical. Recent versions of browsers have allowed Web page designers to create **client-side scripts**, or scripts that the browser itself interprets and runs. Client-side scripts are a key element in allowing DHTML to respond immediately to user actions. For example, the client-side script at the bottom of Figure I-3 changes the text color and adds text to the status window when the mouse pointer moves over certain text.

Cascading Style Sheets (CSS)

In standard HTML, you assign styles and properties to elements of your page—text blocks, images, and other objects—through HTML tags. This system means that each element has its own set of properties. Even if two elements share the same properties, you must assign them separately and make any subsequent changes to each element. Although you can assign similar properties to groups of elements using defined styles, such as <H1>, these styles are defined on each user's browser, and thus you cannot predict exactly how a viewer will see your page in the browser window. **Cascading Style Sheets (CSS)** is a tool that allows you to specify attributes such as color and font size for all page elements marked by a specific tag, name, or ID. CSS not only gives designers a more efficient way to specify style but also more control over an object's attributes as well as how each object should be displayed in certain situations. For example, the Cascading Style Sheet in Figure I-3 assigns attributes to various tags. All text marked with these tags, such as <LI> and <P>, will display the attributes defined for this tag in the style sheet.

FIGURE I-3: Code for Web page incorporating DHTML tools

Cascading
Style Sheet

```
<STYLE TYPE="text/css">
body {background:navy; color:white}
LI {list-style-image: none; list-style: none}
UL.toc {display:none}
UL.expanded {display:block}
A.select {color:white; background:blue}
.over {color:red}
P {margin-top:0; margin-bottom:0}
</STYLE>
```

Client-side
script

```
<SCRIPT LANGUAGE="JavaScript">
<!--
var curSelection = null;

function setStyle(src, toClass) {
        if (null != src)
        src.className = toClass;
}

function mouseEnters() {
        if ((curSelection != event.toElement) && ("A" ==
event.toElement.tagName)) {
                setStyle(event.toElement,"over");
                window.status="Fall registration begins August 15, 2000."
        }
}
```

Clues to Use

Proprietary features

Both Netscape and Microsoft have each introduced unique features, known as **proprietary features**, into their browsers. For example, Netscape Navigator 4 allows use of the <LAYER> tag to overlap screen elements easily. Microsoft Internet Explorer 4 supports the embedding of external tables in a Web page, as well as a set of features that affect element appearance in complex ways. Eventually, some of these technologies become part of new international Web page standards. When proprietary features become part of the industry standard, they eventually become supported by the major browsers and are then no longer considered proprietary features. However, proprietary features that are supported by only one of the two major browsers are most useful only in single-browser settings, such as intranets whose users all run the same browser.

HTML

Touring DHTML Pages

Although DHTML technology may sound intriguing, viewing and interacting with it is the only way to get a true sense of its impact and capabilities. Looking at existing pages, both successful and not, is also a useful way to begin planning the features you want to include in your own pages. ✎ Lydia has downloaded several sample Web pages that incorporate features she has researched. She opens and tests them as she begins collecting ideas for updating the Nomad Ltd Web site.

Steps 1 2 3 4

Trouble?
If you are using Navigator, some text on the page may be arranged differently from that shown in the figures. However, all of the features of the page should still work.

1. **Start your Web browser program, open the file HTML I-1.htm, then scroll down the page to view its layout**
As Figure I-4 shows, this page contains several blocks of text positioned around the page; each of these is an example of DHTML positioning. The designer of this Web page created the sidebar along the right edge of the screen by using DHTML style specifications to position the text, specify its width, and specify a background color for the text block.

2. **Scroll down the page until the heading Blue Ray appears in your document window, then move your mouse pointer over the heading Blue Ray**
If you are using Internet Explorer 4, notice that the text color changes from black to purple and that the text size increases—an example of **dynamic style**. Netscape Navigator 4 does not support most dynamic styles and shows no change when your mouse pointer is over this heading.

3. **Click the heading Blue Ray**
A paragraph of detailed information appears beneath the heading, without the page reloading, as shown in Figure I-5. This is an example of **dynamic content** because user activity can affect the page content.

4. **Watch the text in the status window**
A message continuously scrolls across the status window. This feature, created by a script, is another example of dynamic content.

5. **Scroll to the top of the page, and move your mouse pointer over one of the links under the heading "Learn more about Jim's!"**
As the pointer moves over link text or an image, the link image changes. When the pointer moves off the link, the image returns to its original appearance, which is an instance of dynamic content. Rather than simply changing a graphic's display properties, the position of the pointer over the link triggers a script that changes the source of the image in the image tag. The pointer movement causes the image to toggle between two different source files.

QuickTip
Currently, data binding is a proprietary feature of Internet Explorer 4, but an extension is available from the Microsoft Web site that allows Netscape Navigator 4 to display this and other Internet Explorer 4 features.

6. **If you are using Internet Explorer, open the file HTML I-2.htm and scroll to the bottom of the page**
As Figure I-6 shows, this page contains a data table. Unlike standard HTML tables, however, this table was generated from an external file as the Web page opened. Linking a Web page to an external data file is known as **data binding**. If you added or changed records in the external file, they would be reflected in the Web page the next time you opened it without requiring any changes in the Web page's code. A related feature, known as **data-awareness**, allows a Web page to load all the records from a database but display only some of them. Then, a user can access any record instantly without needing to download more information to the browser.

FIGURE I-4: Sample DHTML Web page

All-natural,
quality berries
and berry
products

Jim's

Blueberry Farm

Learn more about Jim's!

 Tour the farm

 Directions for visiting us

 Picking season and hours

Here's another great blueberry idea from our kitchen!

Blueberry tart

Pastry:
1-1/4 c white flour
2 T sugar

Positioned elements

FIGURE I-5: Dynamic content and style changes

 Picking season and hours

 Products by mail

Click the names of blueberry breeds below to read about our selection:

Blue Ray

highbush type, 4 to 6 ft. at maturity, fruit ripening mid/late July, yields 10 to 20 lbs per bush, fruit size large (approx. 60 berries per cup).

Blue Jay

Pastry:
1-1/4 c white flour
2 T sugar
5/8 cup butter
2 T water or milk
Filling:
1/2 c sugar
2 T white flour
1/4 t cinnamon
1/2 t ground coriander
pinch nutmeg
3-1/2 c blueberries
Topping:
1-1/4 c blueberries

To prepare crust, mix flour and sugar. Cut butter in to mixture with pastry blender. Add 2 T water to moisten (more if required). Roll mixture and place in 9" pie plate.

Text color changes in response to pointer position

New text appears after click

FIGURE I-6: Web page containing bound data

products

The following table summarizes the information on all our blueberry types. Click any table heading to sort the table by that column.

Bush	Type	Height	Fruit maturity	Yield per bush	Berry size	Berries per cup
Blue Ray	high	4-6 ft.	mid/late July	10-20 lb.	large	60
Blue Jay	high	5-7 ft.	late July	7-10 lb.	small/medium	110
Jersey	high	5-7 ft.	late July	7-10 lb.	small/medium	110
Elliott	high	5-7 ft.	late Aug./early Sept.	10-20 lb	small/medium	75
Northland	medium	3-4 ft.	early July	15-20	small	135

Table generated from linked external data source

HTML

Understanding the DHTML Object Model

Developers of early scripting languages created an **object hierarchy**, which is a system of organization that allows Web page developers to describe and work with the Web page elements in a browser window. This hierarchy, officially called the **Document Object Model (DOM)**, categorizes and groups Web page elements into a tree-like structure. Each part of this structure is referred to as an **object**. For example, in the basic JavaScript DOM, a page's images, forms, anchors, and links are all grouped beneath the document object. The document, its location, and its history are, in turn, grouped below the frame object. DOMs allow browsers to identify page elements and to make them available to scripts in Web pages that they display. Although the earliest DOMs were part of scripting languages, Navigator 4 and Internet Explorer 4 have increased the range and versatility of DHTML by including their own extended DOM versions in the browser code itself, which are sometimes referred to as **DHTML Object Models**. DHTML Object Models allow you to reference a particular object the same way in any scripting language on a particular browser. However, because Netscape and Microsoft have developed different DOMs, you must reference some objects differently in Navigator 4 than in Internet Explorer 4. Figure I-7 shows the basic structure of the DOM for Internet Explorer 4, which makes virtually all browser window elements available to scripts. In order to take full advantage of DHTML's capabilities, Lydia reviews the top level of object classes in the Microsoft DHTML Object Model.

 ### Location
The location object contains the URL of the current page.

 ### Frames
The frames object contains a separate Window object for each frame in the current browser window. When the window is not divided into frames, this object is empty and the entire document contents are part of the document object The Microsoft DOM also contains a frames collection within the document object, to reference its <IFRAME> tag.

 ### History
The history object allows access to the browser's list of previously visited URLs.

 ### Navigator
The navigator object makes information about the browser available.

 ### Event
The event object allows interaction with the event currently being processed by the browser, such as mouse movement or the press of a button.

 ### Screen
The screen object makes information about the user's screen setup and display available.

Document
The document object represents the current Web page in the browser window. A document object contains many elements as listed in Figure I-7. These elements, including links, anchors, images, and so on, are what help to give each Web page its unique characteristics.

Trouble?

Don't worry if you don't know the meaning of each element of the Document object. You will learn about some of these elements as you learn more about DHTML.

FIGURE I-7: Microsoft DHTML Object Model

window
- location
- frames
- history
- navigator
- event
- screen
- document
  - links
  - anchors
  - images
  - filters
  - forms
  - applets
  - embeds
  - plug-ins
  - frames
  - scripts
  - all
  - selection
  - stylesheets
  - body

HTML

Understanding Browser Variability

Although DHTML has few current standards, work is underway to change this situation. The **World Wide Web Consortium**, or the **W3C**—an international body whose mission is the creation of standards for WWW technologies—is creating official guidelines for DHTML. Although the W3C has created standards for the DOM and other DHTML technologies, these agreements have not yet resulted in a uniform interpretation of DHTML on the Web. The Microsoft and Netscape corporations, as the manufacturers of the vast majority of browsers in use today, have the greatest influence in DHTML implementation on the Web because the technology depends on each user's browser to interpret and run it. This difference in implementation means that code written for use on one browser may not work on the other, which requires writing two sets of code to incorporate some features into a page. As standards evolve and new browser versions are released, it will become easier to create today's features with a uniform code. However, both companies undoubtedly will continue to incorporate new, incompatible innovations into their browsers, which means that browser variability probably will always be a factor in creating DHTML pages. Lydia researches the implications of the different browsers available on the DHTML pages she is planning.

 Some dynamic HTML code is compatible with the 3.x versions of Navigator and Internet Explorer, known as **third generation** browsers, but most features work only on the 4.x and later versions, the **fourth generation** browsers. Because many users have upgraded to fourth generation browsers already and many more will upgrade eventually, it is often easiest to create DHTML with these browsers in mind. Remember, however, that if you want your pages to reach the largest possible audience, they must still accommodate other browsers. By organizing your pages to display logically even without their DHTML features and adding a few extra tags to allow older browsers to process the code, your content can remain accessible by older browsers that can't interpret DHTML, by text-based browsers, and by Web interfaces for people with disabilities. Testing your pages on different browsers before publishing them is important because standard DHTML code could cause older browsers to stop functioning, or **hang**. Figure I-8 shows a DHTML page in a fourth-generation browser and in Lynx, a text-only browser. Notice that the text-only browser ignores all of the DHTML commands, such as those for positioning, while still displaying all the information logically.

 The differences in DHTML capabilities between fourth-generation browsers and earlier versions make writing interactive Web pages complicated because Internet Explorer 4 and Navigator 4 use and interpret DHTML differently. As you saw in the DHTML tour, therefore, they are not compatible when it comes to creating certain dynamic HTML features. Because DHTML components are still new technologies, many are not yet standardized in the software industry. For now, this incompatibility issue results in some features being available only in one browser and others being available only in the other. For some features to be available in either Web browser, DHTML Web page designers must write separate scripts to create similar features in the fourth-generation browsers.

 Designing dynamic Web pages is easiest when they will reside on a network where all users run the same browser, such as a corporate intranet. When publishing to the WWW, the only way to make sure that most users can view your pages is to write **cross-platform code**, or DHTML code that works on both fourth generation browsers. This often requires two sets of code in your page, along with a script to recognize in which browser the Web page is opening. Using this technique allows you to make interesting and interactive pages without causing compatibility problems for potential users. Although cross-platform coding can be time-consuming, many Web sites freely distribute such code that they have developed for popular features, along with tutorials describing how the code works. Using existing code can save a lot of page-development time.

FIGURE I-8: **One Web page as it displays in two different browsers**

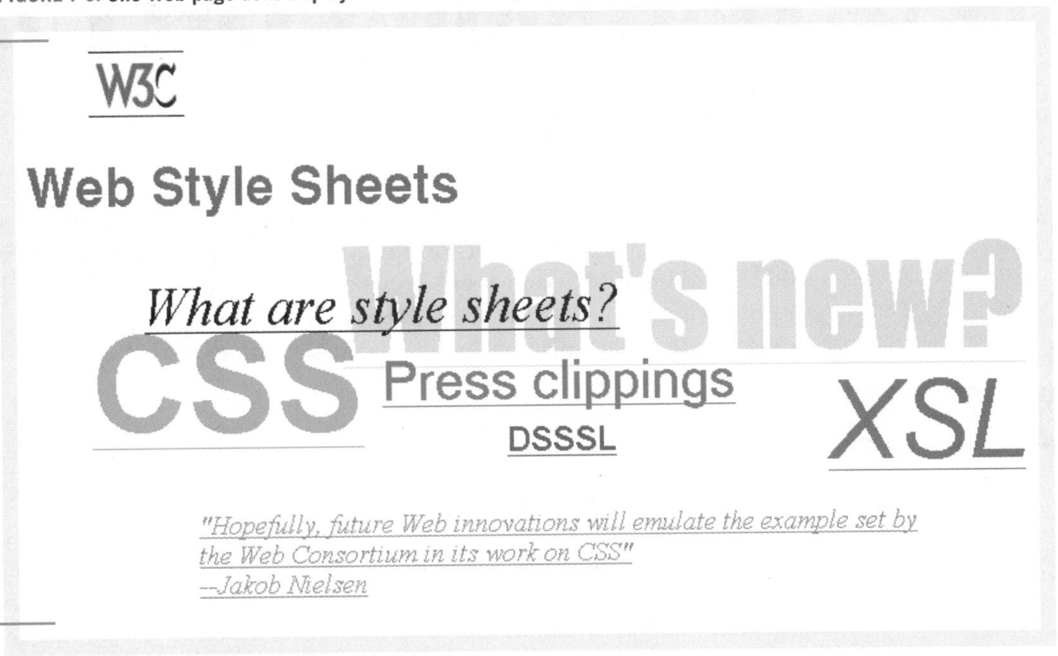

Web page using style sheets and positioning in a fourth generation browser

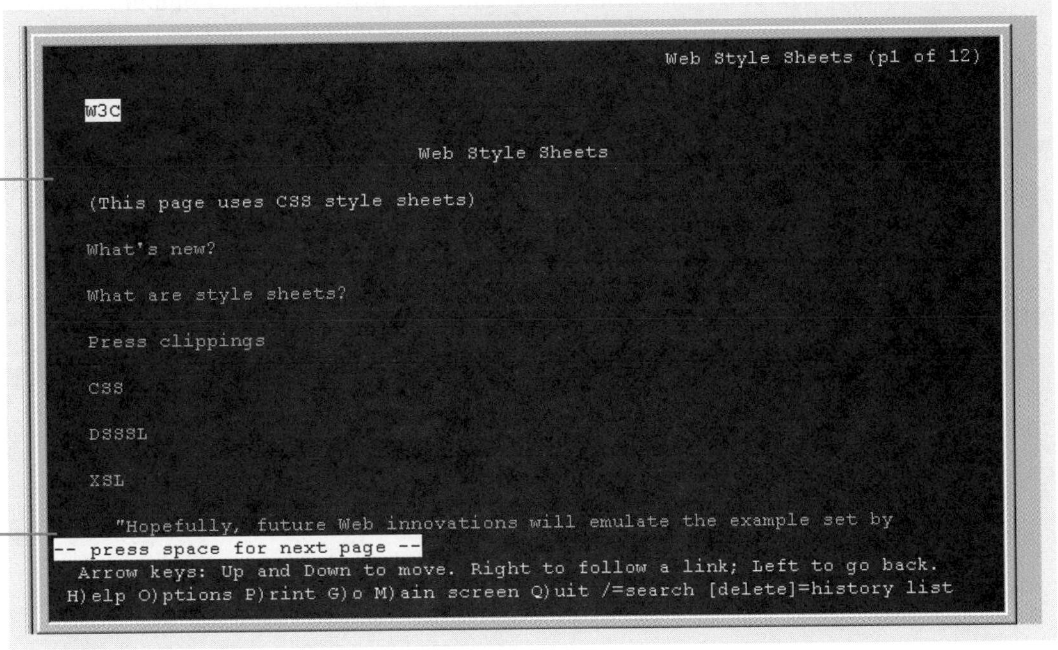

W3C

Web Style Sheets

What are style sheets? **What's new?**

CSS **Press clippings** *XSL*

DSSSL

"Hopefully, future Web innovations will emulate the example set by the Web Consortium in its work on CSS"
--Jakob Nielsen

Page structure and coding creates orderly display without DHTML features

```
                                              Web Style Sheets (p1 of 12)

  W3C
                             Web Style Sheets

  (This page uses CSS style sheets)

  What's new?

  What are style sheets?

  Press clippings

  CSS

  DSSSL

  XSL

       "Hopefully, future Web innovations will emulate the example set by
-- press space for next page --
  Arrow keys: Up and Down to move. Right to follow a link; Left to go back.
  H)elp O)ptions P)rint G)o M)ain screen Q)uit /=search [delete]=history list
```

HTML

Designing DHTML Pages

Like static Web pages, those incorporating DHTML require planning and forethought. Standard HTML rules, such as careful proofreading and judicious use of headings, still apply to dynamic pages. However, DHTML has its own advantages and pitfalls, which are important to keep in mind. In addition to awareness of browser differences, several other guidelines are helpful in working with this new technology. To ensure that her Web pages follow good design principles, Lydia has made a list of recommendations, based on her DHTML research, for designing pages with DHTML.

Details

Organize for dynamic content

Remember that DHTML allows positioning of page elements and lets you show new content in response to user actions. Generally, this means that you can fit more in a dynamic page than in a static HTML page. For example, the hierarchical menu, shown in Figure I-9, allows a single page to contain information that otherwise works best as a list of links and a set of associated pages. This menu works like the one you use when you click the Start button in Windows. With DHTML, you can insert this within your Web pages, for simplified navigation, which keeps the Web page uncluttered. It also organizes the information so that the user can see the interrelationships of choices. Organizing your Web site to take advantage of DHTML capabilities can make the site easier for users to navigate and for you to manage.

Use dynamic features purposefully

Dynamic HTML features appear impressive, and you may be eager to show off your new skills by incorporating many of them into the pages you create. However, just as in static pages, the best Web pages are focused and free of distracting elements. Your Web page's content and message, rather than newly available features, should dictate which dynamic tools you use.

FIGURE I-9: Web page containing a hierarchical menu

ebreference   suggest   forum   new   headlines   search   contents

home / experts / dhtml / column15   ⬤⬤⬤⬤⬤⬤⬤⬤⬤⬤⬤⬤⬤⬤⬤⬤

Cross-Browser Hierarchical Menus
popup site navigation for both DHTML browsers

Webreference
Suggest
Cool
New
Headli
Sea
Conte

This tutorial can be appreciated by users of any browser, any version. The in-... ill work only in Netscape Navigator 4 and Microso... orer 4 for Windows.

| Books |
| Browsers |
| History |
| Magazines |
| Software |
| Standards |
| Statistics |
| Tutorials |

Web/Net	▶
WebMaster	▶
On-Site Originals	▶
About Us	▶

...al menus that we developed last column for ... y appeared on many web sites. (one week

...eate a cross-browser script based on the concepts, methods and functions developed for Navigator 4. An

Pointing to "Contents" opens first level of menu

Pointing to "Web/Net" opens second level of menu

Second level contains list of links to open listed pages

Design resources

One advantage of the browser competition between Microsoft and Netscape is that both companies are eager to show off their browser's features. Both companies keep a list of links to well-designed pages (supporting their own proprietary features) on their corporate Web sites. Reviewing these pages can give you ideas for planning successful dynamic Web pages as well as introduce you to new features.

Researching Code Architecture

After you outline your Web page and identify the DHTML features you want to use in it, the next step is to sit down and write code to make these features work. In many cases, although you have seen a Web page incorporating a certain action, it can be difficult to determine exactly how to create the feature with scripts and style sheets. At this point, research on the Web is indispensable to creating a successful DHTML page. For example, you can use the Web to look at the page source of a Web page that uses a feature you like. You also can find well-documented sample code on Web sites, which often you are allowed to modify and use for your own purposes. ◢━━ Lydia has written the HTML for a new Web page that lists questions and answers. She wants to use DHTML to create a collapsible list on her Web page. In a collapsible list, explanatory text appears only when a user clicks its associated heading. Recently, Lydia saw the collapsible list feature on a page while browsing the Web, and she downloaded a copy of the Web page so that she could examine the code further.

Steps

1. **Open the file HTML I-3.htm in your Web browser**
   The page displays a list of blueberry breeds.

2. **Click the phrase Blue Jay**
   Associated text appears below the berry name, as shown in Figure I-10. Notice in the address bar that clicking the phrase did not open a new page; rather, it simply triggered a change in the appearance of the current Web page.

3. **Start your text editor program, then open the file HTML I-3.htm to display the source code for the Web page**
   Figure I-11 shows part of the script for creating the collapsible list.

4. **Close the text editor without saving the document**

5. **Be sure your computer is connected to the Internet, then open a search engine of your choice**

6. **In the "Search" text box, type DynamicHTML programming and click the Find button, or its equivalent**
   The browser returns a list of links to sites related to DHTML programming.

7. **Review the links returned by the search engine, then follow one to a site that seems likely to contain tutorials or sample code**
   Articles and sample scripts for dynamic HTML applications may be helpful in creating your own pages.

8. **Scan the site's opening page for links to script libraries or articles about DHTML features, then follow the appropriate links**

9. **Locate sample code or a relevant article for an interesting DHTML feature, then download the page to your Project Disk with the name Feature download.htm**
   This downloaded file can be a helpful reference when you plan your own DHTML applications.

FIGURE I-10: Web page containing collapsible list

Click the names of blueberry breeds
below to read about our selection:

Blue Ray

Blue Jay

New text
appears in
response to
mouse click

highbush type, 5 to 7 ft. at maturity, fruit ripening the first
to middle of July, yield is 10 to 20 lbs per bush, fruit
size medium/large (approx. 75 berries per cup).

Jersey

Elliott

Northland

2 T white flour
1/4 t cinnamon
1/2 t ground coriander
pinch nutmeg
3-1/2 c blueberries
Topping:
1-1/4 c blueberries

To prepare crust, mix
flour and sugar. Cut butter
in to mixture with pastry
blender. Add 2 T water
to moisten (more if
required). Roll mixture
and place in 9" pie plate.

For the filling, mix sugar,
flour, cinnamon,
coriander, and nutmeg
thoroughly. Toss with 3-
1/2 c blueberries to coat

FIGURE I-11: Source code for expanding table of contents

Part of code
for expanding
elements in
Internet
Explorer

Part of code
for expanding
elements in
Navigator

```
function expandIE(el) {
        whichEl=eval(el + "Desc");
        if (whichEl.style.display == "none") {
                whichEl.style.display="block";
                whichEl.isExpanded=true;
        }
        else {
                whichEl.style.display="none";
                whichEl.isExpanded=false;
        }
}

function expandNav(el) {
        whichEl=eval("document." + el + "Desc");
        if (whichEl.visibility == "hide") {
                whichEl.visibility="show";
                whichEl.isExpanded=true;
        }
        else {
                whichEl.visibility="hide";
                whichEl.isExpanded=false;
        }
        arrange();
}
```

CLUES TO USE

Code-borrowing etiquette

When you find existing code on the Web that fits a project you are working on, it can save you time and frustration to use the existing code in your page instead of creating it from scratch. However, to be considerate to other designers, you should follow a few simple guidelines. First, be aware that some DHTML code is copyrighted and you cannot use it without permission from its author, which usually involves paying a fee as well. Some pages and sites offer code for free re-use. In this situation, it is still considered courteous to credit the source of the code in your Web page, usually with the creator's name and the source URL. If you find code you'd like to use and are unsure whether you are allowed to, it is best to contact the creator for permission. If you don't have permission to use someone else's code, you can still use its basic framework to help you plan the creation of your page and then augment the features with your own coding.

HTML

Keeping Up with DHTML Changes

Web and software designers have already developed many ideas and methods for using DHTML in Web pages. As with any new technology, this body of knowledge will continue to grow, and in the process, will provide new uses and workarounds for DHTML programming. In addition, browser creators update and expand the capabilities of their products, resulting in ever-expanding possibilities for new DHTML applications. As a consequence of all these factors, it's important to stay current with the latest new developments in DHTML if you want to take full advantage of its possibilities for your Web pages. Predictably, the Web is a rich source of information on DHTML. Lydia wants to see what new DHTML features are on the horizon.

Steps 1 2 3 4

1. Be sure you are connected to the Internet, open your browser, then use a search engine of your choice to search the Web for the keywords DHTML news
   The search engine returns descriptions and links to pages about DHTML.

2. Follow a link on the search results page to a site containing DHTML information

3. Scroll through and scan the opening page for tips on working with DHTML and for news about recent and upcoming developments
   Figure I-12 shows a Web page offering tips and articles on using DHTML.

4. Follow links to explanations of new DHTML features or to news about upcoming additions or changes, then read one of these articles

5. Close your Web browser

FIGURE I-12: **Web page containing DHTML tips**

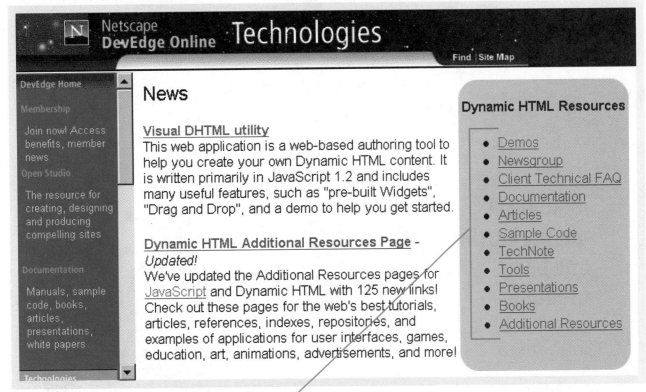

Resources available
on this site

HTML

HTML Practice

► Concepts Review

Label each item in Figure I-13 with the DHTML category that best describes it.

FIGURE I-13

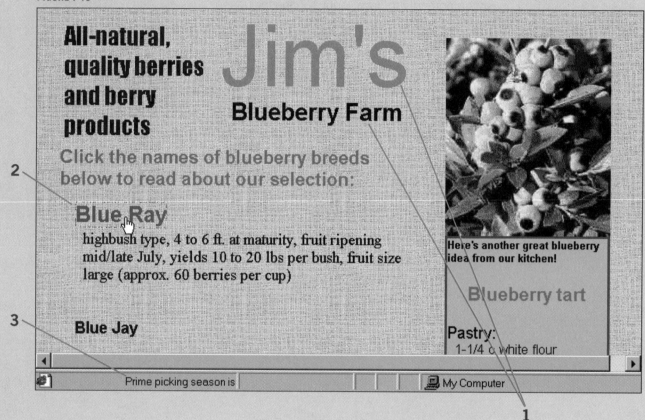

Match each term with its description.

4. **Dynamic style**
5. **Static HTML**
6. **Client-side scripts**
7. **Cascading Style Sheets (CSS)**
8. **DHTML Object Model**
9. **Cross-platform code**
10. **W3C**
11. **Positioning**
12. **Dynamic HTML**

a. Hierarchy organizing browser window elements
b. Collection of Web page technologies allowing quick response to user actions
c. Scripts that the browser itself interprets and runs
d. International body creating Web standards
e. Web page technologies allowing very limited interactivity
f. Ability to specify locations of all Web page elements
g. Component of DHTML allowing precise Web page style specification
h. Style that changes in response to user actions
i. Code that works on both fourth generation browsers

Select the best answer from the list of choices.

13. Which of the following is *not* a feature of DHTML?
    a. Dynamic style
    b. Dynamic content
    c. Server-side scripts
    d. Data awareness

14. Positioning allows Web page designers to
    a. Create interactive page formatting.
    b. Create predictable layouts.
    c. Download Web page data.
    d. Create interactive page content.

15. A collapsible list is a good example of
    a. Dynamic style.
    b. Dynamic content.
    c. Data awareness.
    d. Absolute positioning.

16. DHTML uses an object model called
    a. The World Wide Web Consortium.
    b. JavaScript.
    c. Cascading Style Sheets.
    d. The DHTML Object Model.

17. Fourth generation browsers include
    a. Internet Explorer 5.0.
    b. Navigator 4.0 and Internet Explorer 4.0.
    c. Navigator 3.0 and Internet Explorer 3.0.
    d. Lynx and other text-based browsers.

18. Creating DHTML pages for both fourth generation browsers requires
    a. Excluding CSS from your pages.
    b. Limiting the pages you write to working only on one browser.
    c. Eliminating all dynamic features from your pages.
    d. Using cross-platform code.

19. What should provide the underlying structure for your Web pages?
    a. The page's content and message
    b. The amount of information you want to include
    c. Other pages you see on the Web
    d. The dynamic features you want to include

► Independent Challenges

1. The owners of the Green House plant store have asked you to add to their Web site a list of houseplant products they sell, along with a description of each. You think that a collapsible list would format and display this information easily and concisely. To begin, you design this Web page on paper.

To complete this independent challenge:

a. On a sheet of paper, write the text for one or more titles for the Web page.

b. Below the headings, copy the following list of products, along with description placeholder text:

Potting soil
[description]
Washed gravel
[description]
Peat moss
[description]
Houseplant fertilizer
[description]
Cactus soil mix
[description]

c. On your Web page outline, label each element to indicate what page elements will be part of the collapsible list and what page elements will be appear on the Web page at all times.

d. Indicate how you will format each text item.

e. Indicate next to each of the product names that it will be formatted with dynamic style and add a second style specification for how the text will display when a user interacts with it.

f. Indicate on your sketch any positioning you will use in your page.

g. Add any further text to your sketch, such as that for hypertext links, and label the text with its formatting specifications and any additional features.

2. Sandhills Regional Public Transit wants to discuss with you ways to make their Web pages more interactive. In preparation for meeting with your clients, you want to become more familiar with different DHTML formatting options.

To complete this independent challenge:

a. Log on to the Internet and open a search engine of your choice, then search on the phrase *DHTML formatting*.

b. Click one of the links provided by the search engine to open a Web site containing DHTML formatting resources.

c. Scan the opening page and navigate the site to locate articles or sample scripts for Web page features using DHTML.

d. Read and print the article or the explanatory text accompanying a script.

e. Write a paper detailing two DHTML formatting features you think would be useful in a home page that provides information to a wide range of people. Explain why you would include these features and how they would enhance the page.

3. Community Public School Volunteers has hired you to manage their Web site on an ongoing basis. To stay on top of the latest Web page design trends, you want to regularly research relevant news on the Web. Because you're preparing to create dynamic pages for CPSV, you want to research the state of W3C standards for DHTML.

To complete this independent challenge:

a. Log on to the Internet and search on the keywords *W3C DHTML standards.*

b. Investigate the sites listed on the search results page. Locate and print two articles regarding recommendations or standards released within the past six months.

c. For each article, use the Microsoft and Netscape Web sites to research whether the standard is supported in each company's fourth-generation browser or if the company has announced plans to comply with the standard in a future release.

d. Write a paragraph on each article, summarizing the area of DHTML it covers (for example, scripting or dynamic style), which browsers support it or will support it, and an overview of the article's content.

4. Explore sample DHTML pages on the Web, either at the Microsoft or Netscape Web sites, or by searching on the term *DHTML sample pages* in a search engine. Choose one Web page, print it out from your Web browser, and on the printout areas of the page that demonstrate DHTML features. On a separate sheet of paper, list these elements and, if applicable, describe briefly how they respond to user actions. Submit your printout and list to your instructor.

Specifying
Style Dynamically

Objectives

- ► **Understand Cascading Style Sheets**
- ► **Create an embedded style sheet**
- ► **Create a class**
- ► **Detect browsers**
- ► **Show and hide page elements**
- ► **Change font size dynamically**
- ► **Control font color dynamically**
- ► **Use an external style sheet**

Cascading Style Sheets (CSS) and scripts form the foundation of DHTML. Whereas scripting allows the browser to alter the page, CSS lets you specify in detail how the page and its elements should appear. An understanding of CSS's simple syntax and organization opens the door to many new options for your Web pages' appearance. Lydia is looking forward to adding new effects to the Nomad Ltd Web pages. First, she will look at CSS a bit more in depth, then she will use CSS to create an interactive page for her department.

Understanding Cascading Style Sheets

With CSS, you can organize and expand the style attributes available in a Web page. CSS allows a Web page designer to easily specify attributes such as color, font size, and even position on the page for single objects or groups of objects, including text blocks, images, and all other DOM objects. CSS offers three different ways to specify style, which simplifies creating and changing Web page code. As Lydia reviews how to implement CSS in her Web pages, she studies the three levels of style available.

Inline style

Use **inline style** to take advantage of CSS's extended formatting options for a small text block or other object a single time in your document. You use inline style—the most basic level of using CSS—to specify your selected attributes in the opening tag surrounding the text itself, as shown in Figure J-1. This method allows you to specify a format different from all others on the page. However, formatting all page objects using inline style is impractical, given the amount of typing required.

Embedded style

Use **embedded style** to simplify formatting multiple page elements. Figure J-2 shows the source for a page using embedded style. To create embedded styles, you associate style attributes with HTML tags between the HEAD tags at the top of your Web page, creating a set of HTML code known as an **embedded style sheet**. Then, any place in the Web page code where you use the tags specified in the embedded style sheet, the text or object is formatted automatically with that style. Embedded style rather than inline style is a more efficient way to format an entire Web page. However, you can specify inline styles in a page that uses embedded styles when you have single objects that need their own style or style adjustment. Each inline style supersedes the embedded style defined for the object where it is used.

External style

Use **external style** to apply the global formatting of embedded style to multiple pages. External style allows you to specify formats and apply them to multiple Web pages rather than just one. External style also is known as **linked style** because, instead of listing style specifications at the top of your Web page, you create a link to an external document that contains the style code, known as an **external style sheet**. This method allows you to format a set of Web pages, such as a Web publication, with a uniform style and allows you to change the style for all pages later simply by editing the external style sheet. External style can be used in a page together with both inline and embedded styles. Just as inline style takes precedence over embedded style wherever you use it, embedded styles and inline styles both take precedence over external style. This system of precedence is known as **cascading**, and it gives CSS its name. Cascading allows you to apply a general format for a page or group of pages as well as to make local exceptions to the global style.

FIGURE J-1: Web page containing inline style

```
<LINK REL="stylesheet" HREF="nomadltd.css" TYPE="text/css">

<SCRIPT LANGUAGE="JavaScript">
<!--
NS4 = (document.layers) ? 1:0;
IE4 = (document.all) ? 1:0;
//-->
</SCRIPT>

<STYLE TYPE="text/css">
<!--
H1 {font-family: arial, sans-serif; font-size: 20pt}
H2 {font-family: "times new roman", times, serif; font-size: 14pt; font-
style: italic}
.question {font-family: "times new roman", times, serif; font-size: 12pt;
font-weight: bold}
//-->
</STYLE>

</HEAD>

<BODY BACKGROUND="Egg shell.jpg">
<DIV STYLE="font-color: navy; text-decoration:underline" ALIGN="center">
<H2>Frequently Asked Questions about</H2>
<H1>Dynamic HTML (DHTML)</H1></DIV>
```

Inline style located in formatting tag

FIGURE J-2: Web page containing embedded style

```
<HTML>
<HEAD>
<TITLE>Nomad Ltd DHTML FAQ</TITLE>

<STYLE TYPE="text/css">
<!--
H1 {font-family: arial, sans-serif; font-size: 20pt; font-style: normal}
H2 {font-family: "times new roman", times, serif; font-size: 14pt; font-
style: italic}
//-->
</STYLE>

</HEAD>

<BODY BACKGROUND="Egg shell.jpg">
<DIV ALIGN="center"><IMG SRC="nomad.jpg" ALIGN="right">
<H2>Frequently Asked Questions about</H2>
<H1>Dynamic HTML (DHTML)</H1></DIV><BR>

<UL TYPE="disk">
<LI><DIV>What is Dynamic HTML?</DIV>

<DIV>Dynamic HTML (DHTML) describes a set of new technologies for designing
Web pages that allow new and more precise formatting features, along with
faster access for users.</DIV><BR>
```

Embedded style sheet

CLUES TO USE

<DIV> vs. <SPAN>

Although it's often useful to assign CSS styles to standard formatting tags such as <H1> or <LI>, HTML includes two specialized tags that are especially valuable for CSS. Both the <DIV> and <SPAN> tags can enclose an element or group of elements, which allows you to specify a style for everything they contain. The <DIV> tagset always includes a line break before and after the enclosed elements, which creates a unit divided from the surrounding page. The <SPAN> tagset does not include line breaks before or after, which causes its contents to flow with the objects surrounding them in the page. When formatting text, <DIV> is best for enclosing a paragraph or group of paragraphs, whereas <SPAN> allows you to create a special style for words or sentences within a paragraph.

HTML

Creating an Embedded Style Sheet

An embedded style sheet consists of one or more lines of HTML code specifying style attributes, surrounded by tags marking the section as CSS style specifications. You can associate style attributes with any HTML structuring or formatting tag and then apply them to Web page elements simply by inserting the tags. After completing her basic research, Lydia decides to create a **FAQ** (which is an acronym for Frequently Asked Questions, pronounced "fak") document about DHTML for her co-workers in Nomad Ltd's information systems department. Lydia wants to take advantage of CSS to specify exactly how the page will appear in a user's browser. Because she wants to create a uniform look for the page, she decides to create an embedded style sheet.

Steps

1. Start your text editor, open the file **HTML J-1.htm**, then save it as a text document with the filename **FAQ embedded style.htm**
   This file contains the text of the FAQ Lydia is creating, along with basic HTML structuring tags. Lydia has enclosed each unit of text in opening and closing DIV tags to make it easy for her to add style attributes later.

2. Select the text **[replace with embedded style sheet]**, press **[Delete]**, type **<STYLE TYPE="text/css">** and press **[Enter]**, then type **<!--** and press **[Enter]**
   Embedded style sheets are placed in the Web page's head section, which allows the browser to incorporate the styles in the text it displays in the body section. A browser recognizes the code as an embedded style sheet from the beginning and ending <STYLE> tags. The TYPE property in the STYLE tag tells the browser the language and format of the style sheet it marks. In this case, the language is CSS, and the information is in text format. The <!-- tag tells browsers that are not compatible with embedded style sheets to ignore this section.

3. Type **H1 {font-family: arial, sans-serif; font-size: 20pt; font-style: normal}** and press **[Enter]**
   Lydia associates 20-point arial with the <H1> tag for use with the page's main heading. By putting it first in a list of two, Lydia specifies arial as her font preference. Her second choice, sans-serif, instructs the user's browser to use any sans-serif font if arial is not available.

4. Type **H2 {font-family: "times new roman", times, serif; font-size: 14pt; font-style: italic}** and press **[Enter]**
   Lydia has specified 14 point as the font size to associate with the <H2> tag, which is the subheading.

5. Type **//-->** and press **[Enter]**, then type **</STYLE>**
   Figure J-3 shows the completed Web page source containing the style sheet.

6. Check the document for errors, make changes as necessary, then save FAQ embedded style.htm as a text document

7. Start your browser program, cancel any dialup activities, then open the file FAQ embedded style.htm
   The Web page appears as shown in Figure J-4.

FIGURE J-3: Completed embedded style sheet

Opening and closing embedded style sheet tags

Style specifications for heading tags

```html
<HTML>
<HEAD>
<TITLE>Nomad Ltd DHTML FAQ</TITLE>

<STYLE TYPE="text/css">
<!--
H1 {font-family: arial, sans-serif; font-size: 20pt; font-style: normal}
H2 {font-family: "times new roman", times, serif; font-size: 14pt; font-style: italic}
//-->
</STYLE>

</HEAD>

<BODY BACKGROUND="Egg shell.jpg">
<DIV ALIGN="center"><IMG SRC="nomad.jpg" ALIGN="right">
<H2>Frequently Asked Questions about</H2>
<H1>Dynamic HTML (DHTML)</H1></DIV><BR>

<UL TYPE="disk">
<LI><DIV>What is Dynamic HTML?</DIV>

<DIV>Dynamic HTML (DHTML) describes a set of new technologies for designing
Web pages that allow new and more precise formatting features, along with
faster access for users.</DIV><BR>
```

FIGURE J-4: Web page formatted with embedded style sheet

Text formatted with H2 style specified in embedded style sheet

Text formatted with H1 style specified in embedded style sheet

Frequently Asked Questions about

Nomad Ltd

Dynamic HTML (DHTML)

- What is Dynamic HTML?
  Dynamic HTML (DHTML) describes a set of new technologies for designing Web pages that allow new and more precise formatting features, along with faster access for users.

- Is DHTML a new language?
  DHTML is not a new language. DHTML is simply a snazzy name for a set of new features that recent Web browsers are equipped to interpret and use. DHTML features work only within the context of a standard HTML document.

- How does DHTML work?
  DHTML uses two new pieces in concert with HTML. The first is scripts that run on the user's browser, written in a scripting language such as JavaScript or VBScript. The other is Cascading Style Sheets, a new method of specifying exact styles for a Web page's elements.

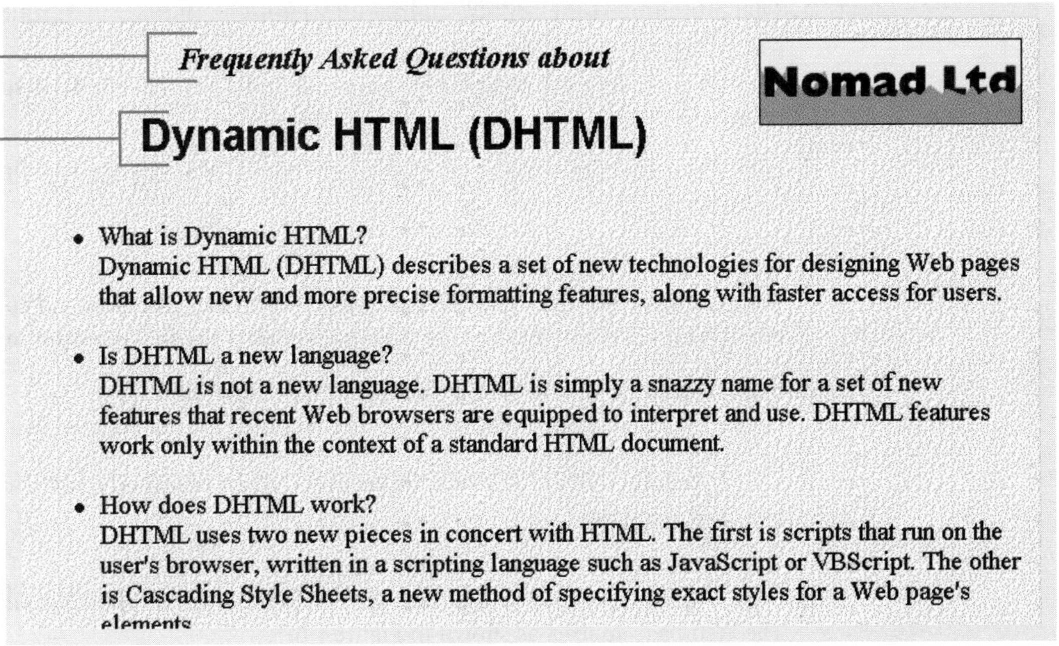

HTML

Creating a Class

In addition to specifying style for all occurrences of a particular HTML tag, you also can name a set of style specifications and then associate, or **call**, this name in tags within your Web page. This named style, known as a **class**, allows you to format selected elements with an embedded style, without requiring that each element be enclosed in the same tag or that every occurrence of a certain tag display the same style. All class names begin with a period to mark them as classes. To apply a class to an element, you add the CLASS attribute to the element's opening HTML tag. ✐ Lydia's bulleted list is a series of questions and answers. Lydia wants to format the headings in her list, which are the questions, differently than the paragraph text, which are the answers. She creates a class that specifies the formatting for the questions and then calls the class within the opening <DIV> tag for each of the questions.

Steps

1. Open the file HTML J-2.htm in your text editor, then save it as a text document with the filename FAQ class.htm

2. Select the text [replace with class style] in the embedded style sheet, then press [Delete]

3. Type .question {font-family: "times new roman", times, serif; font-size: 12pt; font-weight: bold} and press [Enter]
   The dot preceding the style name "question" indicates that the style specification is for a class.

4. Select the text [replace with class] in the <DIV> tag for the first question, then press [Delete]

5. Type CLASS="question"
   The tag now reads <DIV CLASS="question">. This calls the class and applies the style associated with the class "question" to this text, which is the first question in the FAQ.

6. Repeat Steps 4 and 5 for the remaining six questions
   Figure J-5 shows a portion of the completed source for the bulleted list.

7. Check your document for errors, make changes as necessary, then save FAQ class.htm as a text document

8. Click the browser program button on the taskbar, then open the file **FAQ class.htm**
   The Web page appears as shown in Figure J-6.

FIGURE J-5: **Web page source using a class**

Class definition inserted in embedded style sheet

```
H2 {font-family: "times new roman", times, serif; font-size: 14pt; font-
style: italic}
.question {font-family: "times new roman", times, serif; font-size: 12pt;
font-weight: bold}
//-->
</STYLE>

</HEAD>

<BODY BACKGROUND="Egg shell.jpg">
<DIV ALIGN="center"><IMG SRC="nomad.jpg" ALIGN="right">
<H2>Frequently Asked Questions about</H2>
<H1>Dynamic HTML (DHTML)</H1></DIV><BR>

<UL TYPE="disk">
<LI><DIV CLASS="question">What is Dynamic HTML?</DIV>

<DIV>Dynamic HTML (DHTML) describes a set of new technologies for designing
Web pages that allow new and more precise formatting features, along with
faster access for users.</DIV><BR>

<LI><DIV CLASS="question">Is DHTML a new language?</DIV>

<DIV>DHTML is not a new language. DHTML is simply a snazzy name for a set of
new features that recent Web browsers are equipped to interpret and use.
DHTML features work only within the context of a standard HTML
```

Class question called in <DIV> tags

FIGURE J-6: **Web page formatted with new class**

Frequently Asked Questions about

Nomad Ltd

Dynamic HTML (DHTML)

Bold format added using class property

• **What is Dynamic HTML?**
Dynamic HTML (DHTML) describes a set of new technologies for designing Web pages that allow new and more precise formatting features, along with faster access for users.

• **Is DHTML a new language?**
DHTML is not a new language. DHTML is simply a snazzy name for a set of new features that recent Web browsers are equipped to interpret and use. DHTML features work only within the context of a standard HTML document.

• **How does DHTML work?**
DHTML uses two new pieces in concert with HTML. The first is scripts that run on the user's browser, written in a scripting language such as JavaScript or VBScript. The other is Cascading Style Sheets, a new method of specifying exact styles for a Web page's

CLUES TO USE

Creating an ID style

As well as assigning styles to tags and classes in your embedded style sheets, you can define styles for element IDs. Just as each class style name begins with a period, you preface each ID style name with a number sign (#). Because you can assign an ID to only one element, defining global ID styles is no more

efficient than specifying the styles inline. However, ID styles allow you to group style information at the top of the document, rather than inline, which can help make your code less cluttered and easier to read and understand.

HTML

Detecting Browsers

The combination of scripts and CSS allows you to add lag-free interactivity to your Web pages. Although both fourth-generation browsers support DHTML, each does so in a different way. Whereas the methods for creating basic effects in Internet Explorer and Netscape Navigator are the same, the code for most advanced DHTML features is different for each browser. This means that creating code offering dynamic features in both browser platforms, known as **cross-browser code**, often requires writing and integrating two different sets of code into a single page. Additionally, a cross-browser DHTML page requires a **browser-detection script**, which determines the user's browser brand and generation. The browser then uses this information to determine which of the page's DHTML scripts are appropriate for a user's browser. ✐ Lydia wants to add interactive DHTML features to control her FAQ page's display. Before adding the coding to create these features, she inserts a browser-detection script into her page.

Steps

1. Open the file **HTML J-3.htm** in your text editor, then save it as a text document with the filename **FAQ browser detect.htm**
   This copy of the FAQ page contains the CSS features Lydia created in the last lesson.

2. Select the text **[replace with browser-detection script]**, then press **[Delete]**

3. Type the following script, pressing **[Enter]** at the end of each line:

   ```
   <SCRIPT LANGUAGE="javascript">

   <!--

   Nav4 = (document.layers) ? 1:0;

   IE4 = (document.all) ? 1:0;

   //-->

   </SCRIPT>
   ```

   Lydia's completed script, shown in Figure J-7, tells the browser to check for elements of the DOM, one of which is specific to Navigator 4 and the other of which is specific to Internet Explorer 4. The question mark in each line tells the browser to evaluate the preceding condition and to assign the variable the value 1, which equals "true" if the condition is true; otherwise, assign the variable the value 0, which is "false" if it is not true. This script determines if the browser is Netscape Navigator 4 or Internet Explorer 4. Based on the results of the conditional test, the browser reads the appropriate scripts, which create DHTML features in the user's browser.

4. Check the document for errors, then make changes as necessary

5. Save FAQ browser detect.htm as a text document

6. Open the file **FAQ browser detect.htm** in your browser to ensure it displays correctly, and debug the file as necessary until it displays as expected

```
<HTML>
<HEAD>
<TITLE>Nomad Ltd DHTML FAQ</TITLE>

<SCRIPT LANGUAGE="javascript">
<!--
Nav4 = (document.layers) ? 1:0;
IE4 = (document.all) ? 1:0;
//-->
</SCRIPT>

<STYLE TYPE="text/css">
<!--
H1 {font-family: arial, sans-serif; font-size: 20pt}
H2 {font-family: "times new roman", times, serif; font-size: 14pt; font-
style: italic}
.question {font-family: "times new roman", times, serif; font-size: 12pt;
font-weight: bold}
//-->
</STYLE>

</HEAD>

<BODY BACKGROUND="Egg shell.jpg">
<DIV ALIGN="center"><IMG SRC="nomad.jpg" ALIGN="right">
<H2>Frequently Asked Questions about</H2>
```

Browser-detection script

Future cross-browser coding

Much of the difference in browser support between Navigator 4 and Internet Explorer 4 stems from the lack of a DHTML standard. As the W3C organization refines and extends the industry standard, however, future browser releases should match more closely in how they support today's basic features. Although this may make future cross-browser coding as easy as writing for a single browser today, browser-detection routines will probably never become obsolete. As long as the browsers of multiple companies are popular, each company will continue to develop and add its own features, which will be standardized later. Additionally, some Web users will continue to use earlier-generation browsers. Because advanced scripts can hang older browsers, causing them to stop working and sometimes requiring the user to reboot, a browser-detection script can help you develop pages that identify and accommodate less-advanced browsers.

HTML

Showing and Hiding Page Elements

By working together with embedded scripts, CSS can specify how page elements should display in different situations and in response to user actions, which allows you to create the interactive features that are the hallmark of DHTML. Lydia wants her Web page to hide the paragraphs containing the answers and to display each answer only when the user clicks its corresponding question. Lydia can create this feature, known as an **expandable outline**, with a combination of style sheets and scripts. Lydia has already inserted the code to create this feature in Navigator 4. Now, she adds code that Internet Explorer 4 can interpret.

Steps

1. Open the file HTML J-4.htm in your text editor, then save it as a text document with the filename FAQ show and hide.htm
   Notice that this copy of the FAQ page already contains the browser detection script.

2. Scroll and select [replace with expandIE function], then press [Delete]

Trouble?

"El" stands for element. Be sure to type *El* or *el* using the letter l and not the number 1.

3. Type the following code, pressing [Enter] at the end of each line

```
function expandIE(el) {
    theEl=eval(el + "Answer");
    if (theEl.style.display == "none") {
            theEl.style.display="block";
            theEl.expanded=true;
    }
    else {
            theEl.style.display="none";
            theEl.expanded=false;
    }
}
```
   Figure J-8 shows the new code.

4. Scroll down to the <DIV> tag for the first list item "What is Dynamic HTML?", select the text [replace with opening A tag] and the space following it, then press [Delete]

5. Type <A HREF="#" onClick="expand('one'); return false">
   Because Lydia uses an A tag with # as a dummy href, the mouse pointer becomes a hand when it moves over the question which indicates to the user that clicking the text triggers an action. The remaining code uses the onClick event handler to call the function expand and specifies the variable 'one' for the function to process. The function expand checks which browser the user is running and, in Internet Explorer 4, calls the expandIE function you entered earlier.

6. Replace the text [replace with closing A tag] in the next line with </A>

7. Repeat Steps 4 through 6 for the remaining six list items, substituting 'two' for 'one' in item two, and so forth
   Figure J-9 shows a portion of the completed code for the expanding FAQ list.

8. Use Figures J-8 and J-9 to check the document for errors, make changes as necessary, then save FAQ show and hide.htm as a text document

Trouble?

In Navigator 4, all the text is visible briefly when the page opens.

9. Open FAQ show and hide.htm in your browser, then click the first question
   As Figure J-10 shows, the text for the first question is displayed.

FIGURE J-8: FAQ page with added script

```
function expand(el) {
        if (!ver4) return;
        if (IE4) {
                expandIE(el)
        }
        else {
                expandNav(el)
        }
}

function expandIE(el) {
        theEl=eval(el + "Answer");
        if (theEl.style.display == "none") {
                theEl.style.display="block";
                theEl.expanded=true;
        }
        else {
                theEl.style.display="none";
                theEl.expanded=false;
        }
}

function expandNav(el) {
        theEl=eval("document." + el + "Answer");
        if (theEl.visibility == "hide") {
```

Script to make outline expandable in IE4

Change value of display property for a clicked line

FIGURE J-9: <A> tags added to list items

```
<H3>Click any of the popular questions about DHTML below to see its
answer.</H3>

<DIV ID="oneQuestion" CLASS="question"><A HREF="#" onClick="expand('one');
return false"><P>What is Dynamic HTML?</P></A></DIV>

<DIV ID="oneAnswer" CLASS="answer"><P>Dynamic HTML (DHTML) describes a set
of new technologies for designing Web pages that allow new and more precise
formatting features, along with faster access for users.</P></DIV>

<DIV ID="twoQuestion" CLASS="question"><A HREF="#" onClick="expand('two');
return false"><P>Is DHTML a new language?</P></A></DIV>

<DIV ID="twoAnswer" CLASS="answer"><P>DHTML is not a new language. DHTML is
simply a snazzy name for a set of new features that recent Web browsers are
equipped to interpret and use. DHTML features work only within the context
of a standard HTML document.</P></DIV>

<DIV ID="threeQuestion" CLASS="question"><A HREF="#"
onClick="expand('three'); return false"><P>How does DHTML
work?</P></A></DIV>

<DIV ID="threeAnswer" CLASS="answer"><P>DHTML uses two new pieces in concert
with HTML. The first is scripts that run on the user's browser, written in a
scripting language such as JavaScript or VBScript. The other is Cascading
```

Opening <A> tag and event handler inserted

Closing </A> tag inserted

FIGURE J-10: Expanding FAQ list

Mouse pointer becomes hand over question text

Clicking question displays answer text

Frequently Asked Questions about

Nomad Ltd

Dynamic HTML (DHTML)

Click any of the popular questions about DHTML below to see its answer.

What is Dynamic HTML?

Dynamic HTML (DHTML) describes a set of new technologies for designing Web pages that allow new and more precise formatting features, along with faster access for users.

Is DHTML a new language?

How does DHTML work?

What can I do with DHTML?

Changing Font Size Dynamically

In the last lesson, you used a script to modify the style of an element in response to a user action. Using this general formula, you can add dynamic formatting to most style aspects of any object on your Web pages. A popular application of this method has been to change the appearance of text when a user points at it, commonly referred to as a **rollover**. A rollover changes text attributes to make the text stand out. Lydia wants to change the text size of the FAQ questions when the user moves the pointer over them. Although adding this feature to graphics is straightforward in both browsers, Lydia finds that it is difficult to create for text blocks in Navigator. Because the feature is not crucial to the overall layout of her Web page, she decides to focus on creating the feature only in Internet Explorer.

Steps

1. Open the file **HTML J-5.htm** in your text editor, then save it as a text document with the filename **FAQ text size.htm**

2. Scroll down the document to the ending </SCRIPT> tag in the document's head section, select the text **[replace with text size functions]**, press **[Delete]**, then type the following functions, pressing **[Enter]** at the end of each line

   ```
   function changeText(whichQuestion) {
       if (Nav4) {return}
       whichQuestion.style.fontSize="16pt";
   }
   function changeTextBack(whichQuestion) {
       if (Nav4) {return}
       whichQuestion.style.fontSize="12pt";
   }
   ```

   Figure J-11 shows the functions entered into the Web page source. The first function, changeText, changes the font size of the object from which it was called to 16 point. The second function, changeTextBack, changes the font size of the calling object back to 12 point.

3. Scroll down the page to the opening <A> tag for the first list item "What is Dynamic HTML?", select the text **[replace with event handlers]**, then press **[Delete]**

4. Type **onMouseOver="changeText(this)" onMouseOut="changeTextBack(this)"**

   This code adds two new arguments to the heading. The first uses the onMouseOver event handler to call the changeText function you created earlier. The "this" is scripting shorthand to tell the function to make changes to the current object. The second argument calls the changeTextBack function for the current object in response to the mouse moving off the text.

5. Repeat Steps 3 and 4 for the remaining six list items

   Figure J-12 shows source code containing the inline code for dynamically changing text size.

6. Use Figures J-11 and J-12 to check the document for errors, make changes as necessary, then save FAQ text size.htm as a text document

7. Open **FAQ text size.htm** in your browser, then move the pointer over a list item

   Figure J-13 shows the result of this step in Internet Explorer 4. Notice that the text size of the heading increased. However, if you opened FAQ text size.htm in a different browser, such as Netscape Navigator 4, no change occurs.

8. Move the mouse pointer off the first heading

   The first heading returns to its original size.

FIGURE J-11: Page containing new functions

Changes current text to larger font size

Changes larger text back to smaller font size

```
function changeText(whichQuestion) {
      if (Nav4) {return}
      whichQuestion.style.fontSize="16pt";
}
function changeTextBack(whichQuestion) {
      if (Nav4) {return}
      whichQuestion.style.fontSize="12pt";
}
//-->
</SCRIPT>
```

FIGURE J-12: Page containing code to change text size

Calls function to increase text size

Calls function to decrease text size

```
<H3>Click any of the popular questions about DHTML below to see its
answer.</H3>

<DIV ID="oneQuestion" CLASS="question" ><A HREF="#" onClick="expand('one');
return false" onMouseOver="changeText(this)"
onMouseOut="changeTextBack(this)"><P>What is Dynamic HTML?</P></A></DIV>

<DIV ID="oneAnswer" CLASS="answer"><P>Dynamic HTML (DHTML) describes a set
of new technologies for designing Web pages that allow new and more precise
formatting features, along with faster access for users.</P></DIV>

<DIV ID="twoQuestion" CLASS="question" ><A HREF="#" onClick="expand('two');
return false" onMouseOver="changeText(this)"
onMouseOut="changeTextBack(this)"><P>Is DHTML a new language?</P></A></DIV>

<DIV ID="twoAnswer" CLASS="answer"><P>DHTML is not a new language. DHTML is
simply a snazzy name for a set of new features that recent Web browsers are
equipped to interpret and use. DHTML features work only within the context
of a standard HTML document.</P></DIV>

<DIV ID="threeQuestion" CLASS="question"><A HREF="#"
onClick="expand('three'); return false" onMouseOver="changeText(this)"
onMouseOut="changeTextBack(this)"><P>How does DHTML work?</P></A></DIV>

<DIV ID="threeAnswer" CLASS="answer"><P>DHTML uses two new pieces in concert
```

FIGURE J-13: Changed text size in Internet Explorer 4

Question font size increases in response to pointer

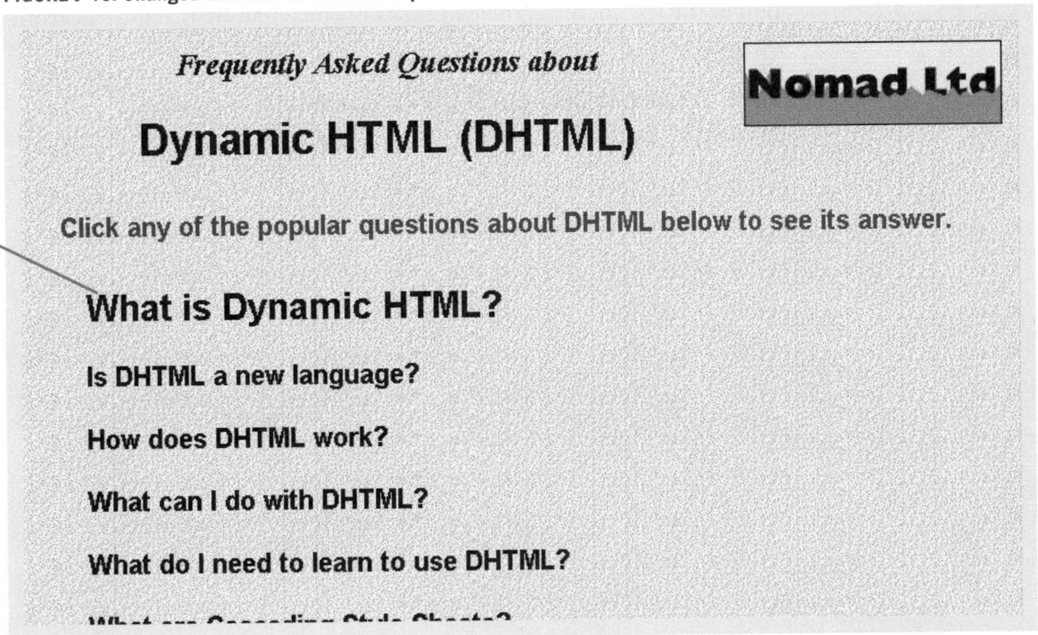

Frequently Asked Questions about

Nomad Ltd

Dynamic HTML (DHTML)

Click any of the popular questions about DHTML below to see its answer.

What is Dynamic HTML?

Is DHTML a new language?

How does DHTML work?

What can I do with DHTML?

What do I need to learn to use DHTML?

HTML

Changing Font Color Dynamically

Just as you can script a page to change text size in response to a user action, you can easily change or modify such scripts to change several other properties that control how text displays. In addition to the increase in text size, Lydia wants the heading font color to change in response to mouse pointing. She can modify the scripts she already created to alter font color at the same time they alter text size in Internet Explorer 4.

Steps

1. Open the file HTML J-6.htm in your text editor, then save it as a text document with the filename FAQ text color.htm

2. Scroll down the page to the changeText function in the page header, select the text [replace with changeText color], then press [Delete]

3. Type whichQuestion.style.color="#9400D3";

4. Select the text [replace with changeTextBack color] in the changeTextBack function in the page header, then press [Delete]

5. Type whichQuestion.style.color="#000000";
   Figure J-14 shows the completed changes in the Web page source containing the color style. The changeText function increases the size of the text as well as changes the color for the selected object. The changeTextBack function returns the text to its original size and color.

6. Check the document for errors, make changes as necessary, then save FAQ text color.htm as a text document

7. Open the file FAQ text color.htm in your browser, then move the pointer over the first heading
   Figure J-15 shows the change, which again takes place only in Internet Explorer 4. In addition to the size increase, the text turns purple, making it stand out from the other questions on the page.

8. Move the mouse pointer off the first heading
   In Internet Explorer 4, the text size and color return to their default settings.

FIGURE J-14: Color change code inserted

```
function changeText(whichQuestion) {
      if (Nav4) {return}
      whichQuestion.style.fontSize="16pt";
      whichQuestion.style.color="#9400D3";
}
function changeTextBack(whichQuestion) {
      if (Nav4) {return}
      whichQuestion.style.fontSize="12pt";
      whichQuestion.style.color="#000000";
}
//-->
</SCRIPT>

<STYLE TYPE="text/css">
<!--
H1 {font-family: arial, sans-serif; font-size: 20pt; font-style: normal}
H2 {font-family: "times new roman", times, serif; font-size: 14pt; font-
style: italic}
H3 {font-family: arial; font-size: 12pt; color: #4619E1; position: relative;
left: 20px; top: -10px}
.question {font-family: "times new roman", times, serif; font-size: 12pt;
font-weight: bold}
.question A {font-family: arial; font-size: 12pt; font-weight: bold; text-
decoration: none; color: black}
.rest {position: absolute; left: 25px}
```

New script lines to change text color

FIGURE J-15: Color change in browser

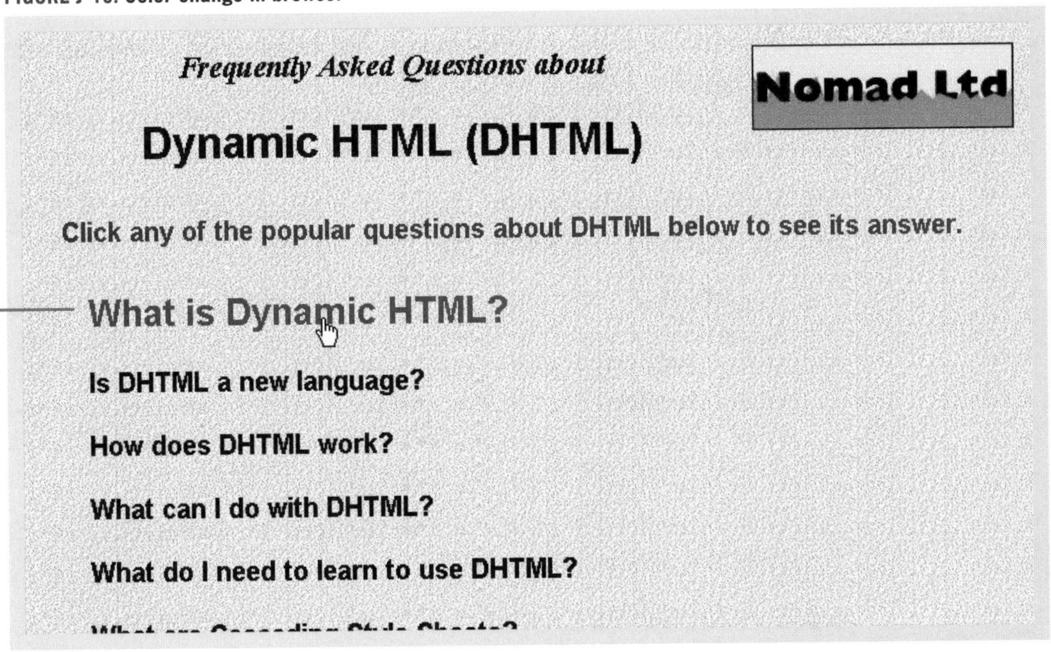

Frequently Asked Questions about

Dynamic HTML (DHTML)

Nomad Ltd

Click any of the popular questions about DHTML below to see its answer.

Changed text color ——— **What is Dynamic HTML?**

Is DHTML a new language?

How does DHTML work?

What can I do with DHTML?

What do I need to learn to use DHTML?

Unit J

HTML

Using an External Style Sheet

When you create or manage a group of related Web pages, it is often helpful to create an external style sheet. Just as you use hyperlinks to refer to external HTML documents, you can link each Web page to the style sheet with a simple line of code. Creating an external style sheet allows you to apply a standard style to a set of Web pages and to easily make changes that apply to all the pages. ▰▰▰ Because Lydia plans to create other FAQ pages for her department, she has created an external style sheet to reflect the styles she wants all the FAQs to use. She also takes into account Nomad Ltd's standard Web page style. She replaces the existing embedded style sheet with a link to the external file. The rules of cascading precedence allow her to leave in place the inline styles that help individualize the Web page by creating her dynamic effects.

Steps 1 2 3 4

QuickTip

Both fourth-generation browsers ignore the highest-level heading definition in an external style sheet. Adding an empty style definition named H0 guarantees that all other heading definitions will display correctly in your documents.

1. Open the file **HTML J-7.css**, then save it as a text document with the filename **nomadltd.css**
This file contains the Nomad Ltd stylesheet. The document consists of text, just like an HTML document, and contains the opening and closing <STYLE> tags that tell browsers how to interpret the contents. A CSS document is formatted just like an embedded style sheet, except that it contains no HTML code outside of the <STYLE> tags. Lydia cut and pasted the styles from her FAQ page that she will apply to other pages she creates.

2. Select the text **#4619E1** in the color definition for the H3 heading, press [Delete], then type **#238E68**
This changes the color for the H3 style, which applies to the directions in Lydia's current page, from blue to green.

3. Save **nomadltd.css** as a text document

4. Open the file **HTML J-8.htm** in your text editor, then save it as a text document with the filename **FAQ external style.htm**
Lydia has removed the heading definitions from the embedded style sheet for her FAQ page because the external style sheet contains these specifications.

5. Scroll down and select **[replace with external style sheet link]** which is just above the embedded style sheet, then press [Delete]

6. Type **<LINK REL="stylesheet" HREF="nomadltd.css" TYPE="text/css">**
Figure J-16 shows the page source containing the insertion. The LINK tag contains information about a file related to the current document. The REL attribute identifies the file type of the related file. The value assigned to HREF is the name and address of the file, just as for a hyperlink. TYPE specifies the format of the associated file because you can code associated information including style sheets in different ways.

7. Check the file for errors, make changes as necessary, then save FAQ external style.htm as a text document

8. Open the file **FAQ external style.htm** in your Web browser
The Web page appears as shown in Figure J-17. Because both Navigator 4 and Internet Explorer 4 support basic CSS, the standardized Nomad Ltd format appears in both browsers. The instruction text color displays in green, which confirms that the page is using the external styles you defined. When Lydia links other FAQ Web pages to this nomadltd.css file as she develops them, then all her FAQ Web pages will have the same style. This helps ensure consistency for all her FAQ Web pages.

FIGURE J-16: Web page code containing link to external style sheet

External style sheet
link text

```
}
//-->
</SCRIPT>

<LINK REL="stylesheet" HREF="nomadltd.css" TYPE="text/css">

<STYLE TYPE="text/css">
<!--
.question {font-family: "times new roman", times, serif; font-size: 12pt;
font-weight: bold}
.question A {font-family: arial; font-size: 12pt; font-weight: bold; text-
decoration: none; color: black}
.rest {position: absolute; left: 25px}
//-->
</STYLE>

</HEAD>

<BODY BACKGROUND="Egg shell.jpg">

<DIV ALIGN="center"><IMG SRC="nomad.jpg" ALIGN="right">
<H2>Frequently Asked Questions about</H2>
<H1>Dynamic HTML (DHTML)</H1></DIV><BR>

<H3>Click any of the popular questions about DHTML below to see its
answer.</H3>
```

FIGURE J-17: Web page linked to external style sheet

Frequently Asked Questions about

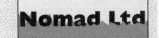

Dynamic HTML (DHTML)

Text color reflects
change made to
external style sheet

Click any of the popular questions about DHTML below to see its answer.

What is Dynamic HTML?

Is DHTML a new language?

How does DHTML work?

What can I do with DHTML?

What do I need to learn to use DHTML?

What are Cascading Style Sheets?

Practice

► Concepts Review

Label each DHTML item marked in Figure J-18.

FIGURE J-18

```
1 ——— <LINK REL="stylesheet" HREF="nomadltd.css" TYPE="text/css">

      <SCRIPT LANGUAGE="JavaScript">
      <!--
      NS4 = (document.layers) ? 1:0;
2 ———  IE4 = (document.all) ? 1:0;
      //-->
      </SCRIPT>

      <STYLE TYPE="text/css">
3 ———  <!--
      H1 {font-family: arial, sans-serif; font-size: 20pt}
      H2 {font-family: "times new roman", times, serif; font-size: 14pt; font-
      style: italic}
4 ———  .question {font-family: "times new roman", times, serif; font-size: 12pt;
      font-weight: bold}
      //-->
      </STYLE>

      </HEAD>

5 ———  <BODY BACKGROUND="Egg shell.jpg">
      <DIV STYLE="font-color: navy; text-decoration:underline" ALIGN="center">
      <H2>Frequently Asked Questions about</H2>
      <H1>Dynamic HTML (DHTML)</H1></DIV>
```

Match each term with its description.

6. Inline style
7. Embedded style
8. External style
9. Cascading
10. Class

a. System of precedence among style-sheet levels
b. Style associated with tags in Web page header
c. Style specified in local occurrence of tag
d. Named set of style specifications created as a tag attribute
e. Style specified in separate linked document

Select the best answer from the list of choices.

11. The most efficient method for assigning style to several text blocks marked with the same tag on one Web page is
    a. Inline style.
    b. Embedded style.
    c. External style.
    d. Linked style.

12. Embedded style sheets begin and end with which tagset?
    a. <SCRIPT> .. </SCRIPT>
    b. <STYLE> .. </STYLE>
    c. <STYLESHEET> .. </STYLESHEET>
    d. <CSS> .. </CSS>

13. **A browser-detection script**
    a. Makes your page's DHTML features viewable with any browser.
    b. Tells the user's browser which version of HTML your page uses.
    c. Tells the user's browser which version of JavaScript your page uses.
    d. Determines and stores the user's browser brand and generation.

14. **Which HTML tags does an external style sheet contain?**
    a. An external style sheet contains no HTML tags.
    b. <SCRIPT> .. </SCRIPT>
    c. <STYLE> .. </STYLE>
    d. <SCRIPT> .. </SCRIPT> and <STYLE> .. </STYLE>

15. **Which HTML tag do you use to associate an external style sheet with a Web page?**
    a. <LINK>
    b. <A>
    c. <CSS>
    d. <STYLE>

 # Skills Review

1. **Create an embedded style sheet.**
   a. Open the file HTML J-9.htm, then save it as a text document with the filename Tours FAQ embedded style.htm.
   b. Select the text [replace with embedded style sheet], press [Delete], type <STYLE TYPE="text/css">, press [Enter], then type <!-- and press [Enter].
   c. Type H1 {font-family: "comic sans ms", arial, sans-serif; font-size: 20pt} and press [Enter].
   d. Type H2 {font-family: "times new roman", times, bookman, serif; font-size: 16pt; font-style: italic} and press [Enter].
   e. Type //--> and press [Enter], then type </STYLE>.
   f. Check the document for errors, make changes as necessary, then save Tours FAQ embedded style.htm as a text document.
   g. Open your Web browser, then open Tours FAQ embedded style.htm to view the Web page.

2. **Create a class.**
   a. Open the file HTML J-10.htm in your text editor, then save it as a text document with the filename Tours FAQ class.htm.
   b. Select the text [replace with class style] in the embedded style sheet, then press [Delete].
   c. Type .title {font-family: garamond, arial, helvetica, sans-serif; font-size: 16pt; font-weight: bold}.
   d. Select the text [replace with class] in the <DIV> tag for the first bulleted list item, then press [Delete].
   e. Type CLASS="title".
   f. Repeat Steps d and e for the remaining two bulleted titles.
   g. Check the document for errors, make changes as necessary, then save Tours FAQ class.htm as a text document.
   h. Open Tours FAQ class.htm in your browser, then view the document.

3. **Detect browsers.**
   a. Open the file HTML J-11.htm in your text editor, then save it as a text document with the filename Tours FAQ browser detect.htm.
   b. Select the text [replace with browser detection script], then press [Delete].

c. Type the following script, pressing [Enter] at the end of each line:

```
<SCRIPT LANGUAGE="javascript">
<!--
NS4 = (document.layers) ? 1:0;
E4 = (document.all) ? 1:0;
//-->
</SCRIPT>
```

d. Check the document for errors, then make changes as necessary.

e. Save Tours FAQ browser detect.htm as a text document.

f. Open Tours FAQ browser detect.htm in your browser, then debug if necessary.

4. **Show and hide page elements.**

a. Open the file HTML J-12.htm in your text editor, then save it as a text document with the filename Tours FAQ show and hide.htm.

b. Scroll down and select the text [replace with expandIE function], then press [Delete].

c. Type the following code, pressing [Enter] at the end of each line

```
function expandIE(el) {
        theEl=eval(el + "ExpI");
        if (theEl.style.display == "none") {
                theEl.style.display="block";
                theEl.expanded=true;
        }
        else {
                theEl.style.display="none";
                theEl.expanded=false;
        }
}
```

d. Scroll down to the <DIV> tag for the first list item "Athlete", select the text [replace with opening A tag] and the space following it, then press [Delete].

e. Type <A HREF="#" onClick="expand('one'); return false">

f. Replace the text [replace with closing A tag] on the next line with </A>.

g. Repeat Steps d through f for the remaining two tour titles, substituting 'two' for 'one' in item two, and so forth.

h. Check the document for errors, making changes as necessary, then save Tours FAQ show and hide.htm as a text document.

i. Open Tours FAQ show and hide.htm in your browser, then click the first title "Athlete".

5. **Change font size dynamically.**

a. Open the file HTML J-13.htm in your text editor, then save it as a text document with the filename Tours FAQ text size.htm.

b. Scroll down the page, select the text [replace with text size functions], press [Delete], then type the following functions, pressing [Enter] at the end of each line

```
function changeText(whichTitle) {
        if (Nav4) {return}
        whichTitle.style.fontSize="24pt";
}
function changeTextBack(whichTitle) {
        if (Nav4) {return}
```

whichTitle.style.fontSize="12pt";
}

c. Scroll down the page to select the text [replace with event handlers] in the opening <A> tag for the first tour title "Athlete", then press [Delete].

d. Type onMouseOver="changeText(this)" onMouseOut="changeTextBack(this)".

e. Repeat Steps c and d for the remaining two list items.

f. Check the document for errors, make changes as necessary, then save Tours FAQ text size.htm as a text document.

g. Open the file Tours FAQ text size.htm in your browser, then move the pointer over the first heading.

6. **Control font color dynamically.**

   a. Open the file HTML J-14.htm in your text editor, then save it as a text document with the filename Tours FAQ text color.htm.

   b. Select the text [replace with changeText color] in the changeText function in the page header, then press [Delete].

   c. Type whichTitle.style.color="#236B8E";

   d. Select the text [replace with changeTextBack color] in the changeTextBack function in the page header, then press [Delete].

   e. Type whichTitle.style.color="#000000";

   f. Check the document for errors, making changes as necessary, then save Tours FAQ text color.htm as a text document.

   g. Open the file Tours FAQ text color.htm in your browser, then move the pointer over the first heading.

7. **Use an external style sheet.**

   a. Open the file HTML J-15.htm, then save it as a text document with the filename Tours FAQ external style.htm.

   b. Scroll down the page, select the text [replace with LINK tag] before the opening <STYLE> tag, then press [Delete].

   c. Type <LINK REL="stylesheet" HREF="nomadltd.css" TYPE="text/css">.

   d. Check the file for errors, make changes as necessary, then save Tours FAQ external style.htm as a text document.

   e. Open the file FAQ external style.htm in your Web browser and notice the green color added to the instruction text.

▶ # Independent Challenges

1. As you update and expand the Sandhills Regional Public Transit Web site, you decide to incorporate DHTML features into your pages. Currently, you are working to make a page on rider tips more interactive and easier to read. You decide to add dynamic size and color to the items on this page.

To complete this independent challenge:

   a. Open the file HTML J-16.htm in your text editor, then save it as a text document with the filename SRPT rider tips.htm.

   b. Select the text [replace with style sheet link] in the head section, press [Delete], then type <LINK REL=stylesheet HREF="HTML J-17.css" TYPE="text/css"> and save SRPT rider tips.htm as a text document.

   c. Select the text [replace with script], press [Delete], and type the following script, pressing [Enter] at the end of each line.

```
<SCRIPT LANGUAGE="javascript">
<!--
Nav4 = (document.layers) ? 1:0;
IE4 = (document.all) ? 1:0;

function changeText(whichTitle) {
```

```
        if (Nav4) {return}
        whichTitle.style.fontSize="24pt";
        whichTitle.style.color="#FF6347"
    }


    function changeTextBack(whichTitle) {
        if (Nav4) {return}
        whichTitle.style.fontSize="16pt";
        whichTitle.style.color="#000000";
    }


    //-->
    </SCRIPT>
```

d. Select the text [replace with event handlers] in the opening <DIV> tag for each of the five tips, press [Delete], then type onMouseOver="changeText(this)" onMouseOut="changeTextBack(this)"

e. Save SRPT rider tips.htm as a text document.

f. Start your browser, cancel any dial-up activities, open SRPT rider tips.htm, then move the cursor over the tips to verify that they change color and increase in font size.

Note: This change will only be noticeable if you are using Internet Explorer 4.

g. If necessary, edit the code in your text editor until the DHTML features work in IE4, and save SRPT rider tips.htm as a text file.

2. While reorganizing the Community Public School Volunteers Web publication, you decide that the pages should have a uniform style. You think the easiest way to create and apply this style would be to make an external style sheet and link each page to it.

To complete this independent challenge:

a. Open the file HTML J-18.htm in your text editor, then save it as a text document with the filename CPSV home.htm.

b. Select the text of the embedded style sheet in the head section, including the opening and closing <STYLE> tags, then copy it to the Clipboard.

c. Open a new text file in your text editor, paste the style sheet from the Clipboard into it, then save this file as a text document with the name CPSV style.css.

d. Reopen CPSV home.htm in your text editor, delete the embedded style sheet from the head section, replace it with <LINK REL=stylesheet HREF="CPSV style.css" TYPE="text/css"> and save CPSV home.htm as a text document.

e. Open CPSV home.htm in your Web browser and notice the formatting created by the external style sheet.

f. If necessary, use your text editor to edit and save your document until it displays correctly.

3. The Green House plant store's most heavily viewed Web page lists popular items available at the store, along with descriptions and prices. The owners would like you to add DHTML features to this page. You decide to convert the list to an expanding outline.

To complete this independent challenge:

a. Open the file HTML J-19.htm in your text editor, then save it as a text document with the filename Green House supplies.htm.

b. Select the text [replace with LINK tag], press [Delete], then type <LINK REL="stylesheet" HREF="HTML J-20.css" TYPE="text/css"> and save Green House supplies.htm as a text document.

c. Select the text [replace with script], press [Delete], then type the following script, pressing [Enter] at the end of each line

Nav4 = (document.layers) ? 1:0;
IE4 = (document.all) ? 1:0;

```
ver4 =(Nav4 II IE4)?1:0;

function expandIE(el) {
    theEl=eval(el + "Desc");
    if (theEl.style.display == "none") {
            theEl.style.display="block";
            theEl.expanded=true;
    }
    else {
            theEl.style.display="none";
            theEl.expanded=false;
    }
}

function changeText(whichProduct) {
    if (Nav4) {return}
    whichProduct.style.fontSize="24pt";
    whichProduct.style.color="#215E21";
}

function changeTextBack(whichProduct) {
    if (Nav4) {return}
    whichProduct.style.fontSize="14pt";
    whichProduct.style.color="#000000";
}
```

d. In the <DIV> tag for the first product name, Potting soil, select the text [replace with opening A tag], press [Delete], then type <A HREF="#" onClick="expand('one'); return false"; onMouseOver="changeText(this)" onMouseOut="changeTextBack(this)">

e. Replace the text [replace with closing A tag] on the next line with </A>.

f. Repeat Steps d and e for the remaining four product names, replacing 'one' with 'two' for the second item, and so forth, then save Green House supplies.htm as a text document.

g. Open your browser, open Green House supplies.htm, then move the cursor over a heading and click it. *Note*: The text size and color events work only in Internet Explorer 4.

h. If necessary, edit the code in your text editor until the expanding outline works and the text size and color changes work in IE4, then save Green House supplies.htm as a text document.

WEB WORK

4. Even though it's complicated, many Web page designers have created cross-browser code to create text-rollover effects in both major fourth-generation browsers. To complete this independent challenge, open a search engine and search on one or more keywords, such as DHTML, cross-browser, or rollover. Using the results from the search engine, open and investigate Web sites that provide tutorials or articles on creating DHTML to find a sample of cross-browser text-rollover code. Print the code, along with any accompanying explanation. After reading the article and scanning the code, make a list on a separate sheet of paper of the compromises the designer found necessary when creating the code. Count the number of code lines necessary to create this feature and, if possible, total those used exclusively by each browser. Submit your printouts and your list to your instructor.

HTML

► Visual Workshop

Add the dynamic size and color features shown in Figure J-19 to each of the five bulleted items in the file HTML J-21.htm. Open HTML J-21 in your text editor, then save it as a text document with the filename Books.htm. Use the script listed in Independent Challenge 1, Step 3 in the page's head section. Use the code from Independent Challenge 1, Step C, in the opening <DIV> tags for the elements that will change color and size. Substitute the color #8E2323 (firebrick), or another color of your choice, to provide contrast to the background.

FIGURE J-19

Book ordering guidelines

In order to search for a book we don't have in stock, we need as much information as you have about it. At a minimum, we recommend one of the following:

- Author's name
- **Full book title**

Controlling
Content Dynamically

- ▶ Understand dynamic content
- ▶ Insert content dynamically
- ▶ Delete content dynamically
- ▶ Modify content dynamically
- ▶ Incorporate an advanced content function
- ▶ Replace graphics dynamically
- ▶ Bind data
- ▶ Manipulate bound data dynamically

Just as dynamic HTML (DHTML) allows you to create pages whose style changes instantly based on user actions, it also provides tools that allow users to immediately modify a page's content. You can use this feature, known as **dynamic content**, to generate all or part of the page when it is opened, or even to alter the page's contents in response to user events. ◢━━ The manager of Nomad Ltd's retail division has heard about dynamic HTML and has asked Lydia to add dynamic content features to some of their Web pages to increase their interactivity. Lydia plans to use dynamic content features that will allow users to adapt the pages to their needs.

HTML

Understanding Dynamic Content

Dynamic HTML includes many tools for altering a Web page's appearance in response to user actions. Using scripts to change text attributes such as color and font size alter the style of elements, leaving the elements themselves, such as text or images, unchanged. Dynamic content tools, however, allow your Web page elements to move or change based on user input. These changes can include the elements themselves as well as the HTML tags associated with elements. Dynamic content can create an effect similar to an expanding outline. The outline actually uses a style attribute, "display" or "appearance," to simply show or hide text while the text remains part of the Web page. True dynamic content involves element reordering and replacing. As she learns about dynamic content, Lydia identifies several of its main uses and thinks about ways she can use it on the Nomad Ltd Web site.

 ### Pointing

Dynamic content allows you to change an element in response to a user's mouse pointer movements. You already have learned about the formatting changes you can create using dynamic style. Now, using dynamic content, you can make your page's text and graphic contents available to user changes. Figure K-1 shows a Web page displaying an alternate graphic in response to user pointing.

 ### Run-time activities

Dynamic content tools can create portions of your Web pages for you at **run time**, the period when a browser first interprets and displays the Web page and runs scripts. A simple case would be a script that displays the text "Good Morning!" or "Good Evening!" based on the time of day according to your computer's clock. You also can program a page to generate a table of contents for the page at run time, which allows you to change the page's structure and contents without also revising the TOC each time you make a change.

HTML tables

In addition to standard tools for working with Web page text, dynamic content includes special features for easily creating and working with tables. You can use dynamic content tools to associate an external database with a Web page, a process known as **data binding**. Data binding allows the user's browser to generate a Web page table from an external data file at run time. By adding some lines of script, you also can allow users to sort the table right on your Web page. Figure K-2 shows a dynamically generated table in a Web page that has been sorted by the Web page user.

FIGURE K-1: Dynamic content responding to user pointing

Color graphic
replaces
original line
art in
response to
pointer

Line art of
tent design

As you narrow your choices, click the Remove button for each tent that you're no longer considering, to remove it from the page.

Tent footprints and descriptions

XTC Starlite
One of the lightest, most compact three-season tents available. Featuring two-pole clip design with a built-in vestibule.

Remove Starlite

Amano Brevifolia
The simple, vaulted design characterized by two doors and two vestibules returns with the 2000 Brevifolia model. New features include: ground level, rainfly with vents, and vaulted sleeves for smoother pole feeding.

Remove Brevifolia

Amano Trifolia

FIGURE K-2: Table sorted by user

Bound data not sorted

Tent	Catalog number	Area (sq ft)	Vestibule (sq ft)	Description	Capacity	Weight	Price
XTC Starlite	BR-370	34	10	Staked	1 person	4 lbs. 3 oz.	$150
Amano Brevifolia	BT-356	38.5	19.6	Freestanding	2 people	5 lbs. 8 oz.	$215
Amano Trifolia	BT-358	49	25.7	Freestanding	2 people	7 lbs.	$250
Vista Hillside	BZ-339	32	15.3	Staked	1 person	4 lbs.	$120
Vista Hilltop	BZ-367	37.5	19.5			5 lbs. 3	
Vista Peak	BZ-323	42.5	24.4				
Vista Summit	BZ-334	51.5	28				

For more information on Nomad Ltd outdoor sup

Table sorted in
response to click
on column head

Tent	Catalog number	Area (sq ft)	Vestibule (sq ft)	Description	Capacity	Weight	Price
XTC Starlite	BR-370	34	10	Staked	1 person	4 lbs. 3 oz.	$150
Vista Hillside	BZ-339	32	15.3	Staked	1 person	4 lbs.	$120
Vista Hilltop	BZ-367	37.5	19.5	Staked	1 person	5 lbs. 3 oz.	$160
Amano Brevifolia	BT-356	38.5	19.6	Freestanding	2 people	5 lbs. 8 oz.	$215
Vista Peak	BZ-323	42.5	24.4	Freestanding	2 people	6 lbs. 3 oz.	$210
Amano Trifolia	BT-358	49	25.7	Freestanding	2 people	7 lbs.	$250
Vista Summit	BZ-334	51.5	28	Freestanding	2 people	7 lbs. 10 oz.	$275

For more information on Nomad Ltd outdoor supplies, please email our sales department

CLUES TO USE

Dynamic HTML features are not discrete

Although you can divide dynamic HTML effects into categories, such as dynamic style and dynamic content, the tools you use to create these effects often overlap. For example, to implement cross-browser dynamic style, you often need to identify the brand of the user's browser and then add lines to the embedded style sheet that are appropriate for the browser. Because you are adding code to the Web page at run time, this is a use of dynamic content to create dynamic style! As you learn more DHTML features and tools, their implementation will overlap increasingly.

Inserting Content Dynamically

Adding content at run time with scripts can allow you to create impressively customized and versatile Web pages. Because the DOM provides access to all the elements of a Web page, you can use scripts to alter any page elements based on conditions on the user's computer or on the page's current contents. ✎ Lydia's first project for the retail department is a Web page that compares the tents that Nomad Ltd sells. She wants to add a statement announcing the number of tent models that users can read about on the page. She can use a script to count the number of tent descriptions on the page and then insert the number dynamically in the page header statement that appears at the bottom of the page when the page loads. This means that the page header statement will still show the correct number even after the sales department adds to or removes tents and their descriptions from its tent selection.

Steps 1 2 3 4

1. **Start your Web browser program and cancel any dial-up activities, then open the file HTML K-1.htm**
   The page shows each tent's floor plan, or footprint, along with the tent's description.

2. **Start your text editor program, open the file HTML K-1.htm, then save it as text document with the filename Tent count.htm**
   Lydia has included a function in the page header that counts the number of tent-description headings in the page and assigns the number to the variable totalTents.

3. **Scroll to the bottom of the page code, highlight the text [replace with tent count code], then press [Delete]**

> **QuickTip**
> Be sure to type a space after the word *describes* and a space before the word *tent*.

4. **Type the following code, pressing [Enter] at the end of each line**

```
<SCRIPT>
<!--
if (IE4) {
    countHeaders()
    document.write("<H1 ALIGN='center'>This page describes ")
    document.write(totalTents)
    document.write(" tent models.</H1>")
}
//-->
</SCRIPT>
```

   Figure K-3 shows the completed Web page code containing the script. The code formats the text "This page describes" and "tent models." as centered on the page with an H1 format. Between the two bits of text, the script uses the document.write method to insert the value counted by the countHeaders function, which is assigned to the variable "totalTents." Because the script that counts the headers works only in Internet Explorer 4, the script begins by checking the browser version.

5. **Check your document for errors, make changes as necessary, then save Tent count.htm as a text document**

6. **Open Tent count.htm in your Web browser, then scroll to the bottom of the page**
   Figure K-4 shows the Web page in Internet Explorer 4. The H1 text Lydia added appears near the bottom of the page. The statement includes the number of tents counted by the countHeaders function and inserted with a script.

FIGURE K-3: Completed Web page code

```
<DIV ID="tent7" name="tent">

<DIV CLASS="tenthead"><IMG SRC="summit.jpg" ALIGN="left">Vista Summit</DIV>

<DIV>Comfortable, rugged, 4-season tent. Quick setup, full rainfly, integral
vestibule, large door. Factory sealed, mesh window and door for
ventilation.</DIV><BR><BR>

<H2 ALIGN="center">Nomad Ltd has a tent that's right for you!</H2>

<SCRIPT>
<!--
if (IE4) {
     countHeaders()
     document.write("<H1 ALIGN='center'>This page describes ")
     document.write(totalTents)
     document.write(" tent models.</H1>")
}
//-->
</SCRIPT>

<DIV>For more information on Nomad Ltd outdoor supplies, please email our <A
HREF="MAILTO:sales@nomadltd.com">sales department</A></DIV>

</BODY>
</HTML>
```

Text and script for tent count statement

FIGURE K-4: Web page displaying tent count

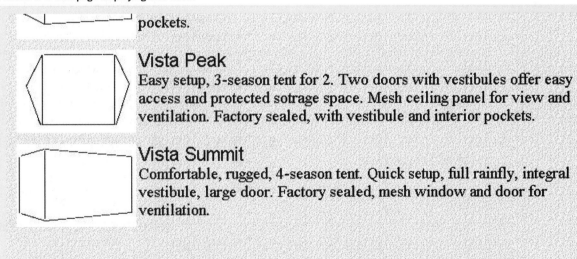

pockets.

Vista Peak
Easy setup, 3-season tent for 2. Two doors with vestibules offer easy access and protected sotrage space. Mesh ceiling panel for view and ventilation. Factory sealed, with vestibule and interior pockets.

Vista Summit
Comfortable, rugged, 4-season tent. Quick setup, full rainfly, integral vestibule, large door. Factory sealed, mesh window and door for ventilation.

Nomad Ltd has a tent that's right for you!

This page describes 7 tent models.

For more information on Nomad Ltd outdoor supplies, please email our sales department

Total calculated by counting script

Deleting Content Dynamically

In addition to adding Web page elements dynamically at run time, you can script your Web page to allow users to tailor it to suit their needs. For example, some scripts can allow users to delete elements from a Web page, including text and graphics. This feature—especially useful in a content-laden page—allows the user to pare down the content in order to view only pertinent elements or sections. Because users of the tent comparison page will be trying to select a tent based on their needs, Lydia thinks it would be helpful to allow users to remove information they are not interested in from the page for tents.

1. Open the file HTML K-2.htm in your text editor, then save it as a text document with the filename Tent delete.htm

2. Scroll down the page to view the body text describing the first tent, the XTC Starlite, select the text [insert button code for tent1], then press [Delete]

3. Type the following code, pressing [Enter] at the end of each line

   ```
   <SCRIPT LANGUAGE="javascript">
   <!--
   if (IE4) {
   ```

Trouble?
To specify the null value, be sure to type single quotes after HTML=.

4. Press [Tab], then type document.write("<BUTTON CLASS='button' onClick=tent1.outerHTML=''>Remove Starlite</BUTTON>") and press [Enter]
   The <BUTTON> tag set creates a button with a customized function in Internet Explorer 4 only. The text between the tags is the label that appears on the button. Lydia has inserted a class definition called .button in the page's embedded style sheet. She uses the onClick event handler to change the **outerHTML** property of the object named tent1, which includes the description and graphic for the first tent. An element's outerHTML property includes the element contents and the tags surrounding it, so changing the property to a null value removes the element and its surrounding tags from the Web page.

5. Type } and press [Enter], then type the following closing script tags, pressing [Enter] at the end of each line

   ```
   //-->
   </SCRIPT>
   ```

6. Repeat Steps 2 through 5 for the remaining six tent descriptions, substituting the button object names and tent names as listed in Table K-1
   Figure K-5 shows the Web page containing the button code for the first two tent descriptions.

7. Check the document for errors, make changes as necessary, then save Tent delete.htm as a text document

8. Open Tent delete.htm in your Web browser and scroll down the page until the Amano Brevifolia description appears in the document window
   Internet Explorer 4 displays the "Remove Brevifolia" button, but other browsers do not show the buttons. Even though the function for deleting content only works in Internet Explorer 4, your cross-browser Web page still displays the basic tent information in other browsers without causing JavaScript errors.

9. If you are using Internet Explorer, click the Remove Brevifolia button
   As Figure K-6 shows, the Web browser removes the tent's description and graphic. Next, Lydia will need to be sure the counter reflects this change by updating the number of tent descriptions displayed.

FIGURE K-5: Web page containing code for delete buttons

Code for first delete button

Tent ID

Code for second delete button

Button text

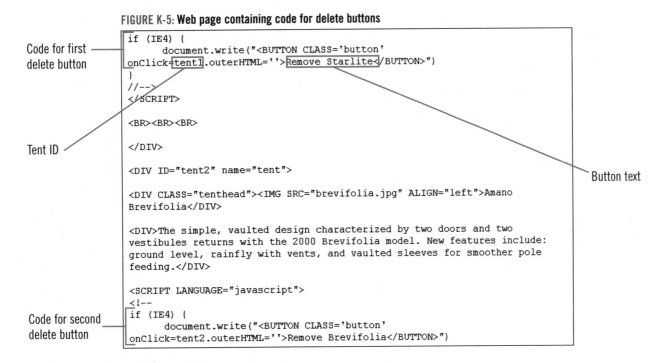

```
if (IE4) {
        document.write("<BUTTON CLASS='button'
onClick=tent1.outerHTML=''>Remove Starlite</BUTTON>")
}
//-->
</SCRIPT>

<BR><BR><BR>

</DIV>

<DIV ID="tent2" name="tent">

<DIV CLASS="tenthead"><IMG SRC="brevifolia.jpg" ALIGN="left">Amano
Brevifolia</DIV>

<DIV>The simple, vaulted design characterized by two doors and two
vestibules returns with the 2000 Brevifolia model. New features include:
ground level, rainfly with vents, and vaulted sleeves for smoother pole
feeding.</DIV>

<SCRIPT LANGUAGE="javascript">
<!--
if (IE4) {
        document.write("<BUTTON CLASS='button'
onClick=tent2.outerHTML=''>Remove Brevifolia</BUTTON>")
```

FIGURE K-6: Web page with Brevifolia removed

Brevifolia deleted from position between Starlite and Trifolia

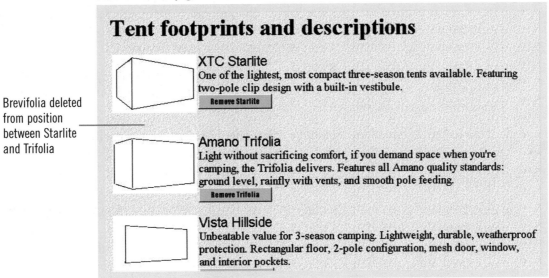

Tent footprints and descriptions

XTC Starlite
One of the lightest, most compact three-season tents available. Featuring
two-pole clip design with a built-in vestibule.
[Remove Starlite]

Amano Trifolia
Light without sacrificing comfort, if you demand space when you're
camping, the Trifolia delivers. Features all Amano quality standards:
ground level, rainfly with vents, and smooth pole feeding.
[Remove Trifolia]

Vista Hillside
Unbeatable value for 3-season camping. Lightweight, durable, weatherproof
protection. Rectangular floor, 2-pole configuration, mesh door, window,
and interior pockets.

TABLE K-1: Tent description IDs and button text

description number	substitute for "tent1"	substitute for "Starlite"
2	tent2	Brevifolia
3	tent3	Trifolia
4	tent4	Hillside
5	tent5	Hilltop
6	tent6	Peak
7	tent7	Summit

HTML

Modifying Content Dynamically

Dynamic content doesn't stop at adding or deleting static Web page content. Also, you can create pages that allow their contents to change in response to various events. You can use this feature to create a basic useful function, such as a DHTML clock, as part of a Web page. A DHTML clock function changes the contents of a text element displaying the time (for example, once per second) in response to the passing of time. You also can add interactivity by modifying page content in response to user actions. ▰▰▰ Because her page allows users to remove descriptions for tents that don't fit their needs, Lydia wants to ensure that the statement showing the number of tents available displays the correct number after user deletions.

Steps

1. Open the file HTML K-3.htm in your text editor, save it as a text document with the filename Tent update.htm, then scroll down the page until the function reCount appears in the document window

   Notice that Lydia has added the function named reCount. The function reCount subtracts 1 from the total count of tent descriptions on the page and then uses the innerHTML property to update the number that appears in the statement at the bottom of the page. InnerHTML replaces an element but leaves its enclosing HTML tags intact. Lydia uses innerHTML because she wants to replace only the number, which is within HTML tags, and not any of the surrounding text or HTML tags. Lydia has written the code so that each of the buttons that removes a tent description from the page triggers the reCount function.

2. Scroll down the page until the opening <BUTTON> tag for tent1 appears

   Notice that Lydia has added a reference to the reCount function in the onClick event handler. She has added this reference for each of the buttons.

3. Scroll to the bottom of the Web page code, select the text [replace with code to write opening SPAN tag], then press [Delete]

4. Type document.write("<SPAN ID='textnum'<>")

5. Select the text [replace with code to write closing SPAN tag], press [Delete], then type document.write("</SPAN>")

   Figure K-7 shows the completed code containing the SPAN tags. By inserting the SPAN tags with an ID value, you create an inline object named "textnum" that you can manipulate with scripts. Lydia's reCount function changes textnum's innerHTML property each time the user clicks one of the delete buttons. This use of dynamic content keeps the contents of the Web page statement current with page changes produced by user actions.

6. Check your document for errors, make changes as necessary, then save Tent update.htm as a text document

7. Open Tent update.htm in your Web browser, then scroll to the bottom of the page

   In Internet Explorer 4, notice that the tent description total, which is currently 7, displays in the statement.

8. If you are using Internet Explorer, click the Remove Summit button

   The browser removes the description for the Vista Summit tent. Simultaneously, it updates the tent description total to 6, as Figure K-8 shows.

9. If you are using Internet Explorer, click the Remove Hilltop button

   The browser removes the Vista Hilltop description, and again changes the tent total to reflect the current number of descriptions on the page.

FIGURE K-7: Code containing SPAN tags

```
</SCRIPT>

<BR><BR>

</DIV>

<H2 ALIGN="center">Nomad Ltd has a tent that's right for you!</H2>

<SCRIPT>
<!--
if (IE4) {
        countHeaders()
        document.write("<H1 ALIGN='center'>This page describes ")
        document.write("<SPAN ID='textnum'>")
        document.write(totalTents)
        document.write("</SPAN>")
        document.write(" tent models.</H1>")
}
//-->
</SCRIPT>

<DIV>For more information on Nomad Ltd outdoor supplies, please email our <A
HREF="MAILTO:sales@nomadltd.com">sales department</A></DIV>

</BODY>
</HTML>
```

JavaScript to write opening and closing SPAN tags inserted

FIGURE K-8: Web page displaying updated total

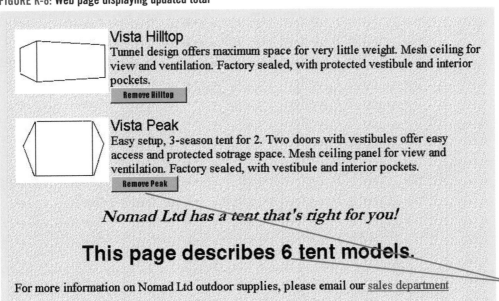

Tent total updated to 6 because Summit tent description deleted

Tool Tips and other floating help

In both Internet Explorer and Netscape Navigator, you can create floating windows that display text relevant to an element when the user moves the cursor over it. This effect is similar to ToolTips in Microsoft applications. These windows are dynamic modifications of the page content in response to user actions. For images, you can use the ALT property to specify the text that displays in a floating window when the user holds the mouse pointer over the image. For other Web page elements, Netscape Navigator versions 3 and 4 require a script to add this effect. However, you can add this effect in Internet Explorer 4 by adding TITLE="text" to the opening tag for the element. Because these floating windows add and remove Web page text, they are part of your set of dynamic content tools.

HTML

Unit K
HTML

Incorporating an Advanced Content Function

Combining different DHTML tools in your scripts allows for a great variety of possible new dynamic content effects, including different ways of presenting or changing your page elements. You can make your Web page unique as well as make it easier for users to read and navigate by incorporating special features into your Web page. These features also can increase your Web page readership. ✦──── Lydia sees a page on the Web containing a script that cycles through different Web page elements in the same spot. This effect is like a slide show, with each new segment of text appearing after a short interval. She decides to use this feature on the tent page she is developing to display some additional information about Nomad Ltd's products.

Steps 1 2 3 4

1. Open the file HTML K-4.htm in your text editor, save it as a text document with the filename Tent cycle.htm, then scroll down the page until the code for the function cycle appears in the document window

   Notice that Lydia entered the function cycle in the page head script. This function replaces an object's contents at regular intervals by using the innerHTML property in conjunction with the script for counting time.

2. Scroll down the Web page code until the top of the body section appears in the document window, select the text [replace with text cycle script], then press [Delete]

3. Type the following script, pressing [Enter] at the end of each line:

   ```
   <SCRIPT LANGUAGE="javascript">
   <!--
   function addCycle() {
   ```

4. Press [Tab], the type cycle(txt1, "Hiking,Bicycling,Camping,Kayaking,Climbing, find all your gear at,nomadltd.com", 30) and press [Enter]

   This line defines the display parameters for the text you want to cycle as follows: txt1 indicates the name of the object whose value will be cycled; the text in quotes separated by commas specifies the different words and phrases that should cycle; and the number 30 tells how long one word or phrase should display before cycling to the next word or phrase.

5. Type the remaining code, pressing [Enter] at the end of each line

   ```
   }
   if (IE4) {window.onload = new Function("addCycle()")}
   //-->
   </SCRIPT>
   ```

   Figure K-9 shows the Web page source code containing the completed script. This script triggers the function cycle, which begins to cycle text after the page loads.

6. Check your document for errors, make changes as necessary, then save Tent cycle.htm as a text document and open it in your Web browser

   In Internet Explorer 4, the cycling text appears in the top right corner of the page, as shown in Figure K-10. The text cycles at a regular 3-second interval as specified by 30 in the script.

Script to invoke text cycling function

```
<IMG SRC="nomad.jpg" ALIGN="left">

<DIV ID="txt1" ALIGN="right" CLASS="tenthead" STYLE="font-size: 18pt"></DIV>

<SCRIPT LANGUAGE="javascript">
<!--
function addCycle() {
        cycle(txt1, "Hiking,Bicycling,Camping,Kayaking,Climbing,find all your
gear at,nomadltd.com", 30)
}

if(IE4) {window.onload = new Function("addCycle()")}
//-->
</SCRIPT>

<BR><BR><BR>
<DIV ALIGN="center" STYLE="font-size: 24pt; font-weight: bold; font-family:
arial; font-style: normal">Tents</DIV>
<H2 ALIGN="center">Selecting one that's right for you</H2>
<BR>

<DIV>Choosing a quality tent that meets your needs can be an intimidating
task. To help you out with this important decision, we've added features to
this page to make it easier to compare the characteristics of our tents.
<BR><BR>
As you narrow your choices, click the Remove button for each tent that
```

Text content changes every few seconds

FIGURE K-10: Web page displaying cycling text

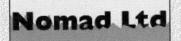

find all your gear at

Tents

Selecting one that's right for you

Choosing a quality tent that meets your needs can be an intimidating task. To help you out with this important decision, we've added features to this page to make it easier to compare the characteristics of our tents.

As you narrow your choices, click the Remove button for each tent that you're no longer considering, to remove it from the page.

Tent footprints and descriptions

HTML

Replacing Graphics Dynamically

All the examples so far have used dynamic content tools to modify a Web page's text, but these features are equally valid for other page elements, including graphics. In a simple scenario, you can use dynamic content features to change the graphic displayed using the onMouseOver event handler. In a more complex scenario, you could gradually change a graphic's size to create the effect of animation. Lydia wants to use color to highlight the element that the user is currently pointing to. However, rather than using dynamic style, she creates colored versions of each of the tent footprint graphics. The color version of a text footprint graphic will appear in response to mouse movement over each graphic or its associated text.

Steps

1. Open the file **HTML K-5.htm** in your text editor, then save it as a text document with the filename **Tent color.htm**

2. Scroll down the Web page code until **<DIV CLASS="tenthead">** appears in the document window, select the text **[replace with star event handlers]**, then press **[Delete]**

3. Type **onMouseOver="star.src='starcolor.jpg'" onMouseOut="star.src='starlite.jpg'"**

4. Scroll down the Web page code, select the text **[replace with brev event handlers]**, press **[Delete]**, then type **onMouseOver="brev.src='brevcolor.jpg'" onMouseOut= "brev.src='brevifolia.jpg'"**

   Figure K-11 shows the completed code for the first two tent items. Notice that the IMG tag for each tent has a unique ID attribute. The onMouseOver event swaps a color graphic of the tent floorplan for the original image source. The onMouseOut event replaces the color image with the original black and white graphic.

5. Repeat Step 4 for the remaining five list items, using the IDs and graphic files listed in Table K-2

6. Check your document for errors, make changes as necessary, then save **Tent color.htm** as a text document

7. Open **Tent color.htm** in your browser

8. Scroll down to the list of tent descriptions, then move your mouse pointer over the heading or graphic for the XTC Starlite

   See Figure K-12. When you move the cursor over the black and white outline or its associated heading in Internet Explorer 4, the image is replaced with a color graphic. Even though you are simply swapping one graphic for another, this action creates the illusion of modifying the original graphic, much like changing text color using style sheets.

9. Move the mouse pointer off the first list item

   The graphic changes back to the black and white version. Notice that if you move the mouse pointer over other tent graphics, they change color in response to the mouse movement.

FIGURE K-11: Event handlers for first and second list items

Event handlers for Starlite inserted in DIV tag

ID attribute

IMG source

Event handlers for Brevifolia inserted in DIV tag

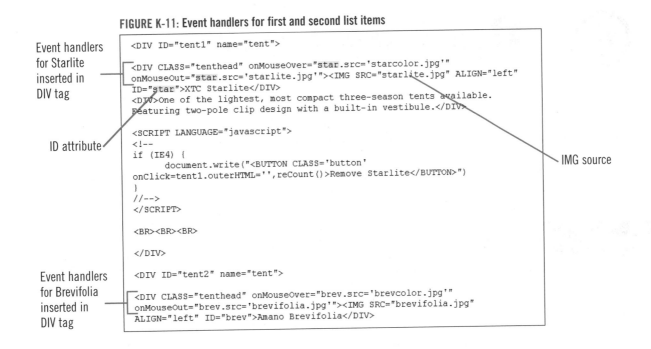

```
<DIV ID="tent1" name="tent">

<DIV CLASS="tenthead" onMouseOver="star.src='starcolor.jpg'"
onMouseOut="star.src='starlite.jpg'"><IMG SRC="starlite.jpg" ALIGN="left"
ID="star">XTC Starlite</DIV>
<DIV>One of the lightest, most compact three-season tents available.
Featuring two-pole clip design with a built-in vestibule.</DIV>

<SCRIPT LANGUAGE="javascript">
<!--
if (IE4) {
        document.write("<BUTTON CLASS='button'
onClick=tent1.outerHTML='',reCount()>Remove Starlite</BUTTON>")
}
//-->
</SCRIPT>

<BR><BR><BR>

</DIV>

<DIV ID="tent2" name="tent">

<DIV CLASS="tenthead" onMouseOver="brev.src='brevcolor.jpg'"
onMouseOut="brev.src='brevifolia.jpg'"><IMG SRC="brevifolia.jpg"
ALIGN="left" ID="brev">Amano Brevifolia</DIV>
```

FIGURE K-12: Web page showing substituted graphic

Color graphic replaces original in response to pointer

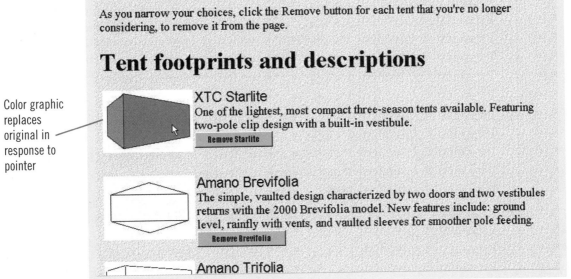

TABLE K-2: List item IDs and graphic filenames

list item	id	color graphic name (onMouseOver)	black and white graphic name (onMouseOut)
1	star	starcolor.jpg	starlite.jpg
2	brev	brevcolor.jpg	brevifolia.jpg
3	tri	trifolia.jpg	tricolor.jpg
4	hillside	hillsidecolor.jpg	hillside.jpg
5	hilltop	hilltopcolor.jpg	hilltop.jpg
6	peak	peakcolor.jpg	peak.jpg
7	summit	summitcolor.jpg	summit.jpg

HTML

Binding Data

DHTML's dynamic content tools offer specialized features for working with tables in your Web pages. One of the most powerful is dynamic table generation, first introduced in Internet Explorer 4. Instead of creating a table using a tag for each element, you can simply create the headers, then add code to reference data located in an external file. Linking an external database with a Web page is known as **data binding**. When the page loads, the browser creates the table at run time. Because the table is re-created each time a user opens the page, you can change the contents of the external data source without changing the Web page code. ◄━━━ Because it's helpful for tent shoppers to be able to compare the details of different models, such as area and weight, Lydia decides to add a tent data table to the Web page. The sales department has provided a text file containing the appropriate information. Lydia binds the file to her Web page to create a dynamic table.

Steps

1. Open the file **HTML K-6.htm** in your text editor, then save it as a text document with the filename **Tent comparison table.htm**

2. Scroll to near the end of the code until the <OBJECT> tags and list of tent descriptions appears in the document window

Figure K-13 shows the code including the OBJECT tags. These tags, which Lydia entered earlier, set up the external file containing the data for her table as a Web page object. The CLASSID attribute calls the Internet Explorer routine for dynamic table generation to format the linked data. The PARAM tags within the beginning and ending OBJECT tags denote parameters for this object. The DataURL parameter identifies the name of the external file to be bound, which is named tents.txt. The True value for the UseHeader attribute specifies that the data in the external file includes a row of information identifying the contents of each column.

3. Select the text [replace with opening TABLE tag], press [Delete], and type <TABLE BORDER="1" ID="elemtbl" DATASRC="#tentlist">

The TABLE tag formats the code that follows as rows in a table. The DATASRC attribute refers to the preceding object, named "tentlist." The number sign indicates that the source is an object in the same Web page.

4. Scroll down, select the text [replace with closing TABLE tag], press [Delete], then type </TABLE>

The rows within the TABLE tags contain row header display information and links to the columns in the external source. The DATAFLD attribute in each DIV tag names the column header in the external file that marks the column to be associated with the tag. Notice that below the closing TABLE tag, Lydia has inserted a script to display extra information for users not running IE4. Because these browsers will not display the bound data, Lydia provides another method for them to obtain the table information.

5. Check your document for errors, make changes as necessary, then save **Tent comparison table.htm** as a text document

6. Open **Tent comparison table.htm** in your browser, then scroll to the bottom of the page

The tent comparison information from the bound data file appears in a table, as shown in Figure K-14. The sales department can add, remove, or edit lines from the external file, and the Web page table will automatically reflect the most current information each time the Web page is loaded.

FIGURE K-13: **OBJECT tags in Web page source**

Code to format imported data

```
<OBJECT ID="tentlist" CLASSID="clsid:333C7BC4-460F-11D0-BC04-0080C7055A83">
      <PARAM NAME="DataURL" VALUE="tents.txt">
      <PARAM NAME="UseHeader" VALUE="True">
</OBJECT>

[replace with opening TABLE tag]

<THEAD>
<TR>
<TD><B><DIV ID=tent>Tent</DIV></B></TD>
<TD><B><DIV ID=catno>Catalog number</DIV></B></TD>
<TD><B><DIV ID=area>Area (sq ft)</DIV></B></TD>
<TD><B><DIV ID=vest>Vestibule (sq ft)</DIV></B></TD>
<TD><B><DIV ID=desc>Description</DIV></B></TD>
<TD><B><DIV ID=cap>Capacity</DIV></B></TD>
<TD><B><DIV ID=weight>Weight</DIV></B></TD>
<TD><B><DIV ID=price>Price</DIV></B></TD>
</TR>
</THEAD>
<TBODY>
<TR>
<TD><DIV DATAFLD="tent"></DIV></TD>
<TD><DIV DATAFLD="catno"></DIV></TD>
<TD><DIV DATAFLD="area"></DIV></TD>
```

FIGURE K-14: **Tent comparison table**

Browser-generated table based on external data source

Tent	Catalog number	Area (sq ft)	Vestibule (sq ft)	Description	Capacity	Weight	Price
XTC Starlite	BR-370	34	10	Staked	1 person	4 lbs. 3 oz.	$150
Amano Brevifolia	BT-356	38.5	19.6	Freestanding	2 people	5 lbs. 8 oz.	$215
Amano Trifolia	BT-358	49	25.7	Freestanding	2 people	7 lbs.	$250
Vista Hillside	BZ-339	32	15.3	Staked	1 person	4 lbs.	$120
Vista Hilltop	BZ-367	37.5	19.5	Staked	1 person	5 lbs. 3 oz.	$160
Vista Peak	BZ-323	42.5	24.4	Freestanding	2 people	6 lbs. 3 oz.	$210
Vista Summit	BZ-334	51.5	28	Freestanding	2 people	7 lbs. 10 oz.	$275

For more information on Nomad Ltd outdoor supplies, please email our sales department

Manipulating Bound Data Dynamically

In addition to dynamic table creation, Internet Explorer 4 introduced other cutting-edge tools for working with tables in Web pages. Perhaps one of the most useful is dynamic sorting, which enables users to sort the data in a table simply by clicking the relevant column heading. ✎ To allow users to compare tent statistics based on the most important categories, Lydia adds a script that sorts the tent information on a given column when a user clicks that column heading.

Steps

1. Open the file HTML K-7.htm in your text editor, then save it as a text document with the filename Tent sortable comparison table.htm

2. Scroll down to the script beneath the table code near the bottom of the page until function tentClick() { is visible
   Notice that Lydia has already entered scripts to sort the table. She created a separate script for each column. Each script sorts the table by the contents of that column using the tentlist.Sort= command, and then regenerates the table to show the sort, with tentlist.Reset(). Accompanying each script is a line of code triggering the script in response to the onclick event for the given column header.

3. Scroll to the bottom of the page, select the text [replace with price script], then press [Delete]

4. Type the following script, pressing [Enter] at the end of each line:
```
function priceClick() {
    tentlist.Sort="price";
    tentlist.Reset();
}
price.onclick=priceClick;
```
   Figure K-15 shows the completed Web page containing the script.

5. Check the script you entered for errors, then save Tent sortable comparison table.htm as a text document

6. Open Tent sortable comparison table.htm in your Web browser, then scroll to the bottom of the page
   The tent comparison table displays in its default order. Notice that the Vestibule (sq ft) column is not displayed in any particular order.

7. Click the Vestibule (sq ft) column heading, then scroll down to see the regenerated table
   The table disappears, then regenerates to show the records in ascending order by vestibule area, as shown in Figure K-16.

8. Click the Price column heading, then scroll down
   The table displays the records in order by price, using the script you entered.

9. Close the Web browser and text editor

```
        tentlist.Sort="weight";
        tentlist.Reset();
}

weight.onclick=weightClick;

function priceClick() {
    tentlist.Sort="price";
    tentlist.Reset();
}

price.onclick=priceClick;

if (!IE4) {
    document.write("If your browser does not display the above table,
please email us at the address below for up-to-date tent details and
prices.<BR><BR>")
}
//-->
</SCRIPT>

<DIV>For more information on Nomad Ltd outdoor supplies, please email our <A
HREF="MAILTO:sales@nomadltd.com">sales department</A></DIV>

</BODY>
</HTML>
```

Script for sorting table on the price column

price Column ID for column to be sorted

Sorts column in ascending order by price

Regenerates the table to show the sort

FIGURE K-16: Table sorted on vestibule area column

Tent	Catalog number	Area (sq ft)	Vestibule (sq ft)	Description	Capacity	Weight	Price
XTC Starlite	BR-370	34	10	Staked	1 person	4 lbs. 3 oz.	$150
Vista Hillside	BZ-339	32	15.3	Staked	1 person	4 lbs.	$120
Vista Hilltop	BZ-367	37.5	19.5	Staked	1 person	5 lbs. 3 oz.	$160
Amano Brevifolia	BT-356	38.5	19.6	Freestanding	2 people	5 lbs. 8 oz.	$215
Vista Peak	BZ-323	42.5	24.4	Freestanding	2 people	6 lbs. 3 oz.	$210
Amano Trifolia	BT-358	49	25.7	Freestanding	2 people	7 lbs.	$250
Vista Summit	BZ-334	51.5	28	Freestanding	2 people	7 lbs. 10 oz.	$275

For more information on Nomad Ltd outdoor supplies, please email our sales department

Table sorted in response to click on column head

Suppressing errors

When creating cross-browser code, you may want to add features to your pages that generate error messages in some browsers. To allow your information to get out to everyone who wants to view it without alarming viewers, you can include a script that keeps error messages from appearing in incompatible browsers. By setting the value of the object window.onerror to "null", you prevent error windows from opening when scripts have problems completing. Take care not to add error suppression until you have completed and debugged your page because error suppression removes an important debugging aid.

HTML

Practice

► Concepts Review

Label the code segments marked in Figure K-17.

FIGURE K-17

```
<DIV ID="tent1" name="tent">

<DIV CLASS="tenthead" onMouseOver="star.src='starcolor.jpg'"
onMouseOut="star.src='starlite.jpg'"><IMG SRC="starlite.jpg" ALIGN="left"
ID="star">XTC Starlite</DIV>
<DIV>One of the lightest, most compact three-season tents available.
Featuring two-pole clip design with a built-in vestibule.</DIV>

<SCRIPT LANGUAGE="javascript">
<!--
if (IE4) {
        document.write("<BUTTON CLASS='button'
onClick=tent1.outerHTML='',reCount()>Remove Starlite</BUTTON>")
}
//-->
</SCRIPT>

<BR><BR><BR>

</DIV>

<DIV ID="tent2" name="tent">

<DIV CLASS="tenthead" onMouseOver="brev.src='brevcolor.jpg'"
onMouseOut="brev.src='brevifolia.jpg'"><IMG SRC="brevifolia.jpg"
ALIGN="left" ID="brev">Amano Brevifolia</DIV>
```

5   4   2   1   3

Match each statement with the term that it decribes.

6. DHTML features that make immediate modifications to a page's actual content
7. Period when a browser first interprets and displays a Web page
8. Associating an external database with a Web page
9. HTML property for replacing an element and the HTML tags enclosing it
10. HTML property for replacing an element but leaving its enclosing HTML tags

a. Data binding
b. InnerHTML
c. Run time
d. OuterHTML
e. Dynamic content

Select the best answer from the list of choices.

11. The outerHTML for the code <DIV>Welcome to the Nomad Ltd home page!</DIV> is
   a. <DIV>Welcome to the Nomad Ltd home page!</DIV>.
   b. <DIV>Welcome to the Nomad Ltd home page!
   c. Welcome to the Nomad Ltd home page!.
   d. Welcome to the Nomad Ltd home page!</DIV>.

12. **A DHTML clock would be an example of**
    a. Deleting content.
    b. Modifying content.
    c. Adding content.
    d. Dynamic table generation

13. **Which HTML tag set do you use to list the properties for a dynamically generated table?**
    a. <TBL>..</TBL>
    b. <TABLE>..</TABLE>
    c. <THEAD>..</THEAD>
    d. <OBJECT>..</OBJECT>

 # Skills Review

1. **Insert content dynamically.**
   a. Open the file HTML K-8.htm in your text editor, then save it as a text document with the filename Pack count.htm.
   b. Scroll to the bottom of the Web page code, highlight the text [replace with pack count code], then press [Delete].
   c. Type the following code, pressing [Enter] at the end of each line:

```
<SCRIPT>
<!--
if (IE4) {
      countHeaders()
      document.write("<H1 ALIGN='center'>This page describes ")
      document.write(totalPacks)
      document.write(" pack models.</H1>")
}
//-->
</SCRIPT>
```

   d. Check your document for errors, make changes as necessary, then save Pack count.htm as a text document.
   e. Open Pack count.htm in your Web browser, then scroll down to the bottom of the page.

2. **Delete content dynamically.**
   a. Open the file HTML K-9.htm, then save it as a text document with the filename Pack delete.htm.
   b. Scroll down below the body text describing the first pack, the Nomad Moonlight, select the text [replace with button code for pack1], then press [Delete].
   c. Type the following code, pressing [Enter] at the end of each line:

```
<SCRIPT LANGUAGE="javascript">
<!--
if (IE4) {
```

   d. Press [Tab], then type document.write("<BUTTON CLASS='button' onClick=pack1.outerHTML="">Remove Moonlight</BUTTON>") and press [Enter].
   e. Type } and press [Enter], then enter the two closing SCRIPT tags.
   f. Repeat Steps b through e for the remaining six pack descriptions, substituting the object names and pack names, as listed in Table K-3.

HTML

TABLE K-3

description number	substitute for "pack1"	substitute for "Moonlight"
2	pack2	Blue Moon
3	pack3	Harvest Moon
4	pack4	New Moon
5	pack5	Full Moon
6	pack6	Trekker
7	pack7	Long Haul

g. Check the document for errors, make changes as necessary, then save Pack delete.htm as a text document.

h. Open Pack delete.htm in your Web browser, then scroll down the Web page until the Nomad Blue Moon pack description appears in the document window.

i. If you are using Internet Explorer, click the Remove Blue Moon button.

3. Modify content dynamically.

a. Open the file HTML K-10.htm in your text editor, then save it as a text document with the filename Pack update.htm.

b. Scroll to the bottom of the Web page code, select the text [replace with opening SPAN tag], then press [Delete].

c. Type document.write("<SPAN ID='textnum'>")

d. Select the text [replace with closing SPAN tag], press [Delete], type document.write("</SPAN>")

e. Check your document for errors, make changes as necessary, then save Pack update.htm as a text document.

f. Open Pack update.htm in your Web browser, then scroll to the bottom of the page.

g. If you are using Internet Explorer, click the Remove Long Haul button.

h. If you are using Internet Explorer, click the Remove Trekker button.

4. Incorporate an advanced function.

a. Open the file HTML K-11.htm in your text editor, then save it as a text document with the filename Pack scroll.htm.

b. Scroll down until the opening body tag appears in the document window, select the text [replace with text scroll script], then press [Delete].

c. Type onload="scrollit('Find all your outdoor supplies at nomadltd.com!');"

d. Check your document for errors, make changes as necessary, then save Pack scroll.htm as a text document.

e. Open Pack scroll.htm in your Web browser and watch the status bar to see the scrolling text that the new function creates. (*Note*: this feature functions in both Internet Explorer and Navigator.)

5. Replace graphics dynamically.

a. Open the file HTML K-12.htm in your text editor, then save it as a text document with the filename Pack color.htm.

b. Scroll down until the line <DIV CLASS="packhead" appears in the document window, select the text [replace with light event handlers], then press [Delete].

c. Type onMouseOver="light.src='lightcolor.jpg'" onMouseOut="light.src='moonlight.jpg'"

d. Scroll down and select the text [replace with blue event handlers], press [Delete], then type onMouseOver="blue.src='bluecolor.jpg'" onMouseOut="blue.src='bluemoon.jpg'"

e. Repeat Step d for the remaining five list items, using the IDs and graphic files listed in Table K-4.

TABLE K-4

list item	id	color graphic name (onMouseOver)	black and white graphic name (onMouseOut)
3	harvest	harvestcolor.jpg	harvest.jpg
4	newmoon	newcolor.jpg	newmoon.jpg
5	full	fullcolor.jpg	fullmoon.jpg
6	trek	trekcolor.jpg	trekker.jpg
7	long	longcolor.jpg	longhaul.jpg

f. Check your document for errors, make necessary changes, then save Pack color.htm as a text document.

g. Open Pack color.htm in your Web browser.

h. If you are using Internet Explorer 4, scroll down to the list of pack descriptions, then move your mouse pointer over the heading or graphic for the Nomad Moonlight.

i. Move your mouse pointer off the selected item.

6. Bind data.

a. Open the file HTML K-13.htm in your text editor, then save it as a text document with the filename Pack comparison table.htm.

b. Scroll to the end of the code for the list of pack descriptions until the <OBJECT> tags appear in the document window.

c. Select the text [replace with opening TABLE tag], press [Delete], then type <TABLE BORDER="1" ID="elemtb" DATASRC="#packlist">

d. Scroll down, select the text [replace with closing TABLE tag], press [Delete], then type </TABLE>

e. Check your document for errors, make necessary changes, then save Pack comparison table.htm as a text document.

f. Open Pack comparison table.htm in your browser, then scroll to the bottom of the page. (*Note*: remember that you will see the bound data only in IE 4.)

7. Manipulate bound data dynamically.

a. Open the file HTML K-14.htm in your text editor, then save it as a text document with the filename Pack sortable comparison table.htm.

b. Scroll to the bottom of the page, select the text [replace with price script], then press [Delete].

c. Type the following script, pressing [Enter] at the end of each line:

```
function priceClick() {
    packlist.Sort="price";
    packlist.Reset();
}
price.onclick=priceClick;
```

d. Check the script you entered for errors, make necessary changes, then save Pack sortable comparison table.htm as a text document.

e. Open Pack sortable comparison table.htm in your Web browser, then scroll to the bottom of the page.

f. If you are using Internet Explorer 4, click the Price column heading, then scroll down to see the regenerated table.

g. Close the Web browser and text editor.

▶ Independent Challenges

1. The owners of the Green House plant store want to allow online ordering on their Web page. On the page listing the Green House plant store's products, you have started adding a check box next to each item. Users can click on a check box next to each item they want to buy. Also, you have begun to add a line that reports the total number of items the user has marked for purchase.

To complete this independent challenge:

a. Open the file HTML K-15.htm in your text editor, then save it as a text document with the filename "Green House supply purchase.htm".

b. Scroll down to the end of the page's head section, select the text [replace with countChecks and reCount functions], then press [Delete].

c. Type the following lines of script, pressing [Enter] at the end of each line:

```
function countChecks() {
    items = 0;
    for (var i = 0; i < document.all.length; i++){
    var el = document.all[i];
    if (el.checked){
            items++;
            }
    }
}

function reCount() {
    countChecks()
    textnum.innerHTML=" " + items;
}
```

d. Check the script you entered for errors, make changes as necessary, then save Green House supply purchase.htm as a text document. *Hint*: To view a model of this script refer to the lesson "Modifying content dynamically" and the student files associated with that lesson.

e. Open "Green House supply purchase.htm" in your browser, then, if you are using Internet Explorer 4, click one of the check boxes and observe the value displayed for total number of items marked for purchase.

f. Check for errors, then use the text editor to make corrections as needed.

g. Close the browser and text editor.

2. You are creating a Web page containing route information for Sandhills Regional Public Transit. You want to allow riders to compare routes that different bus lines follow; and you want to ensure users can remove from the screen lines that do not apply to them.

To complete this independent challenge:

a. Open the file HTML K-16.htm in your text editor, then save it as a text document with the filename "SRPT route comparison.htm".

b. Scroll down to the first list item in the body section, delete the text "[replace with rt11 button code]", then type the following code, pressing [Enter] at the end of each line:

```
<SCRIPT LANGUAGE="javascript">
<!--
if (IE4) {
```

c. Press [Tab], type document.write("<BUTTON CLASS='button' onClick=rt11.outerHTML="">Remove Route 11</BUTTON>")

d. Press [Enter], type } and press [Enter], then add the two closing script tags.

e. Repeat Steps 2 through 4 for the remaining four buttons, replacing the text as indicated in Table K-5.

TABLE K-5

route	replace "rt11" with	replace "Route 11" with
12	rt12	Route 12
13	rt13	Route 13
14	rt14	Route 14
15	rt15	Route 15

f. Check your work, then save SRPT route comparison.htm as a text document.

g. Open "SRPT route comparison.htm" in the browser, and if you are using Internet Explorer, test the buttons to be sure they work.

h. Check for errors, use the text editor to make corrections as needed.

i. Close the browser and text editor.

3. The Community Public School Volunteers organization would like to add a page to their Web site listing schools that currently need volunteers. They also want to include contact information for each school so that potential volunteers can get started immediately. The organization maintains a database of the different schools' volunteer needs. They would like their Web page to reflect the current contents of the database.

To complete this independent challenge:

a. Open the file HTML K-17.htm in your text editor, then save it as a text document with the filename "CPSV volunteer opportunities.htm".

b. Select the text [replace with opening TABLE tag], press [Enter], then type the following code:
<TABLE BORDER="1" ID="elemtbl" DATASRC="#schools">

c. Add the following lines of script after the opening script tags and before the sorting function scripts:
if (!IE4) {
    document.write("If your browser does not display the above table, please contact us to find out about volunteer opportunities.")
}

d. Check your work, make changes as necessary, then save CPSV volunteer opportunities.htm as a text document.

e. Open CPSV volunteer opportunities.htm in the browser, and, if you are using Internet Explorer 4, test the table to verify that the table-generation and table-sorting functions work correctly.

f. Check for errors, use the text editor to make corrections as needed. *Hint*: To view model code, refer to the lessons "Generating a table dynamically" and "Manipulating table contents dynamically" as well as all student files associated with these files.

g. Close the browser and text editor.

4. By creating more complex scripts, you can adapt dynamic content features for a wide range of applications. To complete this independent challenge, connect to the Internet and find two Web pages that incorporate dynamic content in ways that are different than those you learned in this unit. Because you can write cross-browser code for some dynamic content features, you can complete this exercise using either Internet Explorer or Netscape Navigator. Print a copy of each page and circle the area of the page where the content changes dynamically. On another sheet of paper, briefly describe how the content changes, what triggers the change, and what qualifies the feature you circled as dynamic content.

▶ Visual Workshop

You have created a Web page for Touchstone Booksellers that makes their book-inventory database available online. They have provided you a preliminary text file that lists several books. Your task is to bind the text file to the Web page to create a dynamically generated table. The client has asked that you make the table sortable by users, as Figure K-18 illustrates. Open the file HTML K-18.htm, save it as a text document with the filename Touchstone sortable inventory.htm, then replace the text "[replace with sorting script]" with the necessary script to make the list sortable. You need to create a set of script code for each column in the database, as you did in the lesson "Manipulating table contents dynamically" in this unit. The script for the first column is:

```
    function titleClick() {
        booklist.Sort="title";
        booklist.Reset();
}
title.onclick=titleClick;
```

Table K-6 shows the variables to substitute to create the remaining script segments. Remember to include the opening and closing SCRIPT tags.

TABLE K-6

column	replace all four occurrences of "title" with
2	alast
3	afirst
4	year
5	bind
6	copies

FIGURE K-18

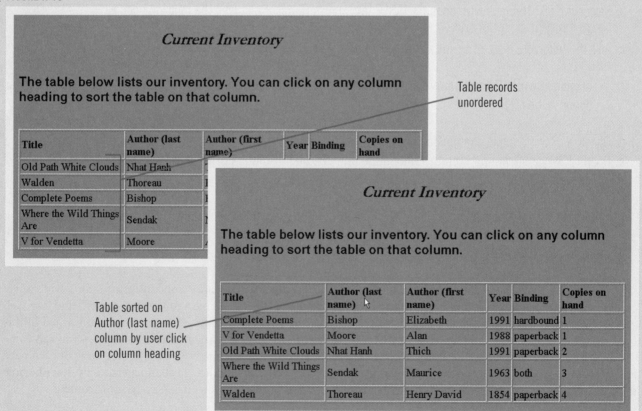

Table records unordered

Table sorted on Author (last name) column by user click on column heading

Positioning
with DHTML

Objectives

► **Understand DHTML positioning**
► **Position an element absolutely**
► **Position an element relatively**
► **Size an element manually**
► **Stack screen elements**
► **Add a scroll bar**
► **Create a sidebar**
► **Incorporate an advanced positioning function**

One of DHTML's greatest contributions to Web page design is a tool for **positioning**, or specifying the precise placement of elements within the page. Just like other DHTML components, DHTML positioning opens doors to many possibilities for new Web page features. Other DHTML features, such as scroll bars, complement positioning to help create effective page layouts.  Lydia wants to enrich the Web page design for the Nomad Ltd Web publication. She will use positioning and other DHTML layout features to create a sophisticated, attractive style.

Understanding DHTML Positioning

A fundamental difference between document layouts in traditional media, such as posters and magazines, and document layouts in HTML is HTML's lack of tools for precise placement of page elements. DHTML allows precise positioning of page elements through an extension of cascading style sheets called **Cascading Style Sheets - Positioning (CSS-P)**. CSS-P allows you to position elements either **absolutely**, at fixed coordinates on a user's screen, or **relatively**, based on the position of other screen elements. To specify positioning, you use the **position** attribute, which is a style sheet property. Although some advanced page layout is possible with basic HTML, CSS-P makes the task much easier to code and offers features not possible with HTML alone. As Lydia researches CSS-P, she learns about several new features that she would like to include in her Web pages, including columns, overlap, and scripted effects.

 ### Columns

Many Web page designers have created advanced layout features using basic HTML formatting. For example, HTML-only pages can use tables to display text in columns, rather than in one single block. However, adding these features in HTML can be difficult and limiting because the tags were not designed originally to provide advanced formatting. CSS-P makes this type of formatting much simpler by allowing you to easily specify each element's width and location on a Web page. CSS-P also places elements more predictably in different screen resolutions. Lydia plans to use the CSS-P float feature to add a sidebar to the Nomad Ltd tents page, similar to the one shown in Figure L-1.

 ### Overlap

A design feature not found in HTML but available in CSS-P, is the ability to overlap screen elements, which facilitates adding labels over graphics. Also, it allows you to create complex layouts such as ones that superimpose words in different colors or that overlap parts of images. The Web page in Figure L-2 uses CSS-P to overlap text and graphics. Lydia wants to use the overlap feature to create a distinctive design effect in her Web pages for Nomad Ltd. She plans to place the general category name for each Web page in large, light-colored text behind the page headings.

 ### Scripted features

As with other DHTML tools, combining CSS-P with scripts allows you to create many new display features for your Web pages. For example, by changing a graphic's dimensions slightly at regular intervals, you can animate with DHTML. You also can use scripting to allow users to drag elements to new positions on the Web page. Lydia plans to add some draggable elements to her tents page to help users visualize the placement of sleeping bags in various tent designs.

FIGURE L-1: Web page containing sidebar

webmonkey/dynamic_html/

Resources

- - - - - - - - -

Inside DHTML

This site by Scott Isaacs, a member of the Internet Explorer design team, provides lots of juicy coverage of Dynamic HTML and excerpts his book - you guessed it, Inside Dynamic HTML.

Toolbox

- - - - - - - - -

Dreamweaver
Platform: Win 95, Power Mac
Cost: not yet set
Company: Macromedia

Taylor's Tutorial

- - - - - - - - -

Taylor's Dynamic HTML Tutorial - Day 1
Dynamic HTML is how Netscape's and Microsoft's 4.0 browsers are pushing the Web to new limits. In the first of five parts, Taylor looks at what dHTML is all about and what skills you need to code for it. *9 Mar 1998*

Taylor's Dynamic HTML Tutorial - Day 2
Taylor digs into dynamic HTML, showing you the basics of using CSS-P to lay out your pages. He even looks at the elusive z-index. *10 Mar 1998*

Taylor's Dynamic HTML Tutorial - Day 3
Today Taylor's series gets tricky: By the end of the day, he'll have you scripting dHTML and making monkeys run around

Sidebar created
using CSS-P

FIGURE L-2: Web page displaying element overlap

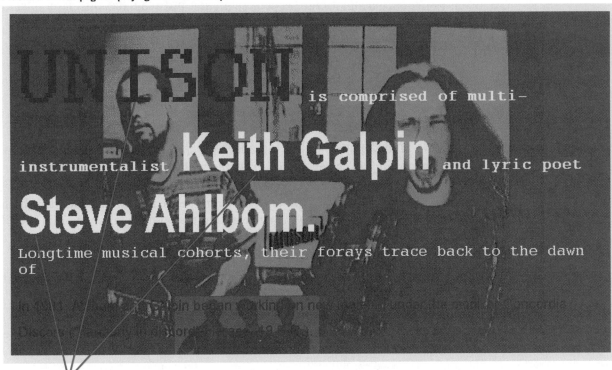

Text overlaps
graphic

Positioning an Element Absolutely

With CSS-P, you can specify an element's position in several different ways. The most straightforward way is to use **absolute positioning**, which lets you specify the left and top coordinates of an element on the Web page. You use the CSS-P **left** and **top** properties to specify an element's location relative to the top-left corner of its **parent**, or the object enclosing it. For example, a <SPAN> element nested within <DIV> tags would be positioned relative to the <DIV> element, its parent. In this case, the <SPAN> element is known as a **child** of the <DIV> element. Any element not enclosed by another element is a child of the browser window and is absolutely positioned with respect to the top-left corner of the window. You can specify left and top values in points (pt), pixels (px), inches (in), millimeters (mm), or centimeters (cm). If you don't specify units, the browser defaults to **pixels**, which are the tiny units of light that create the display on a monitor. The number of pixels visible on a user's screen varies depending on its resolution. However, even when using pixels, it is a good idea to specify units in order to make your code clearer when debugging it and when others read it. As she develops a Web page describing tents available from Nomad Ltd, Lydia wants to reposition the elements located at the top of the page to decrease the amount of blank space in her original design. She adds absolute position information to the elements to create a more compact layout.

Steps

1. **Start your Web browser, cancel any dial-up activities, then open the file HTML L-1.htm**
   Notice how the text flows around the image. In this version of the Web page, because Lydia was using only HTML, she made the text flow by grouping the image and the text together in a DIV tagset. However, text flow created in HTML can be unpredictable depending on the user's display font size and resolution settings.

2. **Start your text editor program, open the file HTML L-1.htm, then save it as a text document with the filename Tent absolute position.htm**

3. **Scroll to the document's HEAD section, select the text [replace with logo absolute position code] in the embedded style sheet, then press [Delete]**

4. **Type #logo {position: absolute; top: 30px; left: 30px}**
   The name #logo associates this style with the ID "logo". Figure L-3 shows the document containing the absolute position code. Lydia placed the logo so that it is 30 pixels from the top of the browser window and 30 pixels from the left edge of the browser window. By positioning the Nomad Ltd logo using absolute positioning, Lydia's headers can move up to fill in the empty area at the top of the page.

5. **Scroll down until the opening DIV tag above the IMG tag for nomad.jpg appears in the document window, select the text [replace with ID], then press [Delete]**
   Lydia wants her layout to work on both fourth-generation browsers. Because Netscape Navigator does not recognize absolute positioning referenced in an IMG tag, she has enclosed the IMG tag in DIV tags. By referencing the position information in the DIV element, Lydia positions the graphic element.

6. **Type ID="logo"**

7. **Check your document for errors, make any necessary changes, then save Tent absolute position.htm as a text document**

8. **Open Tent absolute position.htm in your Web browser**
   As Figure L-4 shows, the Nomad Ltd logo appears in the top-left corner of the window, moved slightly down and to the right from its position in the file HTML L-1.htm. Because the graphic is placed absolutely at a fixed location in the window, the remaining screen elements flow beginning at the top of the window. The presence of the graphic to the left of the headings has no effect on their alignment or flow. As Figure L-4 shows, the result is overlap between the logo and the heading text. Next, Lydia will adjust the position of the heading text to keep it from overlapping the logo.

FIGURE L-3: Web document containing absolute position code

```
<HTML>
<HEAD>

<TITLE>Nomad Ltd - Selecting a tent</TITLE>

<LINK REL=stylesheet HREF="nomadltd.css" TYPE="text/css">

<STYLE>
<!--
.tenthead {font-family: arial, sans-serif; font-size: 14pt}
.button {font-family: impact, arial; font-size: 8pt}
.norm {font-weight: normal}
.noital {font-style: normal}
#logo {position: absolute; top: 30px; left: 30px}
//-->
</STYLE>

<SCRIPT LANGUAGE="javascript">
<!--
Nav4 = (document.layers) ? 1:0;
IE4 = (document.all) ? 1:0;

if(!IE4) {window.onerror=null}

totalTents = 0;
function countHeaders() {
```

Name associates style with ID "logo"

Code to position logo at top-left corner of page

FIGURE L-4: Web page displaying absolutely positioned logo

Logo placed at precise coordinates

Tents

Selecting one that's right for you

Choosing a quality tent that meets your needs can be an intimidating task. To help you out with this important decision, we've added features to this page to make it easier to compare the characteristics of our tents.

As you narrow your choices, click the Remove button for each tent that you're no longer considering, to remove it from the page.

Tent footprints and descriptions

XTC Starlite
One of the lightest, most compact three-season tents available. Featuring two-pole clip design with a built-in vestibule.

Remove Starlite

Cross-browser positioning

Both fourth-generation browsers interpret and display CSS-P formatting, but as with the other parts of DHTML, each browser processes CSS-P differently. This disparity results in unique code to create features in each browser that you need to remember when creating cross-browser code. The main challenge is that Navigator 4 does not correctly interpret positioning information inserted directly in a tag. In fact, inline coding for position removes the style information from all elements in the page that follow the inline code. You can remedy this problem by defining all your positioning code in either embedded or external style sheets. Fortunately, grouping style information at the top or in a separate file brings other benefits because it organizes your code and makes it easier to read and understand.

Positioning an Element Relatively

In addition to placing elements at fixed screen coordinates, CSS-P allows you to simply offset elements from their default positions in the page flow. This format, called **relative positioning**, is useful when you want your document to always display an element before or after other elements, but at a specified horizontal or vertical offset. Lydia wants to indent the page headings, while leaving them in the general page flow. She uses relative positioning to specify the new placement for the headings.

Steps

1. Open the file HTML L-2.htm in your text editor, then save it as a text document with the filename Tent relative position.htm

2. In the embedded style sheet, select the text [replace with head relative position code], then press [Delete]

3. Type #head {position: relative; left: 250px}
   Figure L-5 shows the document containing the relative position code. Similar to the absolute position of the logo, the left property that Lydia used to position the text moves it left in relation to the parent element, which is the browser window. Absolute positioning removes an element from the flow of the document, which causes the elements below it to move up and to overlap its former position in the page flow. This caused the headings to move up in the last lesson. Relatively positioning leaves an element in the document flow. A relatively positioned element moves relative to its default location in the page, but the elements that follow a relatively positioned element do not move up to take that position. This is what Lydia wants to do in her document because she wants the headings indented from the left to appear next to the graphic, but she does not want the text that follows to overlap the headings and graphic.

4. Scroll until <DIV ALIGN="center" appears in the document window, select the text [replace with ID], then press [Delete]

5. Select the adjacent text ALIGN="center" and press [Delete]

6. Type ID="head"
   Lydia references the position information in the DIV element to position the headings.

7. Check your document for errors, make any necessary changes, then save Tent relative position.htm as a text document

8. Open Tent relative position.htm in your Web browser
   As Figure L-6 shows, the main heading and the subheading are indented far enough from the left edge of the window to allow room for the logo. Because the indent was specified using relative positioning, the text after the headings does not move up into the positions previously held by the headings but, rather, continues to flow below them.

FIGURE L-5: Relative position code in Web document

Code to position heading within document flow

```
<HTML>
<HEAD>

<TITLE>Nomad Ltd - Selecting a tent</TITLE>

<LINK REL=stylesheet HREF="nomadltd.css" TYPE="text/css">

<STYLE>
<!--
.tenthead {font-family: arial, sans-serif; font-size: 14pt}
.button {font-family: impact, arial; font-size: 8pt}
.norm {font-weight: normal}
.noital {font-style: normal}
#logo {position: absolute; top: 30px; left: 30px}
#head {position: relative; left: 250px}
//-->
</STYLE>

<SCRIPT LANGUAGE="javascript">
<!--
Nav4 = (document.layers) ? 1:0;
IE4 = (document.all) ? 1:0;

if(!IE4) {window.onerror=null}

totalTents = 0;
```

FIGURE L-6: Web page displaying relatively positioned headings

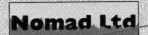

Tents

Selecting one that's right for you

Headings indented within main text flow

Choosing a quality tent that meets your needs can be an intimidating task. To help you out with this important decision, we've added features to this page to make it easier to compare the characteristics of our tents.

As you narrow your choices, click the Remove button for each tent that you're no longer considering, to remove it from the page.

Tent footprints and descriptions

XTC Starlite
One of the lightest, most compact three-season tents available. Featuring two-pole clip design with a built-in vestibule.

Remove Starlite

Sizing an Element Manually

In addition to position on the page, DHTML style properties allow you to specify an element's dimensions using the **height** and **width** properties. You can specify the two dimensions separately by using the same units available for the positioning properties. Additionally, you can size the element relative to its parent by using percentages. If you choose not to specify the height or the width, the browser sizes the element automatically. Lydia wants to reformat the description text for each tent model, so it displays indented and in a narrower column. Because she is changing style information for several screen elements, she adds properties to the page's embedded style sheet.

Steps

1. Open the file HTML L-3.htm in your text editor, then save it as a text document with the filename Tent element size.htm

2. Select the text [replace with tentbody class description] in the embedded style sheet, then press [Delete]

3. Type .tentbody {position: relative; left: 100px; width: 300px}
   Figure L-7 shows the document code including the new width property.

4. Scroll down until the <DIV ID="tent1" name="tent"> tag appears in the document window, then read through the code within this DIV element
   Notice that, in addition to the new style properties, Lydia has inserted CLASS="tentbody" in the DIV tag already, which applies the position information from the tenthead class description she created. She has added this information for each tent.

5. Check your document for errors, make any necessary changes, then save Tent element size.htm as a text document

6. Open Tent element size.htm in your Web browser, then scroll down until the tent descriptions appear in the document window
   As Figure L-8 shows, each description is indented from the left margin and the paragraph width is narrowed, which creates a column.

FIGURE L-7: Web document including width property code

```
<HTML>
<HEAD>

<TITLE>Nomad Ltd - Selecting a tent</TITLE>

<LINK REL=stylesheet HREF="nomadltd.css" TYPE="text/css">

<STYLE>
<!--
.tenthead {font-family: arial, sans-serif; font-size: 14pt; position:
relative; left: 100px}
.button {font-family: impact, arial; font-size: 8pt}
.norm {font-weight: normal}
.noital {font-style: normal}
#logo {position: absolute; top: 30px; left: 30px}
#head {position: relative; left: 250px}
.tentbody {position: relative; left: 100px; width: 300px}
//-->
</STYLE>

<SCRIPT LANGUAGE="javascript">
<!
Nav4 = (document.layers) ? 1:0;
IE4 = (document.all) ? 1:0;

if(!IE4) {window.onerror=null}
```

Width property for tentbody class

FIGURE L-8: Web page displaying adjusted width

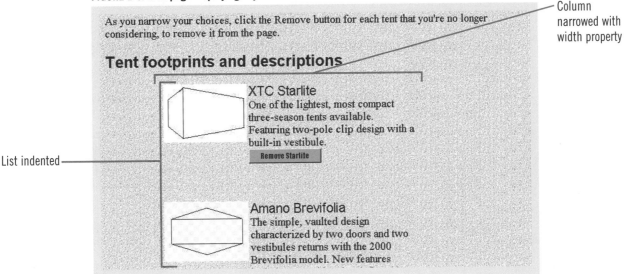

Column narrowed with width property

List indented

As you narrow your choices, click the Remove button for each tent that you're no longer considering, to remove it from the page.

Tent footprints and descriptions

XTC Starlite
One of the lightest, most compact three-season tents available. Featuring two-pole clip design with a built-in vestibule.

Remove Starlite

Amano Brevifolia
The simple, vaulted design characterized by two doors and two vestibules returns with the 2000 Brevifolia model. New features

CLUES TO USE

Positioning and sizing using percentages

Although standard measurement units, such as pixels and points, are most familiar to Web page designers, the ability to use percentage as a positioning and sizing unit offers advantages for some screen elements. Because monitors of different screen resolutions display the document window with a larger or smaller area, a size in pixels or points appears at a different position on the screen at different resolutions. While a column of 150px may fit perfectly in an 800 x 600 display, that same column may be surrounded by space at 1024 x 768, reducing the effectiveness of your layout. Elements sized with percentages, however, automatically adjust to the size of their parent elements. Thus, if you size a graphic element that is a child of the document window at 35%, that graphic element will maintain the same size relative to the document window in different resolutions. You can use the same method to absolutely or relatively position an element as a percentage of its parent. For some applications, specifying an exact measurement is important, but percentage sizing and positioning are important tools in your Web page design toolbox.

HTML

Stacking Screen Elements

Because an absolutely positioned element can appear anywhere on a Web page, including the space occupied by other elements, the browser can't format pages containing these elements as it would standard HTML pages. Instead, each absolutely positioned element is considered to be on a separate **layer**, which is a transparent virtual page that determines overlap order. Web page layers are like sheets of clear plastic with writing or images on them in different areas. When the sheets are superimposed, as layers are in the browser window, all the contents of all sheets are visible; but some contents may block out others, depending on their order in the stack. Each layer's **z-index** property determines its position in the stack. Higher numbers are located closer to the top of the stack, and elements on these layers will block out elements in the same position on lower layers of the stack. An element that is positioned using absolute positioning is placed on a separate layer. An element positioned using relative positioning remains on the same layer as the rest of the standard page elements. ✎ Lydia plans to label each page in Nomad Ltd's Web publication based on its content category. She wants to place the category name at the top of the page so that it appears behind the headings. For the tent page, she wants to add the word *camping* to the heading background in large, light-colored type.

Steps

1. Open the file HTML L-4.htm in your text editor, then save it as a text document with the filename Tent layers.htm

2. In the embedded style sheet, select the text [replace with backtext layer code], then press [Delete]

3. Type #backtext {position: absolute; left: 250px; font-size: 64pt; font-family: arial; color: #7093DB; z-index: -1}
   Figure L-9 shows the document code, including the new background text. The first element positioned in a Web page receives a z-index value of 0. Subsequently placed elements receive higher z-index values, resulting in later elements appearing on top of older elements by default. Because Lydia wants to make sure the word *CAMPING* appears behind the headings, she assigns it a z-index of -1, which is lower than all other default z-index values.

4. Scroll down and select the text [replace with background text], then press [Delete]

5. Type <DIV ID="backtext"> and press [Enter]

6. Type CAMPING and press [Enter], then type </DIV>

7. Check your document for errors, make any necessary changes, then save Tent layers.htm as a text document

8. Open Tent layers.htm in your Web browser
   As Figure L-10 shows, the text *CAMPING* appears behind the headings in a large and light-colored font. This stacked layout allows Lydia to add extra information to the Web page without disrupting the flow of the page. It also adds an interesting, unusual visual effect.

FIGURE L-9: Web document including background text code

```
<HTML>
<HEAD>

<TITLE>Nomad Ltd - Selecting a tent</TITLE>

<LINK REL=stylesheet HREF="nomadltd.css" TYPE="text/css">

<STYLE>
<!--
.tenthead {font-family: arial, sans-serif; font-size: 14pt; position:
relative; left: 100px}
.button {font-family: impact, arial; font-size: 8pt}
.norm {font-weight: normal}
.noital {font-style: normal}
#logo {position: absolute; top: 30px; left: 30px}
#head {position: relative; left: 250px}
.tentbody {position: relative; left: 100px; width: 300px}
#backtext {position: absolute; left: 250px; font-size: 64pt; font-family:
arial; color: #7093DB; z-index: -1}
//-->
</STYLE>

<SCRIPT LANGUAGE="javascript">
<!--
Nav4 = (document.layers) ? 1:0;
IE4 = (document.all) ? 1:0;
```

z-index
property for
background
text

FIGURE L-10: Web page displaying background text

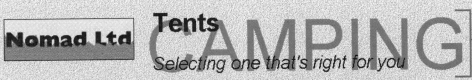

z-index
value places
background
text behind
headings

HTML

Adding a Scroll Bar

You can use CSS-P to associate a scroll bar with an element when the element is too large to fit its defined size. This effect, which you create using the **overflow** property, allows you to create the equivalent of an independent frame anywhere within your browser window. Of the fourth-generation browsers, only Internet Explorer accommodates the overflow property. ✎ To make the tent page layout more concise, Lydia formats the list of tent outlines and descriptions in a box with a scroll bar. This allows users to scroll from top to bottom in the page more quickly and still easily view the tent descriptions if they wish.

Steps 1 2 3 4

1. Open the file **HTML L-5.htm** in your text editor, then save it as a text document with the filename **Tent scroll.htm**

2. In the embedded style sheet, select the text **[replace with list scroll code]**, then press **[Delete]**

3. Type **#list {height: 300px; width: 600px; overflow: auto}**
   Figure L-11 shows the Web page code in the embedded style sheet. Because the list of tent descriptions is much longer than 300 pixels, the height specification creates a display area smaller than the object size. The "auto" value for the "overflow" property instructs the browser to display scroll bars only where necessary. Because the text in this case is longer than 300 pixels, the browser will create a vertical scroll bar for the object. The width of this DIV is not constrained by a style setting, so a horizontal scroll bar is not needed.

4. Scroll until the code for the heading Tent footprints and descriptions appears in the document window, select the text **[replace with opening DIV tag]**, then press **[Delete]**

5. Type **<DIV ID="list">**

Trouble?

The amount of text displayed in your scroll bar box will depend on the size of the font you are using and your screen resolution.

6. Scroll to the end of the tent description list which is after the description for tent 7, select the text **[replace with closing DIV tag]**, press **[Delete]**, then type **</DIV>**

7. Check your document for errors, make any necessary changes, then save **Tent scroll.htm** as a text document

8. Open **Tent scroll.htm** in your Web browser, then scroll down to view the list of tent outlines and descriptions
   As Figure L-12 shows, in IE 4 the tent-description list displays in a limited area with a vertical scroll bar on the right edge.

9. Use the scroll bar for the list to view all of the tent descriptions

FIGURE L-11: Web document including scroll bar code

```
<HTML>
<HEAD>

<TITLE>Nomad Ltd - Selecting a tent</TITLE>

<LINK REL=stylesheet HREF="nomadltd.css" TYPE="text/css">

<STYLE>
<!--
.tenthead {font-family: arial, sans-serif; font-size: 14pt; position:
relative; left: 100px}
.button {font-family: impact, arial; font-size: 8pt}
.norm {font-weight: normal}
.noital {font-style: normal}
#logo {position: absolute; top: 30px; left: 30px}
#head {position: relative; left: 250px}
.tentbody {position: relative; left: 100px; width: 300px}
#backtext {position: absolute; left: 250px; font-size: 64pt; font-family:
arial; color: #7093DB; z-index: -1}
#list {height: 300px; width: 600px; overflow: auto}
//-->
</STYLE>

<SCRIPT LANGUAGE="javascript">
<!--
Nav4 = (document.layers) ? 1:0;
```

overflow property adds scroll bar

FIGURE L-12: List formatted with scroll bar

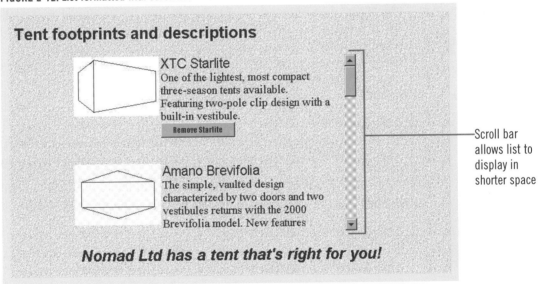

Scroll bar allows list to display in shorter space

Creating a clip region

Sometimes, you want to put a large element on your Web page but don't have room for the full element; other times, you only want to display a portion of a large element. CSS-P's **clip** property allows you to control how much of an element is visible on your Web page by acting as a layer above the element, covering all of it except for a hole you define, called a **clip region**. (Note that Netscape Navigator 4 does not support this property.) To create a clip region, you specify the coordinates of a rectangle, usually with an area smaller than the element, using the syntax **clip: rect(top right bottom left)**. The abbreviation "rect" stands for rectangle, which is the only shape currently supported by this property. Substitute each of the terms in parentheses with a coordinate value, or enter **auto** to leave the default. When the element appears in your Web page, the only portion of the element that will be visible is the section within the rectangle you specified.

HTML

Creating a Sidebar

Using CSS-P's placement and sizing properties, you can create and position text blocks independently of each other. You can use the **float** property to remove an element from the main text flow and display it to the side of the flow. The **left** and **right** values allow you to specify whether the element is positioned on the right or left side of the main document flow. The float feature allows you to create many text effects, including sidebars, which are difficult to create with HTML alone. Lydia wants to add scale outlines of backpacks and sleeping bags to the tents page to give users a better feel for the relative sizes of the tents. To make this area stand out from the page's main text, she creates a sidebar.

Steps

1. Open the file HTML L-6.htm in your text editor, then save it as a text document with the filename Tent sidebar.htm

2. In the embedded style sheet, select the text [replace with sidebar code], then press [Delete]

3. Type #sidebar {width: 350px; float: right; position: absolute; left: 400px; font-family: arial; font-size: 11pt; background: #8FBC8F} and press [Enter]
   The "float" property removes the section from the document flow, and the "right" value specifies that it floats to the right of the flow. Lydia could specify the height, but the height property works in conjunction with the float property only in Internet Explorer. Navigator always adjusts the height of a sidebar to fit its contents, regardless of the height setting. By not assigning the height property, Lydia allows both browsers to automatically adjust the height to ensure uniform appearance.

4. Type .expl {width: 375px}
   To keep the paragraph to the left of the sidebar from overlapping it, Lydia associates it with a fixed width. Figure L-13 shows the Web page code containing the new style specifications.

5. Scroll until the DIV tag before the IMG tags appears in the document window, select the text [replace with ALIGN and ID codes], then press [Delete]

6. Type ALIGN="left" ID="sidebar"
   Sidebars that float to the right of the main text also automatically align text along the right edge. You can override this setting using the HTML ALIGN property.

7. Check your document for errors, make any necessary changes, then save Tent sidebar.htm as a text document

Trouble?

If you are using Netscape Navigator 4 and the sidebar is slow to appear, simply scroll down the page and back to the top to see the scrollbar more quickly.

8. Open Tent sidebar.htm in your Web browser
   As Figure L-14 shows, the text displays in a rectangle with a colored background to the right of the main text flow. Lydia specified absolute positioning settings for the graphics to position them just below the sidebar text.

FIGURE L-13: Web document containing style specifications for sidebar

float property creates sidebar effect

Code added to adjust layout for new text

Absolute position code for pack and bag icons

```
.tentbody {position: relative; left: 100px; width: 300px}
#backtext {position: absolute; left: 250px; font-size: 64pt; font-family:
arial; color: #7093DB; z-index: -1}
#list {height: 300px; width: 600px; overflow: auto}
#sidebar {width: 350px; float: right; position: absolute; left: 400px; font-
family: arial; font-size: 11pt; background: #8FBC8F}
.expl {width: 375px}
#pack1 {position: absolute; left: 505px}
#pack2 {position: absolute; left: 535px}
#pack3 {position: absolute; left: 425px}
#pack4 {position: absolute; left: 460px}
#bag1 {position: absolute; left: 565px}
#bag2 {position: absolute; left: 670px}
//-->
</STYLE>

<SCRIPT LANGUAGE="javascript">
<!--
Nav4 = (document.layers) ? 1:0;
IE4 = (document.all) ? 1:0;

if(!IE4) {window.onerror=null}

totalTents = 0;
function countHeaders() {
    for (var i = 0; i < document.all.length; i++){
```

FIGURE L-14: Web page displaying sidebar

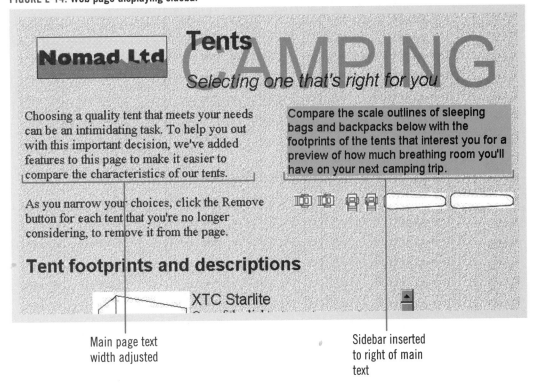

Main page text width adjusted

Sidebar inserted to right of main text

Incorporating an Advanced Positioning Function

By creating scripts to interact with position and layer information, you can add many advanced features to your Web pages. One exciting result of scripting position in Internet Explorer is dragging. A script enabling the drag feature can adjust the position of the selected element based on the coordinates of the pointer and then assign the element to its final position once the user releases the mouse button. This drag feature allows users to rearrange elements into an order that is more useful for them than the page's default organization or to interact with Web page models and games.　　　　Lydia wants to let Internet Explorer users drag the scale outlines of sleeping bags and backpacks over the tent outlines so they can explore how much each tent holds.

Steps

1. Open the file HTML L-7.htm in your text editor, then save it as a text document with the filename Tent drag.htm

   Notice that Lydia has created the class description .drag in the embedded style section for a draggable element.

2. Scroll down until the var elDrag=null code appears in the document window

   Notice that Lydia has created a script in the header section that handles dragging of absolute-positioned elements.

QuickTip

You also can format text elements to be draggable, using DIV or SPAN tags as containers.

3. Scroll down until the IMG SRC code for the first draggable image appears in the document window, select the text [replace with drag code] in the opening DIV tag for the image tag, then press [Delete]

4. Type CLASS="drag" canDrag

   This code associates the image with the "drag" class that Lydia defined in the embedded style sheet, which specifies a z-index of 10. The script Lydia inserted earlier in the code identifies draggable images through the "canDrag" attribute.

5. Repeat Steps 2 and 3 for the remaining five IMG tags

   Figure L-15 shows the draggable image codes for this page.

6. Check your document for errors, make any necessary changes, then save Tent drag.htm as a text document

7. Open Tent drag.htm in your Web browser

8. If you are using IE4, drag some of the backpack and sleeping bag outlines onto a tent footprint

   Look at Figure L-16, and notice that the images move with the mouse pointer. The user can display the images on top of the tent outlines.

FIGURE L-15: Web document containing draggable image codes

Image codes formatted for dragging

```
features to this page to make it easier to compare the characteristics of
our tents.<BR><BR></DIV>

<DIV ID="pack1" CLASS="drag" canDrag>
<IMG SRC="pack.jpg">
</DIV>

<DIV ID="pack2" CLASS="drag" canDrag>
<IMG SRC="pack.jpg">
</DIV>

<DIV ID="pack3" CLASS="drag" canDrag>
<IMG SRC="pack2.jpg">
</DIV>

<DIV ID="pack4" CLASS="drag" canDrag>
<IMG SRC="pack2.jpg">
</DIV>

<DIV ID="bag1" CLASS="drag" canDrag>
<IMG SRC="bag.jpg">
</DIV>

<DIV ID="bag2" CLASS="drag" canDrag>
<IMG SRC="bag.jpg">
</DIV>
```

Attribute marks element as draggable

Class property associates z-index value with each element

FIGURE L-16: Web page showing dragged images

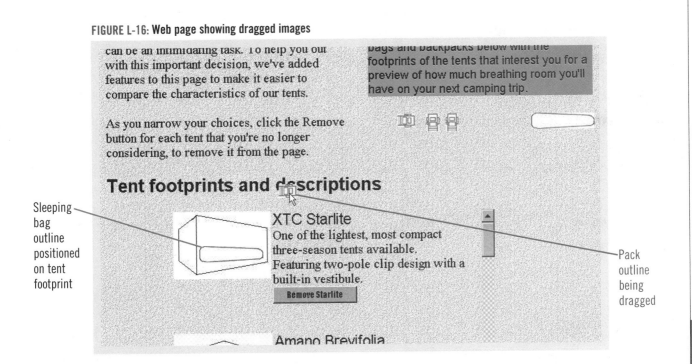

Sleeping bag outline positioned on tent footprint

Pack outline being dragged

Practice

▶ Concepts Review

Label the elements marked in figure L-17 with the CSS-P properties used to create them.

FIGURE L-17

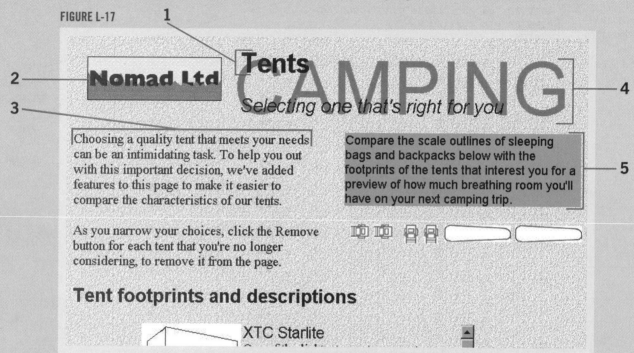

Match each term with its description.

6. **Absolute positioning**
7. **Relative positioning**
8. **Float**
9. **Height and width**
10. **Top and left**

a. Properties for specifying element dimensions
b. Places element at fixed coordinates outside page flow
c. Properties for specifying location
d. Property used to create sidebar
e. Places element relative to parent element's coordinates within page flow

Select the best answer from the list of choices.

11. **An absolutely positioned element is located**
    a. On a separate layer from the rest of the Web page, offset from the parent element.
    b. On a separate layer from the rest of the Web page, offset from the top-left corner of the browser window.
    c. On the same layer as the rest of the page, offset from the parent element.
    d. On the same layer as the rest of the page, offset from the top-left corner of the browser window.

12. **DHTML allows precise positioning of page elements through an extension of Cascading Style Sheets called**
    a. Absolute positioning.
    b. Cascading Style Sheets - Positioning.
    c. The "Position" style property.
    d. Tables.

13. **The browser always places absolutely positioned text**
    a. At the top-left corner of the browser window.
    b. At the specified coordinates relative to the top-left corner of the browser window.
    c. Behind the main page elements in z-index.
    d. At the specified coordinates relative to its parent element.

14. **Which is not a valid measurement unit for specifying dimension and coordinate properties?**
    a. Feet
    b. Inches
    c. Points
    d. Pixels

15. **As you add new layers to a Web page, the elements on the most recent layers receive**
    a. The same z-index value as earlier layers.
    b. Smaller z-index values than earlier layers.
    c. Larger z-index values than earlier layers.
    d. Negative z-index values.

16. **Which property allows you to add scroll bars to specific elements?**
    a. Scroll bar
    b. Float
    c. Layer
    d. Overflow

17. **When adding a scroll bar to an element, assigning the value "auto" results in**
    a. A scroll bar only when the element size requires it.
    b. Both horizontal and vertical scroll bars always appearing .
    c. No scroll bars.
    d. Addition of a vertical scroll bar only.

► Skills Review

1. **Position an element absolutely.**
   a. Open the file HTML L-8.htm in your Web browser.
   b. Open the file HTML L-8.htm in your text editor, then save it as a text document with the filename Pack absolute position.htm.
   c. Scroll to the top of the document's HEAD section, select the text [replace with logo absolute position code] in the embedded style sheet, then press [Delete].
   d. Type #logo {position: absolute; top: 30px; left: 30px}
   e. Scroll and select the text [replace with ID] in the opening DIV tag above the IMG tag for nomad.jpg, then press [Delete].
   f. Type ID="logo"
   g. Check your document for errors, make any necessary changes, then save Pack absolute position.htm as a text document.
   h. Open Pack absolute position.htm in your Web browser.

2. **Position an element relatively.**
   a. Open the file HTML L-9.htm in your text editor and save a copy as Pack relative position.htm.
   b. In the embedded style sheet, select the text [replace with head relative position code], then press [Delete].
   c. Type #head {position: relative; left: 275px}
   d. Scroll and select the text [replace with ID], then press [Delete].
   e. Select the adjacent text ALIGN="center" and press [Delete].
   f. Type ID="head"
   g. Check your document for errors, make any necessary changes, then save Pack relative position.htm as a text document.
   h. Open Pack relative position.htm in your Web browser.

3. **Size an element manually.**
   a. Open the file HTML L-10.htm in your text editor, and save it as a text document with the filename Pack element size.htm.
   b. Select the text [replace with packbody class description] in the embedded style sheet, then press [Delete].
   c. Type .packbody {position: relative; left: 100px; width: 300px}
   d. Check your document for errors, make any necessary changes, then save Pack element size.htm as a text document.
   e. Open Pack element size.htm in your Web browser and scroll down to the pack descriptions.

4. **Stack screen elements.**
   a. Open the file HTML L-11.htm in your text editor, then save it as a text document with the filename Pack layers.htm.
   b. In the embedded style sheet, select the text [replace with backtext layer code], then press [Delete].
   c. Type #backtext {position: absolute; left: 275px; font-size: 64pt; font-family: arial; color: #7093DB; z-index: -1}
   d. Scroll and select the text [replace with background text], then press [Delete].
   e. Type <DIV ID="backtext"> and press [Enter].
   f. Type HIKING and press [Enter], then type </DIV>
   g. Check your document for errors, make any necessary changes, then save Pack layers.htm as a text document.
   h. Open Pack layers.htm in your Web browser.

5. **Add a scroll bar.**

   a. Open the file HTML L-12.htm in your text editor, and save it as a text document with the filename Pack scroll.htm.

   b. In the embedded style sheet, select the text [replace with list scroll code], then press [Delete].

   c. Type #list {height: 300px; width: 600px; overflow: auto}

   d. Scroll and select the text [replace with opening DIV tag], then press [Delete].

   e. Type <DIV ID="list">

   f. Scroll, and select the text [replace with closing DIV tag], press [Delete], then type </DIV>

   g. Check your document for errors, make any necessary changes, then save Pack scroll.htm as a text document.

   h. Open Pack scroll.htm in your Web browser, and scroll down to view the list of pack outlines and descriptions.

   i. Use the scroll bar for the list to view all of the pack descriptions.

6. **Create a sidebar.**

   a. Open the file HTML L-13.htm in your text editor, then save it as a text document with the filename Pack sidebar.htm.

   b. In the embedded style sheet, select the text [replace with sidebar code], then press [Delete].

   c. Type #sidebar {width: 350; float: right; position: absolute; left: 400px; font-family: arial; font-size: 11pt; background: #8FBC8F}

   d. Scroll and select the text [replace with ID], then press [Delete].

   e. Type ALIGN="left" ID="sidebar"

   f. Check your document for errors, make any necessary changes, then save Pack sidebar.htm as a text document.

   g. Open Pack sidebar.htm in your Web browser.

7. **Incorporate an advanced positioning function.**

   a. Open the file HTML L-14.htm in your text editor, then save a copy as Pack drag.htm.

   b. Scroll and select the text [replace with drag code] in the first image tag, then press [Delete].

   c. Type CLASS="drag" canDrag

   d. Repeat Steps b and c for the remaining five IMG tags.

   e. Check your document for errors, make any necessary changes, then save Tent drag.htm as a text document.

   f. Open Tent drag.htm in your Web browser.

   g. If you are using Internet Explorer, drag some of the water bottle and tent outlines onto a backpack outline.

▶ Independent Challenges

1. You are revising the Popular supplies page for the Green House plant store. You have incorporated positioning using style sheets to improve the appearance of the Web page and to make sure it displays similarly in different screen resolutions. Also, you have removed some of the features you added earlier to keep the page from overwhelming users with features. The owners would like to add additional information to the page about how to use it. You think this would fit best in a sidebar next to the headings.

To complete this independent challenge:

a. Open the file HTML L-15.htm in your text editor, then save a copy as "Green House supplies with sidebar.htm".
b. In the embedded style sheet, select the text [replace with #sidebar definition], then press [Delete].
c. Type #sidebar {position: relative; width: 25%; float: right; font-family: arial; font-size: 11pt; background: #8FBC8F}
d. Scroll down to the opening DIV tag for the sidebar text, select the text [replace with ID], then press [Delete].
e. Type ALIGN="left" ID="sidebar"
f. Check your document for errors and make any necessary changes, save Green house supplies with sidebar.htm as a text document and close it, then open it in your Web browser. If necessary, edit your code until the page displays appropriately.

2. You are adding CSS positioning information to the rider tips page for Sandhills Regional Public Transit. To superimpose part of the heading text on the logo graphic, you would like to rearrange the heading section.

To complete this independent challenge:

a. Open the file HTML L-16.htm in your Web browser, then explore the page.
b. Open the file HTML L-16.htm in your text editor, then save a copy as "SRPT positioned rider tips.htm".
c. Create an embedded style sheet, define a style in the embedded style sheet named #logo specifying absolute position, top at 25px, left at 25px, and z-index of -1, then scroll down to the opening DIV tag above the IMG tag for bus.jpg and replace the text [replace with ID] with ID="logo".
d. Define a style in the embedded style sheet named #headtop specifying absolute position, left at 30px, and top at 25px, then scroll down to the opening DIV tag for the first line of the page heading and replace the text [replace with ID] with ID="headtop".
e. Define a style in the embedded style sheet named #headbtm specifying absolute position, left at 60 px, and top at 325px, then scroll down to the opening DIV tag for the second line of the page heading and replace the text [replace with ID] with ID="headbtm".
f. Define a style in the embedded style sheet named #sidetext specifying absolute position, text floating on the right, left at 400px, top at 25px, and width of 350px, then scroll down to the opening DIV tag for the instructions section and replace the text [replace with ID] with ALIGN="left" ID="sidetext".
g. Add style code to the UL tag for the bulleted list specifying relative position and top at 0px.
h. Check your document for errors and make any necessary changes, save and close it, then open it in your Web browser. If necessary, edit your code until the page displays appropriately.

3. You are updating Web pages for the Community Public School Volunteers organization by adding CSS positioning information. You want to improve the layout by placing the CPSV logo graphic behind the heading text.

To complete this independent challenge:

a. Explore the file HTML L-17.htm in your Web browser, then explore the file.

b. Open HTML L-17 in your text editor, then save a copy as "CPSV positioned home.htm".

c. Create a style in the embedded style sheet to place the new, widened logo (which is the colored letters CPSV) behind the heading text at the top of the page with absolute positioning. Use the left and top properties to position it so that it appears centered behind the text. (*Hint*: The heading is positioned relatively to allow it to be displayed in front of the logo in Navigator. Be sure to set a z-index for the logo to place it behind the text.) Reference the style you created in the opening DIV tag for the logo graphic, which is named cpsvlog3.jpg.

d. Create a style in the embedded style sheet for the DIV tagset enclosing the H3 heading and the links to narrow the width of the text area to 50% of the page width, position the section relatively, 25% to the left, change the background color to white (#FFFFFF), and add a 1pt black solid border (the style code for this feature is border: 1pt black solid). Reference the style you created in the opening DIV before the <H3> heading.

e. Save your changes, preview the page in your Web browser, and make any changes necessary to improve the appearance of the Web page.

4. The World Wide Web Consortium (W3C) has included a new set of positioning specifications in its revised Cascading Style Sheet guidelines, known as CSS2. Many of the new features that the W3C has outlined are supported in Microsoft and Netscape fifth-generation browsers. To complete this independent challenge, log on to the Internet, open your Web browser, and use a search engine to locate and open the Web site for the W3C. Locate information about the CSS2 guidelines, then print details of two new positioning features in CSS2. Write a paragraph on each feature, including what it allows a Web programmer to do and suggested syntax for implementing it. Check the Microsoft and Netscape Web sites to find out if their fifth-generation browsers will support either of the features you selected and include this information in your paragraphs. Submit your printout and paragraphs to your instructor.

▶ Visual Workshop

You are improving the layout of the Web pages for Touchstone Booksellers using CSS positioning. Using the file HTML L-18.htm as a starting point, position the heading elements to create the layout in Figure L-18. (*Hint*: Think of the text blocks on the left and right sides of the graphic as two floating sidebars. You should add code only to the two sidebar text blocks.) Save your changes as a text document with the filename Touchstone positioned home.htm.

FIGURE L-18

Touchstone Booksellers

Specializing in nonfiction of all types  *a locally-owned, independent bookstore since 1948*

You can use our Web site to search our current stock, place an order, request a search for an out-of-print book, or find out about upcoming events at our store.

- Search our stock

- Place an order

Implementing
Advanced DHTML Features

Objectives

▶ **Understand advanced features**
▶ **Filter content**
▶ **Scale content**
▶ **Animate element position**
▶ **Create 3D animation**
▶ **Transition elements**
▶ **Create a slideshow**
▶ **Transition between pages**

Using tools such as CSS, dynamic style, dynamic content, and CSS positioning, you can create interactive Web pages with print-quality formatting and layout. By combining these tools and writing scripts to work with them, you can continually create new features. The companies making browsers also continue to simplify the process by adding browser-native features that require little code and no scripting. Lydia Burgos's supervisor has asked her to create a Web-based presentation about Nomad Ltd. In addition to incorporating CSS formatting and positioning to make the page attractive and easy to read, she plans to add advanced effects to keep her users' interest.

HTML

Understanding Advanced Features

In addition to the many effects that the basic DHTML tools offer, you can create complex-looking visual features through a combination of proprietary effects and simple scripts. Although overuse of any dynamic feature can overload users visually and slow down their computers, the limited and precise use of these advanced features can help users focus on the most important aspects of each page. Many proprietary advanced features work only on Internet Explorer 4. However, these innovations will likely be supported by both fifth-generation browsers. Learning these features now is a good way to stay current with trends in Web page design.  As Lydia organizes her presentation, she notes different advanced features that she can use for different effects.

 Modifying an element's appearance

In addition to basic color and sizing formatting for text and graphics alike, Internet Explorer offers predefined element formats that affect appearance in complex ways. These formats, known as **filters**, allow you to create many effects, such as a shadow or glow, as shown in Figure M-1. Another way to affect element appearance is by combining a script with CSS position or size information to create the effect of movement, or **animation**. By slowly changing an element's placement or size with a script, you can create the effect of movement without requiring special software or extensive system resources. To help ensure your page layouts remain attractive at different screen resolutions and browser window sizes, you also can include simple scripts to resize elements, depending on each user's browser size.

 Open and close effects

You can effectively draw attention to a particular page element by scripting its appearance when the page opens. Internet Explorer offers predefined effects called **transitions**, which cause elements to appear gradually and in specific patterns when the page opens or exits. You can apply these effects to selected elements or to the entire page, as shown in Figure M-2. By using an animation script with offscreen starting coordinates and a timer, you can create **presentation effects** in which elements appear on the screen gradually and in a specific order.

Glow filter adds
colored halo to text

Nomad Ltd

Nomad Ltd

Corporate goals

MISSION

Our mission

Nomad Ltd is a national sporting goods
retailer dedicated to delivering high-quality
sporting gear and adventure travel.

Achieving our mission

Nomad Ltd has been in business
for over ten years. During that
time, we have offered tours all
over the world and sold sporting

Tour types:
Art
Leisure
Athlete

Graphic appearing
gradually using
"blend" transition

Nomad Ltd

Nomad Ltd

Corporate goals

MISSION

Our mission

Nomad Ltd is a national sporting goods
retailer dedicated to delivering high-quality
sporting gear and adventure travel.

Achieving our mission

Nomad Ltd has been in business
for over ten years. During that
time, we have offered tours all

Tour types:
Art
Leisure
Athlete

Earth graphic as it
appears at start of
load

Filtering Content

DHTML includes several tools that let you change the basic appearance of text and graphics by varying the size, color, and other characteristics of selected elements. In addition, Internet Explorer supports an extended set of properties, known as **filters**, that allow you to modify element appearance in complex ways. Table M-1 lists and describes the filters available in Internet Explorer 4. Lydia wants to call attention to headings in her presentation page without adding more colored text to the page, so she decides to try filtering the headings instead.

Steps

1. Start your text-editor program, open HTML M-1.htm, then save it as a text document with the filename Presentation filter.htm
2. Select the text [replace with misshead filter code] in the embedded style sheet, then press [Delete]
3. Type {height: 14pt; filter: glow(color=#B8860B)}
   To apply a filter using a DIV or SPAN tag, the text must be absolutely positioned or have a defined height or width. In order to meet this requirement without affecting her layout, Lydia sets the height to 14pt, which is the same height as the heading text.
4. Select the text [replace with second filter code] in the #achieve style definition, then press [Delete]
5. Type height: 12pt; filter: glow(color=#B8860B, strength=3)
   Because the font size in the second heading is smaller than in the first, Lydia decides to lower the intensity of the glow by assigning a strength value. This keeps the glow effect proportional to the text dimensions. Figure M-3 shows the completed code for the glow filters in the embedded style sheet.
6. Scroll down until the <H2> heading "Our mission" appears in the document window
   Lydia wants to apply the filter to the text within the H2 tags. However, filters are incompatible with all heading tags, so she has to embed the H2 tags within DIV tags and then call the filter from the opening DIV tag instead.
7. Type <DIV ID="misshead"> before <H2> Our mission </H2>, then position the insertion point after the closing H2 tag and type </DIV>
8. Check your document for errors, make changes as necessary, then save Presentation filter.htm as a text document
9. Open Presentation filter.htm in your Web browser
   See Figure M-4, which shows the presentation Web page containing the filtered text. If you are using Internet Explorer 4, the filter adds a halo of color around each letter.

Combining filters

In addition to the unique effect that each filter can create on a Web page, you can increase the possibilities by combining filters, a process known as **chaining**. You can add as many filters as you desire to an element by simply listing them in the element's tag or style sheet description. You must separate the code for each filter by a space. For example, you can chain a drop shadow and a glow to a graphic by calling both of these filters in the picture's style sheet description as follows: **#image: {position: absolute; top: 150px; filter: dropshadow(color=#483D8B, OffX=3, OffY=3) glow(color=#9933CC, strength=5)}.** This code would add both drop shadow and glow effects to the graphic.

FIGURE M-3: Web document containing filter code

```
#heading {position: relative; left: 250px}
#mission {width: 375px; font-family: arial}
#misshead {height: 14pt; filter: glow(color=#B8860B) }
#main {position: absolute; left: 60px; width: 275px}
#earth {float: right; position: relative; top: -20px}
.norm {font-weight: normal}
#head1 {font-style: italic; color: #8E236B}
#head2 {font-style: italic; color: #6B8E23}
#head3 {font-style: italic; color: #7093DB}
#head4 {font-style: italic; color: #9400D3}
#achieve {height: 12pt; filter: glow(color=#B8860B, strength=3) }
.font12 {font-size: 12pt}
.bot {color: #3232CD}
.space {line-height: 6pt; position: relative}
.item {position: relative; left: 10px; font-size: 10pt; font-weight: bold}
UL {position: relative; left: -20px; top: -20px; font-size: 10pt; font-
weight: bold}
.sidebar {float: right; position: absolute; left: 375px; font-family: arial;
width: 200px}
</STYLE>

</HEAD>

<BODY BACKGROUND="Egg shell.jpg">

<DIV ID="logo">
```

Style code to add filter effect to text

FIGURE M-4: Web page displaying filtered text

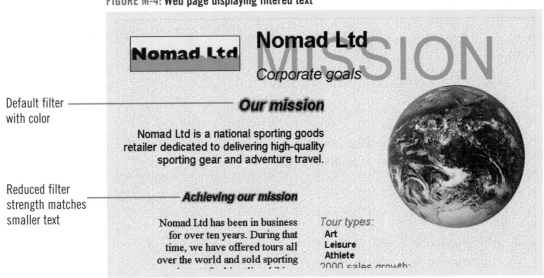

Default filter with color

Reduced filter strength matches smaller text

TABLE M-1: Internet Explorer 4 filter effects

filter effect	description	filter effect	description
Alpha	Sets a transparency level	Grayscale	Drops color information from the image
Blur	Creates the impression of moving at high speed	Invert	Reverses the hue, saturation, and brightness values
Chroma	Makes a specific color transparent	Light	Projects light sources onto an object
Drop Shadow	Creates an offset solid silhouette	Mask	Creates a transparent mask from an object
FlipH	Creates a horizontal mirror image	Shadow	Creates a solid silhouette of the object
FlipV	Creates a vertical mirror image	Wave	Creates a sine wave distortion along the x- and y-axes
Glow	Adds radiance around the outside edges of the object	XRay	Shows just the edges of the object

Scaling Content

One drawback of using basic DHTML positioning is a layout's reliance on a particular window size. For example, an image may fit well in a layout at a certain indentation in a maximized browser window on an SVGA screen. However, on a lower-resolution monitor or on a non-maximized browser window, the element may appear much closer to the right edge of the screen, thus changing the original layout design. Using basic scripts to complement CSS-P, however, you can automatically adjust the position of your Web page elements based on the browser window size. Because Navigator does not recognize changes in style properties (including element dimensions) after the page has loaded, this feature works only in Internet Explorer. Lydia has laid out her page in a maximized browser window set at a resolution of 800 × 600. However, she wants her layout to remain as consistent as possible in smaller windows and at lower resolutions.

Steps

1. Open HTML M-2.htm in your text editor, then save it as a text document with the filename Presentation scale.htm

2. Scroll down to the script tags in the page's head section, select the text [replace with scale script], then press [Delete]

   Lydia has already inserted a browser-detection script, along with a line of code to suppress errors in Navigator.

QuickTip

For elements whose size should remain proportional to the screen dimensions, you can multiply the document.body.clientHeight property (the JavaScript representation of the height of the browser window) by a fixed percentage in your script in order to adjust precisely to different window dimensions.

3. Type the following script, pressing [Enter] at the end of each line:

```
function change() {
        if (document.body.clientWidth < 640) {
                bgword.style.fontSize="48pt"
                earth.style.width="25%"
        }
        else {
                bgword.style.fontSize="64pt"
                earth.style.width="35%"
        }
}

window.onresize=change
window.onload=change
```

   Instead of trying to adjust every screen element to fit on a smaller screen, Lydia focuses on the elements along the right edge of the screen: the heading background text and the earth graphic. Her script adjusts both elements to a size that fits into a maximized browser window set at a 640 × 480 resolution. Figure M-5 shows the Web page document code containing the script.

4. Check your document for errors, make changes as necessary, then save Presentation scale.htm as a text document

5. Open Presentation scale.htm in your Web browser, then make sure your browser window is maximized

Trouble?

If you are in a display mode with resolution greater than 800 × 600, you may need to drag the right edge of the browser window to the left a few inches to see the elements rescale.

6. If you are using Internet Explorer and your display mode is 800 × 600 or greater, click the Restore Window button 🗗 at the top right of the browser window to decrease the size of the document window a fixed amount

   If your display is in 640 × 480 mode, note that the large background text and the earth graphic fit on the screen without requiring you to scroll right. Figure M-6 shows the presentation Web page in a reduced window. The scale script you inserted reduced the background text size and the graphic size to fit better in a limited display area.

FIGURE M-5: Web page document code containing scaling script

```
<SCRIPT LANGUAGE="javascript">
<!--
Nav4 = (document.layers) ? 1:0;
IE4 = (document.all) ? 1:0;

if(!IE4) {window.onerror=null}

function change() {
       if (document.body.clientWidth < 640) {
              bgword.style.fontSize="48pt"
              earth.style.width="25%"
       }
       else {
              bgword.style.fontSize="64pt"
              earth.style.width="35%"
       }
}

window.onresize=change
window.onload=change
//-->
</SCRIPT>

</HEAD>

<BODY BACKGROUND="Egg shell.jpg">
```

Script to resize elements based on window size

FIGURE M-6: Scaled objects in reduced browser window

Browser window size reduced from maximized view

Reduced text and graphic sizes fit in window

CLUES TO USE

Scaling by percent

Specifying element dimensions in percentages, rather than pixels or points, has many applications in DHTML design. Usually, you can simply specify the height, width, or font size in percent. Because percentage measurements reflect a percentage of the parent element dimension, a percentage-sized element automatically resizes when the window size changes. To make sure the element remains proportionally scaled when specifying element dimensions, be sure to specify only height or width, but not both. Sometimes, screen elements need to change position depending on the screen size or when an element such as a graphic would look distorted if it became too big or too small. In these cases, you need a scaling script to resize your pages.

Animating Element Position

By creating simple scripts to interact with position and layer information, you can add impressive features to your Web pages without requiring extensive system resources on a user's computer. To create basic animation, for example, you can script an element's position coordinates to increase or decrease slowly when the user first opens the page, until the element reaches its final, absolute coordinates. ◀━━ Lydia decides to animate the Nomad Ltd logo to move into place when a user first opens the page.

Steps

1. Open the file HTML M-3.htm in your text editor, then save it as a text document with the filename Presentation position animate.htm

2. Scroll down to the function slide() in the head section and examine the script
   The function slide() positions the logo graphic out of screen range on the right side of the page and then incrementally reduces its left coordinate until it reaches the final position of 30. Lydia also has changed the left coordinate for the #logo style to -1000, a value that triggers the slide() function.

3. Scroll down to the opening BODY tag, select the text [replace with event handler], then press [Delete]

4. Type onLoad="slide()"
   The onLoad event handler triggers the "slide" script every time the browser loads the BODY section. Figure M-7 shows the code for the event handler to call the slide() function.

5. Check your document for errors, make any necessary changes, then save Presentation position animate.htm as a text file

6. Open Presentation position animate.htm in your Web browser
   As Figure M-8 shows, the graphic slides into position from the right edge of the window after you open the page. Because Navigator can't change a page's style information after loading, it does not display the logo in its final location.

FIGURE M-7: Web document showing code to call slide() function

Slide function in page head

```
window.onresize=change
window.onload=change

function slide() {
        var pic = document.all.logo;
        if (-1000 == pic.style.pixelLeft) {
                pic.style.pixelLeft = document.body.offsetWidth +
document.body.scrollLeft;
        }
        if (50 <= pic.style.pixelLeft) {
                pic.style.pixelLeft -= 20;
                setTimeout("slide();", 50);
        }
        else {pic.style.pixelLeft =30;}
}
//-->
</SCRIPT>

</HEAD>

<BODY BACKGROUND="Egg shell.jpg" onLoad="slide()">

<DIV ID="logo">
<IMG SRC="nomad.jpg">
</DIV>
```

Event handler triggers slide script when page opens

FIGURE M-8: Nomad Ltd logo sliding into position

Nomad Ltd logo sliding right to left into final position

IMPLEMENTING ADVANCED DHTML FEATURES HTML M-9 ◄

HTML

Creating 3D Animation

You can easily create simple animation on your Web pages with a script that slowly adjusts an element's top or left attribute over a period of time. By incorporating changes in element size, using the width and height properties, you also can create the illusion of 3D movement. Although animation in standard multimedia formats can require special software or browser extensions and significant computer memory, DHTML animation creates the effect of movement using just one image and a small script running on the user's browser. A lot of animation could distract users from the rest of your Web page, but a short animation, or animation of a small element, can make a page interesting and distinctive. Lydia decides that instead of having the Nomad Ltd logo graphic move into position sideways, she would like the earth graphic to appear to approach the user. She creates this effect with 3D animation.

1. Open the file **HTML M-4.htm** in your text editor, save it as a text document with the filename **Presentation 3D animate.htm**

QuickTip

You can use a semicolon to mark the end of a line of code in JavaScript. The semicolon is not required at the end of a line, and it is often used only after short commands in a script.

2. Scroll down and select the text **[replace with 3D animation script]** in the page's head section, press **[Delete]**, then type the following script, pressing **[Enter]** at the end of each line:

```
function grow() {
    if (earthpic.width<250) {
            x=window.setTimeout('grow()', 100)
            earthpic.width=earthpic.width + 10
    }
}

window.onload = grow;
```

Figure M-9 shows the Web page code containing the script. The script uses the graphic's HTML width property, rather than the CSS width, because HTML width is easier to work with in this situation. Lydia has deleted the logo animation script.

3. Scroll down to the IMG tag for the earth graphic, and replace the text **[replace with width property]** with **WIDTH=0**

The script you entered increases the width value by 10 pixels at a time and pauses for a fraction of a second between each increase, which creates the illusion of animation.

4. Check your document for errors, make any necessary changes, then save **Presentation 3D animate.htm** as a text document

5. Open **Presentation 3D animate.htm** in your Web browser

Figure M-10 shows the page as it is loading. As the page loads, the earth graphic appears and slowly grows as it seems to move toward you.

FIGURE M-9: Web document containing grow script

```
window.onload=change

function grow() {
        if (earthpic.width<250) {
                x=window.setTimeout('grow()', 100)
                earthpic.width=earthpic.width + 10
        }
}

window.onload = grow;
//-->
</SCRIPT>

</HEAD>

<BODY BACKGROUND="Egg shell.jpg">

<DIV ID="logo">
<IMG SRC="nomad.jpg">
</DIV>

<DIV ID="bgword">
MISSION
</DIV>

<DIV ID="heading">
```

3D animation script for earth graphic

FIGURE M-10: 3D animation of earth graphic

Gradual size increase on load creates illusion of earth approaching

Animated GIFs

Another popular way to create animation in Web pages is to create **animated GIFs**. A GIF is a graphic file in a specific format. Although most GIFs are static, showing just one image, the GIF format also supports animation. To create an animated GIF, you use special software to combine two or more static graphics and to specify the delay between the display of each frame. You can create a movie-like movement effect with animated GIFs, but one of their most widespread uses on the Web today is in banner advertisements on Web pages. These static GIFs often alternate between two different frames of information, such as an advertising motto and the company logo. Although DHTML animation is easier and cheaper to create, animated GIFs are not limited to fourth-generation browsers and are thus accessible by a wider Web audience.

HTML

Transitioning Elements

Beyond simply hiding and showing an element, or applying filters to an element's display, you can affect the way an element becomes visible or hidden by using filter effects known as **transitions**. For example, one popular transition effect is to make an element appear or disappear gradually in a checkerboard pattern. Because Navigator does not recognize transitions, this feature works only with Internet Explorer. Internet Explorer 4 comes with two transition filters: **blend**, which creates a simple fade-in or fade-out effect, and **reveal**, which allows the more complex filtering effects. These effects, which can be applied to text as well as graphics, can keep a user's interest and distinguish your pages from others on the Web. ✐ Lydia decides to use the blend transition on the Nomad Ltd logo when the page opens.

Steps 1 2 3 4

1. Open the file **HTML M-5.htm** in your text editor, then save it as a text document with the filename **Presentation transition element.htm**

2. Select and replace the text **[replace with style information]** which is in the #logo style specification in the page's embedded style sheet with **visibility: hidden; filter: blendTrans(duration=7)**

   The blend transition can switch from hidden to visible or vice versa. Lydia specifies that she wants the graphic to start out hidden and then become visible using the blendTrans filter. The duration variable details the length of time in seconds of the transition from beginning to end.

3. Scroll down to the end of the page's head section, then replace the text **[replace with transition function]** with the following script, pressing **[Enter]** at the end of each line:

   ```
   function doTrans() {
       logo.filters.blendTrans.Apply();
       logo.style.visibility="visible";
       logo.filters.blendTrans.Play();
   }
   ```

   Unlike standard filters, transition filters require scripts to define what happens when they run. The first line of the doTrans() function calls the transition's Apply method, which creates the final state defined in the next line, which is "visible." Finally, the Play method starts the transition filter itself to create the smooth change from hidden to visible. Figure M-11 shows the Web document code containing the function.

4. Scroll to the bottom of the document just before the closing page tags, delete the text **[replace with function call]**, insert opening and closing script tags, and type **doTrans()** as the body of the script

   This script, shown in Figure M-12, calls the doTrans() function when the page finishes loading in the browser window.

5. Check your document for errors and make any necessary changes, then save **Presentation transition element.htm** as a text document

6. Open **Presentation transition element.htm** in your Web browser

   As Figure M-13 shows, the Nomad Ltd logo slowly fades into view as the page opens.

Trouble?

If the logo does not appear gradually, your video card or monitor is probably not compatible with transitions.

```
window.onload = grow;

function doTrans() {
        logo.filters.blendTrans.Apply();
        logo.style.visibility="visible";
        logo.filters.blendTrans.Play();
}
//-->
</SCRIPT>

</HEAD>
```

Function controlling transition effect

FIGURE M-12: Document code containing script to call function

```
<DIV>For more information on Nomad Ltd, please email our <A
HREF="MAILTO:relations@nomadltd.com">community relations
department</A>.</DIV>

</DIV>

<SCRIPT LANGUAGE="javascript">
<!--
doTrans()
//-->
</SCRIPT>

</BODY>
</HTML>
```

Script triggers doTrans() function after page loads

FIGURE M-13: Nomad Ltd logo showing blend transition

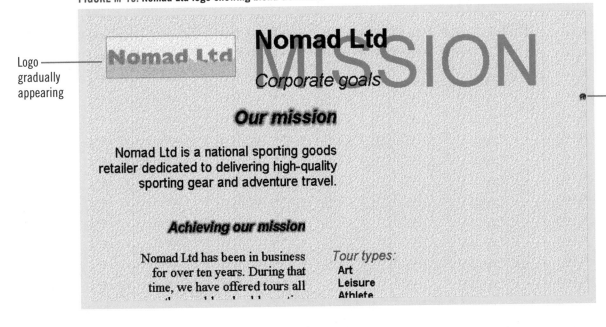

Logo gradually appearing

Earth graphic at start of animation

HTML

Creating a Slideshow

Presentation software, such as Microsoft PowerPoint, allows you to move through a related set of pages, or **slides**, by clicking a mouse button. It is easy to add this effect to Web pages with scripting. Although standard HTML hyperlinks can create a similar effect, DHTML features enable your users to advance by clicking anywhere on the page, rather than scrolling to locate and click a hyperlink. Also, by eliminating navigation-specific elements, you can keep your pages focused on the presentation topic and create a more unified design. ◣◣◣ Lydia has created the second page for her Web presentation. She wants to script the first page to open the second in response to a mouse click, which will allow Internet Explorer users to click anywhere on the Web page to advance to the second Web page.

Steps 1 2 3 4

1. Open the file **HTML M-6.htm** in your text editor, then save it as a text document with the filename **Presentation slideshow.htm**

2. Scroll down to the opening BODY tag, select and replace the text **[replace with event handler]** with **onClick="window.location.href='Presentation page 2.htm'"**
   This event handler changes the window's HREF, or page address, to "Presentation page 2.htm," the second page that Lydia prepared.

3. Scroll down below the text "Corporate goals," then select and replace the text **[replace with instruction text]** with the following script, pressing **[Enter]** at the end of each line:
   <DIV ID="instr">
   Click anywhere to advance to next slide.
   </DIV>
   This text tells users how to navigate through the presentation. Figure M-14 shows the Web page code containing the event handler and the instruction text. Lydia has already added an embedded style for the instructions and has edited the scaling code to reposition the text in smaller window sizes.

4. Check your document for errors, make any necessary changes, then save **Presentation slideshow.htm** as a text document

5. Open **Presentation slideshow.htm** in your Web browser, then click anywhere on the page
   The second presentation page opens, as shown in Figure M-15. By simply adding the event handler to all presentation pages except for the last one, Lydia can enable users to easily page through the presentation online.

FIGURE M-14: Web page code containing event handler and instruction text

Event handler allows easy navigation to second page

Navigation instructions

```
</HEAD>

<BODY BACKGROUND="Egg shell.jpg" onClick="window.location.href='Presentation
page 2.htm'">

<DIV ID="logo">
<IMG SRC="nomad.jpg">
</DIV>

<DIV ID="bgword">
MISSION
</DIV>

<DIV ID="heading">
<H1>Nomad Ltd</H1>
<H2 CLASS="norm">Corporate goals</H2>
</DIV>

<DIV ID="instr">
Click anywhere to advance to next slide.
</DIV>

<DIV ID="earth">
<IMG SRC="earth.jpg" ID="earthpic" WIDTH=0>
</DIV>
```

FIGURE M-15: Second presentation page

Transitioning Between Pages

In addition to creating transition effects for specific elements on a Web page, you can apply transitions when opening or closing a page. In this situation, transitions can grab and hold a viewer's attention, and can help your page to stand out among pages a user has recently seen. Each Web page can trigger transitions upon opening and exiting, independent of the preceding or following page. ✎ As a final touch, Lydia decides she wants Internet Explorer 4 users to see a closing transition to each of the pages in her Web presentation. She starts by adding a closing transition that appears when the first page closes.

Steps 1 2 3 4

1. Open the file **HTML M-7.htm** in your text editor, then save it as a text document with the filename **Presentation page transition.htm**

2. Scroll down below the embedded style sheet in the page's head section and replace the text **[replace with META tag]** with **<META http-equiv="Page-Exit" CONTENT="RevealTrans(Duration=5,Transition=3)">**
   Figure M-16 shows the Web page code containing the META tag. Creating an interpage transition requires no scripting. Instead, you insert an HTML META tag in the page's head section, calling the transition and defining its properties. You can set the http-equiv property, which tells when the transition takes effect, to "Page-Enter" or "Page-Exit." You use the CONTENT property to specify the transition filter name and parameters, just as you do with the STYLE property for element transitions. Lydia uses the reveal transition's "Circle out" pattern, indicated by the Transition number 3. Table M-2 lists other reveal transitions and their number codes.

3. Check your document for errors, make any necessary changes, then save **Presentation page transition.htm** as a text document

4. Open **Presentation page transition.htm** in your Web browser, then click anywhere on the page
   The second presentation page opens in a circle spreading outward from the center of the browser window, as shown in Figure M-17. You can apply other transition patterns, as listed in Table M-2, to open or close pages.

5. Make and save changes in your text-editor program as needed, check changes in your Web browser program, close your Web browser program, then close your text editor program

> **Trouble?**
> Depending on your computer speed, you may see a small white circle in the center of the screen just before the transition starts.

FIGURE M-16: Web page code containing META tag

META tag inserted to control interpage transition

```
.sidebar {float: right; position: absolute; left: 375px; font-family: arial;
width: 200px}
</STYLE>

<META http-equiv="Page-Exit" CONTENT="RevealTrans(Duration=5,Transition=3)">

<SCRIPT LANGUAGE="javascript">
<!--
Nav4 = (document.layers) ? 1:0;
IE4 = (document.all) ? 1:0;

if(!IE4) {window.onerror=null}

function change() {
        if (document.body.clientWidth < 640) {
                bgword.style.fontSize="48pt"
                earth.style.width="25%"
        }
        else {
                bgword.style.fontSize="64pt"
                earth.style.width="35%"
        }
}

window.onresize=change
window.onload=change
```

FIGURE M-17: Web page closing with "Circle out" reveal transition

First presentation page

Second presentation page opening outward in circle

TABLE M-2: Reveal transition effects

reveal transition name	value	reveal transition name	value	reveal transition name	value
Box in	0	Vertical blinds	8	Split horizontal out	16
Box out	1	Horizontal blinds	9	Strips left down	17
Circle in	2	Checkerboard across	10	Strips left up	18
Circle out	3	Checkerboard down	11	Strips right down	19
Wipe up	4	Random dissolve	12	Strips right up	20
Wipe down	5	Split vertical in	13	Random bars horizontal	21
Wipe right	6	Split vertical out	14	Random bars vertical	22
Wipe left	7	Split horizontal in	15	Random	23

Practice

► Concepts Review

Label the advanced DHTML effects indicated on Lydia's Web page in Figure M-18.

FIGURE M-18

Match each term with its description.

4. Filter
5. Position animation
6. 3D animation
7. Transition
8. Scaling

a. Gradually changes element size, using the width and height properties
b. Gradually changes element appearance, becoming visible or hidden
c. Gradually changes element position, using top and left style properties
d. Fits page elements to lower screen resolution or smaller window size
e. Property that modifies element appearance in complex ways

Select the best answer from the list of choices.

9. You can continually create new advanced DHTML features by combining basic features with
   a. CSS.
   b. Dynamic style.
   c. Dynamic content.
   d. Scripts.

10. Which of the following is *not* a filter?
    a. Shadow
    b. Blur
    c. Animation
    d. Blend transition

11. What is the advantage of using DHTML animation rather than other animation methods on the Web?
    a. DHTML animation doesn't require scripts.
    b. DHTML animation uses few system resources.
    c. DHTML animation uses special software.
    d. DHTML animation uses no system resources.

12. Which method will *not* change an element's appearance over a period of time?
    a. Position animation
    b. 3D animation
    c. Glow filter
    d. Blend transition filter

13. Which HTML tag do you use to implement an interpage transition?
    a. <LINK>
    b. <META>
    c. <A>
    d. <SCRIPT>

14. Which is an advantage of using animated GIFs rather than DHTML animation?
    a. Animated GIFs use no system resources.
    b. Animated GIF display is not limited to fourth-generation browsers.
    c. Creating animated GIFs requires no special software.
    d. Animated GIFs can show 3D animation.

Skills Review

1. Filter content.
   a. Open HTML M-8.htm in your Web browser and explore the page.
   b. Open HTML M-8.htm in your text editor and save a copy as Tours filter.htm.
   c. In the embedded style sheet, select the text [replace with histhead filter code], then press [Delete].
   d. Type height: 14pt; filter: glow(color=#6B8E23)
   e. Select the text [replace with second filter code] in the #tourshead style definition, then press [Delete].
   f. Type height: 12pt; filter: glow(color=#6B8E23, strength=3)
   g. Check your document for errors, make changes as necessary, then save Tours filter.htm.
   h. Open Tours filter.htm in your Web browser.

2. Scale content.
   a. Open HTML M-9.htm in your text editor, then save a copy as Tours scale.htm.
   b. Select the text [replace with scale script], then press [Delete].
   c. Enter the opening tags for a JavaScript script, then type the following script, pressing [Enter] at the end of each line:

```
function change() {
        if (document.body.clientWidth < 640) {
                bgword.style.fontSize="48pt"
        }
        else {
                bgword.style.fontSize="64pt"
        }
}

window.onresize=change
window.onload=change
```

   d. Enter the closing script tags, check your document for errors, make changes as necessary, then save Tours scale.htm.
   e. Open Tours scale.htm in your Web browser, then click the Restore Window button to decrease the size of the document window a fixed amount and note the changes to the background text in the heading. If necessary, drag the right edge of the window to the left to decrease the screen width until the change takes place.
   f. Click the browser maximize button.

3. Animate element position.
   a. Open the file HTML M-10.htm in your text editor, then save it as a text document with the filename Tours position animate.htm.
   b. Scroll down to the opening BODY tag, select the text [replace with event handler], then press [Delete].
   c. Type onLoad="slide()"
   d. Check your document for errors, make any necessary changes, then save as Tours position animate.htm.
   e. Open Tours position animate.htm in your Web browser.

4. Create 3D animation.

   a. Open the file HTML M-11.htm in your text editor, then save it as a text document with the filename Tours 3D animate.htm.

   b. Select the text [replace with 3D animation script] in the page's head section, press [Delete], then type the following script, pressing [Enter] at the end of each line:

```
function grow() {
        if (mtnpic.width<180) {
                x=window.setTimeout('grow()', 100)
                mtnpic.width=mtnpic.width + 10
        }
}
```

   c. In the BODY tag, delete the text [replace with event handler], and type onLoad="grow()"

   d. Scroll down to the IMG tag for the mountain graphic and replace the text [replace with width setting] with WIDTH=0

   e. Check your document for errors, make any necessary changes, then save as Tours 3D animate.htm.

   f. Open Tours 3D animate.htm in your Web browser.

5. Use transition elements.

   a. Open the file HTML M-12.htm in your text editor, then save a copy as Tours transition element.htm.

   b. In the #logo style specification in the page's embedded style sheet, replace the text [replace with style information] with visibility: hidden; filter: revealTrans(Transition=12, Duration=5)

   c. Scroll down to the end of the page's head section and replace the text [replace with transition function] with the following, pressing [Enter] at the end of each line:

```
function doTrans() {
        logo.filters.revealTrans.Apply();
        logo.style.visibility="visible";
        logo.filters.revealTrans.Play();
}
```

   d. Scroll to the bottom of the document just before the closing page tags, delete the text [replace with function call], insert opening and closing script tags, and type doTrans() as the body of the script.

   e. Check your document for errors, make any necessary changes, then save as Tours transition element.htm.

   f. Open Tours transition element.htm in your Web browser.

6. Create a slideshow.

   a. Open the file HTML M-13.htm in your text editor, then save it as a text document with the filename Tours slideshow.htm.

   b. Scroll down to the opening BODY tag and replace the text [replace with event handler] with onClick="window.location.href='Tours page 2.htm'"

   c. Scroll down below the text "Tours division", select and replace the text [replace with instruction text] with the following script, pressing [Enter] at the end of each line:

```
<DIV ID="instr">
Click anywhere to advance to next slide.
</DIV>
```

   d. Check your document for errors, make any necessary changes, then save Tours slideshow.htm.

   e. Open Tours slideshow.htm in your Web browser, then click anywhere on the page.

HTML

7. Transition between pages.

    a. Open the file HTML M-14.htm in your text editor, then save a copy as Tours page transition.htm.

    b. Scroll down below the embedded style sheet in the page's head section and replace the text [replace with META tag] with the following: <META http-equiv="Page-Exit" CONTENT="RevealTrans(Duration=5,Transition=10)">

    c. Check your document for errors, make any necessary changes, then save as Tours page transition.htm.

    d. Open Tours page transition.htm in your Web browser, then click anywhere on the page.

▶ Independent Challenges

1. The owners of the Green House plant store have seen transition filters in use on other Web pages and think this effect would make their pages more interesting. You decide to add the "random dissolve" reveal transition to the secondary heading on the "Popular supplies" page.

    To complete this independent challenge:

    a. Open the file HTML M-15.htm in your text editor, then save it as a text document with the filename Green House transition.htm.

    b. Add the following style to the embedded style sheet in the page's head section:
#subhead {visibility: hidden; height: 16pt; filter: revealTrans(Transition=12, Duration=5)}.

    c. Scroll down to the end of the page's head section and replace the text [replace with transition function] with the following script, pressing [Enter] at the end of each line. Be sure to include opening and closing script tags.

```
function doTrans() {
        subhead.filters.revealTrans.Apply();
        subhead.style.visibility="visible";
        subhead.filters.revealTrans.Play();
}
```

    d. In the opening BODY tag, replace the text [replace with function call] with onLoad="doTrans()".

    e. Check your document for errors, make any necessary changes, then save Green House transition.htm.

    f. Open Green House transition.htm in your Web browser and verify that the subhead text appears slowly, in a random dissolve pattern.

2. You've long wanted to add an animated bus graphic to the home page you created for Sandhills Regional Public Transit (SRPT). Now that you know how to animate the position of Web page objects, you want to script this feature at the top of each SRPT Web page.

    To complete this independent challenge:

    a. Open the file HTML M-16.htm in your text editor, then save it as a text document with the filename SRPT animated.htm.

    b. To create space at the top of the page and to avoid overlapping elements, change the "top" values in the embedded style sheet for the following styles to the values indicated:
#bus: 75px
#head1: 60px
#head2: 300px
#instr: 75px

    c. Add the following entry to the embedded style sheet for the moving graphic:
#move {position: absolute; left: -1000px}

    d. You have already inserted the slide() function for this task. Look at the script in the page's HEAD section, noting the differences from the one you used in this unit. Try to predict how this script will behave differently, if at all.

e. Add the following event handler to the opening BODY tag:
onLoad="slide()"

f. Add the following IMG tag for the moving bus graphic immediately after the page's opening BODY tag:
<IMG SRC="busmove.jpg" ID="move">

g. Check your document for errors, then save SRPT animated.htm.

h. Open SRPT animated.htm in your Web browser and verify that the new bus graphic moves across the page without overlapping other elements.

3. The public-relations coordinator of Community Public School Volunteers wants to make sure the organization's Web page has an appealing layout, regardless of the computer's screen resolution or window size. Rather than using a scaling script, however, you decide to specify element dimensions in percentages to ensure uniform appearance.
To complete this independent challenge:

a. Open the file HTML M-17.htm in your text editor, then save it as a text document with the filename CPSV scale.htm.

b. In the #logo definition in the page's embedded style sheet, set the width value to 90%.

c. In the #box definition, change the width value to 75% and the left value to 12.5% (these settings ensure that the box is centered at any window size).

d. In the #instr definition, change the left value to 5% and the width value to 90% (these settings ensure that the text is centered in the box).

e. Check your changes, then save as CPSV scale.htm.

f. Preview CPSV scale.htm in your Web browser, then use your text editor to make any necessary changes, as well as any positioning and sizing changes that you think would improve the page's layout.

4. In addition to the filters and transitions that you've used in this unit, Internet Explorer 4 and 5 offer large selections of each of these features. To complete this independent challenge, connect to the Internet and locate a Web page that explains specific filters and transitions in detail. You can find this information on the Microsoft Web site, as well as on other DHTML sites. Find and print information on one standard filter and one Reveal transition filter that you have not used before. Make sure the information you print includes the name of the filter, the syntax for using it in your style specifications, and an explanation of any special parameters that it allows you to set. Then create a simple Web page named Unit M IC 4.htm, which contains one element. Apply the standard filter to the element and apply the Reveal transition filter to the page exit. Submit the printouts from your research and your file containing the filter and transition to your instructor.

▶ Visual Workshop

The owner of Touchstone Booksellers would like users to see an interesting effect when they first view his page. You decide to try an interpage transition that takes effect when the page opens. Save a copy of the file HTML M-18.htm as Touchstone transition.htm. Insert the necessary code to add the "Random bars vertical" transition, shown in Figure M-19. Use Table M-2 to look up the Transition value for this effect. The http-equiv value for this transition should be "Page-Enter" for the transition to occur as the page first loads. To test your changes, save your file, then open the file "Touchstone open.htm" in your Web browser, and click the link "Touchstone home page" to open the page you created.

FIGURE M-19

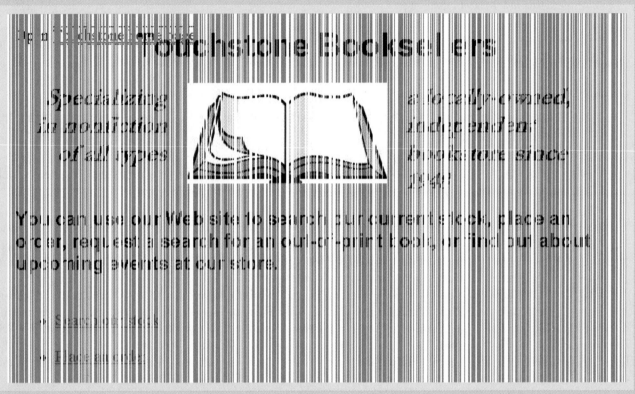

Structuring
Data with XML

Objectives

► **Understand eXtensible Markup Language (XML)**
► **Define XML elements and structure**
► **Enter XML data**
► **Bind XML data to HTML**
► **Format XML data with HTML**
► **Display XML data with HTML**
► **Modify an XML document**
► **Alter XML data view with HTML**

HTML has evolved from a way of structuring information into a language for controlling the format, or display, of Web content. With the vast growth of data on the Web, and the creation of many new applications, it has become critical to have a standard but expandable means to define, structure, and exchange the data on the Web. The **eXtensible Markup Language (XML)** is designed to ensure a **universal data structure** that can be read by any XML-compliant browser yet still allow Web designers the freedom to create **custom data definitions** for an endless variety of applications (e.g., a book or movie database).  Lydia would like to create a "Recommended Backpacking Books" page for backpacking enthusiasts on the Nomad Web site. The HTML page will display book data she stores using XML and custom data definitions.

Understanding eXtensible Markup Language (XML)

XML (**eXtensible Markup Language**) is a text-based syntax especially designed to describe, deliver, and exchange structured data. XML documents use the file extension .xml and, like HTML files, can be created with a simple text editor. XML is not meant as a replacement for HTML but, rather, as a means to vastly extend its descriptive and structural power. XML uses a syntax that is similar to HTML, with four basic differences. These rules guarantee that a document is well-formed. A **well-formed** document requires that data be uniformly structured by tagsets so it can be read correctly by any XML-compliant program. Lydia is new to using XML, so she researches the language before starting to create the backpacking book list. To understand how the syntax of XML differs from HTML, Lydia examines each XML syntax rule carefully.

 All elements must have start and end tags

An **element** consists of the start tag and corresponding end tag along with the content between the tagset. Unlike HTML, where you can mark up a document without using some closing tags (e.g., </P>), XML requires that both opening and closing tags be present. For example, the first line in Figure N-1 shows the correct way to code XML with both the start and end paragraph tags necessary to create a well-formed XML document. The same line in Figure N-2 lacks the required closing "</P>" tag, and thus violates the first rule of XML syntax.

 All elements must be nested correctly

Just as in HTML, when writing XML, you should close first whatever tagset you opened last. However, you cannot overlap elements in XML. The second line of code in Figure N-1 shows the heading tagset "<H2></H2>" correctly nested inside of the paragraph tagset "<P></P>." The same line in Figure N-2 breaks this rule by placing the closing "</H2>" tag after the end paragraph tag "</P>." Although this code would display properly in HTML, it is not well-formed and would not display in XML because of the inherent stricter rule enforcement.

 All attribute values must appear with quotation marks

HTML requires that only certain attribute values, such as URLs and strings, be in quotes. Values such as image and font size may be used without quotes. In XML, attributes must appear in quotes. The third line of code in Figure N-1 illustrates the proper way to code by quoting the font size attribute value "16," whereas the same line in Figure N-2 shows the font attribute value without quotes and, thus, wrongly marked up for XML.

All empty elements must be self-identifying by ending with "/>"

An **empty element** is one that doesn't have a closing tag (e.g., <BR>, <HR>, and <IMG> in HTML). The last tag on the fourth line of code in Figure N-1 demonstrates the proper way to identify an empty element in XML by ending it with "/>." This forward slash at the end of the tag indicates that the element, or container, is not broken (i.e., missing a closing tag) but simply empty. The same tag in Figure N-2 does not contain the necessary ending slash and, hence, would prevent an XML document from being well-formed.

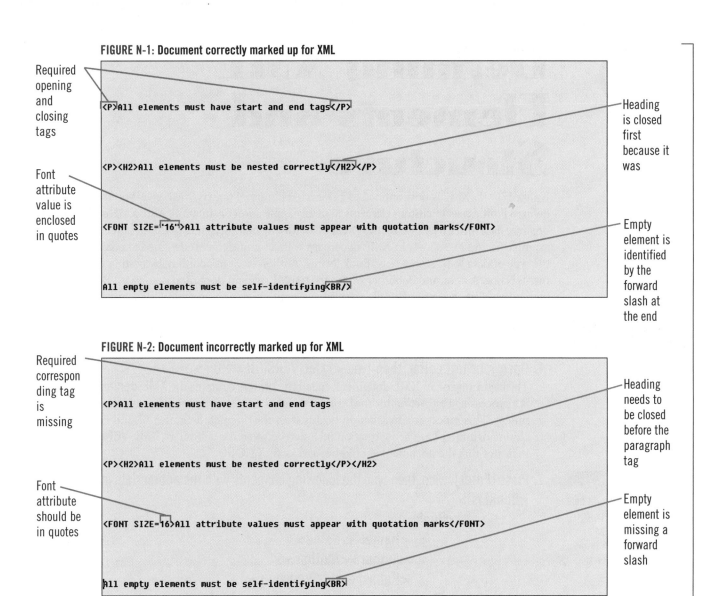

FIGURE N-1: Document correctly marked up for XML

Required opening and closing tags

`<P>All elements must have start and end tags</P>`

`<P><H2>All elements must be nested correctly</H2></P>`

Font attribute value is enclosed in quotes

`<FONT SIZE="16">All attribute values must appear with quotation marks</FONT>`

`All empty elements must be self-identifying<BR/>`

Heading is closed first because it was

Empty element is identified by the forward slash at the end

FIGURE N-2: Document incorrectly marked up for XML

Required corresponding tag is missing

`<P>All elements must have start and end tags`

`<P><H2>All elements must be nested correctly</P></H2>`

Font attribute should be in quotes

`<FONT SIZE=16>All attribute values must appear with quotation marks</FONT>`

`All empty elements must be self-identifying<BR>`

Heading needs to be closed before the paragraph tag

Empty element is missing a forward slash

Benefits of XML

With XML, it is possible to identify data in meaningful ways, much like a database lets you identify and organize data with unique fieldnames and records. XML allows custom "vocabularies," or element sets, to be defined for particular types of data, such as books, movies, auto parts, legal cases, and medical information. In other words, these custom vocabularies act like the fieldnames in a conventional database to clearly identify and segment data. If these highly descriptive elements come into widespread use on the Web, XML has the potential to organize the Web into a coherent body of knowledge. For instance, this new level of semantics should improve the ability of now-overburdened search engines to rapidly find relevant information—in the same way queries can quickly locate relevant data in a database. Additionally, XML offers the means to exchange and process data from otherwise-incompatible information repositories on the Internet. XML and DHTML also enable a significant portion of the processing load to be shifted from Web servers to Web browsers (clients). Consequently, applications that require high-level compatibility and performance, such as those in electronic commerce, will greatly benefit from the implementation of XML. Finally, intelligent Web applications that seek out choice bits of information on the Web to match the preferences of individual users also should realize equally significant gains in accuracy as a result of clearly labeled XML data.

HTML

Defining XML Elements and Structure

Unlike HTML, XML is not confined to a restricted library of tagsets. XML gives you the freedom to define a limitless set of custom elements to fit any application or situation. Also, XML enables you to organize data into a **tree-like hierarchical structure** by nesting elements within other elements. For example, Figure N-3 shows an XML document with a set of elements designed to precisely describe the type of data to be stored (e.g., Book, Name, Author, etc.). In addition, by nesting the **child** elements Name, Author, and Publisher within the **parent** element Book, and nesting the Book elements within BookList, you automatically establish a parent-child, or hierarchical, structure similar to the one illustrated in Figure N-4.  After completing her basic research on XML, Lydia decides to define the XML elements and structure necessary to store the data in the backpacking book list.

1. Open your text editor, then type <?XML VERSION='1.0'?>

The beginning of an XML document, called the **prolog**, contains the **XML declaration**, which is a processing instruction for the browser or other XML-compliant program reading the document. This processing instruction begins with the opening delimiter **<?** and ends with the closing delimiter **?>**. The instruction included between the delimiters, **XML VERSION='1.0'**, indicates that the document should be read as an XML file.

2. Press [Enter] twice, then type the following elements with the appropriate indentations:

```
<BookList>
        <Book>
                <Name></Name>
                <Author></Author>
                <Publisher></Publisher>
        </Book>
</BookList>
```

QuickTip

The indentation shown here is unnecessary for proper processing but helps to more clearly delineate the relationship between the document elements.

The elements in an XML document are **ranked** from the outermost set to the innermost elements. The highest ranked element forms the "root" of a tree-like structure, while the lower ranked elements make up the successive "branches" of the tree, as shown in Figure N-4. Thus, the rank of an element determines how much of the tree it controls.

3. To create two more instances of the Book elements, begin by selecting the highlighted area shown in Figure N-5

4. Press [Ctrl][c] to copy the highlighted area

5. Place the insertion point at the end of the Book element </Book>, then press [Enter] twice

QuickTip

The prefix "XML" is reserved for XML syntax, so you can't use it as a prefix for tag name (e.g., XMLbook).

6. Press [Ctrl][v] to paste a second Book record

A second instance of the Book elements appears in your document.

QuickTip

XML is case-sensitive. For example, the element <Author></Author> is not equivalent to the element <AUTHOR></AUTHOR>.

7. Press [Enter] once, paste another instance of the Book elements, then press [Delete]

Your document should now look like the one shown in Figure N-3.

8. Save the file as a text document with the filename **books.xml**

You are now ready to enter the data into your XML document.

FIGURE N-3: Elements and structure of book list XML document

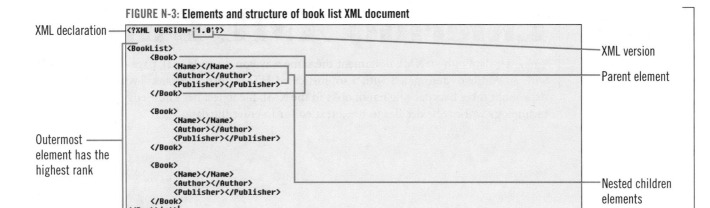

XML declaration

Outermost element has the highest rank

XML version

Parent element

Nested children elements

FIGURE N-4: Tree-like hierarchical structure of XML document

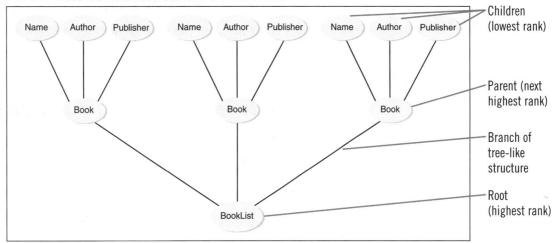

Children (lowest rank)

Parent (next highest rank)

Branch of tree-like structure

Root (highest rank)

FIGURE N-5: Highlighted book elements to copy

```
<?XML VERSION='1.0'?>

<BookList>
        <Book>
                <Name></Name>
                <Author></Author>
                <Publisher></Publisher>
        </Book>
</BookList>
```

Area to copy

CLUES TO USE

Document Type Definition (DTD) and XML schemas

A **Document Type Definition (DTD)** is the formal specification of the rules of an XML document—namely, which elements are allowed and in what combinations. A Web page designer would create a DTD to ensure that any XML document using the DTD will be **valid** (i.e., comply with the formal specification). For example, a DTD could be set up to ensure that all XML files dealing with drug prescriptions include certain data elements (e.g., the prescribing doctor's name, expiration date, and refill information). Although a DTD can be called from an XML file, it uses a different syntax from XML. An **XML schema** combines the concepts of a DTD, relational databases, and object-oriented designs to create a richer and more powerful way to formally define the elements and structure of an XML document. In addition, XML schemas use the same syntax as XML, so they will be able to appear in the same document. However, support for XML schemas are not supported in Internet Explorer 4 and DTDs only enjoy limited support. To learn more about DTDs and XML schemas, visit http://www.microsoft.com/xml/, or search the http://www.microsoft.com for information on XML.

Entering XML Data

You enter data into an XML document the same way you do an HTML page—either manually with an editor or automated with a sophisticated HTML form. Lydia wants to enter data about three backpacking handbooks in the XML file to test her knowledge of how this new technology works. She decides to use a text editor to enter the data.

Steps

1. Make sure that books.xml is open in your text editor

2. Position the insertion point between the first set of <Name></Name> tagsets, as shown in Figure N-6

QuickTip

All the content of an XML element is treated as data, including white space. Make sure not to include unwanted blank space in between any opening and closing tagsets.

3. Type The Backpacker's Field Manual

4. Place the insertion point between the <Author></Author> tagset directly below, then type Rick Curtis

5. Move the insertion point between the <Publisher></Publisher> tagset directly below, then type Crown Publishers Inc.
   The text editor should match the contents of Figure N-7.

6. Type the following data in the appropriate tagsets for the next two instances of the Book elements:

The Modern Backpacker's Handbook	The Backpacker's Handbook
Glenn Randall	Chris Townsend
Lyons and Burford Publishers	Ragged Mountain Press

   The text editor window should look like the one shown in Figure N-8.

7. Save, then close the file

FIGURE N-6: Insertion point position

```
<?XML VERSION='1.0'?>

<BookList>
    <Book>
        <Name>|</Name>
        <Author></<Author>
        <Publisher></Publisher>
    </Book>

    <Book>
        <Name></Name>
        <Author></<Author>
        <Publisher></Publisher>
    </Book>

    <Book>
        <Name></Name>
        <Author></<Author>
        <Publisher></Publisher>
    </Book>
</BookList>
```

Correct insertion
point position

FIGURE N-7: XML document with first data record

```
<?XML VERSION='1.0'?>

<BookList>
    <Book>
        <Name>The Backpacker's Field Manual</Name>
        <Author>Rick Curtis</Author>
        <Publisher>Crown Publishers Inc.</Publisher>
    </Book>

    <Book>
        <Name></Name>
        <Author></Author>
        <Publisher></Publisher>
    </Book>

    <Book>
        <Name></Name>
        <Author></Author>
        <Publisher></Publisher>
    </Book>
</BookList>
```

Data record

FIGURE N-8: XML document with all data entered

```
<?XML VERSION='1.0'?>

<BookList>
    <Book>
        <Name>The Backpacker's Field Manual</Name>
        <Author>Rick Curtis</Author>
        <Publisher>Crown Publishers Inc.</Publisher>
    </Book>

    <Book>
        <Name>The Modern Backpacker's Handbook</Name>
        <Author>Glenn Randall</Author>
        <Publisher>Lyons and Burford Publishers</Publisher>
    </Book>

    <Book>
        <Name>The Backpacker's Handbook</Name>
        <Author>Chris Townsend</Author>
        <Publisher>Ragged Mountain Press</Publisher>
    </Book>
</BookList>
```

Data
record 1

Data
record 2

Data
record 3

Binding XML Data to HTML

XML-compliant browsers such as Internet Explorer 4 support XML by including an XML parser and an XML Data Source Object (XML DSO). An **XML parser** dissects and interprets XML elements, whereas the **XML DSO** enables binding of the XML data to the HTML document using the DHTMLObject Model. Thus, the parser and DSO cooperate to allow the display, or **rendering**, of XML data in HTML.  Lydia wants to display the data in the books.xml file in an HTML document that will become part of Nomad Ltd's Web site. Before she can format the data, Lydia must first create the HTML document and bind the XML data to it.

Steps123**4**

1. Open your text editor, then type
```
<HTML>
<HEAD>
        <TITLE>Backpacking Book List</TITLE>
</HEAD>
<BODY>
<H2>Recommended Backpacking Books</H2>
```
The text editor screen now should look like the one shown in Figure N-9. Lydia is ready to enter the XML DSO Java applet necessary to bind the XML data you created in the last lesson. A **Java applet** is a small program written in the Java programming language that is summoned using the <applet></applet> tagset.

2. Press [Enter] twice, then type
```
<APPLET  CODE="com.ms.xml.dso.XMLDSO.class"  WIDTH="100%"  HEIGHT="25"
ID="xmldso" MAYSCRIPT="true">
    <PARAM NAME="url" VALUE="books.xml">
</APPLET>
```
The document should appear as shown in Figure N-10. Notice that the opening applet tag causes the browser to call the XML DSO Java applet. The parameter tag "<PARAM NAME="url" VALUE="books.xml">" specifies a URL with the name of the XML file to bind to this HTML document.

3. Press [Enter], then type:
```
</BODY>
</HTML>
```
With these closing HTML tags entered, the text editor screen should now match Figure N-11.

4. Save the file as a text document with the filename books.htm
Now Lydia has created an HTML document to which the XML data entered in the previous lesson is bound. The next step is to construct a table to format and display the bound data in your HTML document.

FIGURE N-9: Beginning HTML markup

```
<HTML>
<HEAD>
     <TITLE>Backpacking Book List</TITLE>
</HEAD>
<BODY>
<H2>Recommended Backpacking Books</H2>
```

FIGURE N-10: Applet to call the XML DSO

```
<HTML>
<HEAD>
     <TITLE>Backpacking Book List</TITLE>
</HEAD>
<BODY>
<H2>Recommended Backpacking Books</H2>

<APPLET CODE="com.ms.xml.dso.XMLDSO.class" WIDTH="100%"
HEIGHT="25" ID="xmldso" MAYSCRIPT="true">
     <PARAM NAME="url" VALUE="books.xml">
</APPLET>
```

Parameter name
that specifies
source as a URL

Value that specifies
XML document
filename

Applet to bind XML
document to this
HTML page

FIGURE N-11: HTML document with data-binding code

```
<HTML>
<HEAD>
     <TITLE>Backpacking Book List</TITLE>
</HEAD>
<BODY>
<H2>Recommended Backpacking Books</H2>

<APPLET CODE="com.ms.xml.dso.XMLDSO.class" WIDTH="100%"
HEIGHT="25" ID="xmldso" MAYSCRIPT="true">
     <PARAM NAME="url" VALUE="books.xml">
</APPLET>
</BODY>
</HTML>
```

Formatting XML Data with HTML

Once the data in an XML document has been bound to an HTML page, you can use all of the available formatting capabilities in HTML (plus CSS) to control its presentation in a browser. Because XML data often consists of a list, or database, the table feature in HTML is an ideal vehicle for displaying this tabular data. In addition to the conventional table attributes, several new HTML attributes enable Web page designers to control the binding of XML data to their documents. Table N-1 describes these new attributes. Lydia decides to use a table to format and display her book-list data in the XML file.

Steps

1. Make sure the file books.htm is open in your text editor
2. Place the insertion point below the </APPLET> tag, then press [Enter]

   Lydia wants to use a table to display the data in the books.xml file.

QuickTip

You can use all the power and flexibility of DHTML to manipulate XML data once it appears in an HTML document.

3. Carefully type the following:

```
<TABLE ID="table" BORDER="2" WIDTH="100%" DATASRC="#xmldso"
CELLPADDING="5">
<THEAD>
<FONT FACE="Arial" SIZE="2">
    <TR>
        <TH>TITLE</TH>
        <TH>AUTHOR</TH>
        <TH>PUBLISHER</TH>
    </TR>
</FONT>
</THEAD>
<FONT FACE="Times New Roman" SIZE="2">
    <TR>
        <TD VALIGN="top"><DIV DATAFLD="NAME"
        DATAFORMATAS="HTML"></DIV></TD>
        <TD VALIGN="top"><DIV DATAFLD="AUTHOR"
        DATAFORMATAS="HTML"></DIV></TD>
        <TD VALIGN="top"><DIV DATAFLD="PUBLISHER"
        DATAFORMATAS="HTML"></DIV></TD>
    </TR>
</FONT>
</TABLE>
```

   The text editor screen should match Figure N-12. This code creates a table that uses an Arial font style, with a size of 2, to display the headings TITLE, AUTHOR, and PUBLISHER across the top row. The DATAFLD attributes in this code specify the element from the XML document to be bound to each column. The DATAFORMATAS attributes indicate that the XML-based data should be displayed in HTML format. In other words, the DATAFORMATAS attributes tell your browser to interpret and format the imported XML data as HTML content. This code will create as many rows as necessary to display all the data (records) in your XML file.

4. Check your work to make sure your typing was completely accurate
5. Save, then close the file

FIGURE N-12: **Table code to format and bind XML data**

```
<HTML>
<HEAD>
        <TITLE>Backpacking Book List</TITLE>
</HEAD>
<BODY>
<H2>Recommended Backpacking Books</H2>

<APPLET CODE="com.ms.xml.dso.XMLDSO.class" WIDTH="100%"
HEIGHT="25" ID="xmldso" MAYSCRIPT="true">
        <PARAM NAME="url" VALUE="books.xml">
</APPLET>

<TABLE ID="table" BORDER="2" WIDTH="100%"
DATASRC="#xmldso" CELLPADDING="5">
<THEAD>
<FONT FACE="Arial" SIZE="2">
        <TR>
                <TH>TITLE</TH>
                <TH>AUTHOR</TH>
                <TH>PUBLISHER</TH>
        </TR>
</FONT>
</THEAD>
<FONT FACE="Times New Roman" SIZE="2">
        <TR>
                <TD VALIGN="top"><DIV DATAFLD="NAME"
                DATAFORMATAS="HTML"></DIV></TD>
                <TD VALIGN="top"><DIV DATAFLD="AUTHOR"
                DATAFORMATAS="HTML"></DIV></TD>
                <TD VALIGN="top"><DIV DATAFLD="PUBLISHER"
                DATAFORMATAS="HTML"></DIV></TD>
        </TR>
</FONT>
</TABLE>
```

Font settings for table headings

Font settings for table rows

DATAFORMATAS attribute indicates the bound data should be displayed as HTML

DATAFLD attribute specifies the AUTHOR element be bound to this column

Table column heading for XML data

TABLE N-1: **New table data-binding HTML attributes**

attribute	description
DATASRC	Identifies the XML DSO applet used to bind the data.
DATAFLD	Specifies the particular column to bind the element to.
DATAFORMATAS	Indicates how the bound data should be rendered in the specified column (e.g., in HTML).
DATAPAGESIZE	Controls how many records are displayed in a table at once.

CLUES TO USE

Formatting XML data with the Extensible Style Language (XSL)

In addition to formatting XML data with HTML and CSS, you also can use an XSL (Extensible Style Language) stylesheet. An **XSL stylesheet** is a set of programming rules that determine how XML data is displayed in an HTML document. Because XSL is designed to work with XML, it has the same flexibility and syntax as XML. However, native support for XSL is not built into Internet Explorer 4 or other browsers. To apply an XSL stylesheet to an XML document using Internet Explorer 4, first you must download and install the **Microsoft XSL ActiveX control**. This control is based on Microsoft's object-oriented ActiveX technology and is freely distributed. In fact, you can embed a script in your HTML document to automate the downloading and installation process. For more information on XSL and the XSL ActiveX control, see http://www.microsoft.com/xml/.

HTML

Displaying XML Data with HTML

Once you have created an HTML document to bind and format your XML-based data, you simply need to start your browser and open the HTML page to view the results. The XML document storing the data and the HTML page presenting it can reside on your local computer, network, or a remote Web server on the Internet. ✎ Lydia wants to see the XML data displayed in her HTML document.

Steps

QuickTip

Use Internet Explorer 4 to display XML data with HTML. Netscape Navigator 4 doesn't support XML, Navigator 5 will.

Trouble?

If no error appears, yet the table fails to display correctly, then your installation of Internet Explorer may be missing the Java VM (Virtual Machine). The Java VM is available from the Internet Explorer downloads section at the Microsoft Web site. See your instructor or technical support person for assistance.

1. Start your browser, then open the **books.htm** file

The document shown in Figure N-13 should appear, complete with the formatted data read from your books.xml file. Notice the colored line above the table indicating that the XML was successfully loaded: "file:/A:/books.xml." If the load was unsuccessful, this line indicates an error in parsing the XML file.

2. If your HTML document displays an error when attempting to load the books.xml file like the one shown in Figure N-14, you need to edit your XML document, recheck your typing, and fix any syntax mistakes

Unlike HTML, an XML document won't load correctly unless you obey all the rules of a well-formed document.

3. After successfully viewing the book list in the HTML table, close your browser

FIGURE N-13: **HTML document displaying formatted XML data in a table**

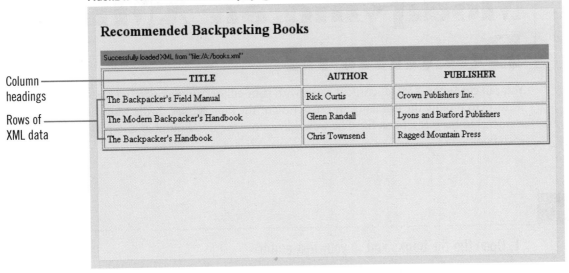

Column headings

Rows of XML data

Recommended Backpacking Books

Successfully loaded XML from "file:/A:/books.xml"

TITLE	AUTHOR	PUBLISHER
The Backpacker's Field Manual	Rick Curtis	Crown Publishers Inc.
The Modern Backpacker's Handbook	Glenn Randall	Lyons and Burford Publishers
The Backpacker's Handbook	Chris Townsend	Ragged Mountain Press

FIGURE N-14: **HTML document displaying a parsing error**

Highlighted line indicates nature of the problem

Recommended Backpacking Books

Error loading XML document 'books.xml'. com.ms.xml.parser.ParseException: Close tag BOOK does not match start tag PUBLISHER

TITLE	AUTHOR	PUBLISHER
The Backpacker's Field Manual	Rick Curtis	Crown Publishers Inc.

CLUES TO USE

Multiple views of data

Once data has been moved into your browser, it can be displayed in many different ways. A Web page designer might build several different views of the same data depending on the audience. For example, in the case of a movie database, the average user might just want to see the title, actors, and general plot of films, whereas some devoted fans will want to view all the particulars like the date the movie was released, who directed it, and so forth. Because XML only describes data, not its appearance, a Web page designer is free to use HTML/CSS to create unique views of the data for different classes of users. In addition, with use of DHTML, the view of XML data can be manipulated easily by the end user to suit his or her needs and tastes.

Modifying an XML Document

You can change an XML document easily with your editor. Simply open the file and use the edit features to modify the elements and structure of the file. ✎ Lydia wants to add two new elements to her XML book file. She would like store the ISBN number and publication date of each book.

Steps

1. Open the file books.xml in your text editor

2. Position the insertion point at the end of the first Publisher element, as shown in Figure N-15

3. Press [Enter] to insert a blank line, use tabs to align the insertion point directly beneath the beginning of the tag above, then type

   <ISBN>0517887835</ISBN>

4. Press [Enter] again, align the insertion point, and type

   <Date>March 1998</Date>

   The text in the editor should now match Figure N-16. All that remains is to enter the new elements for the other two book records.

5. Insert the following elements in the two remaining book records:

   <ISBN>1558212485</ISBN>   <ISBN>0070653151</ISBN>

   <Date>February 1994</Date>   <Date>October 1996</Date>

   The XML document should now contain the text shown in Figure N-17.

6. Save, then close the file

FIGURE N-15: Correct position for insertion point

```
<?XML VERSION='1.0'?>

<BookList>
    <Book>
        <Name>The Backpacker's Field Manual</Name>
        <Author>Rick Curtis</Author>
        <Publisher>Crown Publishers Inc.</Publisher>|
    </Book>

    <Book>
        <Name>The Modern Backpacker's Handbook</Name>
        <Author>Glenn Randall</Author>
        <Publisher>Lyons and Burford Publishers</Publisher>
    </Book>

    <Book>
        <Name>The Backpacker's Handbook</Name>
        <Author>Chris Townsend</Author>
        <Publisher>Ragged Mountain Press</Publisher>
    </Book>
</BookList>
```

Insertion point at the end of the first Publisher element

FIGURE N-16: XML with two new elements

```
<?XML VERSION='1.0'?>

<BookList>
    <Book>
        <Name>The Backpacker's Field Manual</Name>
        <Author>Rick Curtis</Author>
        <Publisher>Crown Publishers Inc.</Publisher>
        <ISBN>0517887835</ISBN>
        <Date>March 1998</Date>
    </Book>

    <Book>
        <Name>The Modern Backpacker's Handbook</Name>
        <Author>Glenn Randall</Author>
        <Publisher>Lyons and Burford Publishers</Publisher>
    </Book>

    <Book>
        <Name>The Backpacker's Handbook</Name>
        <Author>Chris Townsend</Author>
        <Publisher>Ragged Mountain Press</Publisher>
    </Book>
</BookList>
```

ISBN element

Date element

FIGURE N-17: XML file modifications complete

```
<?XML VERSION='1.0'?>

<BookList>
    <Book>
        <Name>The Backpacker's Field Manual</Name>
        <Author>Rick Curtis</Author>
        <Publisher>Crown Publishers Inc.</Publisher>
        <ISBN>0517887835</ISBN>
        <Date>March 1998</Date>
    </Book>

    <Book>
        <Name>The Modern Backpacker's Handbook</Name>
        <Author>Glenn Randall</Author>
        <Publisher>Lyons and Burford Publishers</Publisher>
        <ISBN>1558212485</ISBN>
        <Date>February 1994</Date>
    </Book>

    <Book>
        <Name>The Backpacker's Handbook</Name>
        <Author>Chris Townsend</Author>
        <Publisher>Ragged Mountain Press</Publisher>
        <ISBN>0070653151</ISBN>
        <Date>October 1996</Date>
    </Book>
</BookList>
```

All records include new ISBN and Date elements

Altering XML Data View with HTML

When you add elements to an XML document, you must make corresponding changes to the HTML document you are using to view the data; otherwise, the new data will not be displayed. Fortunately, it is easy to bring the HTML document into alignment with the new XML elements. Simply insert the code necessary to display the new elements in the format you desire. Lydia decides to display the ISBN and publication date in the same table with the rest of her book-list data.

Steps

1. Open the file books.htm in your text editor

2. Change the font face for the Table header from Arial to Arial Black in the opening Table tag

3. Place the insertion point at the end of <TH>PUBLISHER</TH>

4. Press [Enter] to insert a blank line, tab over to align up directly beneath the tag above, then type <TH>ISBN</TH>

5. Press [Enter] to insert a blank line, align with the tag above, then type

   <TH>DATE</TH>

   These tags will create two new column headings—ISBN and DATE—for the data table.

6. Place the insertion point at the end of the last row in the table, as shown in Figure N-18

7. Press [Enter], align the insertion point directly under the beginning of the first tag above, then type

   <TD VALIGN="top"><DIV DATAFLD="ISBN"
   DATAFORMATAS="HTML"></DIV></TD>

8. Press [Enter], align the insertion point, then type

   <TD VALIGN="top"><DIV DATAFLD="DATE"
   DATAFORMATAS="HTML"></DIV></TD>

   The text in the editor should match Figure N-19. Check it carefully to make sure there are no typos.

9. Save the file, then close the document and text editor

Trouble?

If your HTML document displays a parsing error, use your text editor to find the syntax mistake in the books.xml file, then refresh your browser screen.

10. Start your browser, then open the books.htm file to view the changes made to the table

    The HTML document appears with the two new column headings and corresponding data, as shown in Figure N-20.

FIGURE N-18: Position insertion point to enter column data tags

```
<HTML>
<HEAD>
    <TITLE>Backpacking Book List</TITLE>
</HEAD>
<BODY>
<H2>Recommended Backpacking Books</H2>

<APPLET CODE="com.ms.xml.dso.XMLDSO.class" WIDTH="100%"
HEIGHT="25" ID="xmldso" MAYSCRIPT="true">
    <PARAM NAME="url" VALUE="books.xml">
</APPLET>

<TABLE ID="table" BORDER="2" WIDTH="100%"
DATASRC="#xmldso" CELLPADDING="5">
<THEAD>
<FONT FACE="Arial Black" SIZE="2">
    <TR>
        <TH>TITLE</TH>
        <TH>AUTHOR</TH>
        <TH>PUBLISHER</TH>
        <TH>ISBN</TH>
        <TH>DATE</TH>
    </TR>
</FONT>
</THEAD>
<FONT FACE="Times New Roman" SIZE="2">
    <TR>
        <TD VALIGN="top"><DIV DATAFLD="NAME"
        DATAFORMATAS="HTML"></DIV></TD>
        <TD VALIGN="top"><DIV DATAFLD="AUTHOR"
        DATAFORMATAS="HTML"></DIV></TD>
        <TD VALIGN="top"><DIV DATAFLD="PUBLISHER"
        DATAFORMATAS="HTML"></DIV></TD>                    ──── Insertion point at
    </TR>                                                        the end of the line
```

FIGURE N-19: HTML altered to display new XML data

```
<H2>Recommended Backpacking Books</H2>

<APPLET CODE="com.ms.xml.dso.XMLDSO.class" WIDTH="100%"
HEIGHT="25" ID="xmldso" MAYSCRIPT="true">
    <PARAM NAME="url" VALUE="books.xml">
</APPLET>

<TABLE ID="table" BORDER="2" WIDTH="100%"
DATASRC="#xmldso" CELLPADDING="5">
<THEAD>
<FONT FACE="Arial Black" SIZE="2">
    <TR>
        <TH>TITLE</TH>
        <TH>AUTHOR</TH>
        <TH>PUBLISHER</TH>
        <TH>ISBN</TH>                          ──── Inserted column
        <TH>DATE</TH>                               headings
    </TR>
</FONT>
</THEAD>
<FONT FACE="Times New Roman" SIZE="2">
    <TR>
        <TD VALIGN="top"><DIV DATAFLD="NAME"
        DATAFORMATAS="HTML"></DIV></TD>
        <TD VALIGN="top"><DIV DATAFLD="AUTHOR"
        DATAFORMATAS="HTML"></DIV></TD>
        <TD VALIGN="top"><DIV DATAFLD="PUBLISHER"
        DATAFORMATAS="HTML"></DIV></TD>
        <TD VALIGN="top"><DIV DATAFLD="ISBN"         ──── New attributes to
        DATAFORMATAS="HTML"></DIV></TD>                   bind data to
        <TD VALIGN="top"><DIV DATAFLD="DATE"              columns
        DATAFORMATAS="HTML"></DIV></TD>
    </TR>
</FONT>
```

Font face for table headings changed to Arial Black

FIGURE N-20: Five-column table with new data

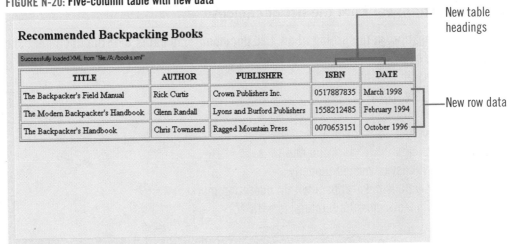

New table headings

New row data

HTML

Practice

► Concepts Review

Label each item marked in Figure N-21.

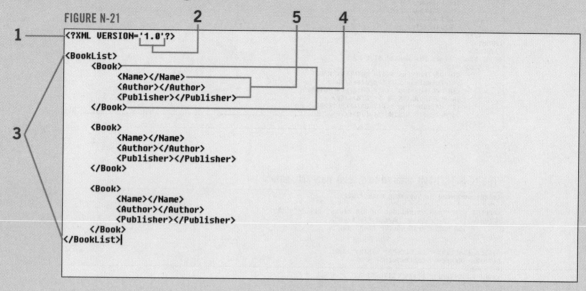

FIGURE N-21

Match each term with its description.

6. **Element**
7. **Parser**
8. **XML**
9. **Correctly nested**
10. **Empty element**

a. An element that doesn't have a closing tag
b. A text-based format that lets you describe, deliver, and exchange structured data
c. No overlapping elements
d. Dissects and interprets XML
e. The start and corresponding end tags, plus the contents in between the tagset

Select the best answer from the list of choices.

11. **The XML declaration, in the prolog of an XML document, indicates that the document should be**
    a. Encoded with XSL.
    b. Processed as an XML file.
    c. Rendered using HTML.
    d. Displayed as HTML.

12. **Which is *not* an XML syntax rule?**
    a. All elements must have start and end tags.
    b. All elements must be nested properly.
    c. All attribute values must appear within quotation marks.
    d. All empty elements must be terminated with "//>".

13. Which statement is False?

a. Blank space appearing in the content of an element is read as data.

b. XML is organized in a tree-like structure.

c. The elements <Wine>red</Wine> and <wine>red</wine> are equivalent in XML.

d. XML brings structure and customization to the Web.

14. Which is *not* a new table data binding attribute for HTML?

a. DATASRC

b. DATAFLD

c. DATAFORMAT

d. DATAPAGESIZE

15. Which one of the following is *not* required to display XML data in a browser?

a. parser

b. Cascading Style Sheet (CSS)

c. data-binding applet

d. data-binding attributes

 # Skills Review

1. Define XML elements and structure.

a. Open your text editor, then type <?XML VERSION='1.0'?>

b. Two lines down, enter the following elements, using the appropriate indentation to signify the structure of the document:

```
<Catalog>
        <Product>
                <Model></Model>
                <Price></Price>
                <Description></Description>
        </Product>

        <Product>
                <Model></Model>
                <Price></Price>
                <Description></Description>
        </Product>

        <Product>
                <Model></Model>
                <Price></Price>
                <Description></Description>
        </Product>
</Catalog>
```

c. Verify your typing and correct any typos.

d. Save the file as a text document with the filename products.xml.

2. Enter XML data.

a. Make sure products.xml is open in your text editor.

b. Position the insertion point between the first instance of the <Model></Model> element and type "Cleaner 100".

c. Type "$495" between the Price tags directly below the first Name element.

d. Type "Domestic robot to vacuum and dust your home." between the Description tags.

e. Enter the following content for the next two Product records:

Whacker 300

$1,195

Yard robot that mows and trims the edges of your lawn.

Nursemaid 400

$4,995

Personal robot to care for purchasers of Cleaner 100 and Whacker 200 robot models.

f. Save and close the document.

3. Bind XML data to HTML.

a. Start your text editor, then in a new document, type the following code with indicated alignments:

```
<HTML>
<HEAD>
<TITLE>Robot Product Catalog</TITLE>
</HEAD>
<BODY>
<H2>Robot Product Catalog</H2>
```

b. Create two blank lines at the bottom the document, then bind the products.xml file to this HTML document by entering the following code:

```
<APPLET CODE="com.ms.xml.dso.XMLDSO.class" WIDTH="100%" HEIGHT="25"
ID="xmldso" MAYSCRIPT="true">
        <PARAM NAME="url" VALUE="products.xml">
</APPLET>
```

c. Type the following HTML closing tags:

```
</BODY>
</HTML>
```

d. Check the document for errors, making changes as necessary.

e. Save the file as a text document with the filename products.htm.

4. Format XML data with HTML.

a. Make sure products.htm is open in your text editor.

b. To create a table to bind, format, and display the data in the products.xml file, type the following HTML code just below the closing applet tag:

```
<TABLE ID="table" BORDER="2" WIDTH="100%" DATASRC="#xmldso" CELLPADDING="5">
<THEAD>
<FONT FACE="Arial" SIZE="2">
<TR>
        <TH>MODEL</TH>
        <TH>PRICE</TH>
        <TH>DESCRIPTION</TH>
```

```
</TR>
        </FONT>
</THEAD>
<FONT FACE="Times New Roman" SIZE="2">
        <TR>
                <TD VALIGN="top"><DIV DATAFLD="MODEL" DATAFORMATAS="HTML"></DIV></TD>
                <TD VALIGN="top"><DIV DATAFLD="PRICE" DATAFORMATAS="HTML"></DIV></TD>
                <TD VALIGN="top"><DIV DATAFLD="DESCRIPTION" DATAFORMATAS="HTML"></DIV></TD>
        </TR>
</FONT>
</TABLE>
```

c. Check the document for errors, making changes as necessary, then save and close the file.

5. **Display XML data with HTML.**
   a. Start your browser, then open the file products.htm.
   b. If you receive a parsing error, use your text editor to find and fix typos in either the products.htm or products.xml documents, then open the products.htm file again with your browser.
   c. When you are done examining the table of data, print the page, then close your browser.

6. **Modifying an XML document.**
   a. Open the file products.xml in your text editor.
   b. In the first Product element, insert the following new elements just below the Description element:
   `<Options>Turbo jet engine</Options>`
   `<Delivery>2-4 weeks</Delivery>`
   c. Enter the following elements for the last two records in your XML file:
   `<Options>Leaf collector</Options>`
   `<Delivery>2-4 weeks</Delivery>`

   `<Options>Medicine tray</Options>`
   `<Delivery>4-6 months</Delivery>`
   d. Check the document for errors, making changes as necessary, then save the file.

7. **Alter XML data view with HTML.**
   a. Open the file products.htm in your text editor.
   b. Insert the following HTML aligned below <TH>DESCRIPTION</TH>:
   `<TH>OPTIONS</TH>`
   `<TH>DELIVERY</TH>`
   c. Type
   `<TD VALIGN="top"><DIV DATAFLD="OPTIONS" DATAFORMATAS="HTML"></DIV></TD>`
   `<TD VALIGN="top"><DIV DATAFLD="DELIVERY" DATAFORMATAS="HTML"></DIV></TD>`
   d. Check the file for errors, making changes as necessary, then save the file and close your text editor.
   e. Open the products.htm file in your browser, and view the newly expanded table.
   f. If you receive a parsing error, use your text editor to find and fix the typing mistakes in either the products.htm or products.xml documents, then open the products.htm file once more with your browser.
   g. Print the document, then close your browser.

HTML

► Independent Challenges

1. You have just started buying music CDs and you would like to keep a list of them on your computer as your collection grows. You decide to use an XML file to store the name, song titles, and type of music for each music CD. At this point, you just want to create the custom elements and hierarchical structure of the XML document.

To complete this independent challenge:

a. Open your text editor.

b. Enter the prolog for an XML document, use the [Enter] key to create a couple of blank lines in the document, then type "<CDlist>".

c. On the next line, press [Tab] once, then type "<CD>".

d. On the next line down, press [Tab] twice, then type "<Name></Name>".

e. On the next line down, press [Tab] three times, then type "<Song1></Song1>".

f. Repeat Step 5 until you have entered tagsets for 10 songs (i.e., <Song2></Song2>...<Song10><Song10>).

g. Below the last Song tagset, type "<Category></Category>".

k. On the next line, press [Tab] once, then type "</CD>".

i. Copy the <CD> element, and all its children elements, three times.

j. At the bottom of the document, at the beginning of a new line, type </CDlist>, then save the file as music list.xml.

k. Print a copy of the document, then close your text editor.

2. Your best friend collects and sells comic books for a living. She asks you to help her create a computerized list of her collection that she can display on her personal Web site. You decide to use XML and HTML as the means of storing and displaying information about her comics. You use five records to test the design.

To complete this independent challenge:

a. Open your text editor, then create an XML file with the root element <ComicList>.

b. Add the parent element <ComicBook> and the children elements <Name></Name>, <Issue></Issue>, <Publisher></Publisher>, and <Value></Value>.

c. Copy the ComicBook element and its children elements four times.

d. At the bottom of the document, on a blank line, type "</ComicList>".

e. Save the XML file as comics.xml.

f. Enter the data from the table below into each ComicBook element in your XML document:

g. Save the document, print it, then open a new document.

h. Create an HTML document to display your XML data. Use the following code to bind the XML data to a table in your HTML file:

```
<APPLET CODE="com.ms.xml.dso.XMLDSO.class"
WIDTH="100%"
HEIGHT="25" ID="xmldso" MAYSCRIPT="true">
<PARAM NAME="url" VALUE="comics.xml">
</APPLET>
<TABLE ID="table" BORDER="2" WIDTH="100%" DATASRC="#xmldso" CELLPADDING="5">
<THEAD>
  <TR>
    <TH>TITLE</TH>
```

name	issue	publisher	value
Bombastic Five	4	Cool Comics	$22,000
Radioactive Dog	12	Cool Comics	$640
Sludge Man	34	Night Owl	$26
Bombastic Five	7	Cool Comics	$18,500
Sludge Man	19	Night Owl	$35

```
        <TH>ISSUE #</TH>
        <TH>PUBLISHER</TH>
        <TH>VALUE</TH>
    </TR>
  </THEAD>
    <TR>
        <TD VALIGN="top"><DIV DATAFLD="NAME" DATAFORMATAS="HTML"></DIV></TD>
        <TD VALIGN="top"><DIV DATAFLD="ISSUE" DATAFORMATAS="HTML"></DIV></TD>
        <TD VALIGN="top"><DIV DATAFLD="PUBLISHER" DATAFORMATAS="HTML"></DIV></TD>
        <TD VALIGN="top"><DIV DATAFLD="VALUE"  DATAFORMATAS=""HTML"></DIV></TD>
    </TR>
  </FONT>
  </TABLE>
```

i. Format the table using the font style Arial with point size of 2.

j. Save the file as a text document called comics.htm, then close your text editor.

k. Open comics.htm in your browser to view your XML data. If the data fails to display, use your text editor to check your typing in comics.xml and comics.htm, and correct any typos.

l. Print a copy of comics.htm from your browser.

3. You have been asked to inventory all the computers in your building at work and make the results available for viewing on your company's Intranet. Management would like to know the make, model, year, and location of each machine.

To complete this independent challenge:

a. Create an XML file called computers.xml with the root element <Computers></Computers>.

b. Add the parent element <Make></Make>, with the children elements <Model></Model>, <Year></Year>, and <Location></Location>. Copy the <Make></Make> element and its children elements five times.

c. Populate the Model elements with data from the table below:

d. Create an HTML file called computers.htm that will display the XML data in a table; use Arial as the font face.

e. Open the HTML file in your browser.

f. Print a copy of the document from your browser.

make	model	year	location
Mega Bite	T-Rex	1998	Office 101
Mega Bite	T-Rex	1998	Office 102
Mega Bite	Raptor	1998	Office 103
Tera Gig	Condor	1997	Office 104
Mega Bite	Raptor	1998	Reception Area

4. You have decided to use XML and HTML to store and display a list of your favorite movies. Be sure to include custom elements (e.g., <MovieTitle></MovieTitle>) to store important information such as the name of the movie, your favorite actor, the plot, and other interesting data. Use the Internet to search for movie data if your information is not complete. In an XML file called movies.xml, structure the movie data so that each movie record is a child element of the parent element <MovieList></MovieList>. Display the data in a table with headings in an HTML file called movies.htm. Open the movies.htm file in your browser, then print the document.

HTML

Visual Workshop

Create a Web application using XML and HTML to display the table of formatted data shown in Figure N-22. Print the document from your browser.

FIGURE N-22

XML Products

Successfully loaded XML from "file:/A:/products.xml"

PRODUCT	COMPANY	DESCRIPTION
HoTMetaL Application Server	SoftQuad	Automates the database-to-XML and XML-to-HTML conversion process.
iNet Developer 4.0	Pictorius	Includes tools for parsing Document Type Definitions (DTD's) and converting HTML documents to XML.
XML Pro	Vervet Logic	A program that allows users to create and edit XML documents.

Appendix

- ► **Put a document on the World Wide Web**
- ► **Increase Web site traffic**
- ► **Review common tasks**
- ► **HTML tag reference**
- ► **HTML color names**
- ► **HTML special characters**
- ► **JavaScript object reference**
- ► **JavaScript operators**
- ► **Cascading Style Sheet reference**
- ► **Filters and Transitions reference**

To create HTML documents for use in a business setting, it is important to know how to construct Web pages as well as how to access and take advantage of resources on the Web. These resources include a variety of search engines and Web sites devoted to helping you have a Web presence. You also should be aware of the many ways of increasing traffic to your Web site. This appendix provides a handy reference as you create and publish your Web pages.

HTML

Putting a Document on the Web

Once you've completed work on your HTML file, you're probably wondering how you place it on the Web for others to see. There are many informative Web sites to assist your efforts. For an example, see Figure AP-1. To make a file available to the Web, you must transfer it to a computer connected to the Web called a **Web server**. Your **Internet Service Provider** (**ISP**)—the company that provides your Internet access—may have a Web server available. Because each ISP has a different procedure for storing Web pages, you should contact them to learn their policies and procedures. Although you may not have to complete each of these steps, when they are done, your work will be available on the Web. Once your site is online, it is important to keep up with current trends; refer to Figure AP-2 for resources for conducting business on the Web.

Your site will be on the Web when the following steps have been completed:

Establish and register your Web site name

Decide on a domain name for your site on the Web (such as "http://www.jackson_electronics.com"). This may take time, so plan to do this process early. Then, when your site is ready, it can be accessed immediately on the Web. You can use your ISP's domain or choose a unique name customers and interested parties can easily remember, such as your company's name followed by the extension .com. If you choose a special domain name for your Web site, you may have to register it. Registration information can be found at **http://www.internic.net** and is necessary to ensure that any name you give to your site is unique. This service may be provided by your ISP on a fee basis; usually, you will have to pay a yearly registration fee to control a unique Web site domain.

Add your site to indexes

While not required, listing your site in indexes makes it easier to locate your site. Each search facility has different policies regarding adding information about Web sites to its index. This process can take several months.

Eliminate errors

Extensively test your files under a variety of browsers and under different display conditions. Weed out any errors and design problems before the page is on the Web.

Modify files

Some Web servers require all Web pages to have the four-letter HTML extension. If your HTML documents have a three-letter HTM extension, you may have to rename those files.

Verify hyperlinks

Confirm that hyperlinks and inline objects in your documents point to the correct filenames. Verify the filenames with respect to upper- and lowercases, because some Web servers distinguish between a file named "Image.jpg" and one named "image.jpg." To be safe, make sure the file references match their sources. If any hyperlinks use absolute pathnames, change them to relative pathnames.

Establish server location

Find out the name of the folder into which you'll be placing your HTML documents from your ISP. (You may need a special user name and password to access this folder.)

QuickTip

In Netscape Navigator, open Composer, click File on the menu bar, then click Publish.

Deliver files

Use **File Transfer Protocol** (**FTP**), a program used on the Internet that transfers files, or e-mail to place your pages in the appropriate folder on your ISP's Web server. Some Web browsers, such as Internet Explorer or Netscape Navigator, have this capability built in, which allows you to transfer your files with a few commands; typically, this capability is on the File menu.

FIGURE AP-1: FAQs about putting a site online

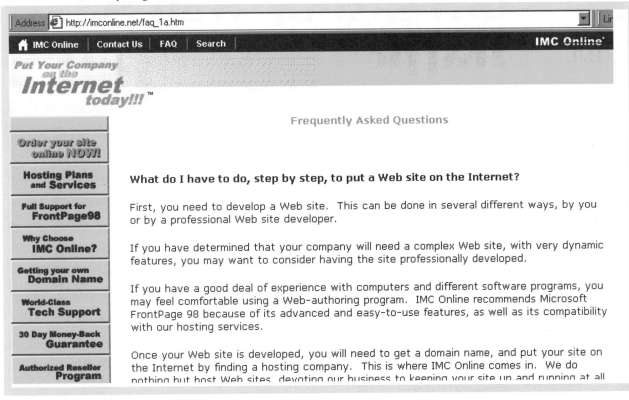

FIGURE AP-2: Library of Congress page for Internet business

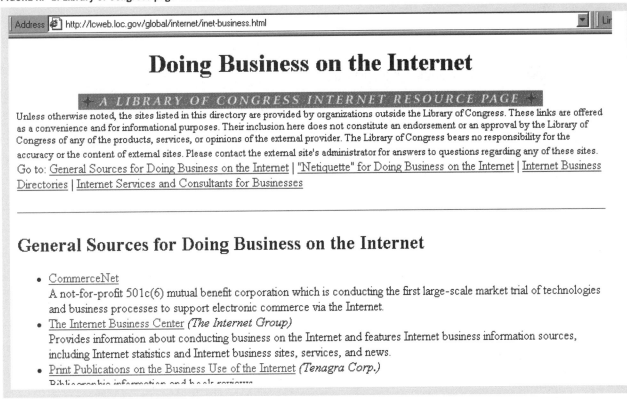

HTML

Increasing Web Site Traffic

Have you ever wondered why a Web site is located using one search engine but not another? How does a site get listed in an index? Some search engines conduct periodic—and laborious—searches of Web sites, and others depend on site submissions to their indices. The key to a successful Internet site is its accessibility to Web users. After all, if no one sees your site, the caliber of its design is irrelevant. Make sure users can access your Web pages using search engines.

Details

Appear in Internet search engines
It is vital that as many Web viewers as possible see a business's Web page. One approach to appearing in listings is to use a service that makes submissions for you. Figure AP-3 shows the AAA Internet Promotions home page. Another such service is shown in Figure AP-4.

Use keywords
Many search engines compile their indices using **keywords**, repetitive words found within the page. Therefore, it is important to use relevant wording in your document title and throughout the body of the page. Many search engines look only at your document title (within the <TITLE> </TITLE> tags) or within the first few lines of text. Therefore, it is important that you choose your words wisely when writing your HTML document.

Consider the time factor
Some search engines can take as long as three months to include your site in their index. This lack of access to a Web site can spell disaster for a business. This time factor may necessitate planning ahead so that your Web presence coincides with your appearance in indices.

Make your page a high priority
Although a search may yield hundreds of sites, most people generally look at the first few entries. You can give your page a higher priority by including a meta tag in your Web site. A **meta tag** is a series of keywords on which search engines find matching Web sites. The page shown in Figure AP-5 includes an area for meta tags.

FIGURE AP-3: AAA Internet Promotions home page

FIGURE AP-4: Submit It! home page

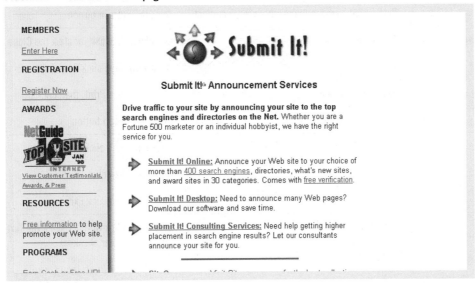

FIGURE AP-5: Meta Master home page

HTML

Reviewing Common Tasks

There are some common tasks that you must do when creating Web pages. These tasks, while functionally similar across programs, are performed using different commands depending on the program you are using. Table AP-1 is provided to help you sort out some of these differences.

TABLE AP-1: Common HTML tasks

program	task	action
Microsoft FrontPage Express	View HTML source	Click View, then click HTML
Microsoft Internet Explorer	Exit the program	Click File, then click Close, or click the Close box
	View HTML source	Click View, then click Source
	Print the document	Click File, click Print, then click OK
	View saved changes in open browser document	Click the Refresh button
Netscape Navigator	Exit the program	Click File, click Exit, or click the Close box
	View HTML source	Click View, then click Page Source
	Print the document	Click File, click Print, then click OK
	View saved changes in open browser document	Click the Reload button
NotePad	Wrap text to ruler	Click Edit, then click Word Wrap
	Print	Click File, then click Print
	Exit	Click File, then click Exit
WordPad	Wrap text to ruler	Click View, click Options, click the Text tab, then click the Wrap to ruler checkbox
	Print	Click File, click Print, then click OK
	Exit	Click File, then click Exit

HTML Tag Reference

The following are currently supported HTML tags and properties. Since the World Wide Web is always in a constant state of change, you should check this information against the current browser versions. Both opening and closing tags are displayed where they are required; a single tag means that no closing tag is needed.

Properties are of the following types:

- *Color*   A recognized color name or color value.
- *CGI Program*   The name of a CGI program on the Web server.
- *Document*   The file name or URL of file.
- *List*   List of items separated by commas. Usually enclosed in double quotes.
- *Options*   Limited to a specific set of values (values are shown below the property.)
- *Text*   Any text string.
- *URL*   The URL for a Web page or file.
- *Value*   A number, usually an integer.

TABLE AP-2: HTML tags

tags and properties	description
Block-Formatting Tags	Block-Formatting are tags that are used to format the appearance of large blocks of text.
<ADDRESS> ... </ADDRESS>	The <ADDRESS> tag is used for information such as addresses, authorship, and so forth. The text is usually italicized and in some browsers it is indented.
<BLOCKQUOTE> ... </BLOCKQUOTE>	The <BLOCKQUOTE> tag is used to set off long quotes or citations by usually indenting the enclosed text on both sides. Some browsers italicize the text as well.

  CLEAR=*Option*
  (LEFT | RIGHT | ALL | NONE)
	The
	 tag forces a line break in the text. Causes the next line to start at the spot in which the specified margin is clear.

<CENTER> ... </CENTER>	The <CENTER> tag centers the enclosed text or image horizontally.
<DFN> ... </DFN>	The <DFN> tag is used for the defining instance of a term, i.e. the first time the term is used. The enclosed text is usually italicized.
<DIV> ... </DIV>	The <DIV> tag is to set the text alignment of blocks of text or images.

<HR>
  ALIGN=*Option*
  (LEFT | CENTER | RIGHT)
  COLOR=*Color*
  NOSHADE
  SIZE=*Value*
  WIDTH=*Value*
	The <HR> tag creates a horizontal line.
	Alignment of the horizontal line. The default is CENTER.
	
	Specifies a color for the line.
	Removes 3D shading from the line.
	The size (height) of the line in pixels.
	The width (length) of the line either in pixels or as a percentage of the display area.

<H1> ... </H1> <H4> ... </H4>
<H2> ... </H2> <H5> ... </H5>
<H3> ... </H3> <H6> ... </H6>
  ALIGN=*Option*
  (LEFT | RIGHT | CENTER)
	The six levels of text headings ranging from the largest (<H1>) to the smallest (<H6>). Text headings appear in a bold face font.
	
	The alignment of the heading.

<NOBR> ... </NOBR>	The <NOBR> tag prevents line breaks for the enclosed text.

<P> ... </P>
  ALIGN=*Option*
  (LEFT | CENTER | RIGHT)
	The <P> tag defines the beginning and ending of a paragraph of text.
	The alignment of the text in the paragraph.

<PRE> ... </PRE>	The <PRE> tag retains the preformatted appearance of the text in the HTML file, including any line breaks or spaces. Text is usually displayed in a fixed width font.

HTML

tags and properties	description
Character Tags	Character tags modify the appearance of individual characters, words, or sentences from that of the surrounding text. Character tags usually appear nested within Block-Formatting tags.
\<B> ... \</B>	The \<B> tag displays the enclosed text in bold type.
\<BIG> ... \</BIG>	The \<BIG> tag increases the size of the enclosed text. The exact appearance of the text depends on the browser and the default font size.
\<BLINK> ... \</BLINK>	The \<BLINK> tag causes the enclosed text to blink on and off.
\<CITE> ... \</CITE>	The \<CITE> tag is used for citations and is usually displayed in italics.
\<CODE> ... \</CODE>	The \<CODE> tag is used for text taken from the code for a computer program. It is usually displayed in a fixed width font.
\<EM> ... \</EM>	The \<EM> tag is used to emphasize text. The enclosed text is usually displayed in italics.
\<FONT> ... \</FONT> COLOR=*Color* FACE=*List* SIZE=*Value*	The \<FONT> tag is used to control the appearance of the text it encloses. The color of the enclosed text. The font face of the text. Multiple font faces can be specified, separated by commas. The browser will try to render the text in the order specified by the list. Size of the font in points, it can be absolute or relative. Specifying SIZE=5 sets the font size to 5 points. Specifying SIZE=+5 sets the font size 5 points larger than default tag.
\<I> ... \</I>	The \<I> tag italicizes the enclosed text.
\<KBD> ... \</KBD>	The \<KBD> tag is used for text made to appear as if it came from a typewriter or keyboard. Text is displayed with a fixed width font.
\<SAMP> ... \</SAMP>	The \<SAMP> tag displays text in a fixed width font.
\<SMALL> ... \</SMALL>	The \<SMALL> tag decreases the size of the enclosed text. The exact appearance of the text depends on the browser and the default font size.
\<STRONG> ... \</STRONG>	The \<STRONG> tag is used to strongly emphasize the enclosed text, usually in a bold font.
\<STYLE> ... \</STYLE>	Contains information that identifies the style sheet in use.
_{... \}	The \<SUB> tag displays the enclosed text as a subscript.
\^{... \}	The \<SUP> tag displays the enclosed text as a superscript.
\<TT> ... \</TT>	The \<TT> tag displays text in a fixed width, teletype style font.
\<U> ... \</U>	The \<U> tag underlines the enclosed text. The \<U> tag should be avoided because it will confuse users with hypertext, which is typically underlined.
\<VAR> ... \</VAR>	The \<VAR> tag is used for text that represents a variable and is usually displayed in italics.
Document Tags	Document tags are tags that specify the structure of the HTML file or control its operations and interactions with the Web server.
\<!>	The \<!> tag is used for comments in documenting the features of your HTML file.

tags and properties	description
<BASE>	The <BASE> tag allows you to specify the URL for the HTML document. It is used by some browsers to interpret relative hyperlinks.
HREF=*URL*	Specifies the URL from which all relative hyperlinks should be based.
TARGET=*Text*	Specifies the default target window or frame for every hyperlink in the document.
<BODY> ... </BODY>	The <BODY> tag encloses all text, images, and other elements that will be visible to the user on the Web page.
ALINK=*Color*	Color of activated hypertext links, which are links the user has pressed with the mouse button but have not yet released.
BACKGROUND=*Document*	The graphic image file used for the Web page background.
BGCOLOR=*Color*	The color of the Web page background.
BGPROPERTIES=FIXED	Keeps the background image fixed so that it does not scroll with the Web page.
LEFTMARGIN=*Value*	Indents the left margin of the page the number of pixels specified in *value*.
LINK=*Color*	Color of all unvisited links.
TEXT=*Color*	Color of all text in the document.
TOPMARGIN=*Value*	Indents the top margin of the page the number of pixels specified in *value*.
VLINK=*Color*	Color of previously visited links.
<HEAD> ... </HEAD>	The <HEAD> tag encloses code that provides information about the document.
<HTML> ... </HTML>	The <HTML> tag indicates the beginning and end of the HTML document.
<LINK>	The <LINK> tag specifies the relationship between the document and other objects.
HREF=*URL*	The URL of the <LINK> tag, hotlinks the user to the specified document.
ID=*Text*	The file, URL, or text that acts as a hypertext link to another document.
REL=*URL*	Directs the browser to link forward to the next page in the document.
REV=*URL*	Directs the browser to go back to the previous link in the document.
TITLE=*Text*	The title of the document named in the link.
<META>	The <META> tag is used to insert information about the document not defined by other HTML tags and properties. It can include special instructions for the Web server to perform.
CONTENT=*Text*	Contains information associated with the NAME or HTTP-EQUIV attributes.
HTTP-EQUIV=*Text*	Directs the browser to request the server to perform different HTTP operations.
NAME=*Text*	The type of information specified in the CONTENT attribute.
<TITLE> ... </TITLE>	The <TITLE> tag is used to specify the text that appears in the Web browser's title bar.
Form Tags	Form tags are used to create user-entry forms.
<FORM> ... </FORM>	The <FORM> tag marks the beginning and end of a Web page form.
ACTION=*URL*	Specifies the URL to which the contents of the form are to be sent.
ENCTYPE=*Text*	Specifies the encoding type used to submit the data to the server.
METHOD=*Option* (POST | GET)	Specifies the method of accessing the URL indicated in the ACTION attribute.
TARGET=*Text*	The frame or window that displays the form's results.
<INPUT> ... </INPUT>	The <INPUT> tag creates an input object for use in a Web page form.
ALIGN=*Option* (LEFT | RIGHT | TOP | TEXTTOP | MIDDLE | ABSMIDDLE | BASELINE | BOTTOM | ABSBOTTOM)	Specifies the alignment of an input image. Similar to the ALIGN attribute with the <IMG> tag.
CHECKED	Specifies that an input checkbox or input radio button is selected.
LOOP=*Value*	Specifies the number of times a moving input image should be played. The value must be either a digit or INFINITE.
LOWSRC=*Document*	A low resolution version of the input image that the browser should initially display before loading the high resolution version.
MAXLENGTH=*Value*	Specifies the maximum number of characters inserted into an input text box.
NAME=*Text*	The label given to the input object.
SIZE=*Value*	The visible size, in characters, of an input text box.
SRC=*Document*	The source file of the graphic used for an input image object.
START=*Option* (FILEOPEN | MOUSEOVER)	Tells the browser when to start displaying a moving image file. Similar to the START property for the <IMG> tag.

HTML

tags and properties	description
TYPE=*Option* (CHECKBOX | HIDDEN | IMAGE | PASSWORD | RADIO | RESET | SUBMIT | TEXT | TEXTAREA)	Specifies the type of input object. CHECKBOX creates a checkbox. HIDDEN creates a hidden object. IMAGE creates an image object. PASSWORD creates a text box which hides the text as the user enters it. RADIO creates a radio button. RESET creates a button that resets the form's fields when pressed. SUBMIT creates a button that submits the form when pressed. TEXT creates a text box. TEXTAREA creates a text box with multiple line entry fields.
USEMAP=*#Map_Name*	Identifies the input image as an image map. Similar to the USEMAP property used with the <IMG> tag.
VALUE=*Value*	Specifies the information that is initially displayed in the input object.
VSPACE=*Value*	The amount of space above and below the image, in pixels.
WIDTH=*Value*	The width of the input image in pixels.
<OPTION> ... </OPTION>	The <OPTION> tag is used for each item in a selection list. This tag must be placed within <SELECT> tags.
SELECTED	The default or selected option in the selection list.
VALUE=*Value*	The value returned to the server when the user selects this option.
<SELECT> ... </SELECT>	The <SELECT> tag encloses a set of <OPTION> tags for use in creating selection lists.
MULTIPLE	Allows the user to select multiple options from the selection list.
NAME=*Text*	The name assigned to the selection list.
SIZE=*Value*	The number of visible items in the selection list.
<TEXTAREA> ... </TEXTAREA>	The <TEXTAREA> tag creates a text box.
COLS=*Value*	The height of the text box in characters.
NAME=*Text*	The name assigned to the text box.
ROWS=*Value*	The width of the text box in characters.
WRAP=*Option* (OFF | VIRTUAL | PHYSICAL)	Specifies how text should be wrapped within the text box. OFF turns off text wrapping. VIRTUAL wraps the text, but sends the text to the server as a single line. PHYSICAL wraps the text and sends the text to the server as it appears in the text box.
Frame Tags	Frame tags are used for creating and formatting frames.
<FRAME>	The <FRAME> tag defines a single frame within a set of frames.
BORDERCOLOR=*Color*	Specifies the color of the frame border.
FRAMEBORDER=*Option* (YES | NO)	Specifies whether the frame border is visible.
FRAMESPACING=*Value*	Specifies the amount of space between frames, in pixels.
MARGINHEIGHT=*Value*	Specifies the amount of space above and below the frame object and the frame borders.
MARGINWIDTH=*Value*	Specifies the amount of space to the left and right of the frame object, in pixels.
NAME=*Text*	Label assigned to the frame.
NORESIZE	Prevents users from resizing the frame.
SCROLLING=*Option* (YES | NO | AUTO)	Specifies whether scroll bars are visible. AUTO (the default) displays scroll bars only as needed.
SRC=*Document*	Specifies the document or URL of the object to be displayed in the frame.
<FRAMESET> ... </FRAMESET>	The <FRAMESET> tag marks the beginning and the end of a set of frames.
BORDER=*Value*	The size of the borders, in pixels.
BORDERCOLOR	The color of the frame borders.
COLS=*List*	The size of each column in set of frames. Columns can be specified either in pixels, as a percentage of the display area, or with an asterisk (*) indicating that any remaining space be allotted to that column. e.g. COLS="40,25%,*".

tags and properties	description
ROWS=*List*	The size of each row in set of frames. Rows can be speicified either in pixels, as a percentage of the display area, or with an asterisk (*) indicating that any remaining space be allotted to that column (e.g. ROWS="40,25%,*").
<NOFRAMES> ... </NOFRAMES>	Enclosing body tags to be used by browsers which do not support frames.
Graphic and Link Tags	Graphic and Link tags are used for hypertext links and inline images.

<A> ... </A>
  HREF=*URL*
  NAME=*Text*
  REL=*Text*
  REV=*Text*
 	
  TARGET=*Text*
  TITLE=*Text*
	The <A> tag marks the beginning and end of a hypertext link.
	Indicates the target, filename, or URL that the hypertext points to.
	Specifies a name for the enclosed text, allowing it to be a target of a hyperlink.
	Specifies the relationship between the current page and the link specified by the HREF property.
	Specifies a reverse relationship between the current page and the link specified by the HREF property.
	Specifies the default target window or frame for the hyperlink.
	Provides a title for the document whose address is given by the HREF property.

<AREA>
  COORDS=*Value 1, value 2...*
 	
  HREF=*URL*
  SHAPE=*Option*
  (RECT | CIRCLE | POLY)
  TARGET=*Text*
	The <AREA> tag defines the type and coordinates of a hotspot within an image map.
	The coordinates of the hotspot. The coordinates depend upon the shape of the hotspot:
	Rectangle: COORDS=*x_left, y_upper, x_right, y_lower*
	Circle: COORDS= *x_center, y_center, radius*
	Polygon: COORDS= $x_1, y_1, x_2, y_2, x_3, y_3, ...$
	Indicates the target, filename, or URL that the hotspot points to.
	The shape of the hotspot.
	
	Specifies the default target window or frame for the hotspot.

<IMG>
  ALIGN=*Option*
  (LEFT | RIGHT | TOP | TEXTTOP |
  MIDDLE | ABSMIDDLE | BASELINE |
  BOTTOM | ABSBOTTOM)
 	
  ALT=*Text*
  BORDER=*Value*
  CONTROLS
  DYNSRC=*Document*
  HEIGHT=*Value*
  HSPACE=*Value*
  ISMAP
  LOOP=*Value*
 	
  LOWSRC=*Document*
 	
  SRC=*Document*
  START=*Item*
  (FILEOPEN | MOUSEOVER)
 	
  USEMAP=*#Map_Name*
 	
  VSPACE=*Value*
  WIDTH=*Value*
	The <IMG> tag is used to insert an inline image into the document.
	Specifies the alignment of the image.
	Specifying an alignment of LEFT or RIGHT aligns the image with the left or right page margin. The other alignment options align the image with surrounding text.
	
	Text to display if the image cannot be displayed by the browser.
	The size of the border around the image in pixels.
	Display VCR-like controls under moving images. Used in conjunction with the DYNSRC property.
	Specifies the file of a video, AVI clip, or VRML worlds displayed inside the page.
	The height of the image in pixels.
	The amount of space to the left and right of the image, in pixels.
	Identifies the graphic as an image map. For use with server-side image maps.
	Specifies the number of times a moving image should be played. The value must be either a digit or INFINITE.
	A low resolution version of the graphic that the browser should initially display before loading the high resolution version.
	The source file of the inline image.
	Tells the browser when to start displaying a moving image file. FILEOPEN directs the browser to start when the file is open. MOUSEOVER directs the browser to start when the mouse moves over the image.
	Identifies the graphic as an image map and specifies the name of image map definition to use with the graphic. For use with client-side image maps.
	The amount of space above and below the image, in pixels.
	The width of the image in pixels.

<MAP> ... </MAP> NAME=*Text*	The <MAP> specifies information about a client-side image map. (Note that it must enclose <AREA> tags.) The name of the image map.
List Tags	List tags are used to create a variety of different kinds of lists.
<DD>	The <DD> tag formats text to be used as relative definitions in a <DL> list.

HTML

tags and properties	description

<DIR> ... </DIR>
  TYPE=*Option*
  (CIRCLE I DISC I SQUARE)
	The <DIR> tag encloses an unordered list of <LI> items, formatted in narrow columns.
	Specifies the type of bullet used for displaying each <LI> item in the <DIR> list.

<DL> ... </DL>	The <DL> tag encloses a definition list in which the <DD> definition term is left-aligned and the <DT> relative definition is indented.
<DT>	The <DT> tag is used to format the definition term in a <DL> list.
<LI>	The <LI> tag identifies list items in a <DIR>, <MENU>, <OL>, or <UL> list.
<MENU> ... </MENU>	The <MENU> tag encloses an unordered list of items, similar to a <UL> or <DIR> list.

<OL> ... </OL>
 	
  START=*Value*
  TYPE=*Option*
  (A I a I I I i I 1)
	The <OL> tag encloses an ordered list of <LI> items. Typically ordered lists are rendered as numbered lists.
	The *value* of the starting number in the ordered list.
	Specifies how ordered items are to be marked.
	A = uppercase letters. a = lowercase letters. I = uppercase Roman numerals. i = lowercase Roman numerals. 1 = Digits. The default is 1.

<UL>
 	
  Type=*Option*
  (CIRCLE I DISK I SQUARE)
	The <UL> tag encloses an unordered list of <LI> items. Typically unordered lists are rendered as bulleted lists.
	Specifies the type of bullet used for displaying each <LI> item in the <UL> list.

Miscellaneous Tags	Miscellaneous tags do not fit into any specific category.

<BGSOUND>
  LOOP=*Value*
 	
  SRC=*Document*
	The <BGSOUND> is used to play a background sound clip when the page is first opened.
	Specifies the number of times the sound clip should be played. LOOP can either be a digit or INFINITE.
	The sound file used for the sound clip.

<MARQUEE> ... </MARQUEE>
  ALIGN=*Option*
  (TOP I MIDDLE I BOTTOM)
  BEHAVIOR=*Option*
  (SCROLL I SLIDE I ALTERNATE)
 	
  BGCOLOR=*Color*
  DIRECTION=*Option*
  (LEFT I RIGHT)
  HEIGHT=*Value*
  HSPACE=*Value*
  LOOP=*Value*
  SCROLLAMOUNT=*Value*
  SCROLLDELAY=*Value*
  VSPACE=*Value*
  WIDTH=*Value*
	The <MARQUEE> tag is used to create an area containing scrolling text.
	The alignment of the scrolling text within the marquee.
	
	Controls the behavior of the text in the marquee. SCROLL causes the text to repeatedly scroll across the page. SLIDE causes the text to slide onto the page and stop at the margin. ALTERNATE causes the text to bounce from margin to margin.
	The background color of the marquee.
	The direction that the text scrolls on the page.
	
	The height of the marquee in either pixels or as a percentage of the display area.
	The amount of space to the left and right of the marquee, in pixels.
	The number of times the marquee will be scrolled, can be either a digit or INFINITE.
	The amount of space between successive draws of the text in the marquee.
	The amount of time between scrolling actions, in milliseconds.
	The amount of space above and below the marquee, in pixels.
	The width of the marquee in either pixels or as a percentage of the display area.

Table Tags	Table tags are used to define the structure and appearance of graphical tables.

<CAPTION> ... </CAPTION>
  ALIGN=*Option*
  (LEFT I RIGHT I CENTER I TOP I
  BOTTOM)
	The <CAPTION> tag encloses the table caption.
	Specifies the alignment of the caption with respect to the table.

tags and properties	description
VALIGN=*Option* (TOP | BOTTOM)	Specifies the vertical alignment of the caption with respect to the table.
<COL> ... </COL> ALIGN=*Option* (CENTER | JUSTIFY | LEFT | RIGHT) SPAN=*Value* VALIGN=*Option* (TOP | MIDDLE | BOTTOM)	The <COL> tag specifies the default settings for a column or group of columns. Specifies the horizontal alignment of text within a column. Specifies the columns modified by the <COL> tag. Specifies the vertical alignment of text within a column.
<COLGROUP> ... </COLGROUP> ALIGN=*Option* (CENTER | JUSTIFY | LEFT | RIGHT) SPAN=*Value* VALIGN=*Option* (TOP | MIDDLE | BOTTOM)	The <COLGROUP> tag encloses a group of <COL> tags, grouping columns together to set their alignment properties. Specifies the horizontal alignment of text within a column group. Specifies the columns within the column group. Specifies the vertical alignment of text within a column group.
<TABLE> ... </TABLE> ALIGN=*Option* (LEFT | CENTER | RIGHT) BACKGROUND=*Document* BGCOLOR=*Color* BORDER=*Value* BORDERCOLOR=*Color* BORDERCOLORDARK=*Color* BORDERCOLORLIGHT=*Color* CELLPADDING=*Value* CELLSPACING=*Value* FRAME=*Option* (ABOVE | BELOW | BOX | HSIDES | LHS | RHS | VOID | VSIDES) HEIGHT=*Value* RULES=*Option* (ALL | COLS | NONE | ROWS) WIDTH=*Value*	The <TABLE> tag is used to specify the beginning and ending of the table. Specifies the horizontal alignment of the table on the page. Specifies a background image for the table. Specifies a background color for the table. Specifies the width of the table border in pixels. Specifies the color of the table border. Specifies the color of the shaded edge of the table border. Specifies the color of the unshaded edge of the table border. Specifies the space between table cells in pixels. Specifies the space between cell text and the cell border in pixels. Specifies the display of table borders. ABOVE = Top border only. BELOW = Bottom border only. BOX = Borders on all four sides. HSIDES = Top and bottom borders. LHS = Left side border. RHS = Right side border. VOID = No borders. VSIDES = Left and right side borders. The height of the table in pixels or as a percentage of the display area. Specifies the display of internal table borders. ALL = Borders between every row and column. COLS = Border between every column. NONE = No internal table borders. ROWS = Borders between every row. The width of the table in pixels or as a percentage of the display area.
<TBODY> ... </TBODY> HALIGN=*Option* (LEFT | CENTER |RIGHT) VALIGN=*Option* (TOP | MIDDLE | BOTTOM)	The <TBODY> tag indentifies text that appears in the table body as opposed to text in the table header (<THEAD> tag) or the table footer (<TFOOT> tag). The horizontal alignment of text in the cells of the table body. The vertical alignment of text in the cells in the table body.
<TD> ... </TD> ALIGN=*Option* (LEFT | CENTER | RIGHT) BACKGROUND=*Document* BGCOLOR=*Color* BORDERCOLOR=*Color* BORDERCOLORDARK=*Color* BORDERCOLORLIGHT=*Color* COLSPAN=*Value* HEIGHT=*Value* NOWRAP ROWSPAN=*Value* VALIGN=*Option* (TOP | MIDDLE | BOTTOM)	The <TD> tag encloses the text that will appear in an individual table cell. Specifies the horizontal alignment of cell text. Specifies a background image for the cell. Specifies a background color for the cell. Specifies the color of the cell border. Specifies the color of the shaded edge of the cell border. Specifies the color of the unshaded edge of the cell border. Specifies the number of columns the cell should span. The height of the cell in pixels or as a percentage of the display area. Prohibits the browser from wrapping text in the cell. Specifies the number of rows the cell should span. Specifies the vertical alignment of cell text.

HTML

HTML

tags and properties	description
WIDTH=*Value*	The width of the cell in pixels or as a percentage of the width of the table.
<TFOOT> ... </TFOOT>	The <TFOOT> tag encloses footer information that will be displayed in the table footer when the table is printed on multiple pages.
HALIGN=*Option* (LEFT I CENTER IRIGHT)	The horizontal alignment of the table footer.
VALIGN=*Option* (TOP I MIDDLE I BOTTOM)	The vertical alignment of the table footer.
<TH> ... </TH>	The <TH> tag encloses the text that will appear in an individual table header cell.
ALIGN=*Option* (LEFT I CENTER I RIGHT)	Specifies the horizontal alignment of header cell text.
BACKGROUND=*Document*	Specifies a background image for the header cell.
BGCOLOR=*Color*	Specifies a background color for the header cell.
BORDERCOLOR=*Color*	Specifies the color of the header cell border.
BORDERCOLORDARK=*Color*	Specifies the color of the shaded edge of the header cell border.
BORDERCOLORLIGHT=*Color*	Specifies the color of the unshaded edge of the header cell border.
COLSPAN=*Value*	Specifies the number of columns the header cell should span.
HEIGHT=*Value*	The height of the header cell in pixels or as a percentage of the display area.
NOWRAP	Prohibits the browser from wrapping text in the header cell.
ROWSPAN=*Value*	Specifies the number of rows the header cell should span.
VALIGN=*Option* (TOP I MIDDLE I BOTTOM)	Specifies the vertical alignment of header cell text.
WIDTH=*Value*	The width of the header cell in pixels or as a percentage of the width of the table.
<THEAD> ... </THEAD>	The <THEAD> tag encloses header information that will be displayed in the table header when the table is printed on multiple pages.
HALIGN=*Option* (LEFT I CENTER IRIGHT)	The horizontal alignment of the table header.
VALIGN=*Option* (TOP I MIDDLE I BOTTOM)	The vertical alignment of the table header.
<TR> ... </TR>	The <TR> tag encloses table cells within a single row.
ALIGN=*Option* (LEFT I CENTER I RIGHT)	Specifies the horizontal alignment of text in the row.
BGCOLOR=*Color*	Specifies a background color for the header cell.
BORDERCOLOR=*Color*	Specifies the color of the header cell border.
BORDERCOLORDARK=*Color*	Specifies the color of the shaded edge of the header cell border.
BORDERCOLORLIGHT=*Color*	Specifies the color of the unshaded edge of the header cell border.
VALIGN=*Option* (TOP I MIDDLE I BOTTOM)	The vertical alignment of the text in the table row.

HTML Color Names

The following is a list of extended color names and their corresponding hexadecimal triplets supported by most Web browsers. To view these colors, you must have a video card and monitor capable of displaying up to 256 colors. As with other aspects of Web page design, you should test these color names on a variety of browsers before committing to their use. Different browsers may render these colors differently, or not at all.

TABLE AP-3: HTML color names

color name	value	preview	color name	value	preview
ALICEBLUE	#F0F8FE		DARKORCHID	#9932CD	
ANTIQUEWHITE	#FAEBD7		DARKPURPLE	#871F78	
AQUA	#00FFFF		DARKSALMON	#E9967A	
AQUAMARINE	#70DB93		DARKSLATEBLUE	#6B238E	
AZURE	#F0FFFF		DARKSLATEGRAY	#2F4F4F	
BEIGE	#F5F5DC		DARKTAN	#97694F	
BLACK	#000000		DARKTURQUOISE	#7093DB	
BLUE	#0000FF		DARKVIOLET	#9400D3	
BLUEVIOLET	#9F5F9F		DARKWOOD	#855E42	
BRASS	#B5A642		DIMGRAY	#545454	
BRIGHTGOLD	#D9D919		DUSTYROSE	#856363	
BRONZE	#8C7853		FELDSPAR	#D19275	
BROWN	#A52A2A		FIREBRICK	#8E2323	
CADETBLUE	#5F9F9F		FORESTGREEN	#238E23	
CHOCOLATE	#D2691E		GOLD	#CD7F32	
COOLCOPPER	#D98719		GOLDENROD	#DBDB70	
COPPER	#B87333		GRAY	#C0C0C0	
CORAL	#FF7F00		GREEN	#00FF00	
CORAL	#FF7F50		GREENCOPPER	#527F76	
CRIMSON	#DC143C		GREENYELLOW	#93DB70	
CYAN	#00FFFF		HOTPINK	#FF69B4	
DARKBLUE	#00008B		HUNTERGREEN	#215E21	
DARKBROWN	#5C4033		INDIANRED	#4E2F2F	
DARKCYAN	#008B8B		INDIGO	#4B0082	
DARKGOLDENROD	#B8860B		IVORY	#FFFFF0	
DARKGRAY	#A9A9A9		KHAKI	#9F9F5F	
DARKGREEN	#006400		LAVENDER	#E6E6FA	
DARKKHAKI	#BDB76B		LIGHTBLUE	#C0D9D9	
DARKMAGENTA	#8B008B		LIGHTCORAL	#F08080	
DARKOLIVEGREEN	#4F4F2F		LIGHTCYAN	#E0FFFF	
DARKORANGE	#FF8C00		LIGHTGRAY	#A8A8A8	

App

HTML

color name	value	preview	color name	value	preview
LIGHTGREEN	#90EE90		PINK	#BC8F8F	
LIGHTPINK	#FFB6C1		PLUM	#EAADEA	
LIGHTSTEELBLUE	#8F8FBD		POWDERBLUE	#B0E0E6	
LIGHTWOOD	#E9C2A6		PURPLE	#800080	
LIME	#00FF00		QUARTZ	#D9D9F3	
LIMEGREEN	#32CD32		RED	#FF0000	
MAGENTA	#FF00FF		RICHBLUE	#5959AB	
MANDARINORANGE	#E47833		ROYALBLUE	#4169E1	
MAROON	#8E236B		SADDLEBROWN	#8B4513	
MEDIUMAQUAMARINE	#32CD99		SALMON	#6F4242	
MEDIUMBLUE	#3232CD		SANDYBROWN	#F4A460	
MEDIUMFORESTGREEN	#6B8E23		SCARLET	#8C1717	
MEDIUMGOLDENROD	#EAEAAE		SEAGREEN	#238E68	
MEDIUMORCHID	#9370DB		SIENNA	#8E6B23	
MEDIUMSEAGREEN	#426F42		SILVER	#E6E8FA	
MEDIUMSLATEBLUE	#7F00FF		SKYBLUE	#3299CC	
MEDIUMSPRINGGREEN	#7FFF00		SLATEBLUE	#007FFF	
MEDIUMTURQUOISE	#70DBDB		SNOW	#FFFAFA	
MEDIUMVIOLETRED	#DB7093		SPICYPINK	#FF1CAE	
MEDIUMWOOD	#A68064		SPRINGGREEN	#00FF7F	
MIDNIGHTBLUE	#2F2F4F		STEELBLUE	#236B8E	
MINTCREAM	#F5FFFA		SUMMERSKY	#38B0DE	
MISTYROSE	#FFE4E1		TAN	#DB9370	
NAVYBLUE	#23238E		TEAL	#008080	
NEONBLUE	#4D4DFF		THISTLE	#D8BFD8	
NEONPINK	#FF6EC7		TOMATO	#FF6347	
NEWMIDNIGHTBLUE	#00009C		TURQUOISE	#ADEAEA	
NEWTAN	#EBC79E		VERYDARKBROWN	#5C4033	
OLDGOLD	#CFB53B		VERYDARKGRAY	#CDCDCD	
OLIVE	#808000		VIOLET	#4F2F4F	
ORANGE	#FF7F00		VIOLETRED	#CC3299	
ORANGERED	#FF2400		WHEAT	#D8D8BF	
ORCHID	#DB70DB		WHITE	#FFFFFF	
PALEGOLDENROD	#EEE8AA		YELLOW	#FFFF00	
PALEGREEN	#8FBC8F		YELLOWGREEN	#99CC32	
PALETURQUOISE	#AFEEEE				

HTML Special Characters

The following table lists a portion of the extended character set for HTML, also known as the ISO Latin-1 Character set. Characters in this table can be entered either by code number or code name. For example, to insert the registered trademark symbol, ®, you would use either &reg or &#174. Not all code names are recognized by all browsers. Some older browsers will not recognize the code name &times, for instance. Code names that may not be recognized by older browsers are marked with an asterisk. If you are planning to use these symbols in your document, you may want to use the code number instead of the code name.

TABLE AP-4: HTML special characters

character	code	code name	character	code	code name
Unused	&#00 - &#08		@	&#64	
[Tab]	&#09		A – Z	&#65 – &#90	
[Line feed]	&#10		[	&#91	
Unused	&#11 – &#31		\	&#92	
[Space]	&#32		]	&#93	
!	&#33		^	&#94	
"	&#34	&quot	_	&#95	
#	&#35		`	&#96	
$	&#36		a – z	&#97 – &#122	
%	&#37		{	&#123	
&	&#38	&amp	|	&#124	
'	&#39		}	&#125	
(	&#40		~	&#126	
)	&#41		Unused	&#127 - &#129	
*	&#42		,	&#130	
+	&#43		ƒ	&#131	
,	&#44		„	&#132	
-	&#45		…	&#133	
.	&#46		†	&#134	
/	&#47		‡	&#135	
0 – 9	&#48 – &#57		ˆ	&#136	
:	&#58		‰	&#137	
;	&#59		Š	&#138	
<	&#60	&lt	‹	&#139	
=	&#61		Œ	&#140	
>	&#62	&gt	Unused	&#141 - &#144	
?	&#63		'	&#145	

HTML

character	code	code name	character	code	code name
'	&#146;		ª	&#170;	&ordf*
"	&#147;		«	&#171;	&laquo*
"	&#148;		¬	&#172;	&not*
•	&#149;			&#173;	&shy*
–	&#150;		®	&#174;	&reg*
—	&#151;		¯	&#175;	&macr*
~	&#152;		°	&#176;	&deg*
™	&#153;	&trade*	±	&#177;	&plusmn*
š	&#154;		²	&#178;	&sup2*
›	&#155;		³	&#179;	&sup3*
œ	&#156;		´	&#180;	&acute*
Unused	&#157 - &#158		µ	&#181;	&micro*
Ÿ	&#159;		¶	&#182;	&para*
[Non-breaking space]		*	·	&#183;	&middot*
¡	&#161;	&iexcl*	¸	&#184;	&cedil*
¢	&#162;	&cent*	¹	&#185;	&sup1*
£	&#163;	&pound*	º	&#186;	&ordm*
¤	&#164;	&curren*	»	&#187;	&raquo*
¥	&#165;	&yen*	¼	&#188;	&frac14*
¦	&#166;	&brvbar*	½	&#189;	&frac12*
§	&#167;	&sect*	¾	&#190;	&frac34*
¨	&#168;	&uml*	¿	&#191;	&iquest*
©	&#169;	&copy*			

JavaScript Object Reference

The following are some of the more important JavaScript objects, properties, methods, and event handlers.

TABLE AP-5: JavaScript objects, properties, methods, and event handlers

JavaScript	descriptions and examples
button	A push button in an HTML form. Buttons can be referred to using their button names. For example, to emulate the action of clicking a button named "RUN," use the following expression: RUN.click();
Properties	
name	The name of the button element
value	The value of the button element
Methods	
click()	Emulates the action of clicking the button
Event Handlers	
onClick	Used to run JavaScript code when the button is clicked
checkbox	A check box in an HTML form. Check boxes can be referred to using their field names. For example, to emulate the action of clicking a check box named "SUBSCRIBE," use the following expression: SUBSCRIBE.click();
Properties	
checked	A Boolean value that indicates whether or not the check box is checked
defaultChecked	A Boolean value that indicates whether or not the check box is selected by default
name	The name of the check box element
value	The value of the check box element
Methods	
click()	Emulates the action of clicking the check box
Event Handlers	
onClick	Used to run JavaScript code when the check box is clicked
date	An object containing information about a specific date or the current date. You can assign a date object to a variable using standard date and time formatting, for example: SomeDay = new Date("June, 15, 2000, 14:35:00").You can also assign the values for each date and time component, such as day or seconds, individually; using this method, the same date object would read: SomeDay = new Date(2000, 5, 15, 14, 35, 0). The values in parentheses are year, month, day, hour, minute, second. You can create a variable containing the current date and time by removing the date and time values. For example: Today = new Date();
Methods	
getDate()	Returns the day of the month from 1 to 31
getDay()	Returns the day of the week from 0 to 6 (Sunday = 0, Monday = 1, ...)

HTML

JavaScript	descriptions and examples
getHours()	Returns the hour in military time from 0 to 23
getMinutes()	Returns the minute from 0 to 59
getMonth()	Returns the value of the month from 0 to 11 (January = 0, February = 1, ...)
getSeconds()	Returns the seconds
getTime()	Returns the date as an integer representing the number of milliseconds since January 1st, 1970 at 00:00:00
getTimesoneOffset()	Returns the difference between the local time and Greenwich Mean Time in minutes
getYear()	Returns the number of years since 1900 (in other words, 1996 is represented by "96.") This value method is inconsistently applied past the year 1999.
setDate(*date*)	Sets the day of the month to the value specified in *date*
setHours(*hour*)	Sets the hour to the value specified in *hour*
setMinutes(*minutes*)	Sets the minute to the value specified in *minutes*
setMonth(*month*)	Sets the month to the value specified in *month*
setSeconds(*seconds*)	Sets the second to the value specified in *seconds*
setTime(*time*)	Sets the time using the value specified in *time*, where *time* is a variable containing the number of milliseconds since January 1st, 1970 at 00:00:00
setYear(*year*)	Sets the year to the value specified in *year*
toGMTString()	Converts the date to a text string in Greenwich Mean Time
toLocaleString()	Converts a date object's date to a text string, using the date format that the Web browser is set up to use
UTC()	Returns the date in the form of the number of milliseconds since January 1st, 1970, 00:00:00
document	**An HTML document**
Properties	
alinkColor	The color of active hyperlinks in the document
anchors	An array of anchors within the document. Use anchors[0] to refer to the first anchor, anchors[1] to refer to the second anchor, and so forth.
bgColor	The background color used in the document
cookie	A text string containing the document's cookie values
fgColor	The text color used in the document
form	A form within the document (the form itself is also an object)
forms	An array of forms within the document. Use forms[0] to refer to the first form, forms[1] to refer to the second form, and so forth.
lastModified	The date the document was last modified

JavaScript	descriptions and examples
linkColor	The color of hyperlinks in the document
links	An array of links within the document. Use links[0] to refer to the first hyperlink, links[1] to refer to the second hyperlink, and so forth.
location	The URL of the document
referrer	The URL of the document containing the link that the user accessed to get to the current document
title	The title of the document
vlinkColor	The color of followed hyperlinks
Methods	
clear()	Clears the contents of the document window
close()	Closes the document stream
open	Opens the document stream
write()	Writes to the document window
writeln()	Writes to the document window on a single line (used only with preformatted text)
elements	**Elements within an HTML form**
Properties	
length	The number of elements within the form
form	**An HTML form within a document. You can refer to a specific form using that form's name. For example, for a form named "REG," you can apply the submit method with the following expression: REG.submit();**
Properties	
action	The location of the CGI script that receives the form values
elements	An array of elements within the form (including input boxes, check boxes, buttons, and other fields). Use elements[0] to refer to the first element, elements[1] to refer to the second element, and so forth. Use the field name of the element to work with a specific element.
encoding	The type of encoding used in the form
method	The type of method used when submitting the form
target	The name of the window into which CGI output should be directed
Methods	
submit()	Submits the form to the CGI script
Event Handlers	
onSubmit	Used to run JavaScript code when the form is submitted by the browser
frame	**A frame window within the Web browser**
Properties	
frames	An array of frames within the frame window. Use frames[0] to refer to the first frame, frames[1] to refer to the second frame and so forth.

App

HTML

JavaScript	descriptions and examples
parent	The name of the window that contains the frame
self	The name of the current frame window
top	The name of the topmost window in the hierarchy of frame windows
window	The name of the current frame window
Methods	
alert(*message*)	Displays the text contained in *message* in a dialog box
clearTimeout(*name*)	Cancels the time out whose value is *name*
close()	Closes the window
confirm(*message*)	Displays the text contained in *message* in a dialog box along with OK and Cancel buttons
prompt(*message*, *default_text*)	Displays the text contained in *message* in a dialog box with a text entry box into which the user can enter a value or text string. The default value or text is specified by the value of *default_text*.
setTimeout(*expression*, *time*)	Evaluates the value of *expression* after the number of milliseconds specified in the value of *time* has passed
hidden	**A hidden field on an HTML form. Hidden fields can be referred to using their field names. For example, to change the value of the hidden field "PWORD" to "newpassword," use the expression: PWORD.value = "newpassword"**
Properties	
name	The name of the hidden field
value	The value of the hidden field
history	**An object containing information about the Web browser's history list**
Properties	
length	The number of items in the history list
Methods	
back()	Goes back to the previous item in the history list
forward()	Goes forward to the next item in the history list
go(*location*)	Goes to the item in the history list specified by the value of *location*. The *location* variable can be either an integer or the name of the Web page.
image	**An embedded image within the document (available only in Netscape Navigator 3.0 or higher)**
Properties	
border	The value of the BORDER property of the <IMG> tag
complete	A Boolean value that indicates whether or not the image has been completely loaded by the browser
height	The height of the image in pixels

hspace	The horizontal space around the image in pixels
lowsrc	The value of the LOWSRC property of the <IMG> tag
src	The source of the inline image
vspace	The vertical space around the image in pixels
width	The width of the image in pixels

link
A link within an HTML document

Properties

target	The target window of the hyperlinks

location
An object that contains information about the location of a Web document

Properties

hash	The location's anchor name
host	The location's hostname and port number
href	The location's URL
pathname	The path portion of the location's URL
port	The port number of the location's URL
protocol	The protocol used with the location's URL

math
A JavaScript object used for advanced mathematical calculations. For example, to calculate the square root of 27 and store this value in the variable "SQ27," use the following JavaScript expression: var SQ27 = math.sqrt(27);

Properties

E	The value of the base of natural logarithms (2.7182...)
LN10	The value of the natural logarithm of 10
LN2	The value of the natural logarithm of 2
PI	The value of pi (3.1416...)

Methods

abs(*number*)	Returns the absolute value of *number*
acos(*number*)	Returns the arc cosine of *number* in radians
asin(*number*)	Returns the arc sine of *number* in radians
atan(*number*)	Returns the arc tangent of *number* in radians
ceil(*number*)	Rounds *number* up to the next highest integer
cos(*number*)	Returns the cosine of *number*, where *number* is an angle expressed in radians
exp(*number*)	Raises the value of E (2.7182...) to the value of *number*
floor(*number*)	Rounds *number* down to the next lowest integer
log(*number*)	Returns the natural logarithm of *number*
max(*number1, number2*)	Returns the greater of *number1* and *number2*

JavaScript	descriptions and examples
min(*number1, number2*)	Returns the lesser of *number1* and *number2*
pow(*number1, number2*)	Returns the value of *number1* raised to the power of *number2*
random()	Returns a random number between 0 and 1
round(*number*)	Rounds *number* to the closest integer
sin(*number*)	Returns the sine of *number*, where *number* is an angle expressed in radians
tan(number)	Returns the tangent of *number*, where *number* is an angle expressed in radians
navigator	**An object representing the Web browser currently in use**
Properties	
appCodeName	The code name of the Web browser
appName	The name of the Web browser
appVersion	The version of the Web browser
userAgent	The user-agent text string sent from the client to the Web server
option	**An option from a selection list**
Properties	
defaultSelected	A Boolean value indicating whether or not the option is selected by default
index	The index value of the option
selected	A Boolean value indicating whether or not the option is currently selected
text	The text of the option as displayed on the Web page
value	The value of the option
password	**A password field in an HTML form. You can refer to a specific password field using the field name. For example, for a password field named "PWORD," you can apply the focus() method with the following expression: PWORD.submit();**
Properties	
defaultValue	The default value of the password
name	The name of the password field
value	The value of the password field
Methods	
blur()	Emulates the action of leaving the text area box
focus()	Emulates the action of moving into the text area box
select()	Emulates the action of selecting the text in a text area box

radio

An array of radio buttons on an HTML form . Use the name of the radio button set to refer to individual buttons. For example if the name of the radio button set is "Products," use Products[0] to refer to the first radio button, Products[1] to refer to the second radio button, and so forth.

Properties

checked	A Boolean value indicating whether or not a specific radio button has been checked
defaultChecked	A Boolean value indicating whether or not a specific radio button is checked by default
length	The number of radio buttons in the set
name	The name of a set of radio buttons
value	The value of a specific radio button

Methods

click()	Emulates the action of clicking the radio button

Event Handlers

onClick	Used to run JavaScript code when the radio button is clicked

reset

A Reset button in an HTML form. You can refer to a specific Reset button using the button's name. For a Reset button named "RELOAD," you can apply the click() method with the following expression: RELOAD.click();

Properties

name	The name of the Reset button
value	The value of the Reset button

Methods

click()	Emulates the action of clicking the Reset button

Event Handlers

onClick	Used to run JavaScript code when the Reset button is clicked

select

A selection list in an HTML form. You can refer to a specific selection list using the selection list's name. For example, to determine the number of options in a selection list named "PRODUCT," use the following expression: PRODUCT.length;

Properties

length	The number of options in the selection list
name	The name of the selection list
options	An array of options within the selection list. Use options[0] to refer to the first option, options[1] to refer to the second option, and so forth. See the options object for more information on working with individual selection list options.
selectedIndex	The index value of the selected option from the selection list

Event Handlers

onBlur	Used to run JavaScript code when the user leaves the selection list
onChange	Used to run JavaScript code when the user changes the selected option in the selection list
onFocus	Used to run JavaScript code when the user enters the selection list

HTML

HTML

JavaScript	descriptions and examples
string	An object representing a text string or string of characters. For example, to italicize the text string "Order Today!", use the following expression: "Order Today!".italics();
Properties	
length	The number of characters in the string
Methods	
anchor(*name*)	Turns the text string into a hyperlink anchor with a name value set to *name*
big()	Modifies the text string to display big characters (similar to the effect of applying the <BIG> tag)
blink()	Modifies the text string to display blinking characters (similar to the effect of applying the <BLINK> tag)
bold()	Modifies the text string to display characters in bold (similar to the effect of applying the <B> tag)
charAt(*index*)	Returns the character in the text string at the location specified by *index*
fixed()	Modifies the text string to display fixed-width characters (similar to the effect of applying the <FIXED> tag)
fontColor(*color*)	Modifies the text string to display text in a color specified by *color* (similar to applying the <FONT> tag to the text along with the COLOR property)
fontSize(*value*)	Modifies the text string to display text in the font size specified by the *value* parameter (similar to applying the <FONT> tag to the text along with the SIZE property)
indexOf(*string, start*)	Searches the text string and returns the index value of the first occurrence of the text string *string*. The search starts at the character indicated by the value of *start*.
italics()	Modifies the text string to display characters in italics (similar to the effect of applying the <I> tag)
lastIndexOf(*string, start*)	Searches the text string and locates the index value of the last occurrence of the text string *string*. The search starts at the character indicated by the value of *start*.
link(*href*)	Turns the text string into a hyperlink pointing to the URL contained in *href*
small()	Modifies the text string to display small characters (similar to the effect of applying the <SMALL> tag)
strike()	Applies the strikeout character to the text string (similar to the effect of applying the <STRIKE> tag)
sub()	Modifies the text string to display subscript characters (similar to the effect of applying the <SUB> tag)
substring(*first, last*)	Returns a substring of characters from the text string, starting with the character at the index number *first* and ending with the character at the index number *last*
sup()	Modifies the text string to display superscript characters (similar to the effect of applying the <SUP> tag)
toLowerCase()	Changes all of the characters in the text string to lowercase
toUpperCase()	Changes all of the characters in the text string to uppercase

submit	A Submit button in an HTML form. You can refer to a specific Submit button using the button's name. For a Submit button named "SAVE," you can apply the click() method with the following expression: SAVE.click();
Properties	
name	The name of the Submit button
value	The value of the Submit button
Methods	
click()	Emulates the action of clicking the Submit button
Event Handlers	
onClick	Used to run JavaScript code when the user clicks the Submit button
text	An input box from an HTML form. You can refer to an input box using the box's name. For example, to move the cursor to an input box named "ADDRESS," use the following expression: ADDRESS.focus();
Properties	
defaultValue	The default value of the input box
name	The name of the input box
value	The value of the input box
Methods	
blur()	Emulates the action of leaving the input box
focus()	Emulates the action of moving into the input box
select()	Emulates the action of selecting the text in an input box
Event Handlers	
onBlur	Used to run JavaScript code when the user leaves the input box
onChange	Used to run JavaScript code when the user changes the value of the input box
onFocus	Used to run JavaScript code when the user enters the input box
onSelect	Used to run JavaScript code when the user selects some or all of the text in the input box
textarea	A text area box in an HTML form. You can refer to a specific text area box using the box's name. For example, to move the cursor out of a text area box named "COMMENTS," use the expression: COMMENTS.blur();
Properties	
defaultValue	The default value of the text area box
name	The name of the text area box
value	The value of the text area box

HTML

JavaScript	descriptions and examples
Methods	
blur()	Emulates the action of leaving the text area box
focus()	Emulates the action of moving into the text area box
select()	Emulates the action of selecting the text in a text area box
Event Handlers	
onBlur	Used to run JavaScript code when the user leaves the text area box
onChange	Used to run JavaScript code when the user changes the value of the text area box
onFocus	Used to run JavaScript code when the user enters the text area box
onSelect	Used to run JavaScript code when the user selects some or all of the text in the text area box
window	**The document window contained within the Web browser**
Properties	
defaultStatus	The default text string displayed in the window's status bar
frames	An array of frames within the window. Use frames[0] to refer to the first frame, frames[1] to refer to the second frame, and so forth. See the frames object for properties and methods that can be applied to individual frames.
length	The number of frames in the parent window
name	The name of the window
parent	The name of the window containing this particular window
self	The name of the current window
status	The text string displayed in the window's status bar
top	The name of the topmost window in a hierarchy of windows
window	The name of the current window
Methods	
alert(*message*)	Displays the text contained in *message* in a dialog box
clearTimeout(*name*)	Cancels the time out whose value is *name*
close()	Closes the window
confirm(*message*)	Displays the text contained in *message* in a dialog box along with OK and Cancel buttons
prompt(*message, default_text*)	Displays the text contained in *message* in a dialog box with a text entry box into which the user can enter a value or text string. The default value or text is specified by the value of *default_text*.
setTimeout(*expression, time*)	Evaluates the value of *expression* after the number of milliseconds specified in the value of *time* has passed

Event Handlers	
onLoad	Used to run JavaScript code when the window or frame finishes loading
onUnload	Used to run JavaScript code when the window or frame finishes unloading

JavaScript Operators

The following are some operators used in JavaScript expressions.

TABLE AP-6: JavaScript operators

operators	description
Assignment	**Assignment operators are used to assign values to variables.**
=	Assigns the value of the variable on the right to the variable on the left (x=y)
+=	Adds the two variables and assigns the result to the variable on the left (x+=y is equivalent to x=x+y)
–=	Subtracts the variable on the right from the variable on the left and assigns the result to the variable on the left (x–=y is equivalent to x=x–y)
*=	Multiplies the two variables together and assigns the result to the left variable (x*=y is equivalent to x=x*y)
/=	Divides the variable on the left by the variable on the right and assigns the result to the variable on the left (x/=y is equivalent to x=x/y)
%=	Divides the variable on the left by the variable on the right and assigns the remainder to the variable on the left (x%=y is equivalent to x=x%y)
Arithmetic	**Arithmetic operators are used for arithmetic functions.**
+	Adds two variables together (x+y)
–	Subtracts the variable on the right from the variable on the left (x–y)
*	Multiplies two variables together (x*y)
/	Divides the variable on the left by the variable on the right (x/y)
%	Calculates the remainder after dividing the variable on the left by the variable on the right (x%y)
++	Increases the value of a variable by 1 (x++ is equivalent to x=x+1)
--	Decreases the value of a variable by 1 (x-- is equivalent to x=x–1)
–	Changes the sign of a variable (–x)
Logical	**Logical operators are used for evaluating true and false expressions.**
&&	Returns true only if both expressions are true (also known as an AND operator)
||	Returns true when either expression is true (also known as an OR operator)
!	Returns true if the expression is false, and false if the expression is true (also known as a *negation* operator)
Comparison	**Comparison operators are used for comparing expressions.**
==	Returns true when the two expressions are equal (x==y)
!=	Returns true when the two expressions are not equal (x!=y)
>	Returns true when the expression on the left is greater than the expression on the right (x > y)
<	Returns true when the expression on the left is less than the expression on the right (x < y)
>=	Returns true when the expression on the left is greater than or equal to the expression on the right (x >= y)
<=	Returns true when the expression on the left is less than or equal to the expression on the right (x <= y)
Conditional (shorthand)	**Conditional operators determine values based on conditions that are either true or false.**
(condition) ? value1 : value2	If *condition* is true, then this expression equals *value1*, otherwise it equals *value2*.

Cascading Style Sheets

The following are CSS1 fourth-generation browser supported styles.

TABLE AP-7: **CSS1 fourth-generation browser supported styles**

property	explanation/syntax	example
Font Properties		
font-style	• *normal* • *oblique* (similar to italic, but created manually rather than using italic typeface) • *italic*	{font-style: italic}
font-variant	• *normal* (default) • *small-caps*	{font-variant: small-caps}
font-weight	• *extra-light* • *demi-light* • *light* • *medium* • *bold* • *demi-bold* • *extra-bold*	{font-weight: extra-bold}
font-size	a number with a unit abbreviation • points (*pt*) • pixels (*px*) • inches (*in*) • centimeters (*cm*) • percentage of default point size (%) • multiple of width of "m" character in current font family (*em*)	{font-size: 16pt}
line-height	sets distance between baselines of two adjacent elements; specify multiplication factor for font size as a value (such as 1.2), percentage (120%), or measurement (1.2em)	{line-height: 1.2}
font-family	any combination of the following, in order of preference • specific typeface name (*times new roman*) • general type family (*times*) • font type (*sans-serif*)	{font-family: "times new roman", times, garamond, serif}
font	shorthand for setting all six font-related attributes at once; no commas, except between font-family settings; order: font-style, font-variant, font-weight, font-size, line-height, font-family	{font: italic small-caps extra-bold 16pt 0.75in "times new roman", times, garamond, serif}
text-decoration	• *none* • *underline* • *italic* • *line-through*	{text-decoration: italic}
Color and Background Properties		
color	hexadecimal or keyword color equivalent for element color	{color: #93DB70}
background-color	hexadecimal or keyword color equivalent for background color	{background-color: navy}

App

HTML

property	explanation/syntax	example
background-image	• *none* • *url*(url)	{background-image: url(me.jpg)}
background-repeat	specifies if and how background image is repeated • *repeat* (tiles over entire background) • *repeat-x* (repeats in single band horizontally) • *repeat-y* (repeats in single band vertically) • *no-repeat* (single image only)	{background-repeat: repeat-x}
background-attachment	• *scroll* (image scrolls with foreground) • *fixed* (image remains fixed as foreground scrolls)	{background-attachment: fixed}
background-position	specifies initial position of background image; coordinates (in percent) match point at those coordinates on image with those coordinates on background	{background-position: 100% 100%}
background	shorthand for setting all five background attributes at once; no commas; order: background-color, background-image, background-repeat, background-attachment, background-position	{background: navy url(me.jpg) repeat-x fixed 100% 100%

Text Properties

property	explanation/syntax	example
word-spacing	specifies additional width to insert between words (default=normal); may be negative	{word-spacing: 0.4em}
letter-spacing	specifies additional width to insert between words (default=normal); may be negative	{letter-spacing: 0.1em}
text-decoration	• *underline* • *overline* • *line-through* • *blink* • *none* (default)	{text-decoration: underline}
vertical-align	• *baseline* • *sub* • *super* • *top* • *text-top* • *middle* • *bottom* • *text-bottom* • percentage value, positive and negative numbers possible, specifies percentage of the element's line-height property in relation to the parent baseline	{vertical-align: super}
text-transform	• *capitalize* capitalizes first character of each word • *uppercase* capitalizes all letters • *lowercase* makes all letters lowercase • *none*	{text-transform: capitalize}

property	explanation/syntax	example
text-align	<ul><li>*left*</li><li>*right*</li><li>*center*</li><li>*justify*</li></ul>	{text-align: center}
text-indent	positive and negative numbers possible, specifies indentation of first line, in an exact measurement, or a percentage of parent element width	{text-indent: 3em}
line-height	sets distance between baselines of two adjacent elements; specify multiplication factor for font size, as a value (such as 1.2), percentage (120%), or measurement (1.2em)	{line-height: 1.2}

Box Properties

property	explanation/syntax	example
margin-top	sets element's top margin as measurement or percentage of parent element width	{margin-top: 2%}
margin-right	sets element's right margin, as measurement or percentage of parent element width	{margin-right: 2em}
margin-bottom	sets element's bottom margin, as measurement or percentage of parent element width	{margin-bottom: 2%}
margin-left	sets element's left margin, as measurement or percentage of parent element width	{margin-right: 2em}
margin	shorthand property for specifying margin-top, margin-right, margin-bottom, and margin-left properties; order: top, right, bottom, left; if only one value given, applies to all four; if one or two values missing, missing value copied from opposite side	{margin 2% 2em}
padding-top	sets an element's top padding, as measurement or percentage of parent element width	{padding-top: 0.3em}
padding-right	sets an element's right padding, as measurement or percentage of parent element width	{padding-right: 20%}
padding-bottom	sets an element's bottom padding, as measurement or percentage of parent element width	{padding-bottom: 0.3em}
padding-left	sets an element's left padding, as measurement or percentage of parent element width	{padding-left: 20%}
padding	shorthand property for specifying padding-top, padding-right, padding-bottom, and padding-left properties; order: top, right, bottom, left; if only one value given, applies to all four; if one or two values missing, missing value copied from opposite side	{padding: 0.3em 20% 0.2em}
border-top-width; border-right-width; border-bottom-width; border-left-width;	<ul><li>*thin*</li><li>*medium*</li><li>*thick*</li><li>measurement</li></ul>	{border-top-width: 2pt}
border-width	shorthand property for specifying all four border thicknesses; order: top, right, bottom, left; if only one value given, applies to all four; if one or two values missing, missing value copied from opposite side	{border-width: 3em}

HTML

property	explanation/syntax	example
border-style	can specify between one and four styles, with same organization as border-width above • *none* • *dotted* • *dashed* • *solid* • *double* • *groove* • *ridge* • *inset* • *outset*	{border-style: groove}
border-color	hexadecimal or keyword color equivalent for element color; can specify between one and four colors, with same organization as border-width above	{border-color: navy red red}
border-top border-right border-bottom border-left	shorthand properties for setting each border's width, style, and color	{border-bottom: thick solid red}
border	shorthand property for setting same width, color, and style on all four borders of an element	{border: thin inset green}
width	element width, as a length or percentage, negative values are allowed (default=auto)	{width: 200px}
height	element height, as a length or percentage, negative values are allowed (default=auto)	{height: 50%}
float	moves element to left or right, and wraps text on opposite side	{float: left}
clear	specifies if an element allows floating elements around it, or should be moved clear of them • *none* • *left* • *right* • *both*	{clear: both}
Classification Properties		
display	• *block* • *inline* • *list-item* • *none*	{display: inline}
white-space	• *normal* white space collapsed • *pre* formatted like HTML PRE element • *nowrap* wrapping triggered only by elements	{white-space: nowrap}

property	explanation/syntax	example
list-style-type	specifies marker style for list items • *disc* • *circle* • *square* • *decimal* • *lower-roman* • *upper-roman* • *lower-alpha* • *upper-alpha* • *none*	{list-style-type: lower-alpha}
list-style-image	specifies an image to use as a list item marker	{list-style-image: url(reddot.jpg)}
list-style-position	• *inside* less space between marker and item • *outside* more space between marker and item (default)	{list-style-position: inside}
list-style	shorthand property for setting list-style-type, list-style-image, and list-style-position	{list-style: lower-alpha url(reddot.jpg) inside}

property	explanation/syntax	example

HTML

The following are CSS-P positioning properties.

TABLE AP-8: CSS-P positioning properties

property	value	description
position	static	normal position in page flow (default)
	absolute	outside normal page flow
	relative	relative to normal position in page flow
top, left	auto	(default)
	[length]	offset from default position in points, pixels, inches, or centimeters with respect to the element's top left corner
	[percent]	offset from default position in percentage of the parent element dimension
width, height	auto	(default)
	[length]	element dimension in points, pixels, inches, or centimeters
	[percent]	element dimension in percentage of parent element dimension
clip	auto	(default)
	rect(top right bottom left)	specifies rectangle coordinates that define document area available for displaying element
z-index	auto	(default)
	number	specifies element's position in the page's set of overlap layers; negative values possible
overflow	visible	entire contents displayed (default)
	hidden	contents that do not fit within the element are hidden
	auto	element contains scroll bar only when some contents do not fit within the element
	scroll	element always contains associated scroll bar
visibility	visible	element displays normally
	hidden	element takes up same space in page as it would normally, but is not visible

Filters and Transitions

The following are options available when creating filters and transitions for Microsoft Internet Explorer 4.

For all true/false parameters, false is represented by 0, and true is represented by 1.

TABLE AP-9: Filters for Microsoft Internet Explorer 4

filter effect	description	parameters	syntax
Filters	Change object or page appearance in complex ways		
Alpha	Sets a transparency level	• *opacity* Ranges from 0 (fully transparent) to 100 (fully opaque) • *finishopacity* (optional) Same values as *opacity*; allows opacity to change across object • *style* Shape of opacity gradient; 0 (uniform), 1(linear), 2 (radial), or 3 (rectangular) • *startX* X coordinate for start of opacity gradient • *startY* Y coordinate for start of opacity gradient • *finishX* X coordinate for end of opacity gradient • *finishY* Y coordinate for end of opacity gradient	{filter: alpha(opacity=*opacity*, finishopacity=*finishopacity*, style=*style*, startX=*startX*, startY=*startY*, finishX=*finishX*, finishY=*finishY*)}
Blur	Creates the impression of moving at high speed	• *add* True/false variable specifying whether original image should be added to motion-blurred image (true; default) or not (false) • *direction* Blur direction, in degrees (0-360) clockwise from vertical, rounded to 45-degree increments; default is 270 (left) • *strength* Number of pixels that blur extends (default=5)	{filter: blur(add=*add*, direction=*direction*, strength=*strength*)}
Chroma	Makes a specific color transparent	• *color* Color subject to transparency, expressed in hexadecimal format (#RRGGBB)	{filter: chroma(color=*color*)}
Drop Shadow	Creates an offset solid silhouette	• *color* Color for drop shadow effect, in hexadecimal format • *offX* X-axis offset of drop shadow, in pixels • *offY* Y-axis offset of drop shadow, in pixels • *positive* drop shadow of any nontransparent pixel (true; default), or drop shadow of any transparent pixel (false)	{filter: dropshadow(color=*color*, offX=*offX*, offY=*offY*, positive=*positive*)}
FlipH	Creates a horizontal mirror image	NONE	{filter: fliph}
FlipV	Creates a vertical mirror image	NONE	{filter: flipv}
Glow	Adds radiance around the outside edges of the object	• *color* Color of radiance around object, in hexadecimal format • *strength* Glow intensity (1-255)	{filter: glow(color=*color*, strength=*strength*)}
Grayscale	Drops color information from the image	NONE	{filter: gray}
Invert	Reverses the hue, saturation, and brightness values	NONE	{filter: invert}

HTML

filter effect	description	parameters	syntax
Light	Projects light sources onto an object	Methods: • *AddAmbient* Adds ambient light source • *AddCone* Adds cone light source • *AddPoint* Adds point light source • *ChangeColor* Changes light color • *ChangeStrength* Changes light strength • *Clear* Clears all lights • *MoveLight* Moves light source	{filter: light}
Mask	Creates a transparent mask from an object	• *color* Color painted on transparent regions, in hexadecimal format	{filter: mask(color=*color*)}
Shadow	Creates a solid silhouette of the object	• *color* Color of shadow effect, in hexadecimal format • *direction* Shadow offset direction, in degrees (0-360) clockwise from vertical, rounded to 45-degree increments; default is 225 (bottom-left)	{filter: shadow(color=color, direction=direction)}
Wave	Creates a sine wave distortion along the x-axis and y-axis	• *add* Adds original image to waved image (true; default) or does not add original image (false) • *freq* Number of waves appearing in distortion • *light* Strength of light on wave effect, in percent • *phase* Phase offset from start of sine wave effect, in percent (default=0) • *strength* Wave intensity	{filter: wave(add=*add*, freq=*freq*, lightstrength=*strength*, phase=*phase*, strength=*strength*)}
XRay	Shows just the edges of the object	NONE	{filter: xray}

TABLE AP-10: Transitions for Microsoft Internet Explorer 4

transition type	description	parameters	syntax
Transitions	Filters that vary over time		
blend	Creates simple fade-in or fade-out with specified duration	• *duration* Length of fade, in seconds	filter: blendTrans(duration=*duration*)
reveal	Allows choice of effects	• *duration* Length of effect, in seconds • *transition* Number corresponding to reveal transition effect, as listed in table that follows	filter: revealTrans(duration=*duration*, transition=*transition*)

TABLE AP-11: Reveal transition effects

reveal transition name	value
Box in	0
Box out	1
Circle in	2
Circle out	3
Wipe up	4
Wipe down	5
Wipe right	6
Wipe left	7
Vertical blinds	8
Horizontal blinds	9
Checkerboard across	10
Checkerboard down	11
Random dissolve	12
Split vertical in	13
Split vertical out	14
Split horizontal in	15
Split horizontal out	16
Strips left down	17
Strips left up	18
Strips right down	19
Strips right up	20
Random bars horizontal	21
Random bars vertical	22
Random	23

HTML

TABLE AP-12: Transition applications

transition application	description
interpage transition	Transition plays when containing page opens or exits Created with the META tag in the page head section; uses *http-equiv* parameter, specifying whether transition should play when page opens ("Page-Enter") or closes ("Page-Exit"), or site opens ("Site-Enter") or closes ("Site-Exit"). For example, the code to create the circle in transition when a page closes could read `<META HTTP-EQUIV="Page-Exit" CONTENT="revealTrans(duration=7, transition=2)">`
object transition	Requires three components: 1. **Transition filter reference** in style description for object to be filtered; for example, to filter an image with the horizontal blinds transition, the code could read `<IMG ID="mypic" SRC="me.jpg" STYLE="filter: revealTrans(duration=5, transition=9)">` 2. **Script to manage filter** consisting of three lines at minimum: `mypic.filters.revealTrans.apply()` *creates the final transition state* `mypic.src= "me2.jpg"` *specifies new condition(s) of transitioned object* `mypic.filters.revealTrans.play()` *animates transition effect* 3. **Event handler** to trigger script

Glossary

_ Underscore; character reserved for built-in frame names.

Begins a comment line in an image map document.

/ Slash symbol replaces the backslash (\ ) symbol used in DOS; also denotes a closing tag.

| Pipe symbol replaces the colon (:) symbol used in DOS.

< > Brackets; symbols that surround tags.

Absolute positioning Positioning option that allows you to place an element at fixed coordinates in the browser window, relative to its parent object; removes positioned object from main page flow; *see also* **relative positioning.**

ALIGN An optional code, physically aligns image on the page. Additional attributes HEIGHT and WIDTH are used to change the size of an image.

ALT An optional code, precedes alternative text.

Animated GIFs A popular way to create animation in Web pages, using the GIF image format to display multiple images in a single area; compatible with browsers older than fourth-generation.

Arithmetic operators Symbols that allow you to program scripts to manipulate variables mathematically.

Attribute Additional code that adds qualities to existing codes.

Background Color added to the area in a Web page or within a table cell.

Blend A transition filter that creates a simple fade-in or fade-out effect.

Border Surrounds a table; adds depth to the table and definition to the page.

Borderless table A table without visible borders around the rows, columns, and cells.

Browser Program that enables the viewing of Web pages.

Browser detection script A script that determines the user's browser brand and generation.

Bug Error in a script, causing it to return unexpected or undesired results.

Bulleted list Each item in a bulleted, or *unordered list*, is preceded by a dark, round circle. Each new line of a bulleted list item forms a hanging indent, in which the text is wrapped around directly underneath the previous text line.

Call To trigger or use a named object, such as a style or function, within your Web page code.

Cascading The system of precedence in CSS; embedded styles take precedence over external styles, and inline style takes precedence over both embedded and external style.

Cascading Style Sheet (CSS) A tool that allows you to specify attributes such as color and font size for all page elements marked by a specific tag, name, or ID.

Cascading Style Sheets - Positioning (CSS-P) An extension of cascading style sheets that allows precise positioning of page elements.

Case-sensitive Treats capital and lower-case versions of the same letter as different characters.

Cell An individual box within a table: the intersection of a column and a row.

Cellpadding The amount of space surrounding each cell in a table.

Chaining The process of combining filters to create complex effects.

Checkbox Form device that enables a user to choose one item from many.

CHECKED Determines default value; works only with CHECKBOX and RADIO. Commonly used codes, or attributes, used with a tag.

Child element The element enclosed by another element, the parent.

Class An HTML property allowing you to assign a category name to multiple Web page elements; allows application of a named style to elements marked by different tags.

Client-side scripts Scripts that a browser interprets and runs; *see also* **server-side scripts.**

Clip Property that allows you to control how much of an element is visible on your Web page by acting as a layer above the element; *see also* **clip region.**

Clip region The hole you define with the clip property, through which the page contents are visible.

Comma-delimited text file A file containing no formatting "frills"; only a header row and data entry.

Conditional Programming decision point that allows your script to choose one of two paths, depending on a condition that you specify.

Containers *See* **tags.**

Cross-platform code DHTML code that works on both fourth-generation browsers.

CSS *See* **Cascading Style Sheets.**

CSS-P *See* **Cascading Style Sheets – Positioning.**

Custom data definitions In XML, tags that describe a specific type of data.

Data-awareness A DHTML feature allowing a user to instantly view and manipulate a database in a Web page; *see also* **data binding.**

Data binding The linking of a Web page to an external data file.

Data source object An embedded object containing fields referenced in an HTML document.

DATAFLD An HTML attribute that indicates the element from an XML document to be bound to a column.

DATAFORMATAS An HTML attribute that specifies how XML-based data should be displayed in HTML.

Debugging The process of systematically identifying and fixing a code or script's bugs.

Definition list Displays a term or short group of words with an indented explanation underneath.

DHTML *See* **Dynamic HTML**.

DHTML Object Models Extended DOM versions included in the browser code for Navigator 4 and Internet Explorer 4, which increase the range and versatility of DHTML.

Directory list Text displays in multiple columns across a Web page.

Document Object Model (DOM) A Web browser's hierarchical system of organization that allows Web page developers to describe and work with the Web page elements in a browser window; categorizes and groups Web page elements into a tree-like structure.

Document Type Definition (DTD) The formal specification of the rules of an XML document, namely which elements are allowed and in what combinations.

DOM *See* **Document Object Model**.

Dot syntax A method of referencing objects in an object hierarchy by beginning on the document level, and separating each level name with a period.

DTD *See* **Document Type Definition**.

Dynamic content A DHTML feature allowing a page to display different content based on a user's activities.

Dynamic HTML (DHTML) A varied set of technologies that allow near-immediate response to user actions in a Web page without accessing the Internet server; *see also* **static HTML**.

Dynamic style A DHTML feature that facilitates immediate style changes in response to user actions.

Element A start tag and corresponding end tag, plus the content between the tagset.

Embedded style CSS style formatting associated with HTML tags, class names, or IDs between the HEAD tags at the top of your Web page; *see also* **embedded style sheet**.

Embedded style sheet The set of code between a page's HEAD tags, consisting of a page's embedded styles.

Empty container An HTML code that does not require a closing tag.

Empty element *See* **empty container**.

Event Each action by a user.

Event handlers Terms that specify possible user actions.

Expandable outline A Web page feature that hides the explanatory paragraphs in a bulleted list, displaying each only when the user clicks its corresponding bulleted item.

Extensible Markup Language *See* **XML**.

External style A style sheet contained in an external file and linked to a Web page; *also called* **linked style**; *see also* **external style sheet**.

External style sheet CSS style formatting contained in an external file and linked to a Web page; *see also* **external style**.

FAQ An acronym for Frequently Asked Questions, pronounced "fak".

Filters Predefined element formats in Internet Explorer 4 that affect element appearance in complex ways; *see also* **transition filters**.

HTML

Float Property to remove an element from the main text flow and display it to the side of the flow.

Form A method of collecting information for later use. A form can accept input from a user in the form of typed text, or by clicking the mouse on radio buttons, checkboxes, or labeled buttons.

Format Change to text size, color, and/or font.

Fourth-generation browsers The 4.x versions of Navigator and Internet Explorer.

Frame document An HTML file that dictates the number and location of horizontal and vertical frames within its windows.

Frames Scroll-capable windows that are created independently and tiled together.

Function A set of script code that performs a certain task, grouped into a named unit.

Gamma settings The degree of contrast between mid-level gray values in an image; varies across platforms.

Graphic image Electronic art file that is referenced in an HTML document and displayed by a Web browser.

Hang To stop functioning.

Hexadecimal value Code values for the colors in a Web page; give you more control over colors' appearance because these values translate more precisely between various browsers and computer platforms.

Hot spot Clickable area in an image that allows you to jump to other Web locations.

.htm Suffix used to indicate a file in HTML format.

HTML (HyperText Markup Language) A series of codes, sometimes called tags.

HTML editor Allows creation/modification of Web documents using tags from drop-down lists and toolbar buttons.

Hyperlink Using HTML tags to reference another Web location.

Image map Defines areas (or hot spots) within an image that can be clicked to jump to other Web locations.

IMG The image tag.

Inline image A graphic file in a Web page that is aligned with text using special HTML tags.

Inline style CSS style formatting specified in the opening tag surrounding an element.

INPUT Creates the following form fields: single text lines, radio buttons, checkboxes, and Submit and Reset buttons.

innerHTML A property that includes only an element's contents, but not the tags surrounding it; *see also* **outerHTML**.

ISMAP An optional code; specifies that image is an image map.

Java applet A small program written in the Java programming language; it is summoned using the <applet></applet> tagset.

JavaScript Scripting language adapted from Sun Microsystems' Java programming language; supported by both Internet Explorer 4 and Navigator 4.

JPG Commonly used graphic file format.

Jscript Microsoft's adaptation of Sun Microsystems' Java programming language for Web use; *see also* **JavaScript**, **VBScript**.

Layer A transparent virtual page that determines overlap order.

Linked style CSS style formatting contained in an external file and linked to a Web page; *also called* **external style**; *see also* **external style sheet**.

Links Connections to other Web site addresses (URLs) that are coded into an HTML document. Created using an anchor and hyperlink.

Logical formatting Code indicating how text should look in comparison to other text on the page.

MAILTO Attribute that allows readers to send e-mail with a single mouse click.

MAXLENGTH Determines the maximum number of allowable characters.

Media Player Program that plays sound files.

Menu list Items display left-justified one beneath another; they contain neither numbers nor bullets, and have no hanging indent.

Method Action an object can carry out.

Microsoft XSL ActiveX control An object-oriented ActiveX program that applies XSL style sheets to format and display XML-based data in an HTML document.

Multimedia Full-motion videos and sound files. Full-motion videos tend to have large file sizes and can be cumbersome on the Internet. Audio files have varying sizes.

MULTIPLE Allows more than one selection to be made; displays as a scroll box.

NAME Defines the name of the data; a required field.

Nested list Lets you create expanded ordered and unordered lists by combining the <UL> </UL> and <OL> </OL> tags within an existing list.

Null A value equal to zero or nothing.

Numbered list Sometimes referred to as an *ordered list*, each line of text in the list is preceded by a number.

Object An element in the browser window identified by JavaScript as a distinct unit; each object has a default name and set of descriptive features based on its location and function; *see also* **methods**, **properties**, **object hierarchy**.

Object hierarchy JavaScript's organization of objects; much like the system of folders used by Windows to keep track of disk contents.

Ordered List Items listed in numeric order.

outerHTML A property that includes an element's contents and the tags surrounding it; *see also* **innerHTML**.

Overflow Property that allows you to create the equivalent of an independent frame, anywhere within your browser window.

HTML

Parent element The element enclosing another element, the child element.

Physical formatting Code indicating how text should look; gives you more control over its appearance.

Pixel coordinates Points within an image that are clicked; they can be identified using a variety of graphics programs.

Placeholder Text (or objects) designed to be replaced at a later date.

Platform The computer/operating system combination.

Plug-in programs Additional programs that enable multimedia files to run.

Position A style sheet attribute used to specify absolute or relative positioning.

Positioning A DHTML feature allowing Web page designers to specify precisely the location of all page elements; *see also* **Cascading Style Sheets – Positioning.**

Preformatted text Text that displays exactly as it is typed in the HTML document; it can include enhancements, such as bolding and italics, and allows you to include your own line spaces and breaks.

Presentation effects Web page effects in which elements appear in the browser window gradually and in a specific order.

Properties An object's qualities such as size, location, and type.

Proprietary features Features unique to just one of the two major Web browsers.

Pull-down menu Form device that enables a user to choose one item from many. Takes up less room than checkboxes or radio buttons.

Push button Form device that has a preset function and performs a task.

Radio button Form device that enables a user to choose one item from many.

Refresh/Reload Command button used to replace the currently displayed browser image with a revised HTML document.

Relative positioning Positioning option that allows you to place an element at coordinates in the browser window based on the position of other screen elements; *see also* **absolute positioning.**

Resolution The number of pixels displayed on the screen. In many cases, the default setting is 640×480, but many people set their resolution at 800×600 or 1024×768.

Reveal A transition filter that allows complex transitions.

Rollover A feature that changes the appearance of text when a user points at it.

Run time The period when a browser first interprets and displays a Web page and runs scripts.

Schema *See* **XML Schema.**

Script Program in a Web page that runs on the viewer's browser; extends and expands the capabilities of a Web page.

Scripting The process of writing scripts.

Scriptlet A script located in an external file that you can link to a Web page.

Scroll box Form device that enables a user to choose one item from many.

SELECT Creates scroll box and pull-down menu fields in a form.

SELECTED Determines default value; works only with OPTION.

Server-side scripts Scripts stored and run on a Web server, rather than on a user's computer; *see also* **client-side scripts**.

SIZE, in a scroll list Determines how many items display. If omitted, choices display as pull-down menu; if set to 2 or more, displays as scroll box.

SIZE, in a text box Determines the size of the field; measured in characters.

Slide A single Web page that is part of a multi-page Web presentation.

Spanned column or row Rows and columns made larger by combining them with adjacent cells using the COLSPAN or ROWSPAN attribute.

SRC The source tag; necessary when defining an inline image.

Static HTML Coding style used to create simple Web documents whose interactivity is limited to hyperlinks; *see also* **dynamic HTML**.

Style Sheet An embedded or separate document that specifies formatting rules.

Styles Used to determine an element's position more precisely. Can be embedded in an HTML file or a separate file.

Table Composed of columns and rows, with data contained in individual cells.

Table header First row in a table, usually shown bold and centered.

Tags HTML codes; can be written in upper– or lower-case, are enclosed in brackets "<>", and sometimes occur in pairs (both before and after the text they surround). The ending tag differs from the beginning tag: it contains a / (slash) as the first character within the brackets.

Text box Used in a form to collect information; a user types entries in a box, as in a paper form.

Text editor Program that creates documents that can be saved in a text format, such as WordPad.

TEXTAREA Creates a form field that accepts multiple lines of user text.

Third-generation browsers The 3.x versions of Navigator and Internet Explorer.

Transition filters Predefined effects in Internet Explorer that cause elements to appear gradually and in specific patterns when a page opens or exits; *also called* **transitions**.

Transitions *See* **transition filters**.

TYPE Sets the input field to either "text," "password," "radio," "checkbox," "Reset," or "Submit."

Universal data structure Standardized structure for defining, describing, and exchanging data on the Web.

HTML

VALUE The value to be assigned to a choice; an optional attribute that doesn't have to have the same value displayed on the page.

Values Pieces of information that you specify to JavaScript, often with instructions to perform functions on them.

Variable A nickname for a value, making repeated references easier and more efficient.

VBScript Microsoft's adaptation of its Visual Basic programming language for Web use.

Visual hierarchy The organizational scheme of graphic design. Tools used within this hierarchy include color, typography, and layout.

W3C See **World Wide Web Consortium**.

Watermark A light-toned image used as a background in a Web page.

Web page Document containing HTML codes that can be viewed by multiple platforms on the World Wide Web.

Web Page Wizard Helps you lay out a variety of Web pages that meet specific needs.

Well-formed Adheres to the strict rules of structure necessary to be correctly parsed by an XML-compliant program.

White space Area on the page that has no text or graphics.

World Wide Web Consortium (W3C) An international body whose mission is the creation of standards for World Wide Web technologies.

WYSIWYG An acronym for "What you see is what you get".

XML (Extensible Markup Language) A text-based syntax especially designed to describe, deliver, and exchange structured data.

XML DSO Enables binding of XML data to an HTML document using the DHTML Object Model; included in XML-compliant browsers.

XML parser Dissects and interprets XML elements; included in XML-compliant browsers.

XML schema Combines the concepts of a DTD, relational databases, and object-oriented designs to create a way to formally define the elements and structure of an XML document.

XSL stylesheet A set of programming rules that determine how XML data is formatted and displayed in an HTML document.

Z-index The property that determines a layer's position in a page's stack.

Index

Index

Index

Index

Index